Research Computational Semantics

Volume 1

Semantics in Text Processing

STEP 2008

Conference Proceedings

Volume 1
Semantics in Text Processing. STEP 2008 Conference Proceedings
Johan Bos and Rodolfo Delmonte, editors.

Research in Computational Semantics Series editor
Johan Bos   jbos@inf.ed.ac.uk

Semantics in Text Processing

STEP 2008
Conference Proceedings

Edited by:

Johan Bos

and

Rodolfo Delmonte

ISBN 978-1-904987-93-2

College Publications
Scientific Director: Dov Gabbay
Managing Director: Jane Spurr
Department of Computer Science
King's College London, Strand, London WC2R 2LS, UK

http://www.collegepublications.co.uk

Original cover design by orchid creative   www.orchidcreative.co.uk
Printed by Lightning Source, Milton Keynes, UK

Contents

Preface ix

A New Life for Semantic Annotations?
Bunt 1

PART I   REGULAR PAPERS   3

**Combining Knowledge-based Methods and Supervised Learning
for Effective Italian Word Sense Disambiguation**
Basile, de Gemmis, Lops, and Semeraro 5

**Semantic Representations of Syntactically Marked Discourse Status
in Crosslinguistic Perspective**
Bender and Goss-Grubbs 17

High Precision Analysis of NPs with a Deep Processing Grammar
Branco and Costa 31

Augmenting WordNet for Deep Understanding of Text
Clark, Fellbaum, Hobbs, Harrison, Murray, and Thompson 45

**How Well Do Semantic Relatedness Measures Perform?
A Meta-Study**
Cramer 59

**KnowNet: A Proposal for Building Highly Connected and Dense
Knowledge Bases from the Web**
Cuadros and Rigau 71

Combining Word Sense and Usage for Modeling Frame Semantics
De Cao, Croce, Pennacchiotti, and Basili 85

Answering Why-Questions in Closed Domains from a Discourse Model
Delmonte and Pianta 103

**Analyzing the Explanation Structure of Procedural Texts:
Dealing with Advice and Warnings**
Fontan and Saint-Dizier 115

**From Predicting Predominant Senses to Local Context for
Word Sense Disambiguation**
Koeling and McCarthy 129

Automatic Fine-Grained Semantic Classification for Domain Adaptation
Liakata and Pulman 139

Analysis of ASL Motion Capture Data towards Identification of Verb Type
Malaia, Borneman, and Wilbur 155

The Idiom–Reference Connection
McShane and Nirenburg 165

**Resolving Paraphrases to Support Modeling Language Perception
in an Intelligent Agent**
Nirenburg, McShane, and Beale 179

Everyday Language is Highly Intensional
Ramsay and Field 193

Refining the Meaning of Sense Labels in PDTB: "Concession"
Robaldo, Miltsakaki, and Hobbs 207

**Connective-based Local Coherence Analysis: A Lexicon for
Recognizing Causal Relationships**
Stede 221

Open Knowledge Extraction through Compositional Language Processing
Van Durme and Schubert 239

PART II SHARED TASK   255

Introduction to the Shared Task on Comparing Semantic Representations
Bos 257

Boeing's NLP System and the Challenges of Semantic Representation
Clark and Harrison 263

Wide-Coverage Semantic Analysis with Boxer
Bos 277

Semantic and Pragmatic Computing with GETARUNS
Delmonte 287

**LXGram in the Shared Task "Comparing Semantic Representations"
of STEP 2008**
Branco and Costa 299

Baseline Evaluation of WSD and Semantic Dependency in OntoSem
Nirenburg, Beale, and McShane 315

The TEXTCAP Semantic Interpreter
Callaway 327

Deep Semantic Analysis of Text
Allen, Swift, and de Beaumont 343

PART III SHORT PAPERS 355

Textual Entailment as an Evaluation Framework for Metaphor Resolution: A Proposal
Agerri, Barnden, Lee, and Wallington 357

Representing and Visualizing Calendar Expressions in Texts
Battistelli, Couto, Minel, and Schwer 365

Addressing the Resource Bottleneck to Create Large-Scale Annotated Texts
Chamberlain, Poesio, and Kruschwitz 375

A Resource-Poor Approach for Linking Ontology Classes to Wikipedia Articles
Reiter, Hartung, and Frank 381

Top-Down Cohesion Segmentation in Summarization
Tatar, Mihis, and Serban 389

Preface

Background and Motivation

Thanks to both statistical approaches and finite state methods, natural language processing (NLP), particularly in the area of robust, open-domain text processing, has made considerable progress in the last couple of decades. It is probably fair to say that NLP tools have reached satisfactory performance at the level of syntactic processing, be the output structures chunks, phrase structures, or dependency graphs. Therefore, the time seems ripe to extend the state-of-the-art and consider deep semantic processing as a serious task in wide-coverage NLP.

This is a step that normally requires syntactic parsing, as well as integrating named entity recognition, anaphora resolution, thematic role labelling and word sense disambiguation, and other lower levels of processing for which reasonably good methods have already been developed.

The goal of the STEP workshop is to provide a forum for anyone active in semantic processing of text to discuss innovative technologies, representation issues, inference techniques, prototype implementations, and real applications. The preferred processing targets are large quantities of texts — either specialised domains, or open domains such as newswire text, blogs, and wikipedia-like text. Implemented rather than theoretical work is emphasised in STEP.

Featuring in STEP 2008 workshop is a "shared task" on comparing semantic representations as output by state-of-the-art NLP systems. Participants were asked to supply a (small) text, before the workshop. The test data for the shared task is composed out of all the texts submitted by the participants, allowing participants to "challenge" each other. The output of these systems will be judged on a number of aspects by a panel of experts in the field, during the workshop.

Welcome to STEP 2008

STEP 2008 is organised as a three-day event at Ca' Dolfin, at the Università Ca' Foscari in Venice, Italy, taking place on September 22–24. In reply to our call for papers we received 40 submissions: 24 regular papers, 8 short papers, and 8 shared task papers. We accepted 30 of these: 18 regular papers, 5 short papers, and 7 shared task papers (yielding an overall acceptance rate of 75%). We would like to thank the referees and members of the programme committee for helping us to review and select the papers:

Roberto Basili (University of Rome "Tor Vergata", Italy)
Johan Bos (University of Rome "La Sapienza", Italy)
Ann Copestake (University of Cambridge, UK)

Rodolfo Delmonte (University of Venice "Ca' Foscari")
Nicola Guarino (ISTC-CNR, Trento, Italy)
Sanda Harabagiu (HLT, University of Texas, USA)
Alexander Koller (University of Edinburgh, UK)
Leonardo Lesmo (DI, University of Tourin, Italy)
Katja Markert (University of Leeds, UK)
Eva Mok (ICSI, Berkeley, USA)
Dan Moldovan (HLT, University of Texas, USA)
Srini Narayanan (ICSI, Berkeley, USA)
Sergei Nirenburg (University of Maryland, USA)
Malvina Nissim (University of Bologna, Italy)
Vincenzo Pallotta (University of Freiburg, Switzerland)
Emanuele Pianta (ITC, Trento, Italy)
Massimo Poesio (University of Trento, Italy)
Stephen Pulman (Oxford University, UK)
Michael Schiehlen (IMS Stuttgart, Germany)
Bonnie Webber (University of Edinburgh, UK)

We also would like to thank Malvina Nissim and Daniel Bos for advice on formatting the proceedings, Gertjan Bos for designing the STEP logo, and Suhel Jaber for
maintaining the STEP 2008 web site. We also thank Jane Spurr from College Publications for her general support and her advice on preparing the camera-ready version of
this book. Finally, we're very grateful to Harry Bunt (Tilburg University) and Sanda
Harabagiu (University of Texas at Dallas) for giving invited presentations at STEP
2008.

Johan Bos & Rodolfo Delmonte
Italy, July 2008

A New Life for Semantic Annotations?

Harry Bunt

Tilburg University (The Netherlands)

email: harry.bunt@uvt.nl

Semantic annotation has so far been approached in essentially the same way as annotation at other levels of linguistic information, namely as the business of labeling text with certain tags which add certain information to the text, in this case, semantic information. Semantic role labeling is a case in point. This may be very useful, for instance for determining the variety of ways in which certain types of semantic information tend to be expressed, but it seems to me that semantic annotations can and should have a deeper significance and a more important role to play.

Since semantic annotations are intended to capture some of the meaning of the annotated text, it ought to be possible to use such annotations in reasoning, and hence to apply that information in language processing tasks. However, reasoning with semantic annotations presupposes that the annotation language has a formal semantics. (In fact, one may wonder how much sense it makes to use a semantic annotation language *without* a semantics, since there is *a priori* little reason to assume that semantically undefined annotations would capture the meanings of natural language expressions any better than the expressions themselves.)

Still, existing work in this area, for instance on semantic role annotation (as in the FrameNet and PropBank initiatives) or on the annotation of temporal information (as in the TimeML effort) makes use of uninterpreted annotation languages.

In this talk, I will discuss some of the possibilities, perspectives, and problems in defining semantic annotation languages with a well-defined semantics. I will do this by starting from an attempt to integrate intermediate results from the design of a standard for temporal annotation in the International Organisation for Standards (ISO), and from the definition of annotation schemas for coreference annotation and semantic role labeling in the European project LIRICS. I will indicate the requirements for integrated and multilayered semantic annotation approaches, and certain general principles for semantic annotation. Moreover, I hope to address issues concerning the relations between using semantic annotations with a formal semantics on the one hand, and using underspecified semantic representations on the other. Finally, I will consider some of the potential applications of the use of interpreted semantic annotations in areas such as information extraction, paraphrase generation, and textual entailment.

PART I

REGULAR PAPERS

Combining Knowledge-based Methods and Supervised Learning for Effective Italian Word Sense Disambiguation

Pierpaolo Basile
Marco de Gemmis
Pasquale Lops
Giovanni Semeraro
University of Bari (Italy)
email: basilepp@di.uniba.it

Abstract

This paper presents a WSD strategy which combines a knowledge-based method that exploits sense definitions in a dictionary and relations among senses in a semantic network, with supervised learning methods on annotated corpora. The idea behind the approach is that the knowledge-based method can cope with the possible lack of training data, while supervised learning can improve the precision of a knowledge-based method when training data are available. This makes the proposed method suitable for disambiguation of languages for which the available resources are lacking in training data or sense definitions. In order to evaluate the effectiveness of the proposed approach, experimental sessions were carried out on the dataset used for the WSD task in the EVALITA 2007 initiative, devoted to the evaluation of Natural Language Processing tools for Italian. The most effective hybrid WSD strategy is the one that integrates the knowledge-based approach into the supervised learning method, which outperforms both methods taken singularly.

1 Background and Motivations

The inherent ambiguity of human language is a greatly debated problem in many research areas, such as information retrieval and text categorization, since the presence of polysemous words might result in a wrong relevance judgment or classification of documents. These problems call for alternative methods that work not only at the lexical level of the documents, but also at the *meaning* level.

The task of Word Sense Disambiguation (WSD) consists in assigning the most appropriate meaning to a polysemous word within a given context. Applications such as machine translation, knowledge acquisition, common sense reasoning and others, require knowledge about word meanings, and WSD is essential for all these applications. The assignment of senses to words is accomplished by using two major sources of information (Nancy and Véronis, 1998):

1. the *context* of the word to be disambiguated, e.g. information contained within the text in which the word appears;

2. *external knowledge sources*, including lexical resources, as well as hand-devised knowledge sources, which provide data useful to associate words with senses.

All disambiguation work involves matching the context of the instance of the word to be disambiguated with either information from an external knowledge source (also known as *knowledge-driven* WSD), or information about the contexts of previously disambiguated instances of the word derived from corpora (*data-driven* or *corpus-based* WSD).

Corpus-based WSD exploits semantically annotated corpora to train machine learning algorithms to decide which word sense to choose in which context. Words in such annotated corpora are tagged manually using semantic classes chosen from a particular lexical semantic resource (e.g. WORDNET (Fellbaum, 1998)). Each sense-tagged occurrence of a particular word is transformed into a feature vector, which is then used in an automatic learning process. The applicability of such supervised algorithms is limited to those few words for which sense tagged data are available, and their accuracy is strongly influenced by the amount of labeled data available.

Knowledge-based WSD has the advantage of avoiding the need of sense-annotated data, rather it exploits lexical knowledge stored in machine-readable dictionaries or thesauri. Systems adopting this approach have proved to be ready-to-use and scalable, but in general they reach lower precision than corpus-based WSD systems.

Our hypothesis is that the combination of both types of strategies can improve WSD effectiveness, because knowledge-based methods can cope with the possible lack of training data, while supervised learning can improve the precision of knowledge-based methods when training data are available.

This paper presents a method for solving the semantic ambiguity of *all words* contained in a text[1]. We propose a hybrid WSD algorithm that combines a knowledge-based WSD algorithm, called JIGSAW, which we designed to work by exploiting WORDNET-like dictionaries as sense repository, with a supervised machine learning

---

[1] *all words* task tries to disambiguate all the words in a text, while *lexical sample* task tries to disambiguate only specific words

algorithm (K-Nearest Neighbor classifier). WORDNET-like dictionaries are used because they combine the characteristics of both a dictionary and a structured semantic network, supplying definitions for the different senses of words and defining groups of synonymous words by means of *synsets*, which represent distinct lexical concepts. WORDNET also organize synsets in a conceptual structure by defining a number of semantic relationship (IS-A, PART-OF, etc.) among them.

Mainly, the paper concentrates on two investigations:

1. First, corpus-based WSD is applied to words for which training examples are provided, then JIGSAW is applied to words not covered in the first step, with the advantage of knowing the senses of the context words already disambiguated in the first step;

2. First, JIGSAW is applied to assign the most appropriate sense to those words that can be disambiguated with a high level of confidence (by setting a specific parameter in the algorithm), then the remaining words are disambiguated by the corpus-based method.

The paper is organized as follows: After a brief discussion about the main works related to our research, Section 3 gives the main ideas underlying the proposed hybrid WSD strategy. More details about the K-NN classification algorithm and JIGSAW, on which the hybrid WSD approach is based, are provided in Section 4 and Section 5, respectively. Experimental sessions have been carried out in order to evaluate the proposed approach in the critical situation when training data are not much reliable, as for Italian. Results are presented in Section 6, while conclusions and future work close the paper.

2 Related Work

For some Natural Language Processing (NLP) tasks, such as part of speech tagging or named entity recognition, there is a consensus on what makes a successful algorithm, regardless of the approach considered. Instead, no such consensus has been reached yet for the task of WSD, and previous work has considered a range of knowledge sources, such as local collocational clues, common membership in semantically or topically related word classes, semantic density, and others. In recent SENSEVAL-3 evaluations[2], the most successful approaches for *all words* WSD relied on information drawn from annotated corpora. The system developed by Decadt et al. (2002) uses two cascaded memory-based classifiers, combined with the use of a genetic algorithm for joint parameter optimization and feature selection. A separate word expert is learned for each ambiguous word, using a concatenated corpus of English sense tagged texts, including SemCor, SENSEVAL datasets, and a corpus built from WORDNET examples. The performance of this system on the SENSEVAL-3 English all words dataset was evaluated at 65.2%. Another top ranked system is the one developed by Yuret (2004), which combines two Naïve Bayes statistical models, one based on surrounding collocations and another one based on a bag of words around the target word. The statistical models are built based on SemCor and WORDNET, for an overall disambiguation accuracy of 64.1%. All previous systems use supervised methods, thus

---

[2]http://www.senseval.org

requiring a large amount of human intervention to annotate the training data. In the context of the current multilingual society, this strong requirement is even increased, since the so-called "sense-tagged data bottleneck problem" is emphasized.

To address this problem, different methods have been proposed. This includes the automatic generation of sense-tagged data using monosemous relatives (Leacock et al., 1998), automatically bootstrapped disambiguation patterns (Mihalcea, 2002), parallel texts as a way to point out word senses bearing different translations in a second language (Diab, 2004), and the use of volunteer contributions over the Web (Mihalcea and Chklovski, 2003). More recently, Wikipedia has been used as a source of sense annotations for building a sense annotated corpus which can be used to train accurate sense classifiers (Mihalcea, 2007). Even though the Wikipedia-based sense annotations were found reliable, leading to accurate sense classifiers, one of the limitations of the approach is that definitions and annotations in Wikipedia are available almost exclusively for nouns.

On the other hand, the increasing availability of large-scale rich (lexical) knowledge resources seems to provide new challenges to knowledge-based approaches (Navigli and Velardi, 2005; Mihalcea, 2005). Our hypothesis is that the complementarity of knowledge-based methods and corpus-based ones is the key to improve WSD effectiveness. The aim of the paper is to define a cascade hybrid method able to exploit both linguistic information coming from WORDNET-like dictionaries and statistical information coming from sense-annotated corpora.

3   A Hybrid Strategy for WSD

The goal of WSD algorithms consists in assigning a word w_i occurring in a document d with its appropriate meaning or sense s. The sense s is selected from a predefined set of possibilities, usually known as *sense inventory*. We adopt ITALWORDNET (Roventini et al., 2003) as sense repository. The algorithm is composed by two procedures:

1. **JIGSAW** - It is a knowledge-based WSD algorithm based on the assumption that the adoption of different strategies depending on Part-of-Speech (PoS) is better than using always the same strategy. A brief description of JIGSAW is given in Section 5, more details are reported in Basile et al. (2007b), Basile et al. (2007a) and Semeraro et al. (2007).

2. **Supervised learning procedure** - A K-NN classifier (Mitchell, 1997), trained on MultiSemCor corpus[3] is adopted. Details are given in Section 4. MultiSemCor is an English/Italian parallel corpus, aligned at the word level and annotated with PoS, lemma and word senses. The parallel corpus is created by exploiting the SemCor corpus[4], which is a subset of the English Brown corpus containing about 700,000 running words. In SemCor, all the words are tagged by PoS, and more than 200,000 content words are also lemmatized and sense-tagged with reference to the WORDNET lexical database. SemCor has been used in several supervised WSD algorithms for English with good results. MultiSemCor contains less annotations than SemCor, thus the accuracy and the coverage of the supervised learning for Italian might be affected by poor training data.

---

[3]http://multisemcor.itc.it/
[4]http://www.cs.unt.edu/~rada/downloads.html\#semcor

The idea is to combine both procedures in a hybrid WSD approach. A first choice might be the adoption of the supervised method as first attempt, then JIGSAW could be applied to words not covered in the first step. Differently, JIGSAW might be applied first, then leaving the supervised approach to disambiguate the remaining words. An investigation is required in order to choose the most effective combination.

4   Supervised Learning Method

The goal of supervised methods is to use a set of annotated data as little as possible, and at the same time to make the algorithm general enough to be able to disambiguate all content words in a text. We use MultiSemCor as annotated corpus, since at present it is the only available semantic annotated resource for Italian. The algorithm starts with a preprocessing stage, where the text is tokenized, stemmed, lemmatized and annotated with PoS.

Also, the collocations are identified using a sliding window approach, where a collocation is considered to be a sequence of words that forms a compound concept defined in ITALWORDNET (e.g. artificial intelligence). In the training step, a semantic model is learned for each PoS, starting with the annotated corpus. These models are then used to disambiguate words in the test corpus by annotating them with their corresponding meaning. The models can only handle words that were previously seen in the training corpus, and therefore their coverage is not 100%. Starting with an annotated corpus formed by all annotated files in MultiSemCor, a separate training dataset is built for each PoS. For each open-class word in the training corpus, a feature vector is built and added to the corresponding training set. The following features are used to describe an occurrence of a word in the training corpus as in Hoste et al. (2002):

- **Nouns** - 2 features are included in feature vector: the first noun, verb, or adjective before the target noun, within a window of at most three words to the left, and its PoS;

- **Verbs** - 4 features are included in feature vector: the first word before and the first word after the target verb, and their PoS;

- **Adjectives** - all the nouns occurring in two windows, each one of six words (before and after the target adjective) are included in the feature vector;

- **Adverbs** - the same as for adjectives, but vectors contain adjectives rather than nouns.

The label of each feature vector consists of the target word and the corresponding sense, represented as *word#sense*. Table 1 describes the number of vectors for each PoS.

To annotate (disambiguate) new text, similar vectors are built for all content-words in the text to be analyzed. Consider the target word *bank*, used as a noun. The algorithm catches all the feature vectors of *bank* as a noun from the training model, and builds the feature vector v_f for the target word. Then, the algorithm computes the similarity between each training vector and v_f and ranks the training vectors in decreasing order according to the similarity value.

Table 1: Number of feature vectors

PoS	#feature vectors
Noun	38,546
Verb	18,688
Adjective	6,253
Adverb	1,576

The similarity is computed as Euclidean distance between vectors, where POS distance is set to 1, if POS tags are different, otherwise it is set to 0. Word distances are computed by using the *Levenshtein* metric, that measures the amount of difference between two strings as the minimum number of operations needed to transform one string into the other, where an operation is an insertion, deletion, or substitution of a single character (Levenshtein, 1966). Finally, the target word is labeled with the most frequent sense in the first K vectors.

5   JIGSAW - Knowledge-based Approach

JIGSAW is a WSD algorithm based on the idea of combining three different strategies to disambiguate nouns, verbs, adjectives and adverbs. The main motivation behind our approach is that the effectiveness of a WSD algorithm is strongly influenced by the POS tag of the target word.

JIGSAW takes as input a document $d = (w_1, w_2, \ldots, w_h)$ and returns a list of synsets $X = (s_1, s_2, \ldots, s_k)$ in which each element s_i is obtained by disambiguating the *target word* w_i based on the information obtained from the sense repository about a few immediately surrounding words. We define the *context C* of the target word to be a window of n words to the left and another n words to the right, for a total of $2n$ surrounding words. The algorithm is based on three different procedures for nouns, verbs, adverbs and adjectives, called $JIGSAW_{nouns}$, $JIGSAW_{verbs}$, $JIGSAW_{others}$, respectively.

JIGSAW$_{nouns}$ - Given a set of nouns $W = \{w_1, w_2, \ldots, w_n\}$, obtained from document d, with each w_i having an associated sense inventory $S_i = \{s_{i1}, s_{i2}, \ldots, s_{ik}\}$ of possible senses, the goal is assigning each w_i with the most appropriate sense $s_{ih} \in S_i$, according to the *similarity* of w_i with the other words in W (the context for w_i). The idea is to define a function $\varphi(w_i, s_{ij})$, $w_i \in W$, $s_{ij} \in S_i$, that computes a value in $[0, 1]$ representing the confidence with which word w_i can be assigned with sense s_{ij}. In order to measure the relatedness of two words we adopted a modified version of the Leacock and Chodorow (1998) measure, which computes the length of the path between two concepts in a hierarchy by passing through their *Most Specific Subsumer* (MSS). We introduced a constant factor *depth* which limits the search for the MSS to *depth* ancestors, in order to avoid "poorly informative" MSSs. Moreover, in the similarity computation, we introduced both a Gaussian factor $G(pos(w_i), pos(w_j))$, which takes into account the distance between the position of the words in the text to be disambiguated, and a factor $R(k)$, which assigns s_{ik} with a numerical value, according to the frequency score in ITALWORDNET.

JIGSAW$_{verbs}$ - We define the *description* of a synset as the string obtained by concatenating the gloss and the sentences that ITALWORDNET uses to explain the usage of a synset. *JIGSAW$_{verbs}$* includes, in the context C for the target verb w_i, all the nouns in the window of $2n$ words surrounding w_i. For each candidate synset s_{ik} of w_i, the algorithm computes $nouns(i,k)$, that is the set of nouns in the description for s_{ik}. Then, for each w_j in C and each synset s_{ik}, the following value is computed:

$$(1) \quad max_{jk} = max_{w_l \in nouns(i,k)} \left\{ \text{sim}(w_j, w_l, depth) \right\}$$

where $\text{sim}(w_j, w_l, depth)$ is the same similarity measure adopted by *JIGSAW$_{nouns}$*. Finally, an overall similarity score among s_{ik} and the whole context C is computed:

$$(2) \quad \varphi(i,k) = R(k) \cdot \frac{\sum_{w_j \in C} G(pos(w_i), pos(w_j)) \cdot max_{jk}}{\sum_h G(pos(w_i), pos(w_h))}$$

where both $R(k)$ and $G(pos(w_i), pos(w_j))$, that gives a higher weight to words closer to the target word, are defined as in *JIGSAW$_{nouns}$*. The synset assigned to w_i is the one with the highest φ value.

JIGSAW$_{others}$ - This procedure is based on the WSD algorithm proposed in Banerjee and Pedersen (2002). The idea is to compare the glosses of each candidate sense for the target word to the glosses of all the words in its context.

6 Experiments

The main goal of our investigation is to study the behavior of the hybrid algorithm when available training resources are not much reliable, e.g. when a lower number of sense descriptions is available, as for Italian. The hypothesis we want to evaluate is that corpus-based methods and knowledge-based ones can be combined to improve the accuracy of each single strategy.

Experiments have been performed on a standard test collection in the context of the *All-Words-Task*, in which WSD algorithms attempt to disambiguate all words in a text. Specifically, we used the EVALITA WSD All-Words-Task dataset[5], which consists of about 5,000 words labeled with ITALWORDNET synsets.

An important concern for the evaluation of WSD systems is the agreement rate between human annotators on word sense assignment.

While for natural language subtasks like part-of-speech tagging, there are relatively well defined and agreed-upon criteria of what it means to have the "correct" part of speech assigned to a word, this is not the case for word sense assignment. Two human annotators may genuinely disagree on their sense assignment to a word in a context, since the distinction between the different senses for a commonly used word in a dictionary like WORDNET tend to be rather fine.

What we would like to underline here is that it is important that human agreement on an annotated corpus is carefully measured, in order to set an upper bound to the performance measures: it would be futile to expect computers to agree more with the reference corpus that human annotators among them. For example, the inter-annotator agreement rate during the preparation of the SENSEVAL-3 WSD English All-Words-Task dataset (Agirre et al., 2007) was approximately 72.5%.

---

[5]http://evalita.itc.it/tasks/wsd.html

Unfortunately, for EVALITA dataset, the inter-annotator agreement has not been measured, one of the reasons why the evaluation for Italian WSD is very hard. In our experiments, we reasonably selected different baselines to compare the performance of the proposed hybrid algorithm.

6.1   Integrating JIGSAW into a supervised learning method

The design of the experiment is as follows: firstly, corpus-based WSD is applied to words for which training examples are provided, then JIGSAW is applied to words not covered by the first step, with the advantage of knowing the senses of the context words already disambiguated in the first step. The performance of the hybrid method was measured in terms of precision (P), recall (R), F-measure (F) and the percentage A of disambiguation attempts, computed by counting the words for which a disambiguation attempt is made (the words with no training examples or sense definitions cannot be disambiguated). Table 2 shows the baselines chosen to compare the hybrid WSD algorithm on the All-Words-Task experiments.

Table 2: Baselines for Italian All-Words-Task

Setting	P	R	F	A
1st *sense*	58.45	48.58	53.06	83.11
Random	43.55	35.88	39.34	83.11
JIGSAW	55.14	45.83	**50.05**	83.11
K-NN	59.15	11.46	**19.20**	19.38
K-NN + 1st *sense*	57.53	47.81	52.22	83.11

The simplest baseline consists in assigning a random sense to each word (*Random*), another common baseline in Word Sense Disambiguation is first sense (1st *sense*): each word is tagged using the first sense in ITALWORDNET that is the most commonly (frequent) used sense. The other baselines are the two methods combined in the hybrid WSD, taken separately, namely JIGSAW and K-NN, and the basic hybrid algorithm "K-NN + 1st *sense*", which applies the supervised method, and then adopts the first sense heuristic for the words without examples into training data. The K-NN baseline achieves the highest precision, but the lowest recall due to the low coverage in the training data (19.38%) makes this method useless for all practical purposes. Notice that JIGSAW was the only participant to EVALITA WSD All-Words-Task, therefore it currently represents the only available system performing WSD All-Words task for the Italian language.

Table 3: Experimental results of K-NN+JIGSAW

Setting	P	R	F	A
K-NN + JIGSAW	56.62	47.05	**51.39**	83.11
K-NN + JIGSAW ($\varphi \geq 0.90$)	61.88	26.16	36.77	42.60
K-NN + JIGSAW ($\varphi \geq 0.80$)	61.40	32.21	42.25	52.06
K-NN + JIGSAW ($\varphi \geq 0.70$)	60.02	36.29	45.23	60.46
K-NN + JIGSAW ($\varphi \geq 0.50$)	59.58	37.38	45.93	62.74

Table 3 reports the results obtained by the hybrid method on the EVALITA dataset. We study the behavior of the hybrid approach with relation to that of JIGSAW, since this specific experiment aims at evaluating the potential improvements due to the inclusion of JIGSAW into K-NN. Different runs of the hybrid method have been performed, each run corresponding to setting a specific value for φ (the confidence with which a word w_i is correctly disambiguated by JIGSAW). In each different run, the disambiguation carried out by JIGSAW is considered reliable only when φ values exceed a certain threshold, otherwise any sense is assigned to the target word (this the reason why A decreases by setting higher values for φ).

A positive effect on precision can be noticed by varying φ between 0.50 and 0.90. It tends to grow and overcomes all the baselines, but a corresponding decrease of recall is observed, as a consequence of more severe constraints set on φ. Anyway, recall is still too low to be acceptable.

Better results are achieved when no restriction is set on φ (K-NN+JIGSAW in Table 3): the recall is significantly higher than that obtained in the other runs. On the other hand, the precision reached in this run is lower than in the others, but it is still acceptable.

To sum up, two main conclusions can be drawn from the experiments:

- when no constraint is set on the knowledge-based method, the hybrid algorithm K-NN+JIGSAW in general outperforms both JIGSAW and K-NN taken singularly (F values highlighted in bold in Tables 3 and 4);

- when thresholding is introduced on φ, no improvement is observed on the whole compared to K-NN+JIGSAW.

A deep analysis of results revealed that lower recall was achieved for verbs and adjectives rather than for nouns. Indeed, disambiguation of Italian verbs and adjectives is very hard, but the lower recall is probability due also to the fact that *JIGSAW* uses glosses for verbs and adjectives disambiguation. As a consequence, the performance depends on the accuracy of word descriptions in the glosses, while for nouns the algorithm relies only the semantic relations between synsets.

6.2 Integrating supervised learning into JIGSAW

In this experiment we test whether the supervised algorithm can help JIGSAW to disambiguate more accurately. The experiment has been organized as follows: JIGSAW is applied to assign the most appropriate sense to the words which can be disambiguated with a high level of confidence (by setting the φ threshold), then the remaining words are disambiguated by the K-NN classifier. The dataset and the baselines are the same as in Section 6.1.

Note that, differently from the experiments described in Table 3, run JIGSAW+K-NN has not been reported since JIGSAW covered all the target words in the first step of the cascade hybrid method, then the K-NN method is not applied at all. Therefore, for this run, results obtained by JIGSAW+K-NN correspond to those get by JIGSAW alone (reported in Table 2).

Table 4 reports the results of all the runs. Results are very similar to those obtained in the runs K-NN+JIGSAW with the same settings on φ. Precision tends to grow,

Table 4: Experimental results of JIGSAW+K-NN

Setting	P	R	F	A
JIGSAW ($\varphi \geq 0.90$) + K-NN	61.48	27.42	37.92	44.61
JIGSAW ($\varphi \geq 0.80$) + K-NN	61.17	32.59	42.52	53.28
JIGSAW ($\varphi \geq 0.70$) + K-NN	59.44	36.56	**45.27**	61.52

while a corresponding decrease in recall is observed. The main outcome is that the overall accuracy of the best combination JIGSAW+K-NN ($\varphi \geq 0.70$, F value highlighted in bold in Table 4) is outperformed by K-NN+JIGSAW. Indeed, this result was largely expected because the small size of the training set does not allow to cover words not disambiguated by JIGSAW.

Even if K-NN+JIGSAW is not able to achieve the baselines set on the 1st sense heuristic (first and last row in Table 2), we can conclude that a step toward these hard baselines has been moved. The main outcome of the study is that the best hybrid method on which further investigations are possible is K-NN+JIGSAW.

7 Conclusions and Future Work

This paper presented a method for solving the semantic ambiguity of *all words* contained in a text. We proposed a hybrid WSD algorithm that combines a knowledge-based WSD algorithm, called JIGSAW, which we designed to work by exploiting WORDNET-like dictionaries as sense repository, with a supervised machine learning algorithm (K-Nearest Neighbor classifier). The idea behind the proposed approach is that JIGSAW can cope with the possible lack of training data, while K-NN can improve the precision of JIGSAW method when training data are available. This makes the proposed method suitable for disambiguation of languages for which the available resources are lacking in training data or sense definitions, such as Italian.

Extensive experimental sessions were performed on the EVALITA WSD All-Words-Task dataset, the only dataset available for the evaluation of WSD systems for the Italian language. An investigation was carried out in order to evaluate several combinations of JIGSAW and K-NN. The main outcome is that the most effective hybrid WSD strategy is the one that runs JIGSAW after K-NN, which outperforms both JIGSAW and K-NN taken singularly. Future work includes new experiments with other combination methods, for example the *JIGSAW* output could be used as feature into supervised system or other different supervised methods could be exploited.

References

Agirre, E., B. Magnini, O. L. de Lacalle, A. Otegi, G. Rigau, and P. Vossen (2007). SemEval-2007 Task 1: Evaluating WSD on Cross-Language Information Retrieval. In *Proceedings of SemEval-2007*. Association for Computational Linguistics.

Banerjee, S. and T. Pedersen (2002). An adapted lesk algorithm for word sense disambiguation using wordnet. In *CICLing '02: Proceedings of the Third International*

Conference on Computational Linguistics and Intelligent Text Processing, London, UK, pp. 136–145. Springer-Verlag.

Basile, P., M. de Gemmis, A. Gentile, P. Lops, and G. Semeraro (2007a). JIGSAW algorithm for Word Sense Disambiguation. In *SemEval-2007: 4th International Workshop on Semantic Evaluations*, pp. 398–401. ACL press.

Basile, P., M. de Gemmis, A. L. Gentile, P. Lops, and G. Semeraro (2007b). The JIG-SAW Algorithm for Word Sense Disambiguation and Semantic Indexing of Documents. In R. Basili and M. T. Pazienza (Eds.), *AI*IA*, Volume 4733 of *Lecture Notes in Computer Science*, pp. 314–325. Springer.

Decadt, B., V. Hoste, W. Daelemans, and A. V. den Bosch (2002). Gambl, Genetic Algorithm optimization of Memory-based WSD. In *Senseval-3: 3th International Workshop on the Evaluation of Systems for the Semantic Analysis of Text*.

Diab, M. (2004). Relieving the data acquisition bottleneck in word sense disambiguation. In *Proceedings of ACL*. Barcelona, Spain.

Fellbaum, C. (1998). *WordNet: An Electronic Lexical Database*. MIT Press.

Hoste, V., W. Daelemans, I. Hendrickx, and A. van den Bosch (2002). Evaluating the results of a memory-based word-expert approach to unrestricted word sense disambiguation. In *Proceedings of the ACL-02 workshop on Word sense disambiguation: recent successes and future directions*, Volume 8, pp. 95–101. Association for Computational Linguistics Morristown, NJ, USA.

Leacock, C. and M. Chodorow (1998). *Combining local context and WordNet similarity for word sense identification*, pp. 305–332. MIT Press.

Leacock, C., M. Chodorow, and G. Miller (1998). Using corpus statistics and Word-Net relations for sense identification. *Computational Linguistics 24*(1), 147–165.

Levenshtein, V. I. (1966). Binary codes capable of correcting deletions, insertions, and reversals. *Soviet Physics Doklady 10*(8), 707–710.

Mihalcea, R. (2002). Bootstrapping large sense tagged corpora. In *Proceedings of the 3rd International Conference on Language Resources and Evaluations*.

Mihalcea, R. (2005). Unsupervised large-vocabulary word sense disambiguation with graph-based algorithms for sequence data labeling. In *HLT '05: Proceedings of the conference on Human Language Technology and Empirical Methods in Natural Language Processing*, Morristown, NJ, USA, pp. 411–418. Association for Computational Linguistics.

Mihalcea, R. (2007). Using Wikipedia for Automatic Word Sense Disambiguation. In *Proceedings of the North American Chapter of the Association for Computational Linguistics*.

Mihalcea, R. and T. Chklovski (2003). Open Mind Word Expert: Creating Large Annotated Data Collections with Web Users' Help. In *Proceedings of the EACL Workshop on Linguistically Annotated Corpora, Budapest*.

Mitchell, T. (1997). *Machine Learning*. New York: McGraw-Hill.

Nancy, I. and J. Véronis (1998). Introduction to the special issue on word sense disambiguation: The state of the art. *Computational Linguistics 24*(1), 1–40.

Navigli, R. and P. Velardi (2005). Structural semantic interconnections: A knowledge-based approach to word sense disambiguation. *IEEE Transactions on Pattern Analysis and Machine Intelligence 27*(7), 1075–1086.

Roventini, A., A. Alonge, F. Bertagna, N. Calzolari, J. Cancila, C. Girardi, B. Magnini, R. Marinelli, M. Speranza, and A. Zampolli (2003). ItalWordNet: building a large semantic database for the automatic treatment of Italian. *Computational Linguistics in Pisa - Linguistica Computazionale a Pisa. Linguistica Computazionale, Special Issue XVIII-XIX, Tomo II*, 745–791.

Semeraro, G., M. Degemmis, P. Lops, and P. Basile (2007). Combining learning and word sense disambiguation for intelligent user profiling. In *Proceedings of the Twentieth International Joint Conference on Artificial Intelligence IJCAI-07*, pp. 2856–2861. M. Kaufmann, San Francisco, California. ISBN: 978-I-57735-298-3.

Yuret, D. (2004). Some experiments with a naive bayes WSD system. In *Senseval-3: 3th Internat. Workshop on the Evaluation of Systems for the Semantic Analysis of Text*.

Semantic Representations of Syntactically Marked Discourse Status in Crosslinguistic Perspective

Emily M. Bender
David Goss-Grubbs
University of Washington (USA)
email: ebender@u.washington.edu

Abstract

This paper presents suggested semantic representations for different types of referring expressions in the format of Minimal Recursion Semantics and sketches syntactic analyses which can create them compositionally. We explore cross-linguistic harmonization of these representations, to promote interoperability and reusability of linguistic analyses. We follow Borthen and Haugereid (2005) in positing COG-ST ('cognitive status') as a feature on the syntax-semantics interface to handle phenomena associated with definiteness. Our proposal helps to unify the treatments of definiteness markers, demonstratives, overt pronouns and null anaphora across languages. In languages with articles, they contribute an existential quantifier and the appropriate value for COG-ST. In other languages, the COG-ST value is determined by an affix. The contribution of demonstrative determiners is decomposed into a COG-ST value, a quantifier, and proximity information, each of which can be contributed by a different kind of grammatical construction in a given language. Along with COG-ST, we posit a feature that distinguishes between pronouns (and null anaphora) that are sensitive to the identity of the referent of their antecedent and those that are sensitive to its type.

1   Introduction

In this paper, we discuss the compositional construction of semantic representations reflecting discourse status across a range of phenomena. Borthen and Haugereid (2005) propose COG-ST ('cognitive-status')[1] as a feature on the syntax-semantics interface to handle phenomena associated with definiteness. We explore how their approach leads to cross-linguistically unified treatments of demonstratives, overt pronouns and null anaphora as well. We find that cross-linguistic studies motivate different representations than we might have arrived at from just one language.

Our work grows out of the Grammar Matrix, a multilingual grammar engineering project (Bender et al., 2002; Bender and Flickinger, 2005) which strives to harmonize semantic representations across diverse languages. The Grammar Matrix is couched within the Head-driven Phrase Structure Grammar (HPSG) framework (Pollard and Sag, 1994). We use Minimal Recursion Semantics (Copestake et al., 2001, 2005) as our semantic representation system.

2   Background

2.1   Minimal Recursion Semantics

Grammar Matrix-derived grammars associate surface strings with MRS representations (or MRSs), in a bidirectional mapping that allows both parsing and generation. An MRS consists of a multiset of elementary predications (eps), each of which is a single relation with its associated arguments, labeled by a handle; a set of handle constraints relating the labels of eps to argument positions within other eps; and a top handle indicating which of the labels has outermost scope (Copestake et al., 2001, 2005). The MRSs produced by these grammars are underspecified for scope, allowing multiple different fully-scoped variants, according to the handle constraints.

Each ep has a predicate (PRED) value and one or more argument positions, usually labeled ARG0 through ARGn. By convention, we refer to elementary predications by their PRED values. For scope-taking eps (including quantifiers as well as clause-embedding predicates such as **_believe_v_rel** and scopal modifiers such as negation), at least one argument position is handle-valued, and related (in a well-formed structure) to the label of another ep. For non-scopal predications, the values of the argument positions are variables (also called indices) which may themselves be associated with 'variable properties', such as person, number and gender on individual variables, or tense, aspect, sentential force and mood on event variables.

One benefit of MRS is that it is designed to be compatible with feature-structure grammars. We build up MRSs through an HPSG implementation of the MRS algebra in Copestake et al. (2001), in which each constituent bears features recording the eps and handle constraints contributed within the constituent, as well as a set of properties exposed through the feature HOOK to facilitate further composition. These properties include pointers to the local top handle (LTOP), the constituent's primary index (INDEX), and the external argument, if any (XARG).

Eps are canonically contributed by lexical entries, with one ep per lexical entry. Lexical entries can, however, contribute more than one ep or no eps at all. In addition, syntactic constructions can also contribute eps of their own.

---

[1] Original feature name: COGN-ST.

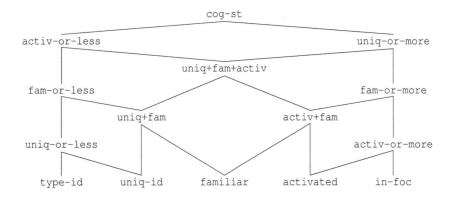

Figure 1: Cognitive status hierarchy

2.2 Harmonization of Representations

The semantic representations used in the Grammar Matrix were originally derived from those used in the English Resource Grammar (Flickinger, 2000), a wide-coverage grammar of English. In this paper, we propose to refine the semantic representations for phenomena connected to discourse status in light of the constraints on the syntax-semantics interface we find in a range of languages. This is not to say that we are promoting working towards an interlingua: indeed, even if it were possible to define a suitable interlingual set of representations, we believe it wouldn't be possible to map from surface strings to such representations in one compositional step.

Nonetheless, it is useful to harmonize representations across languages while still allowing for necessary differences, for at least two reasons. First, when semantic representations are as similar as they practically can be, this simplifies both the transfer component in transfer-based machine translation systems (e.g., Oepen et al., 2007) and the design of downstream components that make use of semantic representations in multilingual NLP systems in general. Second, harmonized semantic representations facilitate the creation of libraries in a resource like the Grammar Matrix, which in turn promotes both the reuse of analyses within implemented grammars and the exploration of computational linguistic typology.

2.3 Discourse/Cognitive Status

This paper builds on a tradition of work investigating the way the discourse status of referents influences the form of the referring expressions used to refer to them, or alternatively, the way that speakers use contrasts in form to signal to their interlocutors the discourse (or cognitive) status of their intended referents (Chafe, 1976, 1994; Prince, 1981; Gundel et al., 1993; Borthen and Haugereid, 2005; Arnold, 2008).

Borthen and Haugereid (2005) (henceforth B&H) present arguments from a range of languages that the discourse status associated with referring expressions can be constrained by multiple intersecting syntactic factors. They use this to motivate embedding the discourse status information within the semantic features of a sign, rather than on the contextual features. They adapt the implicational scale proposed by Gundel et al. (1993) and Prince (1981), representing discourse referents as having a range of values from 'type identifiable' through 'in focus'. In Gundel et al. and Prince's work, this is an implicational scale, where a discourse status of 'in focus', for example, also entails a discourse status of 'activated'. B&H argue that it needs to be represented within the syntax by a type hierarchy that makes each discourse status type incompatible with the others, while also creating supertypes that represent ranges of discourse status values. Their intuition is that the syntactic constraints restrict the distribution of certain forms based on the highest discourse status they are compatible with, rather than on the actual discourse status of the referent they are used to evoke in a given context. The cognitive status hierarchy, as we adopt it from Borthen and Haugereid (2005) is shown in Fig 1.

3   Markers of Definiteness

The first phenomenon we consider is markers of definiteness. In English, these are syntactically identified with determiners, and thus the English Resource Grammar represents the semantic contrast between *the* and *a* with the PRED value of the ep contributed by the determiner: **_the_q_rel** vs. **_a_q_rel** (where 'q' stands for 'quantifier'). Crosslinguistically, however, definiteness is not always marked in lexical determiners which might plausibly contribute quantifier relations. For example, in Norwegian, definiteness is signaled in part by an affix on the noun:

(1)   Jeg så   bilen.
      I   saw car.DEF

      'I saw the car.' [nob]

This does not lend itself to the analysis of definiteness in English provided by the ERG: First, the definite suffix can co-occur with something else in the determiner role, as in (2).[2] Second, even if the affix did contribute a **_def_q_rel**, this would lead to ill-formed MRSs as soon as there were any intersective modifiers: Eps introduced by intersective modifiers (such as *nye* in (2)) should be labeled with the same handle as the ep introduced by the noun. But according to the MRS model of semantic compositionality, the label of the noun's relation is not available for further composition once the quantifier has attached.

(2)   Jeg så   den nye   bilen
      I   saw the new.DEF car.DEF

      'I saw the new car.' [nob]

Third, adjectives can also take definite forms. We would like to enforce the compatibility of this information, rather than having each instance of the definite suffix contribute an additional ep. Per B&H, this supports treating definiteness in terms of a feature rather than through eps.

---

[2]Note that the determiner is required when there is an adjective in a definite NP, and pragmatically very restricted when there is not.

Following B&H, we note that the apparently binary distinction between definites and indefinites is better assimilated to the cognitive status hierarchy. There are morphosyntactic phenomena in various languages which divide the cognitive status hierarchy into two separate ranges, though the division point may vary across languages and within languages across phenomena. Using a single feature for cognitive status that takes its values from the type hierarchy in Fig 1 allows these various distinctions to be modeled elegantly.

B&H propose wrapping semantic indices in a new structure *ref-prop*, which contains COG-ST as well as other features related to the referential properties of a noun phrase. In this paper, we focus on COG-ST and leave the other dimensions to future work. However, we differ from B&H in proposing that COG-ST, at least, should be a feature of semantic indices, rather than inside a parallel structure (i.e., their *ref-prop*). This has the benefit of causing the COG-ST information from particular words or affixes to be included in the compositionally created semantic representations of phrases and sentences without any further effort: wherever the index so marked appears, it will carry its COG-ST value with it. It also makes the (correct, we believe) prediction that whenever an index appears in multiple places in the semantic representation, it should bear the same cognitive status information in all of them. For example, the MRS for (3) is as in (4), where the variable 'x5' represents the cat, and appears as a value in four separate elementary predications: ARG0 of **_cat_n_rel**, ARG0 of **_exist_q_rel**, ARG1 of **_want_v_rel**, and ARG1 of **_go+out_v_rel**. We claim that in all of these guises, the cognitive status of the referent is the same; there is only one mental representation of the referent involved.

(3)   The cat wanted to go out.

(4)
$$
\begin{bmatrix}
\text{LTOP} & \text{h0} \\
\text{INDEX} & \text{e1} \\
\text{RELS} & \left\langle
\begin{bmatrix}
\text{\_exist\_q\_rel} \\
\text{LBL} \quad \text{h3} \\
\text{ARG0} \quad \text{x5}[uniq\text{-}id] \\
\text{RSTR} \quad \text{h6} \\
\text{BODY} \quad \text{h4}
\end{bmatrix},
\begin{bmatrix}
\text{\_cat\_n\_rel} \\
\text{LBL} \quad \text{h7} \\
\text{ARG0} \quad \text{x5}
\end{bmatrix},
\begin{bmatrix}
\text{\_want\_v\_rel} \\
\text{LBL} \quad \text{h8} \\
\text{ARG0} \quad \text{e2} \\
\text{ARG1} \quad \text{x5} \\
\text{ARG2} \quad \text{h9}
\end{bmatrix},
\begin{bmatrix}
\text{\_go+out\_v\_rel} \\
\text{LBL} \quad \text{h10} \\
\text{ARG0} \quad \text{e11} \\
\text{ARG1} \quad \text{x5}
\end{bmatrix}
\right\rangle \\
\text{HCONS} & \left\langle \text{h6} =_q \text{h7, h9} =_q \text{h10} \right\rangle
\end{bmatrix}
$$

B&H consider this possibility and dismiss it on the grounds that coreferential noun phrases don't necessarily share the same cognitive status. However, placing the COG-ST value on the index does not necessarily entail that the expressions *The cat, herself*, and *her* impute the same cognitive status to their discourse referent in (5). As far as the syntactic processing is concerned, these expressions introduce distinct indices. It is up to a separate reference resolution component to identify them, and that component could merge their COG-ST values or not, as appropriate.

(5)   The cat opened the door herself with her paw.

Thus rather than having English *the* and similar elements introduce a specialized quantifier relation, we instead do a small amount of semantic decomposition: *the* introduces just an existential quantifier (**_exist_q_rel**), but constrains the variable it

```
a.  def-noun-lex-rule := inflecting-lexeme-to-word-rule &
    %prefix (ha- *)
      [ SYNSEM.LOCAL.CONT.HOOK.INDEX.COG-ST uniq-id,
        DTR noun-lex ].
b.  def-adj-lex-rule := inflecting-lexeme-to-word-rule &
    %prefix (ha- *)
      [ SYNSEM.LOCAL.CAT.HEAD.MOD.LOCAL.CONT.HOOK.INDEX.COG-ST
        uniq-or-more, DTR adj-lex ].
c.  indef-noun-lex-rule := constant-lexeme-to-word-rule &
      [ SYNSEM.LOCAL.CAT.HEAD.MOD.LOCAL.CONT.HOOK.INDEX.COG-ST
        type-id, DTR adj-lex ].
```

Figure 2: Sample lexical rules for definiteness affixes

binds to be [COG-ST *uniq-id*]. This signals to the hearer that s/he should be able to assign a unique representation to the referent (but not that the referent itself is unique in the world or in the previous discourse, cf. Gundel et al., 2001).

In other languages affixes can also constrain COG-ST to *uniq-or-more* or *uniq-id*. We illustrate here with the Hebrew definite prefix *ha-*, shown in (6) (from Wintner, 2000:322).

(6) koll šešš ha-smalot   ha-yapot ha-'elle   šelli mi-'rhb
     all six DEF-dresses DEF-nice DEF-these mine   from-US

     'all these six nice dresses of mine from the US' [heb]

ha- is added by a lexical rule (sketched in Fig 2a) which adds information about the COG-ST to the noun's own INDEX value.[3] When *ha-* attaches to an adjective in Hebrew, it instead adds the information that the noun the adjective is modifying must have the COG-ST value *uniq-or-more*, as sketched in Fig 2b. This rule is paired with a non-inflecting lexical rule Fig 2c which produces adjectives which can only modify nouns that are [COG-ST *type-id*], i.e., indefinite. This will enforce definiteness agreement across the noun phrase.[4]

This section has briefly outlined an adaptation of B&H's proposal for definiteness marking. The main difference to their proposal is in the location of COG-ST in the feature geometry. In the following two sections, we extend the approach to demonstratives and a variety of null anaphora.

4   Demonstratives

Demonstratives can stand alone as noun phrases (demonstrative pronouns) or function as nominal dependents. Starting again with English, we find that demonstratives in their nominal-dependent guise, like the markers of definiteness, fill the spec-

---

[3]The lexical rules in Fig 2 are non-branching productions that apply at the bottom of the parse tree, before any syntactic rules can apply. The SYNSEM value represents the mother and the DTR value the daughter. The types they inherit from (e.g., *inflecting-lexeme-to-word-rule*) enforce identity of most of the information between mother and daughter. The rules add information about COG-ST, which must be compatible with what's provided by the lexical entries for the rules to apply.

[4]For the rule for unmarked nouns, see §4 below.

ifier slot of the noun phrase and function as determiners. Accordingly, the ERG represents their semantic contribution through the PRED value of the quantifier relation: **_this_q_dem_rel** and **_that_q_dem_rel**. Crosslinguistically, however, demonstratives functioning as nominal dependents can also appear as adjectives or affixes (Dryer, 2008). In such languages, within the general constraints of composition of MRS, it is not elegant or natural-seeming to have an adjective contribute a quantifier relation or constrain the PRED value of a relation contributed by a separate determiner or non-branching NP construction.

Instead, it seems more appropriate to decompose the semantic representation of determiners into a quantifier relation (**_exist_q_rel**) and a separate one-place modifier relation (e.g., **_distal+dem_a_rel**, for 'that'). In languages with demonstrative adjectives, the demonstrative form contributes only the modifier relation. In languages with demonstrative determiners, the demonstrative forms contribute both.

Demonstratives also constrain the COG-ST value of the nouns the modify, typically to *activ-or-fam*. In some languages, (e.g., Irish Gaelic), the demonstratives require additional marking of discourse status. Typically this takes the form of a definite article (see (7) from McCloskey (2004)), but demonstratives can also attach to pronouns and proper nouns (McCloskey, 2004).

(7)   an fear mór téagartha groí   seo
      the man big stocky   cheerful DEM

      'this big stocky cheerful man' [gle]

(8)   *fear mór téagartha groí seo

Such languages are straightforwardly countenanced within this system: the definite article and article-less NPs have incompatible COG-ST values, and only the former is compatible with the COG-ST constraints contributed by the demonstrative adjective.[5]

The situation in Hebrew is slightly more complex: Demonstratives can occur with or without the *ha-* prefix, so long as they agree with the noun they modify. Conversely, nouns without the *ha-* prefix are interpreted as indefinite, unless they are modified by a demonstrative adjective. It is unclear at this point whether there is a difference in interpretation between (9) and (10) (from Wintner, 2000:334), but it seems likely that *type-id* is not the correct cognitive status for (9); that is, it is most likely not an indefinite.

(9)   sepr ze   nimkar heiteb
      book this is.sold well

      'This book sells well.' [heb]

(10) ha-sepr   ha-ze   nimkar heiteb
      DEF-book   DEF-this is.sold well

      'This book sells well.' [heb]

---

[5]McCloskey points out that the demonstratives can attach to coordinated NPs, each with their own article. This raises difficulties for treating the demonstratives as adjectives, as it would require the demonstrative adjectives to attach outside the determiner (cf. Bender et al., 2005). We leave this issue to future work.

Here, we postpone the assignment of a COG-ST value to an unmarked noun until the NP level, filling in *type-id* in case no demonstrative has attached. This requires an additional syntactic feature to control the application of the NPs rules, but this seems motivated: As Wintner notes, *ha-* is functioning as an agreement marker; its distribution has become grammaticized and drifted somewhat from what purely semantic constraints would predict.

To provide complete representations for demonstratives, we also need to address the additional information they carry in many languages, such as the relative proximity of the referent to the speaker and/or the hearer, its visibility or elevation (Diessel, 1999). These distinctions appear to be at least partially independent of the COG-ST dimension. In addition, in the absence of any evidence for syntactically-mediated agreement between elements of a sentence along this dimension, for now we represent this part of the meaning of demonstratives as an elementary predication rather than as a feature.

Some languages (e.g., Lithuanian) have a demonstrative element which does not express any distance contrast, in addition to ones that do (Diessel, 2008). In this case, it might make sense to reduce the contribution of the former sort of element to the constraints it places on the noun's COG-ST value. However, in the interests of uniformity within the system, we continue to assign it an elementary predication.

Other languages (e.g., French and German) don't mark any distance contrast on the primary demonstrative element. In all such languages, there are optional, deictic adverbials which can be added to mark the contrast (Diessel, 2008).

(11)   Das Bild   hier gefällt mir besser als   das   da.
       DEM picture here like   me better than DEM there.

       'I like this picture better than that one (over there).' [deu]

In light of such data, we could decompose demonstratives with distance contrasts in all languages into separate demonstrative and deictic/distance relations. Alternatively, we could do that decomposition only in languages like German and French. To the extent that the deictic elements (e.g., German *hier* and *da*) have other uses as ordinary adverbs which can be syntactically assimilated to the same lexical entry, we would want to at least make sure that the ep they contribute is the same in both cases.

5   Overt pronouns and zero anaphora

Pronouns in the ERG are currently represented by an index which is bound by the quantifier **_pronoun_q_rel** and modified by **_pronoun_n_rel**. The quantifier ep marks the pronoun as definite, and the modifier ep serves as the restriction for the quantifier as well as identifying the index as a pronoun.

Following the treatment of other nominals presented here, however, we do away with the quantifier ep in favor of the COG-ST feature. Similarly, we replace the modifier ep with a feature PRON-TYPE, which indicates whether an index is to be interpreted as pronominal, and if so, the type of the pronoun (as discussed below). Not only is this representation simpler, there is no prediction that pronouns participate in quantifier scope relations, as there is when using **_pronoun_q_rel**.

Overt pronouns, clitics and zero pronominals are generally assumed to take a COG-ST value of *in-focus* (Gundel et al., 1993; Borthen and Haugereid, 2005). In general, we agree. We assume that most overt pronouns and many forms of zero anaphora do take that value. However, there are forms which require us to make exceptions to this.

First let us consider the English indefinite pronoun *one*, as in (12). Clearly in this case the referent of *one* is not in focus. Rather, such a pronoun should bear the COG-ST value *type-id*.

(12)   Kim bought a computer and Sandy borrowed one.

B&H make a distinction between what they call *token pronouns* and *type pronouns*, where the former are the standard pronouns, which corefer with their antecedents, and the latter are like English *one*, which refer to a new token whose type is taken from its antecedent. We propose that the PRON-TYPE feature take a value of type *pron-type*, with subtypes *not-pron* for non-pronouns and *type-or-token* for pronouns. The latter will have two further subtypes, *token-pron* and *type-pron*. English *one* will be lexically specified as [PRON-TYPE *type-pron*].

Certain cases of zero anaphora similarly get their type information from their antecedents. A couple of instances of the Italian null subject construction appear in (13) and (14).

(13)   John ha fatto   la torta. La-ha mangiata
       John has make.PPRT the cake. it-has eat.PPRT

       'John baked the cake. (He) ate it.' [ita]

(14)   Se uno bambino vuole un biscotto, gli-arriva
       if a   child   wants a   cookie   to.him-arrives

       'If a child wants a cookie, he gets one.' [ita]

In (13), the referent of the null subject is indeed an entity which is in focus, namely John. On the other hand, in (14) the referent of the null subject is a new token of a type which is in focus, namely the type 'cookie'.

To handle this situation, we propose that Italian null subjects are associated with COG-ST *in-focus*, and with PRON-TYPE *type-or-token*. The grammar for Italian contains a 'subject drop' construction which discharges the subject requirement of the verb without realizing any overt dependent. Because the verb will have linked the appropriate argument position of its own ep to the HOOK.INDEX value inside the feature recording its subject requirement, the subject drop construction can constrain the properties of this index. In particular, it will specify that its PRON-TYPE is *type-or-token* (i.e., it is a pronominal), and that its COG-ST is *in-focus*. The subject-drop construction is sketched in Fig 3. When further processing determines the nature of the antecedent, the PRON-TYPE value will get further specified. If it is a non-specific indefinite, e.g. it is an indefinite in an intensional context, the pronominal will be specified *type-pron*, otherwise it will be specified *token-pron*.

The next type of zero pronominal we consider are Japanese dropped arguments, which present a counterexample to Gundel et al. (1993)'s claim that all zero pronominals are COG-ST *in-focus*. To be sure, Japanese zero anaphora can be understood

```
head-opt-subj-phrase := head-valence-phrase & head-only &
[ SYNSEM.LOCAL.CAT.VAL.SUBJ < >,
  HEAD-DTR.SYNSEM.LOCAL.CAT [ HEAD verb & [ FORM fin ],
                              VAL.SUBJ < [ LOCAL.CONT.HOOK.INDEX
                                         [ COG-ST in-focus,
                                           PRON-TYPE type-or-token ]] > ]].
```

Figure 3: Subject drop construction for Italian

similarly to overt token pronouns, as in (15). However, there are also examples where it can be understood like an overt type pronoun, like English *one*, as in (16). Note that (16) is different from (14) in that the antecedent of the null anaphor is not in an intensional context.

(15)   Mi-ta.
       see.PAST

       '(He/she) saw (it).' [jpn]

(16)   Zyon-wa konpyuutaa-o kat-ta.   Mearii-wa kari-ta.
       John.TOP computer.ACC buy.PAST Mary.TOP borrow.PAST

       'John bought a computer. Mary borrowed one.' [jpn]

We propose that Japanese dropped arguments are underspecified with respect to cognitive status and pronoun type. They are associated with indices specified as COG-ST *cog-st* and PRON-TYPE *type-or-token*.

Finally, we turn to lexically licensed null instantiation in English, beginning with definite null instantiation. Fillmore et al. (2003) define definite null instantiation as a phenomenon whereby some conceptually necessary participant in a situation is left unexpressed, but its identity is derivable from context. In lexically licensed null instantiation, the possibility of argument drop and the interpretation of the dropped argument are dependent on the selecting head. In English, lexically licensed DNI is typically a kind of token pronominal, as in (17). But some items can also license type-pronominal DNI, as in (18). In (17), the thing that was won is the previously mentioned game. In (18), there is no particular job that is being sought, although we do know from the context that it is a job.

(17)   Kim played a game with Sandy, and Sandy won.

(18)   I can't find a job, but I'm still looking.

We model lexical licensing of null instantiation through a feature called OPT which allows selecting heads to record whether or not their arguments are 'optional'. Since the interpretation of dropped arguments is also constrained by the lexical heads, we propose two additional features OPT-CS and OPT-PT which encode the cognitive status and pronoun type to assign to that argument in case it is dropped. The complement-drop construction and the lexical constraints on *look* are sketched in Fig 4a-b.

In this figure, strings prefixed with # indicate reentrancy in the feature structure. The feature KEYREL in lexical entries is a pointer to the main ep they contribute. The

```
a.  head-opt-comp-phrase := head-valence-phrase & head-only &
    [ SYNSEM.LOCAL.CAT.VAL.COMPS #comps, HEAD-DTR.SYNSEM.LOCAL.CAT
      [ VAL.COMPS [ FIRST [ OPT +,
                           OPT-CS #cog-st,
                           OPT-PT #pron-type,
                           LOCAL.CONT.HOOK.INDEX [ COG-ST #cog-st,
                                                   PRON-TYPE #pron-type ]],
                   REST #comps ]]].
b.  look := pp-transitive-verb-lex &
    [ STEM < "look" >,
      SYNSEM [ LOCAL.CAT.VAL.COMPS < [ OPT-CS in-focus,
                                       OPT-PT type-or-token ] >,
               LKEYS.KEYREL.PRED "_look_v_rel" ]].
c.  read := transitive-verb-lex &
    [ STEM < "read" >,
      SYNSEM [ LOCAL.CAT.VAL.COMPS < [ OPT-CS type-id,
                                       OPT-PT non-pron ] >,
               LKEYS.KEYREL.PRED "_read_v_rel" ]].
d.  devour := transitive-verb-lex &
    [ STEM < "devour" >,
      SYNSEM [ LOCAL.CAT.VAL.COMPS < [ OPT - ] >,
               LKEYS.KEYREL.PRED "_devour_v_rel" ]].
```

Figure 4: Lexically licensed complement drop for English

type *transitive-verb-lex* inherits from its supertypes the linking constraints which identify the HOOK.INDEX values of the syntactic arguments with the appropriate ARG*n* values in the ep contributed by the verb.[6]

Indefinite null instantiation is similar, except that the identity of the missing element is either unknown or immaterial. An example of this is (19). INI differs from other null nominals in that it is not a kind of anaphor. There is nothing in the context that helps to identify its referent.

(19)   Kim is reading.

We propose that indices in INI constructions are specified as COG-ST *type-id* and PRON-TYPE *non-pron*. In English, these constructions are also lexically licensed, and can be handled with the same features described for DNI. The lexical constraints on *read* are illustrated in Fig 4c. For completeness, we also include in Fig 4d an example of a lexical item which does not license missing complements.

6   Summary and Future Work

In this paper we have explored the construction of semantic representations for a variety of forms of referring expressions. Building on Borthen and Haugereid (2005)'s proposal to treat cognitive status as a semantic feature within HPSG, we have developed representations for definite, demonstrative and null NPs, and sketched means of arriving at them compositionally.

---

[6]The constraints shown on the COMPS value of lexical entries would actually be implemented as constraints on types that the lexical entries inherit from, allowing the grammar to capture generalizations across lexical entries. They are shown as constraints on the lexical entries here for ease of exposition only.

In future work, we plan to expand the range of these analyses to cover phenomena such as Irish demonstratives taking scope over coordinated noun phrases and cross-linguistic variation in the marking of generics as definite or indefinite.

On the basis of these analyses, we plan to develop libraries for the Grammar Matrix customization system covering the topics discussed here. The Grammar Matrix customization system (Bender and Flickinger, 2005; Drellishak and Bender, 2005) presents the linguist-user with a typological questionnaire which elicits information about the language to be described. On the basis of the user's responses to the questionnaire, the customization system compiles a working starter grammar out of the Matrix core grammar and analyses stored in libraries. The new libraries will cover argument optionality (both general pro-drop and lexically-licensed), as well as demonstratives of different syntactic types (pronouns, determiners, adjectives and affixes), the marking of definiteness, and definiteness agreement.

Acknowledgments

We would like to thank Toshiyuki Ogihara, Laurie Poulson, Jeanette Gundel, Jennifer Arnold, Francesca Gola, and the reviewers for STEP 2008 for helpful comments and discussion. Any remaining errors are our own. This material is based upon work supported by the National Science Foundation under Grant No. BCS-0644097.

References

Arnold, J. E. (2008). Reference production: Production-internal and addressee-oriented processes. *Language and Cognitive Processes 23*(4), 495–527.

Bender, E. M., M. Egg, and M. Tepper (2005). Semantic construction for nominal expressions in cross-linguistic perspective. In *IWCS-6*.

Bender, E. M. and D. Flickinger (2005). Rapid prototyping of scalable grammars: Towards modularity in extensions to a language-independent core. In *Proceedings of the 2nd International Joint Conference on Natural Language Processing IJCNLP-05 (Posters/Demos)*, Jeju Island, Korea.

Bender, E. M., D. Flickinger, and S. Oepen (2002). The Grammar Matrix: An open-source starter-kit for the rapid development of cross-linguistically consistent broad-coverage precision grammars. In J. Carroll, N. Oostdijk, and R. Sutcliffe (Eds.), *Proceedings of the Workshop on Grammar Engineering and Evaluation at the COLING19*, Taipei, Taiwan, pp. 8–14.

Borthen, K. and P. Haugereid (2005). Representing referential properties of nominals. *Research on Language and Computation 3*(2), 221–246.

Chafe, W. (1976). Givenness, contrastiveness, definiteness, subjects, topics, and point of view. In C. Li (Ed.), *Subject and Topic*, pp. 25–56. New York: Academic Press.

Chafe, W. (1994). *Discourse, Consciousness, and Time*. Chicago: Chicago University Press.

Copestake, A., D. Flickinger, C. Pollard, and I. A. Sag (2005). Minimal recursion semantics: An introduction. *Research on Language and Computation 3*(4), 281–332.

Copestake, A., A. Lascarides, and D. Flickinger (2001). An algebra for semantic construction in constraint-based grammars. In *Proc. ACL.*

Diessel, H. (1999). *Demonstratives: Form, Function, and Grammaticalization.* Amsterdam: John Benjamins.

Diessel, H. (2008). Distance contrasts in demonstratives. In M. Haspelmath, M. Dryer, D. Gil, and B. Comrie (Eds.), *The World Atlas of Linguistic Structures Online*, Chapter 41. Munich: Max Planck Digital Library.

Drellishak, S. and E. M. Bender (2005). A coordination module for a crosslinguistic grammar resource. In S. Müller (Ed.), *Proc. HPSG*, Stanford, pp. 108–128. CSLI Publications.

Dryer, M. S. (2008). Order of demonstrative and noun. In M. Haspelmath, M. Dryer, D. Gil, and B. Comrie (Eds.), *The World Atlas of Linguistic Structures Online*, Chapter 88. Munich: Max Planck Digital Library.

Fillmore, C., C. Johnson, and M. Petruck (2003). Background to FrameNet. *International Journal of Lexicography 16*, 235–250.

Flickinger, D. (2000). On building a more efficient grammar by exploiting types. *Natural Language Engineering 6 (1) (Special Issue on Efficient Processing with HPSG)*, 15–28.

Gundel, J., N. Hedberg, and R. Zacharski (1993). Cognitive status and the from of referring expressions in discourse. *Language 69*, 274–307.

Gundel, J., N. Hedberg, and R. Zacharski (2001). Definite descriptions and cognitive status in English: Why accommodation is unnecessary. *English Language and Linguistics 5*, 273–295.

McCloskey, J. (2004). Irish nominal syntax I: Demonstratives. UC Santa Cruz.

Oepen, S., E. Velldal, J. T. Lønning, P. Meurer, V. Rosén, and D. Flickinger (2007). Towards hybrid quality-oriented machine translation. On linguistics and probabilities in MT. In *TMI 2007*, Skövde, Sweden.

Pollard, C. and I. A. Sag (1994). *Head-Driven Phrase Structure Grammar.* Studies in Contemporary Linguistics. Chicago: University of Chicago Press.

Prince, E. (1981). Toward a taxonomy of given-new information. In P. Cole (Ed.), *Radical Pragmatics*, pp. 223–255. New York: Academic Press.

Wintner, S. (2000). Definiteness in the Hebrew noun phrase. *Journal of Linguistics 36*, 319–363.

High Precision Analysis of NPs with a Deep Processing Grammar

António Branco
Francisco Costa
Universidade de Lisboa (Portugal)
email: Antonio.Branco@di.fc.ul.pt

Abstract

In this paper we present LXGram, a general purpose grammar for the deep linguistic processing of Portuguese that aims at delivering detailed and high precision meaning representations. LXGram is grounded on the linguistic framework of Head-Driven Phrase Structure Grammar (HPSG). HPSG is a declarative formalism resorting to unification and a type system with multiple inheritance. The semantic representations that LX-Gram associates with linguistic expressions use the Minimal Recursion Semantics (MRS) format, which allows for the underspecification of scope effects. LXGram is developed in the Linguistic Knowledge Builder (LKB) system, a grammar development environment that provides debugging tools and efficient algorithms for parsing and generation. The implementation of LXGram has focused on the structure of Noun Phrases, and LX-Gram accounts for many NP related phenomena. Its coverage continues to be increased with new phenomena, and there is active work on extending the grammar's lexicon. We have already integrated, or plan to integrate, LXGram in a few applications, namely paraphrasing, treebanking and language variant detection. Grammar coverage has been tested on newspaper text.

1 Introduction

In this paper we present LXGram, a hand-built, general purpose computational grammar for the deep linguistic processing of Portuguese, specially geared to high precision processing of Noun Phrases. This grammar is based on the framework of Head-Driven Phrase Structure Grammar (HPSG; Pollard and Sag (1994)), one of the most prominent linguistic theories being used in natural language processing. Like several other computational HPSGs, LXGram uses Minimal Recursion Semantics (MRS; Copestake et al. (2005)) for the representation of meaning.

LXGram is developed in the Linguistic Knowledge Builder (LKB) system (Copestake, 2002), a development environment for constraint-based grammars. This environment provides a GUI, debugging tools and very efficient algorithms for parsing and generation with the grammars developed there (Malouf et al., 2000; Carroll et al., 1999).

Several broad-coverage grammars have been developed in the LKB. Currently, the largest ones are for English (Copestake and Flickinger, 2000), German (Müller and Kasper, 2000) and Japanese (Siegel and Bender, 2002). The grammars developed with the LKB are also supported by the PET parser (Callmeier, 2000), which allows for faster parsing times due to the fact that the grammars are compiled into a binary format in a first step. As the LKB grammars for other languages, LXGram is in active development, and it is intended to be a broad-coverage, open-domain grammar for Portuguese. At the same time, it produces detailed representations of meaning in tandem with syntactic structures, making it useful for a wide range of applications.

In Section 2, we describe the framework foundations of the grammar. The major design features of the grammar are introduced in Section 3. We talk about the coverage of LXGram in Section 4. Section 5 presents some of the phenomena treated within the NP domain and shows examples of implemented analyses relating to NP syntax and semantics. In Section 6, results on the performance of the grammar are reported, and in Section 7, we discuss applications where the grammar is or is being integrated. Finally, the paper closes with concluding remarks in Section 8.

2 Foundations

LXGram adopts the HPSG framework, a popular linguistic theory with a large body of literature covering many natural language phenomena. These insights can be directly incorporated in the implementation of a computational grammar.

2.1 HPSG

HPSG resorts to a declarative formalism to model linguistic data. It employs a type system (supporting multiple inheritance) and typed feature structures (recursive data structures defining "has-a" relations) in order to describe the properties of linguistic objects (words, phrases, rules). Unification of types and feature structures is central to HPSG, used to ensure that the various elements have compatible properties. For instance, the fact that a transitive verb takes an NP as its complement is captured in HPSG by defining a lexical type for transitive verbs, say *transitive-verb-lex(eme)*, with constraints like the following (among others), presented in the Attribute-Value Matrix (AVM) format widely employed in HPSG:

$$
\begin{bmatrix}
\textit{transitive-verb-lex} \\[4pt]
\text{SYNSEM}|\text{LOCAL}|\text{CAT}|\text{VAL}|\text{COMPS} \left\langle \begin{bmatrix} \text{LOCAL}|\text{CAT} \begin{bmatrix} \text{HEAD} & \textit{noun} \\ \text{VAL} & \begin{bmatrix} \text{SPR} & \langle\rangle \\ \text{COMPS} & \langle\rangle \end{bmatrix} \end{bmatrix} \end{bmatrix} \right\rangle
\end{bmatrix}
$$

The NP complement of the verb is represented in this AVM as the value of the attribute COMPS. This attribute takes a list as its value (indicated by the angle brackets). In this case the sole element of this list describes an object with a HEAD feature of the type *noun* and empty complements (the attribute COMPS) and specifier (the feature SPR) (i.e. they have been saturated at the point where the verb combines with this element), which is the HPSG description of an NP.

2.2 MRS

Minimal Recursion Semantics (MRS) is used as the format of semantic representations that LXGram associates with expressions from Portuguese. MRS has several properties that are interesting for applications. A relevant one is the use of pointers to represent scope effects that are handled via recursion in traditional formal semantics. This use of pointers (called *handles*) allows for the underspecification of scope relations, which avoids listing all scope possibilities for ambiguous sentences (although they can still be computed on demand with the LKB machinery). This is a useful property: scope does not need to be resolved in all applications (e.g. machine translation does not require it), but at the same time scoped formulas can be obtained on demand if required (e.g. for automated inference).

We provide an example MRS representation derived for the sentence "todas as equipas podem vencer" (*all teams can win*) in Figure 1. This MRS describes the

$$
\begin{bmatrix}
\textit{mrs} \\
\text{LTOP} & \boxed{h1}\, h \\
\text{INDEX} & \boxed{e2}\, e \\[6pt]
\text{RELS} & \left\langle
\begin{bmatrix} \_todo\_q\_rel \\ \text{LBL} & \boxed{h3}\, h \\ \text{ARG0} & \boxed{x6}\, x \\ \text{RSTR} & \boxed{h5}\, h \\ \text{BODY} & \boxed{h4}\, h \end{bmatrix},
\begin{bmatrix} \_equipa\_n\_rel \\ \text{LBL} & \boxed{h7}\, h \\ \text{ARG0} & \boxed{x6} \end{bmatrix},
\begin{bmatrix} \_poder\_v\_rel \\ \text{LBL} & \boxed{h8} \\ \text{ARG0} & \boxed{e2} \\ \text{ARG1} & \boxed{h9}\, h \end{bmatrix},
\begin{bmatrix} \_vencer\_v\_rel \\ \text{LBL} & \boxed{h10} \\ \text{ARG0} & \boxed{e11} \\ \text{ARG1} & \boxed{x6} \end{bmatrix}
\right\rangle \\[6pt]
\text{HCONS} & \left\langle
\begin{bmatrix} \textit{qeq} \\ \text{HARG} & \boxed{h1} \\ \text{LARG} & \boxed{h8} \end{bmatrix},
\begin{bmatrix} \textit{qeq} \\ \text{HARG} & \boxed{h5} \\ \text{LARG} & \boxed{h7} \end{bmatrix},
\begin{bmatrix} \textit{qeq} \\ \text{HARG} & \boxed{h9} \\ \text{LARG} & \boxed{h10} \end{bmatrix}
\right\rangle
\end{bmatrix}
$$

Figure 1: MRS for the sentence "Todas as equipas podem vencer" (*all teams can win*)

two following scoped formulas, where the predicate *_todo_q* stands for a universal quantifier:

- $\_todo\_q(x_6, \_equipa\_n(x_6), \_poder\_v(e_2, \_vencer\_v(e_{11}, x_6)))$
- $\_poder\_v(e_2, \_todo\_q(x_6, \_equipa\_n(x_6), \_vencer\_v(e_{11}, x_6)))$

The first reading is the one that says that each team has a chance to win, while the second reading says that it is possible for there to be a situation in which all teams win (false assuming common sense knowledge). A single MRS representation is obtained for these two readings by instantiating the ARG1 feature of the relation _poder_v (can) with the handle h_9, which is related to the handle h_{10} labeling the relation _vencer_v (win) via a qeq relation (equality modulo intervening quantifiers). This is the way of saying that these two handles are the same (first reading) or that there is an intervening generalized quantifier relation (second reading).

Semantic representations abstract from many grammatical and superficial details of language, like word order, syntactic structure and morphology. As such, they are very similar across different natural languages (modulo predicate names). This is also true of MRS. Furthermore, semantic representations hide grammar implementation. As such, they are the preferred grammar's interface for applications, that do not need any knowledge of the grammatical properties of Portuguese and may not need to look at syntactic analysis.

The MRS format is also used with several other computational HPSGs, for other languages. Several applications (e.g. Machine Translation) have been used with other HPSGs that communicate with these grammars via the MRSs (Bond et al., 2004). These applications can be easily integrated with grammars for different languages that also use MRS: they are almost completely language independent.

3 Design Features

Given the foundational options, LXGram adheres to a number of important design features.

Bidirectionality LXGram is bidirectional. The formalism employed is completely declarative. It can be used for parsing (yielding syntactic analyses and semantic representations from natural language input) and also for generation (yielding natural language from meaning representations). As such it can be useful for a wide range of applications.

Precision LXGram aims at high precision of linguistic processing. Modulo bugs, the grammar cannot parse ungrammatical input. Although this feature may have a negative impact on robustness, it is an important aspect of the grammar when it is used for generation, as it means it is not possible to generate ungrammatical strings.[1] It is indeed possible to mark some rules and some lexical entries to only be used for parsing and not for generation. In the configuration files for the LKB one can list these rules and lexical items. We are currently using this feature in order to be able to parse input that is not ungrammatical but is marked with respect to register, but preventing the grammar from generating such strings.

Importantly, the fact that it cannot parse ungrammatical input also means that the grammar will not produce impossible analyses for grammatical sentences.

Broad Coverage LXGram development is aimed at a broad coverage. We also seek to make LXGram neutral with respect to regional variation as much as possible. Currently, the grammar accommodates both European Portuguese and Brazilian

---

[1] We believe that dealing with ill-formed input is best done via other means (rather than let the grammar overgenerate so it can parse more), like partial parsing or the integration with/falling back to other tools.

Portuguese. Aspects of variation that are accounted for include lexical differences (merely affecting spelling or more substantial ones) as well as syntactic discrepancies (e.g. definite articles before possessives, word order between clitic pronouns and the verb).

Efficiency The processors on which LXGram runs (LKB, PET) are very efficient. In addition, there are grammar engineering techniques that improve efficiency (e.g. (Flickinger, 2000)) that are also exploited in our implementation.

Robustness The LKB and PET systems provide several ways to combine a grammar with the output of shallow tools, like part-of-speech taggers. Such integration can improve grammar coverage, as the grammar needs information about all words in the input, and some words may be missing in the grammar's lexicon. We have successfully combined LXGram with a part-of-speech tagger and a morphological analyzer (more in Section 6). The grammar code includes mappings from the input format (XML) to the feature structures that are manipulated by the grammar.

Availability A version of LXGram is publicly available at `http://nlxgroup.di.fc.ul.pt/lxgram`. LXGram can be used by applications without any knowledge of the grammar's implementation or internal workings. The LKB allows for applications to communicate with the grammar via sockets, accepting parser input in XML or raw text and returning semantic representations in XML, for which a DTD is available. It is also possible to automatically produce a list of all the predicates known by the grammar together with their arity and argument types (from the lexicon and syntax rules), that can be manually annotated with comments and examples. The predicates corresponding to lexical items are however quite transparent once the naming conventions that are used are explained.

4 Coverage

4.1 Lexical Coverage

When one is using a lexicalist framework like HPSG, lexical coverage is a key issue because all tokens in the input should be known by the grammar in order for the grammar to produce a parse. Furthermore, the amount of information included in the lexicon that is used by an HPSG is very large. Part-of-speech and morphological information is not sufficient. For the correct assignment of semantic representations, subcategorization frames as well as other information pertaining to semantics must be correctly associated with every lexical item, something that cannot be known with sufficient quality by just using shallower tools, like part-of-speech taggers.

In LXGram a hand-crafted lexicon containing several hundreds of nouns, adjectives and verbs was developed. However, the manual creation of lexica with this amount of information is time consuming and error prone. We are exploring methods to alleviate this problem. An option is to combine the grammar with shallower tools in order to have access to some of the information needed and assume default values for the information that cannot be obtained this way. We have already integrated the grammar with a set of shallow tools (a part-of-speech tagger, a lemmatizer and a morphological analyzer) in order to guess information about unknown words. Preliminary results indicate an increase in coverage on unrestricted newspaper text from 2% to 13%. Although this approach cannot guarantee correct semantic representations (or even syntactic trees, since subcategorization frames constrain syntactic structure), it can be useful in applications that only require some restricted amount of linguistic information.

4.2 Overall Grammatical Coverage

In order to get a quantitative overview of the grammar, it can be characterized as follows:

- 24,484 lines of code, including comments and excluding the lexicon;

- 53 syntax rules;

- 40 lexical rules, mostly inflectional;

- 3,154 total types;

- 414 types for lexical items;

- 2,718 hand-built lexical entries.

For a qualitative overview, these are the linguistic phenomena covered so far:

- **Declarative sentences**

- **Yes-no questions** e.g.: "Portanto o Estado tem um gosto?" (So does the State have preferences?)

- **Imperative sentences** e.g.: "Dá-me um desses bolos." (Give me one of those cakes)

- **Some subcategorization frames of verbs, nouns and adjectives** e.g.: "a Polónia *empatou* com a França" (Poland *tied* with France); "eu já *disse* que *pode ser* um dos mais baratos" (I *told* you already that it *can be* one of the cheapest); "*filho* de um professor dos *arredores* de Viena" (*son* of a teacher from the *outskirts* of Vienna)

- **Comparative constructions** e.g.: "a vida é maior *do que* o cinema" (life is larger *than* cinema)

- **Noun phrase structure, including determiners, possessives, cardinal and ordinal numerals, prepositional phrases, adjectives, etc.** (examples in the next section)

- **Modification of verbal projections by prepositional and adverbial phrases** e.g.: "*No CAPC* termina *hoje* a exposição" (the exhibit ends *today at CAPC*);

- **Relative clauses** e.g.: "sete outros suspeitos *que a polícia ainda procura*" (seven other suspects *that the police are still looking for*)

- **Null subjects and objects** e.g.: "Saímos depois do jantar." ((We) left after dinner); "Podemos comer lá perto." (We can eat near there)

- **Floated Quantifiers** e.g.: "os índices subiram *todos*" (the indices have *all* gone up)

The development of the grammar is going on and this grammar is getting its coverage increased with important phenomena that are missing. In particular, for the near future, we are working towards including more subcategorization frames for verbs, nouns and adjectives, and implementing wh-questions, coordination and adverbial subordination.

5 Noun Phrases

A special design feature of LXGram is that it includes a comprehensive implementation of Portuguese Noun Phrase structure, covering:

- **Bare noun phrases** (i.e. NPs lacking a determiner) e.g.: "boa gestão" (good management); "imagens da bancada" (images of the seats)

- **Determiners and predeterminers** e.g.: "*esta* sua última produção" (*this* last production of his); "*todos estes* problemas" (*all these* problems); "*todos os* partidos políticos" (*all the* political parties), "*aquele* tempo *todo*" (*all that* time)

- **Word order constraints among NP elements** e.g.: "as duas primeiras instituições" (the two first institutions); "os primeiros sete meses deste ano" (the first seven months of this year); "sete outros suspeitos que a polícia ainda procura" (seven other suspects that the police are still looking for); "os outros três membros do conselho" (the other three members of the council); "os seus dois primeiros anos polémicos na Casa Branca" (his first two polemic years in the White House); "o primeiro grande conflito que aportava em Belém" (the first great conflict that reached Berlin); "outro lugar qualquer" (any other place); "um lugar qualquer" (any place); "qualquer outra solução" (any other solution)

- **Prenominal and postnominal possessives** e.g.: "o *seu* terceiro maior parceiro comercial" (*its* third major commercial partner); "um adjunto *seu* que atendeu ali o telefonema" (an assessor *of his* who answered the phone call there)

- **Modification of adjectives** e.g.: "os escritores *mais* importantes" (the *most* important writers); "o discurso *razoavelmente* optimista" (the *reasonably* optimistic speech)

- **Missing nouns** e.g.: "dois que são gémeos" (two who are twins)

- **Word order between adjectives and complements of nouns** e.g.: "o conhecimento *essencial* das pessoas" (the *essential* knowledge about people)

- **Adjectives with the semantics of arguments of nouns** e.g.: "o veto *americano* à renovação do mandato" (the *American* veto to the renewal of the position)

Precision was given a lot of attention. For instance, many items are constrained not to appear more than once in a given NP (determiners, possessives, cardinals, ordinals, etc.). Scope phenomena are also handled (motivated by semantics), as well as order constraints. Agreement is enforced.

We present some examples of phenomena for which LXGram provides interesting semantic representations and that we have not found in the literature pertaining to implemented grammars.

5.1 Floated Quantifiers

The first example relates to floated quantifiers. For all the sentences in (1), which are all grammatical in Portuguese, LXGram provides the MRS equivalent of $all(x, price(x), will(go\_up(x)))$:

(1) a. Todos os preços vão subir.
         all   the prices will go up

     b. Os preços todos vão subir.
         the prices all   will go up

     c. Os preços vão todos subir.
         the prices will all   go up

     d. Os preços vão subir todos.
         the prices will go up all

In all of these cases we associate empty semantics to the definite article ("os"). Semantic information is percolated around the syntactic trees so that the universal quantifier, which can be realized at several different places, ends up being linked to the semantics of the NP subject in the semantic representations for all these sentences. We also make sure that definite articles always carry quantifier semantics when no floated quantifier is present.

The implementation revolves around allowing floated quantifiers to attach to verbs, resulting in verb-headed nodes that combine with NP subjects lacking quantifier semantics. Raising verbs, like the form "vão" in this example, constrain their subject according to the constraints of the subject of their VP complement. For instance, the last example (1d) receives a syntactic analysis like the one described by the following tree:

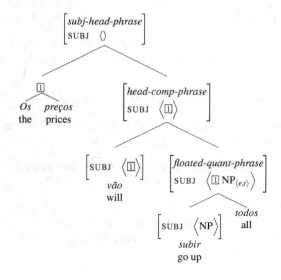

Here, NP abbreviates a feature structure that describes a noun phrase (of the semantic type $\langle\langle e,t\rangle,t\rangle$), and NP$_{\langle e,t\rangle}$ abbreviates the constraints that describe an NP introduced by a determiner lacking quantifier semantics (i.e. an NP with an MRS representation that is similar to that of constituents with the the semantic type $\langle e,t\rangle$).

In HPSG, the SUBJ feature encodes the constraints on the subject that a constituent selects. We use a dedicated syntax rule to combine "subir" and "todos" (*floated-quant-phrase*), that creates a node requiring an NP with the semantic type $\langle e,t\rangle$ as its subject. The verb form "vão" is treated as a raising verb: in HPSG the syntactic requirements on the subject of a raising verb are the same as the requirements on the subject of the VP complement that that verb selects for. This is denoted by the boxed integers in this tree (which represent unification).

In this example, the VP complement of "vão" is the phrase "subir todos", as these two constituents are combined via the *head-comp-phrase* rule (selection of complements is represented in a way similar to the selection of subjects, but via the feature COMPS instead of the feature SUBJ). The subject of the *head-comp-phrase* is the subject of its head daughter ("vão"). The topmost node is the result of applying a syntactic rule to project subjects to the left of their head (*subj-head-phrase*).

The example in (1c) is processed in a similar fashion:

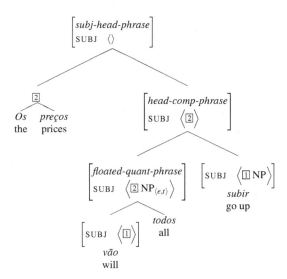

In this example, the complement of "vão" is the node spanning "subir", which selects for a quantified subject. The subject of the raising verb is accordingly also a quantified NP. Here, the rule to project a floated quantifier applies lower than the construction that projects complements, creating a node that requires a non-quantified subject. The SUBJ feature of head-complement constructions comes from the head daughter (the *floated-quant-phrase* node in this example). Therefore, the node produced by the *head-comp-phrase* rule also requires a non-quantified subject.

Note that the composition of semantics with MRS in based on the concatenation of the RELS and HCONS lists associated to the various constituents and passing around the values of the features LTOP and INDEX (see Figure 1). It is not based on function application. The composition of semantics with MRS is quite flexible.

5.2   Scope of Adjectives and Relative Clauses

The second example that we show here relates to the semantic scope between different elements of noun phrases. In particular, we can see a distinction in the interpretation of the two following examples:

(2)   a.   um possível médico chinês
           a   possible doctor Chinese

           a possible Chinese doctor

      b.   um possível médico que é chinês
           a   possible doctor who is Chinese

           a possible doctor who is Chinese

In the first NP an entity is described as possibly being a Chinese doctor. The second NP describes an entity as possibly being a doctor and certainly being Chinese. Accordingly, LXGram delivers slightly different semantic representations for these two NPs. The first case produces something similar to

$$\lambda P.\, a(x, possible(doctor(x) \land chinese(x)), P(x)).$$

The second NP is treated along the lines of

$$\lambda P.\, a(x, possible(doctor(x)) \land chinese(x), P(x)).$$

These two different readings are derived simply by constraining the relative syntactic scope of adjectives and relative clauses. Namely, LXGram forces prenominal adjectives to attach higher than postnominal adjectives (2a) but lower than relative clauses (2b). In this case, the scope differences in the semantic representations are simply derived from the differences in syntactic scope:

Of course, the following examples receive equivalent semantics:

(3)   a.   um médico chinês
           a   doctor chinese

           a Chinese doctor

      b.   um médico que é chinês
           a   doctor who is Chinese

           a doctor who is Chinese

6   Evaluation

Some evaluation experiments were conducted to test LXGram's coverage. In one of them, a corpus with newspaper text (self-reference) was used, with 145 sentences. For this experiment, we used a part-of-speech tagger and a morphological analyzer (self-reference) in order to guess some information about out-of-vocabulary words. A default value was assumed for the missing subcategorization information (all unknown verbs were treated as transitive verbs). The average sentence length was 22 words. In this experiment, 13.1% of all sentences received at least one parse by the grammar.[2] On the same test corpus, the average time it took for a sentence to parse was 1.1 seconds on a P4 machine at 3GHz. The average amount of memory required to analyze a sentence was 145.5MB.

In another experiment, with 180,000 short sentences (5 to 9 words) selected randomly from two newspaper corpora (CETEMPúblico and CETENFolha), LXGram had achieved 26% coverage, using a similar approach to handle unknown words (self-reference).

During the development of LXGram we maintain several test suites, consisting of example sentences for the implemented phenomena. The test suites use a controlled vocabulary. Also, several examples attest several phenomena, in order to test the interaction of the different modules. They are very useful to test the syntax rules of the grammar and the semantics that LXGram produces, and for regression testing. The test suite for NPs contains 851 sentences (429 of which are negative examples, that the grammar should not parse). The average sentence length is 5.3 words (2–16). On this test suite LXGram has 100% coverage and 0% overgeneration. The average time needed to analyze a sentence is 0.11 seconds, with an average memory requirement of 15.5MB. Plotting parse time by sentence length, we see an approximately linear increase in parse time with this test suite.

7   Applications and Further Work

We have used LXGram to automatically discriminate between texts written in European Portuguese and Brazilian Portuguese, with encouraging results, which match the results obtained with other dialect detection methodologies. (self-reference).[3]

Additionally, we are working towards integrating it with an existing question answering system (self-reference).[4] This is in part the reason for the special focus on NPs, as these constituents are often short answers to factoid questions.

Because the grammar is entirely bidirectional, a paraphraser is gained for free from the implementation of LXGram: the grammar can simply be used to generate from the semantic representations that it derives from an input sentence, thus producing paraphrases of the textual input. We are also working to integrate the grammar, running under this functionality, into the QA system.

---

[2] Note that one of the HPSGs with the broadest coverage at the moment, the ERG, covers 17% of the British National Corpus. The main cause of parse failure is out-of-vocabulary words.

[3] In particular, the results obtained with LXGram were quite similar to the results obtained with the standard methods (based on character n-grams) that are used to identify the language in which a given text is written, when used for this purpose.

[4] See (Bobrow et al., 2007) for a similar approach, where an LFG is employed in a question answering system aiming at high precision.

On a par with the above lines of research, we are intensively using the grammar to semi-automatically produce a treebank that contains syntactic representations and semantic descriptions of the sentences in a newspaper corpus. LXGram has also served in the past to implement and experiment with novel linguistic analyses of interesting phenomena (self-reference). By making it freely available, we intend to encourage this sort of experimentation also by other researchers. One can reap important benefits from computationally implementing linguistic analyses: the debugging tools allow for fast checking of correctness; the impact on other analyses that are already implemented can be immediately assessed via regression testing, making it possible to test the interaction between linguistic analyses for different phenomena; it is possible to automatically compare different competing analyses for efficiency, based on test suites or corpora.

8 Conclusions

In this paper we presented LXGram, a computational grammar for the deep linguistic processing of Portuguese. LXGram is implemented in a declarative formalism. It can be used for analysis as well as generation. It produces high precision syntactic analyses and semantic representations. LXGram supports the two main varieties of Portuguese: European and Brazilian Portuguese. It is not dependent on a particular domain or genre.

So far the focus of the implementation was on noun phrases and basic sentence structure, a coverage that is being extended in ongoing work. The outcome of different evaluation experiments shows scores that are in line with those obtained with similar grammars for other languages.

References

Bobrow, D. G., B. Cheslow, C. Condoravdi, L. Karttunen, T. H. King, R. Nairn, V. de Paiva, C. Price, and A. Zaenen (2007). PARC's bridge and question answering system. In T. H. King and E. M. Bender (Eds.), *Proceedings of the GEAF07 Workshop*, Stanford, CA, pp. 46–66. CSLI Publications.

Bond, F., S. Fujita, C. Hashimoto, K. Kasahara, S. Nariyama, E. Nichols, A. Ohtani, T. Tanaka, and S. Amano (2004). The Hinoki treebank: Working toward text understanding. In S. Hansen-Schirra, S. Oepen, and H. Uszkoreit (Eds.), *COLING 2004 5th International Workshop on Linguistically Interpreted Corpora*, Geneva, Switzerland, pp. 7–10. COLING.

Callmeier, U. (2000). PET — A platform for experimentation with efficient HPSG processing techniques. *Natural Language Engineering* 6(1), 99–108. (Special Issue on Efficient Processing with HPSG).

Carroll, J., A. Copestake, D. Flickinger, and V. Poznański (1999). An efficient chart generator for (semi-)lexicalist grammars. In *Proceedings of the 7th European Workshop on Natural Language Generation (EWNLG'99)*, Toulouse, pp. 86–95.

Copestake, A. (2002). *Implementing Typed Feature Structure Grammars*. Stanford: CSLI Publications.

Copestake, A. and D. Flickinger (2000). An open-source grammar development environment and broad-coverage English grammar using HPSG. In *Proceedings of the Second conference on Language Resources and Evaluation (LREC-2000)*, Athens, Greece.

Copestake, A., D. Flickinger, I. A. Sag, and C. Pollard (2005). Minimal Recursion Semantics: An introduction. *Journal of Research on Language and Computation 3*(2–3), 281–332.

Flickinger, D. (2000). On building a more efficient grammar by exploiting types. *Natural Language Engineering 6*(1), 15–28. (Special Issue on Efficient Processing with HPSG).

Malouf, R., J. Carrol, and A. Copestake (2000). Efficient feature structure operations without compilation. *Natural Language Engineering 6*(1), 29–46. (Special Issue on Efficient Processing with HPSG).

Müller, S. and W. Kasper (2000). HPSG analysis of German. In W. Wahlster (Ed.), *Verbmobil: Foundations of Speech-to-Speech Translation* (Artificial Intelligence ed.)., pp. 238–253. Berlin Heidelberg New York: Springer-Verlag.

Pollard, C. and I. Sag (1994). *Head-Driven Phrase Structure Grammar*. Stanford: Chicago University Press and CSLI Publications.

Siegel, M. and E. M. Bender (2002). Efficient deep processing of Japanese. In *Proceedings of the 3rd Workshop on Asian Language Resources and International Standardization. Coling 2002 Post-Conference Workshop*, Taipei, Taiwan, pp. 31–38.

Augmenting WordNet for Deep Understanding of Text

Peter Clark[1]
Christiane Fellbaum[2]
Jerry R. Hobbs[3]
Phil Harrison[1]
William R. Murray[1]
John Thompson[1]

[1]The Boeing Company (USA)
[2]Princeton University (USA)
[3]University of Southern California (USA)

email: peter.e.clark@boeing.com

Abstract

One of the big challenges in understanding text, i.e., constructing an over-all coherent representation of the text, is that much information needed in that representation is unstated (implicit). Thus, in order to "fill in the gaps" and create an overall representation, language processing systems need a large amount of world knowledge, and creating those knowledge resources remains a fundamental challenge. In our current work, we are seeking to augment WordNet as a knowledge resource for language understanding in several ways: adding in formal versions of its word sense definitions (glosses); classifying the morphosemantic links between nouns and verbs; encoding a small number of "core theories" about WordNet's most commonly used terms; and adding in simple representations of scripts. Although this is still work in progress, we describe our experiences so far with what we hope will be a significantly improved resource for the deep understanding of language.

1 Introduction

Much information that text is intended to convey is not explicitly stated. Rather, the reader constructs a mental model of the scene described by the text, including many "obvious" features that were not explicitly mentioned. By one estimate, the ratio of explicit to implicit facts is 1:8 (Graesser, 1981), making the task of understanding text, i.e., constructing a coherent representation of the scene that the author intended to convey, very difficult, even given the generally reasonable quality of syntactic interpretation that today's systems produce. For example, given the sentence:

A soldier was killed in a gun battle.

a reader will infer that (probably):

The soldier was shot; The soldier died; There was a fight; etc.

even though none of these facts are explicitly stated. A person is able to draw these plausible conclusions because of the large amounts of world knowledge he/she has, and his/her ability to use them to construct an overall mental model of the scene being described.

A key requirement for this task is access to a large body of world knowledge. However, machines are currently poorly equipped in this regard. Although a few knowledge encoding projects are underway, e.g., Cyc (Lenat and Guha, 1989), developing such resources continues to be a major challenge, and any contribution to this task has significant potential benefit. WordNet (Miller, 1995; Fellbaum, 1998) presents an unique avenue for making inroads into this problem: It already has broad coverage, multiple lexicosemantic connections, and significant knowledge encoded (albeit informally) in its glosses. It can thus be viewed as on the way to becoming an extensively leveragable, "lightweight" knowledge base for reasoning. In fact, WordNet already plays a central role in many question-answering systems e.g., 21 of the 26 teams in the recent PASCAL RTE3 challenge used WordNet (Giampiccolo et al., 2007), and most other large-scale resources already include mappings to it and thus can leverage it easily. In our work we are developing several augmentations to WordNet to improve its utility further, and we report here on our experiences to date.

Although we are performing experiments with recognizing textual entailment (RTE) (determining whether a hypothesis sentence H follows from some text T), it is important to note that RTE is not our end-goal. Many existing RTE systems, e.g., (Adams et al., 2007; Chambers et al., 2007) largely work by statistically scoring the match between T and H, but this to an extent sidesteps "deep" language understanding, namely building a coherent, internal representation of the overall scenario the input text was intended to convey. RTE is one way of measuring success in this endeavor, but it is also possible to do moderately well in RTE without the system even attempting to "understand" the scenario the text is describing. It is yet to be seen whether very high performance in RTE can be obtained without some kind of deep language understanding of the entire scene that a text conveys.

We are testing our work with BLUE, Boeing's Language Understanding Engine, which we first describe. We then present the WordNet augmentations that we are developing, and our experience with these as well as with the DIRT paraphrase database.

The contribution of this paper is some preliminary insight into avenues and challenges for creating and leveraging more world knowledge, in the context of WordNet, for deeper language understanding.

2 Text Interpretation and Subsumption

2.1 Text Interpretation

For text interpretation we are using BLUE, Boeing's Language Understanding Engine (Clark and Harrison, 2008), comprising a parser, logical form (LF) generator, and final logic generator. Parsing is performed using SAPIR, a mature, bottom-up, broad coverage chart parser (Harrison and Maxwell, 1986). The parser's cost function is biased by a database of manually and corpus-derived "tuples" (good parse fragments), as well as hand-coded preference rules. During parsing, the system also generates a logical form (LF), a semi-formal structure between a parse and full logic, loosely based on Schubert and Hwang (1993). The LF is a simplified and normalized tree structure with logic-type elements, generated by rules parallel to the grammar rules, that contains variables for noun phrases and additional expressions for other sentence constituents. Some disambiguation decisions are performed at this stage (e.g., structural, part of speech), while others are deferred (e.g., word senses, semantic roles), and there is no explicit quantifier scoping. A simple example of an LF is shown below (items starting with underscores _âĂİ denote variables):

```
;;; LF for "A soldier was killed in a gun battle."
(DECL ((VAR _X1 "a" "soldier")
       (VAR _X2 "a" "battle" (NN "gun" "battle")))
      (S (PAST) NIL "kill" _X1 (PP "in" _X2)))
```

The LF is then used to generate ground logical assertions of the form r(x,y), containing Skolem instances, by applying a set of syntactic rewrite rules recursively to it. Verbs are reified as individuals, Davidsonian-style. An example of the output is:

```
;;; logic for "A soldier was killed in a gun battle."
object(kill01,soldier01)
in(kill01,battle01)
modifier(battle01,gun01)
```

plus predicates associating each Skolem with its corresponding input word. At this stage of processing, the predicates are syntactic relations (subject(x,y), object(x,y), modifier(x,y), and all the prepositions, e.g., in(x,y)). Definite coreference is computed by a special module which uses the (logic for the) referring noun phrase as a query on the database of assertions. Another module performs special structural transformations, e.g., when a noun or verb should map to a predicate rather than an individual. Two additional modules perform (currently naive) word sense disambiguation (WSD) and semantic role labelling (SRL), described further in Clark and Harrison (2008). However, for our RTE experiments we have found it more effective to leave senses and roles underspecified, effectively considering all valid senses and roles (for the given lexical features) during reasoning until instantiated by the rules that apply.

2.2 Subsumption

A basic operation for reasoning is determining if one set of clauses subsumes (is more general than, is thus implied by) another, e.g., (the logic for) "A person likes a person" subsumes "A man loves a woman". This basic operation is used both to determine if an axiom applies, and in RTE to determine if a text H subsumes (is implied by) a text T or its axiom-expanded elaboration. A set S1 of clauses subsumes another S2 if each clause in S1 subsumes some (different) member of S2. A clause C1 subsumes another C2 if both (for binary predicates) of C1's arguments subsume the corresponding arguments in C2, and C1 and C2's predicates "match". An argument A1 subsumes another A2 if some word sense for A1's associated word is equal or more general (a hypernym of) some word sense of A2's associated word (thus effectively considering all possible word senses for A1 and A2)[1]. We also consider adjectives related by WordNet's "similar" link, e.g., "clean" and "pristine", to be equal. Two syntactic predicates "match" (i.e., are considered to denote the same semantic relation) according to the following rules:

1. both are the same;
2. either is the predicate "of" or "modifier";
3. the predicates "subject" and "by" match (for passives);
4. the two predicates are in a small list of special cases that should match e.g., "on" and "onto".

These rules for matching syntactic roles are clearly an approximation to matching semantic roles, but have performed better in our experiments than attempting to explicitly assign (with error) semantic roles early on and then matching on those.

In addition, in language, ideas can be expressed using different parts of speech (POS) for the same basic notion, e.g., verb or noun as in "The bomb destroyed the shrine" or "The destruction of the shrine by the bomb" (Gurevich et al., 2006). To handle these cross-POS variants, when finding the word senses of a word (above) our system considers all POS, independent of its POS in the original text. Combined with the above predicate-matching rules, this is a simple and powerful way of aligning expressions using different POSs, e.g.:

- "The bomb destroyed the shrine" and "The destruction of the shrine by the bomb" (but not "The destruction of the bomb by the shrine") are recognized as equivalent.
- "A person attacks with a bomb" and "There is a bomb attack by a person" are recognized as equivalent.
- "There is a wrecked car", "The car was wrecked", and "The car is a wreck" (adjective, verb, and noun forms) are recognized as equivalent.

Although clearly these heuristics can go wrong, they provide a basic mechanism for assessing simple equivalence and subsumption between texts.

---

[1] Clearly this can go wrong, e.g., if the contexts of T and H are different so repeated/matching words have incompatible intended senses, although such discontinuities are unusual in natural text.

2.3 Experimental Test Bed

As an experimental test bed we have developed a publically available RTE-style test suite[2] of 250 pairs (125 entailed, 125 not entailed). As our goal is deeper semantic processing, the texts are syntactically simpler than the PASCAL RTE sets (at www. pascal-network.org) but semantically challenging to process. We use examples from this test suite (and others) in this paper.

3 Exploiting Lexical & World Knowledge

3.1 Use of WordNet's Glosses

Translation to Logic WordNet's word sense definitions (glosses) appear to contain substantial amounts of world knowledge that could help with semantic interpretation of text, and we have been exploring leveraging these by translating them into first-order logic. We have also experimented with Extended WordNet (XWN), a similar database constructed several years ago by Moldovan and Rus (2001).

To do the translation, a different language interpreter, developed by ISI, was used (for historic reasons — BLUE was not available at the time the translations were done, and has not been exercised or extended for definition processing). ISI's system works as follows: First each gloss is converted into a sentence of the form "word is gloss" and parsed using the Charniak parser. Then the parse tree is then converted into a logical syntax by a system called LFToolkit, developed by Nishit Rathod. In LFToolkit, lexical items are translated into logical fragments involving variables. Finally, as syntactic relations are recognized, variables in the constituents are identified as equal. For example, "John works" is translated into John($x1$) & work($e,x2$) & present(e), where e is a working event, and then a rule which recognizes "John" as the subject of "works" sets $x1$ and $x2$ equal to each other. Rules of this sort were developed for a large majority of English syntactic constructions. ISI's system was then used to translate the modified WordNet glosses into axioms. For example (rewritten from the original eventuality notation):

```
;;; "ambition#n2: A strong drive for success"
ambition(x1) -> a(x1) & strong(x1) & drive(x1) & for(x1,x6) & success(x6)
```

Predicates are assigned word senses using the new-ly released WordNet sense-tagged gloss corpus[3]. This process was applied to all $\approx$ 110,000 glosses, but with particular focus on glosses for the 5,000 "core" (most frequently used) synsets. It resulted in good translations for 59.4% of the 5,000 core glosses, with lower quality for the entire gloss corpus. Where there was a failure, it was generally the result of a bad parse, with constructions for which no LFToolkit rules had been written. In these cases, the constituents are translated into logic, so that no information is lost; what is lost is the equalities between variables that provides the connections between the constituents. For instance, in the "John works" example, we would know that there was someone named John and that somebody works, but we would not know that they were the same person. Altogether 98.1% of the 5,000 core glosses were translated into correct axioms (59.4%) or axioms that had all the propositional content but were

---

[2]http://www.cs.utexas.edu/~pclark/bpi-test-suite/
[3]http://wordnet.princeton.edu/glosstag

disconnected in this way (38.7%). The remaining 1.9% of these glosses had bizarrely wrong parses due to noun-adjective ambiguities or to complex conjunction ambiguities.

Using the Glosses   We have used a combination of these logicalized glosses and those from XWN to infer implicit information from text. Although the quality of the logic is generally poor (for a variety of reasons, in particular that the glosses were never intended for machine processing in the first place), our software was able to infer conclusions that help answer a few entailment problems, for example:

> T: Britain puts curbs on immigrant labor from Bulgaria and Romania.
> H: Britain restricted workers from Bulgaria.

using the logic for the definition:

```
restrict#v1: "restrict", "restrain": place limits on.
```

plus WordNet's knowledge that: "put" and "place" are synonyms; "curb" and "limit" are synonyms; and a laborer is a worker. In our experiments, the glosses were used to answer 5 of the 250 entailment questions (4 correctly). More commonly, the glosses came "tantalizingly close" to providing the needed knowledge. For example, for:

> T: A Union Pacific freight train hit five people.
> H: A locomotive was pulling the train.

it seems that the definition:

```
train#n1: "train", "railroad train": public transport provided
by a line of railway cars coupled together and drawn by a locomotive.
```

is very close to providing the needed knowledge. However, unfortunately it defines a train as "public transport provided by cars pulled by a locomotive" rather than just "cars pulled by a locomotive" (the locomotive pulls the cars, not the train/public-transport), hence the hypothesis H is not concluded. Similarly:

> T: The Philharmonic orchestra draws large crowds.
> H: Large crowds were drawn to listen to the orchestra.

essentially requires knowledge that crowds (typically) listen to orchestras. WordNet's glosses come very close to providing this, with knowledge that:

> orchestra = collection of musicians
> musician = someone who plays musical instrument
> music = sound produced by musical instruments
> listen = hear = perceive sound

However, the connection that the playing results in sound production is missing, and hence again H cannot be inferred. These experiences with the WordNet glosses were very common. In summary, our experience is the WordNet glosses provided some value, being used 5 times (4 correctly) on the 250 examples in our test suite, with the short, simple definitions (e.g., bleed = lose blood) being the most reliable. The low quality of the logic was a problem (definitional text is notoriously difficult to interpret automatically (Ide and Veronis, 1993)), although often the knowledge came close. Finally, 110,000 rules (approx. one per gloss) is actually quite a small number; typically only 10's of rules fired per sentence, rarely containing the implications we were looking for.

3.2 Typed Morphosemantic Links

WordNet contains approximately 21,000 links connecting derivationally related verb and noun senses, e.g., employ#v2-employee#n1; employ#v2-employment#n3. These links turn out to be essential for mapping between verbal and nominalized expressions (e.g. using "destroy"-"destruction", as mentioned earlier). However, the current links do not state the semantic type of the relation (e.g., that employee#n1 is the UNDER-GOER of an employ#v2 event; employment#n3 is the employ#v2 EVENT itself), which limits WordNet's ability to help perform semantic role labeling. In addition, not being able to distinguish the semantics of the relationships can cause errors in reasoning, for example distinguishing between H1 and H2 in:

> T: Detroit produces fast cars.
> H1: Detroit's product is fast.
> H2*: Detroit's production is fast. [NOT entailed]

> T: The Zoopraxiscope was invented by Mulbridge.
> H1: Mulbridge was the inventor of the Zoopraxiscope.
> H2*: Mulbridge was the invention of the Zoopraxiscope. [NOT entailed]

To type these links, we have used a semi-automatic process: First, the computer makes a "guess" at the appropriate semantic relation based on the morphological relationship between the noun and the verb (e.g., âĂIJ-erâĂİ nouns usually refer to the agent), and the location of the two synsets in WordNet's taxonomy. Second, a human validates and corrects these, a considerably faster progress than entering them from scratch. 9 primary semantic relations (as well as 5 rarer ones) were used, namely:

> agent (e.g., employ#v2-employer#n1)
> undergoer/patient (e.g., employ#v2-employee#n1)
> instrument (e.g., shred#v1-shredder#n1)
> recipient (e.g., grant#v2-grantee#n1)
> result (e.g., produce#v2-product#n2)
> body-part (e.g., adduct#v1-adductor#n1)
> vehicle (e.g., cruise#v4-cruiser#n3)
> location (e.g., bank#v3-bank#n4)
> identity/equality (eg employ#v2-employment#n1)

The resulting database of 21,000 typed links was recently completed, constituting a major new addition to WordNet in support of deep language processing. One of the surprising side results of this effort was discovering how often the normal morphological defaults (e.g., "-er" nouns refer to agents) are violated, described in more detail in Fellbaum et al. (2007). We are now in the process of incorporating the database into our software.

3.3 Core Theories

While WordNet's glosses and links contain world knowledge about specific entities and relations, there is also more fundamental knowledge about language and the world — e.g., about space, time, and causality — which is essential for understanding many types of text, yet is unlikely to be expressed in dictionary definitions or automatically learnable. To address this need, we are also encoding by hand a number of theories to support deeper reasoning (in the style of lexical decomposition). We have axiomatized a number of abstract core theories that underlie the way we talk about events and event structure (Hobbs, 2008). Among these are theories of composite entities (things made of other things), scalar notions (of which space, time, and number are specializations), change of state, and causality. For example, in the theory of change of state, the predication change(e1,e2) says there is a change of state from state e1 to state e2. The predication changeFrom(e1) says there is a change out of state e1. The predication changeTo(e2) says there is a change into state e2. An inference from changeFrom(e1) is that e1 no longer holds. An inference from changeTo(e2) is that e2 now does hold. In the theory of causality (Hobbs, 2005), the predication cause(e1,e2), for e1 causes e2, is explicated. One associated inference is that if the causing happens, then the effect e2 happens. A defeasible inference is that not-cause-not often is the same as cause:

$$not(cause(x,not(e))) \leftrightarrow cause(x,e)$$

In the rightward direction this is of course sometimes wrong, but if we go to the trouble of saying that the negation of something was not caused, then very often it is a legitimate conclusion that the causing did happen.

We are connecting these theories with WordNet by mapping the core (5,000 most common) WordNet synsets to the theory predicates. For example, the core part of WordNet contains 450 word senses having to do with events and event structure, and we are in the process of encoding their meanings in terms of core theory predicates. For example, if x lets e happen (WordNet sense let#v1), then x does not cause e not to happen:

$$let\#v1(x,e) \leftrightarrow not(cause(x,not(e)))$$

One sense of "go" is "changeTo", as in "I go crazy"

$$go\#v4(x,e) \leftrightarrow changeTo(e)$$

(The entity x is the subject of the eventuality e.) If x frees y (the verb sense of "free"), then x causes a change to y being free (in the adjective sense of "free"):

$$free\#v1(x,y) \leftrightarrow cause(x,changeTo(free\#a1(y)))$$

Given these mappings and the core theories themselves, this is enough to answer the entailment pair:

T: The captors freed the hostage.
H: The captors let the hostage go free.

via successive application of the above axioms:

(part of) H interpretation → let(x,go(y,free(y)))
    ↔ not(cause(x,not(changeTo(free#a1(y)))))
    ↔ cause(x,changeTo(free#a1(y)))
    ↔ free#v1(x,y)

We are still in the early stages of developing this resource and have not yet evaluated it, but we have already seen a number of examples of its potential utility in the text inference problem such as above.

3.4 Scripts

Simple inference rules, such as in the above resources, provide a direct means of drawing conclusions from a few words in the input text. However, they are largely context-independent, i.e., not sensitive to the bigger picture which the surrounding text provides. Consider the following example:

T: A dawn bomb attack devastated a major shrine.
H: The bomb exploded.

In this case, it is hard to express the required knowledge (to conclude H follows from T) as simple rules (e.g., the rules "bomb âĘŠ bomb explode" or "bomb attack → bomb explode" are not adequate, as we do not want H to follow from "The police destroyed the bomb." or "The bomb attack was thwarted"). Rather, when a person reads T, he/she recognizes a complete scenario from multiple bits of evidence (possibly in multiple sentences), and integrates what is read with that scenario. This kind of top-down, expectation-driven process seems essential for creating an overall, coherent representation of text.

Although scripts are an old idea (e.g., (Schank and Abelson, 1977)) there are reasons their use may be more feasible today. First, rapid advances in paraphrasing suggests that the matching problem — deciding if some text is expressing part of of a script — may be substantially eased. (Script work in the '70s required stories to be worded in exactly the right way to fire a script). Second, two new approches for amassing knowledge are available today that were not available previously, namely automated learning from corpora, and use of Web volunteers (e.g., (Chklovski, 2005)), and may be applicable to script acquisition (Script work in the '70s typically worked with tiny databases of scripts). Finally, techniques for language processing have substantially improved, making core tasks (e.g., parsing) less problematic, and opening the possibility to easy authoring of scripts in English, followed by machine interpretation. FrameNet (Baker et al., 1998) already provides a few small scripts, but does not currently encode the complex scenarios that we would like; a vastly expanded resource would be highly useful.

We are in the early stages of exploring this avenue, encoding scripts as a list of simple English sentences, which are then automatically translated to WordNet-sense tagged logic using our software. For example, a "bombing" script looks:

A building is bombed by an attacker.
The attacker plants the bomb in the building.

The bomb explodes.
The explosion damages or destroys the building.
The explosion injures or kills people in the building.

In addition, some of these sentences are flagged as "salient". If any salient sentence matches (subsumes) part of the text, then the script is triggered. When triggered, a standard graph-matching algorithm searches for the maximal overlap between the clauses in the (interpreted) script and the clauses in the text, and then the script is unified with the text according to that maximal overlap, thus asserting the additional facts contained in the script to the text under consideration. In the example earlier, the script is triggered by, and matched with, the text, thus aligning "building" with "shrine", and asserting additional facts including (the logic representation of) "The bomb explodes" and "The bomb was planted in the building.".

3.5 Using DIRT Paraphrases

Like others, we have also explored the use of the DIRT paraphrase database for reasoning, and we report our experiences here for comparison. The database contains 12 million rules, discovered automatically from text, of form (X relation1 Y) → (X relation2 Y), where relation is a path in the dependency tree/parse between constitutents X and Y. Although they are noisy (informally, about 50% seem reliable), they provided some leverage for us also, for example correctly answering:

T: William Doyle works for an auction house in Manhattan.
H*: William Doyle never goes to Manhattan. [NOT entailed]

using the DIRT rule "IF Y works in X THEN Y goes to X" combined with negation, and

T: The president visited Iraq in September.
H: The president traveled to Iraq.

using the (slightly strange but plausible) DIRT rule "IF Y is visited by X THEN X flocks to Y" and that âĂIJflockâĂİ is a type (hyponym) of âĂIJtravelâĂİ. In our experiments, DIRT rules were used 47 times (27 correctly) on our 250 example test suite. The main cause of incorrect answers was questionable/incorrect rules in the database, e.g.:

T: The US troops stayed in Iraq.
H*: The US troops left Iraq. [NOT entailed]

was found to be entailed using the DIRT rule "IF Y stays in X THEN Y leaves X". In addition, DIRT does not distinguish word senses (e.g., according to DIRT, shooting a person/basket implies killing the person/basket and scoring a person/basket), also contributing errors.

Despite this, the DIRT rules were useful because they go beyond just the definitional knowledge in WordNet. For example, according to DIRT "X marries Y" implies, among other things: Y marries X; X lives with Y; X kisses Y; X has a child with Y; X loves Y — all examples of plausible world knowledge. The main limitations we found were they were noisy, did not account for word senses, and only cover one rule pattern (X r1 Y → X r2 Y). So, for example, a rule like "X buys Y → X pays Money" is outside the expressive scope of DIRT.

4   Preliminary Evaluation

Although this is work in progress, we have evaluated some of these augmentations using our test suite. As our ultimate goal is deeper understanding of text, we have deliberately eschewed using statistical similarity measures between T and H, and instead used abductive reasoning to create an axiom-elaborated representation of T, and then seen if it is subsumed by H. Although not using statistical similarity clearly hurts our score, in particular assuming "no entailment" when the elaborated representation of T is not subsumed by H, we believe this keeps us appropriately focused on our longer-term goal of deeper understanding of text. The results on our 250 pairs currently are:

H or ¬H predicted by:	Correct	Incorrect
Simple syntax manipulation	11	3
WordNet taxonomy + morphosemantics	14	1
WordNet logicalized glosses	4	1
DIRT paraphrase rules	27	20
H or ¬H not predicted:	**Correct**	**Incorrect**
(assumed not entailed)	97	72

Thus our overall score on this test suite is 61.2%. We have also run our software on the PASCAL RTE3 dataset (Giampiccolo et al., 2007), scoring 55.7% (excluding cases where no initial logical representation could be constructed due to parse/LF generation failures). In some cases, other known limitations of WordNet (eg. hypernym errors, fine-grained senses) also caused errors in our tests (outside the scope of this paper). However, the most significant problem, at least for these tests, was lack of world knowledge.

5   Conclusion

A big challenge for deep understanding of text — constructing a coherent representation of the scene it is intended to convey — is the need for large amounts of world knowledge. We have described our work-in-progress to augment WordNet in various ways so it can better provide some of this knowledge, and described some initial experiences with those augmentations, as well as with the DIRT database. Existing WordNet already provides extensive leverage for language processing, as evidenced by the large number of groups using it. The contribution of this paper is some preliminary insight into avenues and challenges for further developing this resource. Although somewhat anecdotal at this stage, our experience suggests the augmentations have promise for further improving deep language processing, and we hope will result in a significantly improved resource.

Acknowledgements   This work was performed under the DTO AQUAINT program, contract N61339-06-C-0160.

References

Adams, R., G. Nicolae, C. Nicolae, and S. Harabagiu (2007). Textual entailment through extended lexical overlap and lexico-semantic matching. In *Proc. ACL-PASCAL Workshop on Textual and Entailment and Paraphrasing*, pp. 119–124.

Baker, C. F., C. J. Fillmore, and J. B. Lowe (1998). The Berkeley FrameNet project. In C. Boitet and P. Whitelock (Eds.), *Proc 36th ACL Conf.*, CA, pp. 86–90. Kaufmann.

Chambers, N., D. Cer, T. Grenager, D. Hall, C. K. MacCartney, M.-C. de Marneffe, D. R. Yeh, and C. D. Manning (2007). Learning alignments and leveraging natural logic. In *Proc. ACL-PASCAL Workshop on Textual and Entailment and Paraphrasing*, pp. 165–170.

Chklovski, T. (2005). Collecting paraphrase corpora from volunteer contributors. In *Proc 3rd Int Conf on Knowledge Capture (KCap'05)*, NY, pp. 115–120. ACM.

Clark, P. and P. Harrison (2008, September). Boeing's NLP System and the Challenges of Semantic Representation. In J. Bos and R. Delmonte (Eds.), *Semantics in Text Processing. STEP 2008 Conference Proceedings*, Venice, Italy.

Fellbaum, C. (1998). *WordNet: An Electronic Lexical Database*. Cambridge, MA: MIT Press.

Fellbaum, C., A. Osherson, and P. Clark (2007). Putting semantics into wordnet's morphosemantic links. In *Proc. 3rd Language and Technology Conference*, Poznan, Poland.

Giampiccolo, D., B. Magnini, I. Dagan, and B. Dolan (2007). Textual entailment through extended lexical overlap and lexico-semantic matching. In *Proc. ACL-PASCAL Workshop on Textual and Entailment and Paraphrasing*, pp. 1–9.

Graesser, A. C. (1981). *Prose Comprehension Beyond the Word*. NY: Springer.

Gurevich, O., R. Crouch, T. King, and V. de Paiva (2006). Deverbal nouns in knowledge representation. In *Proc. FLAIRS'06*.

Harrison, P. and M. Maxwell (1986). A new implementation of GPSG. In *Proc. 6th Canadian Conf on AI (CSCSI-86)*, pp. 78–83.

Hobbs, J. (2005). Toward a useful notion of causality for lexical semantics. *Journal of Semantics 22*, 181–209.

Hobbs, J. (2008). Encoding commonsense knowledge. Technical report, USC/ISI. http://www.isi.edu/~hobbs/csk.html.

Ide, N. and J. Veronis (1993). Extracting knowledge-bases from machine-readable dictionaries: Have we wasted our time? In *Proc KB&KB'93 Workshop*, pp. 257–266.

Lenat, D. and R. Guha (1989). *Building Large Knowledge-Based Systems.* MA: Addison-Wesley.

Miller, G. (1995). WordNet: a lexical database for english. *Comm. of the ACM 38*(11), 39–41.

Moldovan, D. and V. Rus (2001). Explaining answers with extended wordnet. In *Proc. ACL'01.*

Schank, R. and R. Abelson (1977). *Scripts, Plans, Goals and Understanding.* Hillsdale, NJ: Erlbaum.

Schubert, L. and C. Hwang (1993). Episodic logic: A situational logic for NLP. In *Situation Theory and Its Applications*, pp. 303–337.

How Well Do Semantic Relatedness Measures Perform? A Meta-Study

Irene Cramer

Dortmund University of Technology (Germany)

email: irene.cramer@udo.edu

Abstract

Various semantic relatedness, similarity, and distance measures have been proposed in the past decade and many NLP-applications strongly rely on these semantic measures. Researchers compete for better algorithms and normally only few percentage points seem to suffice in order to prove a new measure outperforms an older one. In this paper we present a meta-study comparing various semantic measures and their correlation with human judgments. We show that the results are rather inconsistent and ask for detailed analyses as well as clarification. We argue that the definition of a shared task might bring us considerably closer to understanding the concept of semantic relatedness.

1   Introduction

Various applications in Natural Language Processing, such as Question Answering
(Novischi and Moldovan, 2006), Topic Detection (Carthy, 2004), and Text Summarization (Barzilay and Elhadad, 1997), rely on semantic relatedness (similarity or distance)[1] measures either based on word nets and/or corpus statistics as a resource. In
the HyTex project, funded by the German Research Foundation, we develop strategies
for the text-to-hypertext conversion using text-grammatical features. One strand of
research in this project consists of topic-based linking methods using lexical chaining as a resource (Cramer and Finthammer, 2008). Lexical chaining is a well-known
method to calculate partial text representations; it relies on semantic relatedness values as basic input. We therefore implemented[2] eight semantic relatedness measures
— (Hirst and St-Onge, 1998; Jiang and Conrath, 1997; Leacock and Chodorow, 1998;
Lin, 1998; Resnik, 1995; Wu and Palmer, 1994) — based on GermaNet[3] Lemnitzer
and Kunze (2002) and three based on Google co-occurrence counts (Cilibrasi and Vitanyi, 2007). In order to evaluate the performance of these measures we conducted
two human judgment experiments and computed the correlation between the human
judgment and the values of the eleven semantic measures. We also compared our
results with those reported in the literature and found that the correlations between
human judgments and semantic measures are extremely scattered. In this paper we
compare the correlation of our own human judgment experiments and the results of
three similar studies. In our opinion this comparison points to the necessity of a thorough analysis of the methods used in these experiments. We argue that this analysis
should aim at answering the following questions:

- How does the setting of the human judgment experiment influence the results?

- How does the selection of the word-pairs influence the results?

- Which aspects of semantic relatedness are included in human judgments? Thus,
  what do these experiments actually measure?

- Are the semantic relatedness measures proposed in the literature able to capture
  all of these aspects?

In this paper we intend to open the above mentioned analysis and therefore assembled
a set of aspects which we consider to be important in order to answer these questions.
Consequently, the remainder of this paper is structured as follows: In Section 2 we

---

[1] The notions of semantic relatedness, similarity, and distance measure are controversially discussed in
the literature, e.g. Budanitsky and Hirst (2006). However, semantic similarity and relatedness seem to be
the predominant terms in this context. Budanitsky and Hirst (2006) define them as follows: word-pairs are
considered to be semantically similar if a synonymy or hypernymy relation holds. In contrast, word-pairs
are considered to be semantically related if a systematic relation, such as synonymy, antonymy, hypernymy,
holonymy, or an unsystematic relation holds. Thus relatedness is the more general (broader) concept since
it includes intuitive associations as well as linguistically formalized relations between words (or concepts).
The focus of this paper is on relatedness.

[2] Since GermaNet — e.g. in terms of internal structure — slightly differs from Princeton WordNet we
could not simply use the measure implementations of the latter and therefore had to reimplement and adapt
them for GermaNet.

[3] GermaNet is the German counterpart of WordNet (Fellbaum, 1998).

present our own human judgment experiments. In Section 3 we describe three similar studies, two conducted with English data and one with German. In Section 4 we compare the results of the four studies and discuss (with respect to the experimental setting and goals) potential differences and possible causes for the observed inconsistency of the results. Finally, we summarize our work and outline some ideas for future research.

2   Our Human Judgement Experiments

In order to evaluate the quality of a semantic measure, a set of pre-classified (i.e. judged with respect to their semantic relatedness by subjects) word-pairs is necessary. In previous work for English data, most researchers used the word-pair list by Rubenstein and Goodenough (1965) as well as the list by Miller and Charles (1991) as an evaluation resource. For German there are — to our knowledge — two research groups, which compiled lists of word-pairs with respective human judgment:

- Gurevych et al. constructed three lists (a translation of Rubenstein and Goodenough's list (Gurevych, 2005), a manually generated set of word-pairs, and a semi-automatically generated one (Zesch and Gurevych, 2006)).

- While investigating lexical chaining for German corpora, we additionally compiled a total of six lists, each of which consists of 100 word-pairs with respective human judgments.

The goal of our experiments was to cover a wide range of relatedness types, i.e. systematic and unsystematic relations, and relatedness levels, i.e. various degrees of relation strength. However, we only included nouns in the construction of our sets of word-pairs, since we consider cross-part-of-speech (cross-POS) relations to be an additional challenge[4], which we intend to address in a continuative experiment. Furthermore, in order to identify a potential bias of the lists and the impact of this bias on the results, we applied two different methods for the compilation of word-pairs.

For our first human judgment experiment (Cramer and Finthammer, 2008) we collected nouns (analytically)[5] of diverse semantic classes, e.g. abstract nouns, such as das Wissen (Engl. knowledge), and concrete nouns, such as das Bügeleisen (Engl. flat-iron). By this means, we constructed a list of approximately 300 word-pairs. We picked approximately 75 and randomized them. For the remaining 25 word-pairs, we selected five words and constructed word-pairs such as Sonne-Wind (Engl. sun-wind), Sonne-Wärme (Engl. sun-warmth), Sonne-Wetter (Engl. sun-weather) etc. We arranged these 25 pairs into sequences in order to focus our subjects' attention on small semantic relatedness distinctions.

---

[4] Since in most word nets cross-POS relations are very sparse, researchers currently investigate relation types able to connect the noun, verb, and adjective sub-graphs (e.g. Marrafa and Mendes (2006) or Lemnitzer et al. (2008)). However, these new relations are not yet integrated on a large scale and therefore should not (or even cannot) be used in semantic relatedness measures. Furthermore, calculating semantic relatedness between words with different POS might introduce additional challenges potentially as yet unidentified, which calls for a careful exploration.

[5] In this paper and in most comparable studies, the term *analytical* means that the word-pairs are handpicked. Obviously, the disadvantage of this approach is its sensibility to idiosyncrasies, which might extremely bias the outcome of the experiments.

For the five remaining lists (WP2-WP6), we applied a different method: firstly, we again analytically collected word-pairs which are part of collocations, i.e. the two nouns Rat and Tat (mit Rat und Tat helfen, Engl. to help with words and deeds) or Qual and Wahl (die Qual der Wahl haben, Engl. to be spoilt for choice). Secondly, we assembled word-pairs which feature association relations, i.e. Afrika (Engl. Africa) and Tiger (Engl. tiger) or Weihnachten (Engl. Christmas) and Zimt (Engl. cinnamon). Thirdly, we automatically constructed a list of random word-pairs using the Wacky corpus (Baroni and Bernardini, 2006) as a resource and manually excluded ad-hoc-constructions. Finally, out of these three resources we compiled five sets of 100 randomized word-pairs with no more than 20% of the collocation and association word-pairs.

We asked subjects to rate the word-pairs on a 5-level scale (0 = *not related* to 4 = *strongly related*). The subjects were instructed to base the rating on their intuition about any kind of conceivable relation between the two words. WP1 was rated by 35 subjects and WP2 to WP6 were each rated by 15 subjects. We then calculated the average judgment per word-pair and ranked the word-pairs accordingly.

The correlation between the human judgments and the eleven semantic measures is shown in Table 1. The difference between the correlation coefficients of WP1 and WP2-WP6 suggests that the method of construction might have an impact on the results of the experiments. The manual compilation of word-pairs seems to lead to better correlation coefficients and might therefore cause an overestimation of the performance of the semantic measures. Furthermore, with respect to the list construction methods, the two resources and respective measures, namely GermaNet (TreePath–Lin) and Google (GoogleQ–GooglePMI), seem to respond differently: whereas the correlation coefficients of the eight GermaNet based measures drop to a greater or lesser extend (Table 1: r for WP1 and r for WP2-WP6), the correlation coefficients of the three Google based measures approximately level off.

Table 1: Our Correlation Coefficients: Correlation between Average Human Judgment and Semantic Measure Values

r	Tree Path	Graph Path	Wu-Palm.	Leac.-Chod.	Hirst-St-O.	Resnik	Jiang-Conr.	Lin	Google Norm.	Google Quot.	Google PMI
WP1	0.41	0.42	0.36	0.48	0.47	0.44	0.45	0.48	0.27	0.37	0.37
WP2	0.09	0.31	0.33	0.16	0.26	0.37	0.18	0.36	0.24	0.29	0.27
WP3	0.03	0.22	0.24	0.11	0.28	0.19	0.15	0.26	0.46	0.45	0.40
WP4	0.07	0.39	0.11	0.11	0.31	0.11	0.25	0.16	0.34	0.38	0.34
WP5	0.27	0.39	0.26	0.32	0.38	0.31	0.41	0.34	0.19	0.32	0.28
WP6	0.09	0.27	0.15	0.17	0.39	0.24	0.29	0.25	0.26	0.38	0.43
mean	**0.16**	**0.33**	**0.24**	**0.23**	**0.35**	**0.28**	**0.29**	**0.31**	**0.29**	**0.36**	**0.35**

In any case, since the correlation coefficients are rather low, there is much room for improvement. However, as all measures scatter in the same range — independently of the precise algorithm or resource used, as it seems — we argue that the reason for this critical performance might be one of the following two aspects (most probably a combination of both):

- Word nets (and/or corpora) do not cover the (all) types of semantic information required.

- Human judgment experiments are (without clear and standardized specification of the experimental setup) an inappropriate way to evaluate semantic measures.

Both aspects are discussed in Section 4. However, we first should have a look at three similar studies, two for English and one for German.

3 Three Similar Studies

As mentioned above various researchers rely on human judgment experiments as an evaluation resource for semantic relatedness measures. In this section, three such studies are summarized in order to identify differences with respect to the methods adopted and results obtained.[6]

3.1 Budanitsky and Hirst

Budanitsky and Hirst (2006) specify the purpose of their paper *Evaluating WordNet-based Measures of Lexical Semantic Relatedness* as a comparison of the performance of various relatedness measures. Accordingly, they sketch a number of measures and identify three evaluation methods: firstly, the theoretical examination (of e.g. the mathematical properties of the respective measure); secondly, the comparison with human judgments; thirdly, the evaluation of a measure with respect to a given NLP-application. They regard the second and third method as being the most appropriate ones and therefore focus on them in their empirical work presented in the paper. As a basis for the second evaluation method, i.e. the comparison between semantic measure and human judgments, they use two word-pair lists: the first compiled by Rubenstein and Goodenough (1965) and containing 65 word-pairs[7], the second compiled by Miller and Charles (1991) and containing 30 word-pairs. In order to evaluate the performance of five different measures (and potentially in order to find a ranking), Budanitsky and Hirst (2006) compute the semantic relatedness values for the word-pairs and compare them with the human judgments. They thus find the correlation coefficients summarized in Table 2.

Budanitsky and Hirst (2006) regard this evaluation method, i.e. comparing measure values and human judgments, as the ideal approach. However, in examining the results of this comparison, they identify several limitations; i.e. they point out that the amount of data available (65 word-pairs) might be inadequate for real NLP-applications. They additionally emphasize that the development of a large-scale data set would be time-consuming and expensive. Moreover, they argue that the experiments by Rubenstein and Goodenough (1965) as well as Miller and Charles (1991) focus on relations between words rather than relations between word-senses (concepts), which would be

---

[6]There are many more relevant studies; however, they all point to the same issue, namely, the incompatibility of the results.

[7]Rubenstein and Goodenough (1965) investigated the relationship between 'similarity of context' and 'similarity of meaning'. They asked 51 subjects to rate on a scale of 0 to 4 the similarity of meaning for the 65 word-pairs. Miller and Charles (1991) selected 30 out of the 65 original word-pairs (according to their relatedness strength) and asked 38 subjects to rate this list. They used the same experimental setup as Rubenstein and Goodenough (1965).

Table 2: Correlation Coefficients by Budantisky and Hirst

r	Leac.-Chod.	Hirst-StO.	Resnik	Jiang-Conr.	Lin
M&C	0.816	0.744	0.774	0.850	0.82
R&G	0.838	0.786	0.779	0.781	0.819
mean	**0.83**	**0.77**	**0.78**	**0.82**	**0.82**

— especially when taking potential NLP-applications into account — more appropriate. They note that it might however be difficult to trigger a specific concept without biasing the subjects.

3.2 Boyd-Graber, Fellbaum, Osherson, and Schapire

In contrast to the above mentioned experiments by Budanitsky and Hirst (2006), the research reported in *Adding Dense, Weighted Connections to WordNet* aims at the development of a new, conceptually different layer of relations to be included into a word net. Boyd-Graber et al. (2006) are motivated in their work by three widely acknowledged shortcomings of word nets:

- The lack of cross-POS links connecting the sub-graphs containing nouns, verbs, or adjectives, respectively.

- The low density of relations in the sub-graphs, i.e. potentially missing types of relations such as 'actor' or 'instrument'.

- The absence of weights assigned to the relations, i.e. representing the degrees of semantic distance of different subordinates of the same superordinate.

In order to address these shortcomings, Boyd-Graber et al. ask subjects to assign values of 'evocation' representing the relations between 1,000 synsets. They ask 20 subjects to rate evocation in 120,000 pairs of synsets (these pairs form a random selection of all possible pairs of the above mentioned 1,000 core synsets considered in the experiment). The subjects are given a manual explaining a couple of details about the task and are trained on a sample of 1,000 (two sets of 500) randomly selected pairs. Although the research objective of the work presented in this paper is to construct a new relations layer for Princeton WordNet rather than to evaluate semantic relatedness measures, Boyd-Graber et al. compare the results of their human judgment experiment with the relatedness values of four different semantic measures. The correlation coefficients of this comparison are summarized in Table 3.

Boyd-Graber et al. arrive at the conclusion that — given the obvious lack of correlation (see Table 3) — evocation constitutes an empirically supported semantic relation type which is still not captured by the semantic measures (at least not by those considered in this experiment).

3.3 Gurevych et al.

Similar to the study by Budanitsky and Hirst (2006), Gurevych (2005) gives insight into a human judgment experiment conducted in order to compare the performance

Table 3: Correlation Coefficients by Boyd-Graber et al.

r	Lesk	Path	LC	LSA
all	0.008			
verbs		0.046		
nouns		0.013	0.013	
closest				0.131

Table 4: Correlation Coefficients by Gurevych (with $Lesk_1$ = Lesk (DWDS); $Lesk_2$ = Lesk (radial); $Lesk_3$ = Lesk (hypernym); Resn. = Resnik)

r	Google	$Lesk_1$	$Lesk_2$	$Lesk_3$	Resn.
R&G German	0.57	0.53	0.55	0.60	0.72

of her own semantic relatedness measure[8] with established ones. For this purpose (Gurevych, 2005) translates the word-pair list by Rubenstein and Goodenough (1965) and asks 24 native speakers of German to rate the word-pairs with respect to their semantic relatedness on a 5-level scale; she thus replicates the study by Rubenstein and Goodenough (1965) for German. Gurevych (2005) finally compares the human judgments with several semantic measures. The correlation coefficients of this comparison are summarized in Table 4.

Gurevych (2005) comments on (among others) the following four issues: firstly, she emphasizes the difference between semantic similarity and relatedness; she argues that most word-pair lists were constructed in order to measure semantic similarity rather than relatedness and that these lists might therefore be inappropriate for the task at hand. Secondly, Gurevych (2005) observes that, in contrast to the concept of semantic similarity, semantic relatedness is not well defined. Thirdly, as the experiments are based on words rather than concepts, the results attained thus far might exhibit additional noise. Finally, she notes that the amount of data is too limited in size and that analytically created word-pair lists are inherently biased. Accordingly, Zesch and Gurevych (2006) propose a corpus based method for automatically constructing test data and list a number of advantages of this approach: i.e. lexical-semantic cohesion in texts accounts for various relation types, domain-specific and technical terms can easily be included, and, in contrast to manually constructed, corpus based lists are probably more objective.

4 Meta-Level Evaluation

Table 5 shows the minimum, maximum, and mean correlations reported in the three studies as well as our own results. The table illustrates the broad statistical spread: the mean correlation coefficients range between 0.8 and 0.04 for English and between 0.61 and 0.29 for German. Admittedly, the experimental setup and the goals of the

---

[8] Her measure is able to manage limitations of some of the previously published measures.

Table 5: Comparison of the Correlation Coefficients of the Different Experiments (with B&G: Budanitsky and Hirst / B-G et al.: Boyd-Graber et al. / G et al.: Gurevych et al. / C&F, C: our results)

	B&H	B-G et al.	G et al.	C&F, C
max	0.83	0.131	0.72	0.36
min	0.77	0.008	0.53	0.16
mean	**0.80**	**0.04**	**0.61**	**0.29**
stdv	0.03	0.05	0.08	0.06

four studies differ in several aspects[9]. However, the principle idea — i.e. using human judgments as a baseline or evaluation resource — is the same.

We argue that — given the statistical spread shown in Table 5 — as long as the reasons for this discrepancy have not been determined and the methods have not been harmonized as far as possible, the results of these experiments should not be used as a basis for e.g. the evaluation or comparison of semantic measures. As mentioned in Section 1 we suspect that (no fewer than) the following aspects influence the results of the human judgment experiments and thus the correlation between humans and semantic measures:

- **Research objective:** The goals of the studies differ with respect to several aspects. Firstly, some studies, e.g. Budanitsky and Hirst (2006), aim at comparing the performance of different semantic (relatedness) measures, whereas Boyd-Graber et al. (2006) intend to construct a new relations layer (potentially able to substitute or complement established relatedness measures). Secondly, in some cases, e.g. Cramer and Finthammer (2008), relations between words are considered, whereas e.g. Boyd-Graber et al. (2006) examine relations between concepts. Thirdly, it seems to be unclear which types of relations are actually searched for (relatedness, similarity, evocation, distance) and in what aspects these correspond or differ. Interestingly, in computational linguistics and psycholinguistics there is an additional strand of research investigating the so-called 'association relation', e.g. Schulte im Walde and Melinger (2005) and Roth and Schulte im Walde (2008), which is not yet considered or integrated in the research on semantic relatedness measures. We argue that such an integration might be fruitful for both research strands.

- **Setting of the human judgment experiment:** In all studies summarized above, the subjects are students (mostly of linguistics, computer sciences, and computational linguistics). In most cases, they are given a short manual explaining the task, which certainly differs in many aspects, e.g. due to the above mentioned fact that the relation type searched for is a still unsettled issue. Furthermore, no training phase is included in most of the studies except the one by Boyd-Graber

---

[9] It seems unfeasible to determine all possible differences of the studies because, among other things, the papers do not specify the experimental setup in detail. We therefore assume that the definition of a shared task might bring us considerably closer to understanding the questions raised in this paper.

et al. (2006), who are therefore able to identify potential training effects. Again only Boyd-Graber et al. (2006) account for the handling of idiosyncrasies.

- **Construction of experimental data:** In Boyd-Graber et al. (2006) the concept-pairs were randomly selected, whereas the word-pairs used by Budanitsky and Hirst (2006) were constructed analytically. In the studies by Gurevych (2005), Zesch and Gurevych (2006), and Cramer and Finthammer (2008), some were analytically constructed and some randomly (semi-automatically) selected. In addition, the data sets vary with respect to their size: Budanitsky and Hirst (2006), Gurevych (2005), and Cramer and Finthammer (2008) only use small sets of word-pairs (concept-pairs), i.e. a few hundred pairs, whereas Boyd-Graber et al. (2006) investigate a huge amount of data; their experiment therefore certainly constitutes the most representative one. All studies also indicate the (mean/median) inter-subject correlation[10] which varies from 0.48 (concept-pair based) in Zesch and Gurevych (2006) and 0.72 (concept-pair based) in Boyd-Graber et al. (2006) to 0.85 (word-pair based) in Budanitsky and Hirst (2006).

We think that this comparison of the various experiments points to two aspects which probably cause the large statistical spread shown in Table 5: the selection of the word-pairs (concept-pairs) and the type of relation (relatedness, similarity, evocation, distance). We assume that it should be possible to condense the comparison into one (more or less simple) rule: the narrower the relation concept (similarity < relatedness < evocation) and the narrower the data considered (lexical semantic selection rule < any kind of selection rule < random selection) the better the correlation between human judgment and semantic measure[11]. In any case, it seems essential to determine which relation types the subjects (knowingly or unknowingly) bear in mind when they judge word-pairs with respect to semantic relatedness. In order to achieve this goal and be able to integrate all relevant relations into the resources used for calculating semantic relatedness, the human judgments collected in the above-mentioned studies should be dissected into components (i.e. components for which systematic/unsystematic lexical semantic relations account etc.); such a decomposition certainly also helps render more precisely the definition of semantic relatedness.

Furthermore, it is — in our opinion — an unsettled issue whether the three types of semantic relation at hand, thus the relations

1. represented in a word net or corpus (both computed via semantic measure),

2. existing between any given word-pair in a text (which is mostly relevant for NLP-applications),

3. and the one assigned by subjects in a human judgment experiment

---

[10]The inter-subject correlation depends on various parameters, e.g. the complexity of the task, the subjects (and their background, age, etc.) as well as the experimental setup (task definition, training phase, etc.).

[11]... and obviously the easier the task!

correspond at all. In principle, word nets, corpus statistics, and human judgments should be related to (theoretically even represent) the (at least partially) shared knowledge of humans about the underlying 'lexical semantic system', whereas relations between words in a concrete text represent an instantiation of a system. From this point of view, at least the human judgments should correspond to the semantics encoded in a word net (or corpus statistics). Instead of using human judgments as an evaluation resource (for e.g. word net based semantic measures), they might as well be directly integrated into the word net as a (preferably dense) layer of (potentially cognitively relevant, weighted but unlabeled) semantic relations, which is best adopted in Boyd-Graber et al. (2006), as summarized in Section 3. This approach has several advantages: firstly, the calculation of a semantic relatedness value is — given such a layer — trivial, since it merely consists in a look-up procedure. Secondly, NLP-applications using word nets as a resource would certainly benefit from the thus enhanced density of relations, i.e. cross-POS relations. Thirdly, an elaborate and standardized experimental setup for human judgment experiments could be used for the construction of such a layer in different languages (and domains) and would also guarantee the modeling quality. Finally, such a new word net layer would hopefully resolve the above mentioned open issue of the diverging correlation coefficients.

Alternatively, since it is completely unclear if the evocation relation can really act as a substitute for classical semantic relatedness measures in NLP-applications, current word nets should be enhanced by systematically augmenting existing relation types and integrating new ones. On that condition and given that a common evaluation framework exists, it should be possible to determine which semantic relatedness measure performs best under what conditions.

Last but not least, in order to determine the relation between an underlying semantic system (represented by a semantic measure or as mentioned above the evocation layer) and the instantiation of this system in a concrete text, a study similar to the one reported in Zesch and Gurevych (2006) should be conducted. Such a study probably also shows if the evocation relation is able to substitute (or at least complement) semantic relatedness measures typically used in NLP-applications.

5   Conclusions and Future Work

We have presented our own human judgment experiments for German and compared them with three similar studies. This comparison illustrates that the results of these studies are incompatible. We therefore argue that the experimental setup should be clarified and, if possible, harmonized. We also think that the notion of association should be considered carefully, since it is an established concept for measuring related phenomena in several psycholinguistic and computational linguistic communities.

We now plan to continue our work on three levels. Firstly, we intend to conduct a study similar to the one reported by Boyd-Graber et al. (2006) with a small amount of German data. We hope that this will provide us with insight into some of the open issues mentioned in Section 1 and Section 4. Secondly, we plan to investigate if the evocation relation is able to substitute the semantic relatedness measures typically used in lexical chaining and similar NLP-applications. Thirdly, we intend to run experiments using the database of noun associations in German constructed by Melinger and Weber (2006) as a resource for the evaluation of semantic relatedness measures.

Acknowledgements The author would like to thank Michael Beißwenger, Christiane Fellbaum, Sabine Schulte im Walde, Angelika Storrer, Tonio Wandmacher, Torsten Zesch, and the anonymous reviewers for their helpful comments. This research was funded by the DFG Research Group 437 (HyTex).

References

Baroni, M. and S. Bernardini (Eds.) (2006). *Wacky! Working papers on the Web as Corpus*. GEDIT, Bologna.

Barzilay, R. and M. Elhadad (1997). Using lexical chains for text summarization. In *Proceedings of the Intelligent Scalable Text Summarization Workshop*, pp. 10–17.

Boyd-Graber, J., C. Fellbaum, D. Osherson, and R. Schapire (2006). Adding dense, weighted, connections to wordnet. In *Proceedings of the 3rd Global WordNet Meeting*, pp. 29–35.

Budanitsky, A. and G. Hirst (2006). Evaluating wordnet-based measures of semantic relatedness. *Computational Linguistics 32 (1)*, 13–47.

Carthy, J. (2004). Lexical chains versus keywords for topic tracking. In *Computational Linguistics and Intelligent Text Processing*, Lecture Notes in Computer Science, pp. 507–510. Springer.

Cilibrasi, R. and P. M. B. Vitanyi (2007). The google similarity distance. *IEEE Transactions on Knowledge and Data Engineering 19*(3), 370–383.

Cramer, I. and M. Finthammer (2008). An evaluation procedure for word net based lexical chaining: Methods and issues. In *Proceedings of the 4th Global WordNet Meeting*, pp. 120–147.

Fellbaum, C. (1998). *WordNet. An Electronic Lexical Database*. The MIT Press.

Gurevych, I. (2005). Using the structure of a conceptual network in computing semantic relatedness. In *Proceedings of the IJCNLP 2005*, pp. 767–778.

Hirst, G. and D. St-Onge (1998). Lexical chains as representation of context for the detection and correction malapropisms. In C. Fellbaum (Ed.), *WordNet: An Electronic Lexical Database*, pp. 305–332. The MIT Press.

Jiang, J. J. and D. W. Conrath (1997). Semantic similarity based on corpus statistics and lexical taxonomy. In *Proceedings of ROCLING X*, pp. 19–33.

Leacock, C. and M. Chodorow (1998). Combining local context and wordnet similarity for word sense identification. In C. Fellbaum (Ed.), *WordNet: An Electronic Lexical Database*, pp. 265–284. The MIT Press.

Lemnitzer, L. and C. Kunze (2002). Germanet - representation, visualization, application. In *Proceedings of the 4th Language Resources and Evaluation Conference*, pp. 1485–1491.

Lemnitzer, L., H. Wunsch, and P. Gupta (2008). Enriching germanet with verb-noun relations - a case study of lexical acquisition. In *Proceedings of the 6th International Language Resources and Evaluation*.

Lin, D. (1998). An information-theoretic definition of similarity. In *Proceedings of the 15th International Conference on Machine Learning*, pp. 296–304.

Marrafa, P. and S. Mendes (2006). Modeling adjectives in computational relational lexica. In *Proceedings of the COLING/ACL 2006 poster session*, pp. 555–562.

Melinger, A. and A. Weber (2006). A database of noun associations in german. Online available database: http://www.coli.uni-saarland.de/projects/nag.

Miller, G. A. and W. G. Charles (1991). Contextual correlates of semantic similiarity. *Language and Cognitive Processes 6*(1), 1–28.

Novischi, A. and D. Moldovan (2006). Question answering with lexical chains propagating verb arguments. In *Proceedings of the 21st International Conference on Computational Linguistics and 44th Annual Meeting of the Association for Computational Linguistics*, pp. 897–904.

Resnik, P. (1995). Using information content to evaluate semantic similarity in a taxonomy. In *Proceedings of the IJCAI 1995*, pp. 448–453.

Roth, M. and S. Schulte im Walde (2008). Corpus co-occurrence, dictionary and wikipedia entries as resources for semantic relatedness information. In *Proceedings of the 6th Conference on Language Resources and Evaluation*.

Rubenstein, H. and J. B. Goodenough (1965). Contextual correlates of synonymy. *Communications of the ACM 8*(10), 627–633.

Schulte im Walde, S. and A. Melinger (2005). Identifying semantic relations and functional properties of human verb associations. In *Proceedings of Human Language Technology Conference and Conference on Empirical Methods in Natural Language Processing*, pp. 612–619.

Wu, Z. and M. Palmer (1994). Verb semantics and lexical selection. In *Proceedings of the 32nd Annual Meeting of the Association for Computational Linguistics*, pp. 133–138.

Zesch, T. and I. Gurevych (2006). Automatically creating datasets for measures of semantic relatedness. In *Proceedings of the Workshop on Linguistic Distances at COLING/ACL 2006*, pp. 16–24.

KnowNet:
A Proposal for Building Highly Connected and Dense Knowledge Bases from the Web

Montse Cuadros

TALP Research Center, UPC, Barcelona (Spain)

email: cuadros@lsi.upc.edu

German Rigau

IXA NLP Group, UPV/EHU, Donostia (Spain)

email: german.rigau@ehu.es

Abstract

This paper presents a new fully automatic method for building highly dense and accurate knowledge bases from existing semantic resources. Basically, the method uses a wide-coverage and accurate knowledge-based Word Sense Disambiguation algorithm to assign the most appropriate senses to large sets of topically related words acquired from the web. KnowNet, the resulting knowledge-base which connects large sets of semantically-related concepts is a major step towards the autonomous acquisition of knowledge from raw corpora. In fact, KnowNet is several times larger than any available knowledge resource encoding relations between synsets, and the knowledge that KnowNet contains outperform any other resource when empirically evaluated in a common multilingual framework.

1   Introduction

Using large-scale knowledge bases, such as WordNet (Fellbaum, 1998), has become a usual, often necessary, practice for most current Natural Language Processing (NLP) systems. Even now, building large and rich enough knowledge bases for broad–coverage semantic processing takes a great deal of expensive manual effort involving large research groups during long periods of development. In fact, hundreds of person-years have been invested in the development of wordnets for various languages (Vossen, 1998). For example, in more than ten years of manual construction (from 1995 to 2006, that is from version 1.5 to 3.0), WordNet passed from 103,445 to 235,402 semantic relations[1]. But this data does not seems to be rich enough to support advanced concept-based NLP applications directly. It seems that applications will not scale up to working in open domains without more detailed and rich general-purpose (and also domain-specific) semantic knowledge built by automatic means. Obviously, this fact has severely hampered the state-of-the-art of advanced NLP applications.

However, the Princeton WordNet is by far the most widely-used knowledge base (Fellbaum, 1998). In fact, WordNet is being used world-wide for anchoring different types of semantic knowledge including wordnets for languages other than English (Atserias et al., 2004), domain knowledge (Magnini and Cavaglià, 2000) or ontologies like SUMO (Niles and Pease, 2001) or the EuroWordNet Top Concept Ontology (Álvez et al., 2008). It contains manually coded information about nouns, verbs, adjectives and adverbs in English and is organised around the notion of a *synset*. A synset is a set of words with the same part-of-speech that can be interchanged in a certain context. For example, <*party, political_party*> form a synset because they can be used to refer to the same concept. A synset is often further described by a gloss, in this case: "an organisation to gain political power" and by explicit semantic relations to other synsets.

Fortunately, during the last years the research community has devised a large set of innovative methods and tools for large-scale automatic acquisition of lexical knowledge from structured and unstructured corpora. Among others we can mention eXtended WordNet (Mihalcea and Moldovan, 2001), large collections of semantic preferences acquired from SemCor (Agirre and Martinez, 2001, 2002) or acquired from British National Corpus (BNC) (McCarthy, 2001), large-scale Topic Signatures for each synset acquired from the web (Agirre and de la Calle, 2004) or knowledge about individuals from Wikipedia (Suchanek et al., 2007). Obviously, all these semantic resources have been acquired using a very different set of processes (Snow et al., 2006), tools and corpora. In fact, each semantic resource has different volume and accuracy figures when evaluated in a common and controlled framework (Cuadros and Rigau, 2006).

However, not all available large-scale resources encode semantic relations between synsets. In some cases, only relations between synsets and words have been acquired. This is the case of the Topic Signatures (Agirre et al., 2000) acquired from the web (Agirre and de la Calle, 2004). This is one of the largest semantic resources ever built with around one hundred million relations between synsets and semantically related

---

[1] Symmetric relations are counted only once.

words.[2]

A knowledge net or KnowNet, is an extensible, large and accurate knowledge base, which has been derived by semantically disambiguating the Topic Signatures acquired from the web. Basically, the method uses a robust and accurate knowledge-based Word Sense Disambiguation algorithm to assign the most appropriate senses to the topic words associated to a particular synset. The resulting knowledge-base which connects large sets of topically-related concepts is a major step towards the autonomous acquisition of knowledge from raw text. In fact, KnowNet is several times larger than WordNet and the knowledge contained in KnowNet outperforms WordNet when empirically evaluated in a common framework.

Table 1 compares the different volumes of semantic relations between synset pairs of available knowledge bases and the newly created KnowNets[3].

Table 1: Number of synset relations

Source	#relations
Princeton WN3.0	235,402
Selectional Preferences from SemCor	203,546
eXtended WN	550,922
Co-occurring relations from SemCor	932,008
New KnowNet-5	231,163
New KnowNet-10	689,610
New KnowNet-15	1,378,286
New KnowNet-20	2,358,927

Varying from five to twenty the number of processed words from each Topic Signature, we created automatically four different KnowNets with millions of new semantic relations between synsets.

After this introduction, Section 2 describes the Topic Signatures acquired from the web. Section 3 presents the approach we plan to follow for building highly dense and accurate knowledge bases. Section 4 describes the methods we followed for building KnowNet. In Section 5, we present the evaluation framework used in this study. Section 6 describes the results when evaluating different versions of KnowNet and finally, Section 7 presents some concluding remarks and future work.

2 Topic Signatures

Topic Signatures (TS) are word vectors related to a particular topic (Lin and Hovy, 2000). Topic Signatures are built by retrieving context words of a target topic from large corpora. In our case, we consider word senses as topics. Basically, the acquisition of TS consists of:

- acquiring the best possible corpus examples for a particular word sense (usually characterising each word sense as a query and performing a search on the corpus

---
[2] Available at http://ixa.si.ehu.es/Ixa/resources/sensecorpus
[3] These KnowNet versions can be downloaded from http://adimen.si.ehu.es

Table 2: TS of party#n#1 (first 10 out of 12,890 total words)

tammany#n	0.0319
alinement#n	0.0316
federalist#n	0.0315
whig#n	0.0300
missionary#j	0.0229
Democratic#n	0.0218
nazi#j	0.0202
republican#n	0.0189
constitutional#n	0.0186
organization#n	0.0163

for those examples that best match the queries)

- building the TS by deriving the context words that best represent the word sense from the selected corpora.

The Topic Signatures acquired from the web (hereinafter TSWEB) constitutes one of the largest available semantic resources with around 100 million relations (between synsets and words) (Agirre and de la Calle, 2004). Inspired by the work of Leacock et al. (1998), TSWEB was constructed using monosemous relatives from WN (synonyms, hypernyms, direct and indirect hyponyms, and siblings), querying Google and retrieving up to one thousand snippets per query (that is, a word sense), extracting the salient words with distinctive frequency using TFIDF. Thus, TSWEB consist of a large ordered list of words with weights associated to each of the senses of the polysemous nouns of WordNet 1.6. The number of constructed topic signatures is 35,250 with an average size per signature of 6,877 words. When evaluating TSWEB, we used at maximum the first 700 words while for building KnowNet we used at maximum the first 20 words.

For example, Table 2 present the first words (lemmas and part-of-speech) and weights of the Topic Signature acquired for party#n#1.

3   Building highly connected and dense knowledge bases

It is our belief, that accurate semantic processing (such as WSD) would rely not only on sophisticated algorithms but on knowledge intensive approaches. In fact, the cycling arquitecture of the MEANING[4] project demonstrated that acquiring better knowledge allow to perform better Word Sense Disambiguation (WSD) and that having improved WSD systems we are able to acquire better knowledge (Rigau et al., 2002).

Thus, we plan to acquire by fully automatic means highly connected and dense knowledge bases from large corpora or the web by using the knowledge already available, increasing the total number of relations from less than one million (the current number of available relations) to millions.

---

[4]http://www.lsi.upc.edu/~nlp/meaning

The current proposal consist of:

- to follow Cuadros et al. (2005) and Cuadros and Rigau (2006) for acquiring highly accurate Topic Signatures for all monosemous words in WordNet (for instance, using InfoMap (Dorow and Widdows, 2003)). That is, to acquire word vectors closely related to a particular monosemous word (for instance, airport#n#1) from BNC or other large text collections like GigaWord, Wikipedia or the web.

- to apply a very accurate knowledge–based all–words disambiguation algorithm to the Topic Signatures in order to obtain sense vectors instead of word vectors (for instance, using a version of Structural Semantic Interconnections algorithm (SSI) (Navigli and Velardi, 2005)).

For instance, consider the first ten weighted words (with Part-of-Speech) appearing in the Topic Signature (TS) of the word sense airport#n#1 corresponding to the monosemous word airport, as shown in Table 3. This TS has been obtained from BNC using InfoMap. From the ten words appearing in the TS, two of them do not appear in WN (corresponding to the proper names heathrow#n and gatwick#n), four words are monosemous (airport#n, airfield#n, travelling#n and passenger#n) and four other are polysemous (flight#n, train#n, station#n and ferry#n).

Table 3: First ten words with weigths and number of senses in WN of the Topic Signature for airport#n#1 obtained from BNC using InfoMap

word+pos	weight	#senses
airport#n	1.000000	1
heathrow#n	0.843162	0
gatwick#n	0.768215	0
flight#n	0.765804	9
airfield#n	0.740861	1
train#n	0.739805	6
travelling#n	0.732794	1
passenger#n	0.722912	1
station#n	0.722364	4
ferry#n	0.717653	2

SSI-Dijkstra

We have implemented a version of the Structural Semantic Interconnections algorithm (SSI), a knowledge-based iterative approach to Word Sense Disambiguation (Navigli and Velardi, 2005). The SSI algorithm is very simple and consists of an initialisation step and a set of iterative steps. Given W, an ordered list of words to be disambiguated, the SSI algorithm performs as follows. During the initialisation step, all monosemous words are included into the set I of already interpreted words, and the polysemous words are included in P (all of them pending to be disambiguated). At each step, the

Table 4: Minimum distances from airport#n#1

Synsets	Distance
4	6
4530	5
64713	4
29767	3
597	2
20	1
1	0

set I is used to disambiguate one word of P, selecting the word sense which is closer to the set I of already disambiguated words. Once a sense is disambiguated, the word sense is removed from P and included into I. The algorithm finishes when no more pending words remain in P.

Initially, the list I of interpreted words should include the senses of the monosemous words in W, or a fixed set of word senses[5]. However, in this case, when disambiguating a TS derived from a monosemous word m, the list I includes since the beginning at least the sense of the monosemous word m (in our example, airport#n#1).

In order to measure the proximity of one synset (of the word to be disambiguated at each step) to a set of synsets (those word senses already interpreted in I), the original SSI uses an in-house knowledge base derived semi-automatically which integrates a variety of online resources (Navigli, 2005). This very rich knowledge-base is used to calculate graph distances between synsets. In order to avoid the exponential explosion of possibilities, not all paths are considered. They used a context-free grammar of relations trained on SemCor to filter-out inappropriate paths and to provide weights to the appropriate paths.

Instead, we use part of the knowledge already available to build a very large connected graph with 99,635 nodes (synsets) and 636,077 edges (the set of direct relations between synsets gathered from WordNet and eXtended WordNet). On that graph, we used a very efficient graph library to compute the Dijkstra algorithm.[6] The Dijkstra algorithm is a greedy algorithm that computes the shortest path distance between one node an the rest of nodes of a graph. In that way, we can compute very efficiently the shortest distance between any two given nodes of a graph. This version of the SSI algorithm is called *SSI-Dijkstra*.

For instance, Table 4 shows the volumes of the minimum distances from airport#n#1 to the rest of the synsets of the graph. Interestingly, from airport#n#1 all synsets of the graph are accessible following paths of at maximum six edges. While there is only one synset at distance zero (airport#n#1) and twenty synsets directly connected to airport#n#1, 95% of the total graph is accessible at distance four or less.

SSI-Dijkstra has very interesting properties. For instance, SSI-Dijkstra always pro-

---

[5]If no monosemous words are found or if no initial senses are provided, the algorithm could make an initial guess based on the most probable sense of the less ambiguous word of W.

[6]See http://www.boost.org

vides an answer when comparing the distances between the synsets of a word and all the synsets already interpreted in I. That is, the Dijkstra algorithm always provides an answer being the minimum distance close or far[7]. At each step, the SSI-Dijkstra algorithm selects the synset which is closer to I (the set of already interpreted words).

Table 5 presents the result of the word–sense disambiguation process with the SSI-Dijkstra algorithm on the TS presented in Table 3[8]. Now, part of the TS obtained from BNC using InfoMap have been disambiguated at a synset level resulting on a word–sense disambiguated TS. Those words not present in WN1.6 have been ignored (heathrow and gatwick). Some others, being monosemous in WordNet were considered already disambiguated (travelling, passenger, airport and airfield). But the rest, have been correctly disambiguated (flight with nine senses, train with six senses, station with four and ferry with two).

Table 5: Sense disambiguated TS for airport#n#1 obtained from BNC using InfoMap and SSI-Dijkstra

Word	Offset-WN	Weight	Gloss
flight#n	00195002n	0.017	a scheduled trip by plane between designated airports
travelling#n	00191846n	0	the act of going from one place to another
train#n	03528724n	0.012	a line of railway cars coupled together and drawn by a locomotive
passenger#n	07460409n	0	a person travelling in a vehicle (a boat or bus or car or plane or train etc) who is not operating it
station#n	03404271n	0.019	a building equipped with special equipment and personnel for a particular purpose
airport#n	02175180n	0	an airfield equipped with control tower and hangers as well as accommodations for passengers and cargo
ferry#n	02671945n	0.010	a boat that transports people or vehicles across a body of water and operates on a regular schedule
airfield#n	02171984n	0	a place where planes take off and land

This sense disambiguated TS represents seven direct new semantic relations between airport#n#1 and the first words of the TS. It could be directly integrated into a new knowledge base (for instance, airport#n#1 –related–> flight#n#9), but also all the indirect relations of the disambiguated TS (for instance, flight#n#9 –related–> travelling#n#1). In that way, having n disambiguated word senses, a total of $(n^2 - n)/2$ relations could be created. That is, for the ten initial words of the TS of airport#n#1, twenty-eight new direct relations between synsets could be created.

This process could be repeated for all monosemous words of WordNet appearing in the selected corpus. The total number of monosemous words in WN1.6 is 98,953. Obviously, not all these monosemous words are expected to appear in the corpus. However, we expect to obtain in that way several millions of new semantic relations between synsets. This method will allow to derive by fully automatic means a huge knowledge base with millions of new semantic relations.

---

[7]In contrast, the original SSI algorithm not always provides a path distance because it depends on the grammar.

[8]It took 4.6 seconds to disambiguate the TS on a modern personal computer.

Furthermore, this approach is completely language independent. It could be repeated for any language having words connected to WordNet.

It remains for further study and research, how to convert the relations created in that way to more specific and informed relations.

4   Building KnowNet

As a proof of concept, we developed KnowNet (KN), a large-scale and extensible knowledge base obtained by applying the SSI-Dijkstra algorithm to each topic signature from TSWEB. That is, instead of using InfoMap and a large corpora for acquiring new Topic Signatures for all the monosemous terms in WN, we used the already available TSWEB. We have generated four different versions of KonwNet applying SSI-Dijkstra to the first 5, 10, 15 and 20 words for each TS. SSI-Dijkstra used only the knowledge present in WordNet and eXtended WordNet which consist of a very large connected graph with 99,635 nodes (synsets) and 636,077 edges (semantic relations).

We generated each KnowNet by applying the SSI-Dijkstra algorithm to the whole TSWEB (processing the first words of each of the 35,250 topic signatures). For each TS, we obtained the direct and indirect relations from the topic (a word sense) to the disambiguated word senses of the TS. Then, as explained in Section 3, we also generated the indirect relations for each TS. Finally, we removed symmetric and repeated relations.

Table 6 shows the percentage of the overlapping between each KnowNet with respect the knowledge contained into WordNet and eXtended WordNet, the total number of relations and synsets of each resource. For instance, only an 8,6% of the total relations included into WN+XWN are also present in KN-20. This means that the rest of relations from KN-20 are new. This table also shows the different KnowNet volumes.

As expected, each KnowNet is very large, ranging from hundreds of thousands to millions of new semantic relations between synsets among increasing sets of synsets. Surprisingly, the overlapping between the semantic relations of KnowNet and the knowledge bases used for building the SSI-Dijkstra graph (WordNet and eXtended WordNet) is very small, possibly indicating disjunct types of knowledge.

Table 6: Size and percentage of overlapping relations between KnowNet versions and WN+XWN

KB	WN+XWN	#relations	#synsets
KN-5	3.2%	231,164	39,837
KN-10	5.4%	689,610	45,770
KN-15	7.0%	1,378,286	48,461
KN-20	8.6%	2,358,927	50,705

Table 7 presents the percentage of overlapping relations between KnowNet versions. The upper triangular part of the matrix presents the overlapping percentage covered by larger KnowNet versions.That is, most of the knowledge from KN-5 is also contained in larger versions of KnowNet. Interestingly, the knowledge contained into KN-10 is only partially covered by KN-15 and KN-20. The lower triangular part of the matrix presents the overlapping percentage covered by smaller KnowNet versions.

Table 7: Percentage of overlapping relations between KnowNet versions

overlapping	KN-5	KN-10	KN-15	KN-20
KN-5	100	93,3	97,7	97,2
KN-10	31,2	100	88,5	88,9
KN-15	16,4	44,4	100	97.14
KN-20	9,5	26,0	56,7	100

5 Evaluation framework

In order to empirically establish the relative quality of these KnowNet versions with respect already available semantic resources, we used the noun-set of Senseval-3 English Lexical Sample task which consists of 20 nouns.

Trying to be as neutral as possible with respect to the resources studied, we applied systematically the same disambiguation method to all of them. Recall that our main goal is to establish a fair comparison of the knowledge resources rather than providing the best disambiguation technique for a particular resource. Thus, all the semantic resources studied are evaluated as Topic Signatures. That is, word vectors with weights associated to a particular synset (topic) which are obtained by collecting those word senses appearing in the synsets directly related to the topics.

A common WSD method has been applied to all knowledge resources. A simple word overlapping counting is performed between the Topic Signature and the test example[9]. The synset having higher overlapping word counts is selected. In fact, this is a very simple WSD method which only considers the topical information around the word to be disambiguated. All performances are evaluated on the test data using the fine-grained scoring system provided by the organisers. Finally, we should remark that the results are not skewed (for instance, for resolving ties) by the most frequent sense in WN or any other statistically predicted knowledge.

5.1 Baselines

We have designed a number of baselines in order to establish a complete evaluation framework for comparing the performance of each semantic resource on the English WSD task.

RANDOM: For each target word, this method selects a random sense. This baseline can be considered as a lower-bound.

SEMCOR-MFS: This baseline selects the most frequent sense of the target word in SemCor.

WN-MFS: This baseline is obtained by selecting the most frequent sense (the first sense in WN1.6) of the target word. WordNet word-senses were ranked using SemCor and other sense-annotated corpora. Thus, WN-MFS and SemCor-MFS are similar, but not equal.

---

[9]We also consider the multiword terms.

TRAIN-MFS: This baseline selects the most frequent sense in the training corpus of the target word.

TRAIN: This baseline uses the training corpus to directly build a Topic Signature using TFIDF measure for each word sense. Note that in WSD evaluation frameworks, this is a very basic baseline. However, in our evaluation framework, this "WSD baseline" could be considered as an upper-bound. We do not expect to obtain better topic signatures for a particular sense than from its own annotated corpus.

5.2 Large-scale Knowledge Resources

In order to measure the relative quality of the new resources, we include in the evaluation a wide range of large-scale knowledge resources connected to WordNet.

WN (Fellbaum, 1998): This resource uses the different direct relations encoded in WN1.6 and WN2.0. We also tested WN^2 using relations at distance 1 and 2, WN^3 using relations at distances 1 to 3 and WN^4 using relations at distances 1 to 4.

XWN (Mihalcea and Moldovan, 2001): This resource uses the direct relations encoded in eXtended WN.

WN+XWN: This resource uses the direct relations included in WN and XWN. We also tested $(WN+XWN)^2$ (using either WN or XWN relations at distances 1 and 2).

spBNC (McCarthy, 2001): This resource contains 707,618 selectional preferences acquired for subjects and objects from BNC.

spSemCor (Agirre and Martinez, 2002): This resource contains the selectional preferences acquired for subjects and objects from SemCor.

MCR (Atserias et al., 2004): This resource uses the direct relations of WN, XWN and spSemCor (we excluded spBNC because of its poor performance).

TSSEM (Cuadros et al., 2007): These Topic Signatures have been constructed using the part of SemCor having all words tagged by PoS, lemmatized and sense tagged according to WN1.6 totalizing 192,639 words. For each word-sense appearing in SemCor, we gather all sentences for that word sense, building a TS using TFIDF for all word-senses co-occurring in those sentences.

6 KnowNet Evaluation

We evaluated KnowNet using the framework of Section 5, that is, the noun part of the test set from the Senseval-3 English lexical sample task.

Table 8 presents ordered by F1 measure, the performance in terms of precision (P), recall (R) and F1 measure (F1, harmonic mean of recall and precision) of each knowledge resource on Senseval-3 and its average size of the TS per word-sense. The different KnowNet versions appear marked in bold and the baselines appear in italics. In this table, TRAIN has been calculated with a vector size of at maximum 450 words. As expected, RANDOM baseline obtains the poorest result. The most frequent senses obtained from SemCor (SEMCOR-MFS) and WN (WN-MFS) are both below the most frequent sense of the training corpus (TRAIN-MFS). However, all of them are far below to the Topic Signatures acquired using the training corpus (TRAIN).

The best resources would be those obtaining better performances with a smaller number of related words per synset. The best results are obtained by TSSEM (with F1 of 52.4). The lowest result is obtained by the knowledge directly gathered from WN mainly because of its poor coverage (R of 18.4 and F1 of 26.1). Interestingly, the knowledge integrated in the MCR although partly derived by automatic means performs much better in terms of precision, recall and F1 measures than using them separately (F1 with 18.4 points higher than WN, 9.1 than XWN and 3.7 than spSem-Cor).

Despite its small size, the resources derived from SemCor obtain better results than its counterparts using much larger corpora (TSSEM vs. TSWEB and spSemCor vs. spBNC).

Regarding the baselines, all knowledge resources surpass RANDOM, but none achieves neither WN-MFS, TRAIN-MFS nor TRAIN. Only TSSEM obtains better results than SEMCOR-MFS and is very close to the most frequent sense of WN (WN-MFS) and the training (TRAIN-MFS).

The different versions of KnowNet consistently obtain better performances as they increase the window size of processed words of TSWEB. As expected, KnowNet-5 obtain the lower results. However, it performs better than WN (and all its extensions) and spBNC. Interestingly, from KnowNet-10, all KnowNet versions surpass the knowledge resources used for their construction (WN, XWN, TSWEB and WN+XWN).

Furthermore, the integration of WN+XWN+KN−20 performs better than MCR and similarly to MCR^2 (having less than 50 times its size). It is also interesting to note that WN+XWN+KN−20 has a better performance than their individual resources, indicating a complementary knowledge. In fact, WN+XWN+KN−20 performs much better than the resources from which it derives (WN, XWN and TSWEB).

These initial results seem to be very promising. If we do not consider the resources derived from manually sense annotated data (spSemCor, MCR, TSSEM, etc.), KnowNet-10 performs better that any knowledge resource derived by manual or automatic means. In fact, KnowNet-15 and KnowNet-20 outperforms spSemCor which was derived from manually annotated corpora. This is a very interesting result since these KnowNet versions have been derived only with the knowledge coming from WN and the web (that is, TSWEB), and WN and XWN as a knowledge source for SSI-Dijkstra (eXtended WordNet only has 17,185 manually labelled senses).

7 Conclusions and future research

The initial results obtained for the different versions of KnowNet seem to be very promising, since they seem to be of a better quality than other available knowledge resources encoding relations between synsets derived from non-annotated sense corpora.

We tested all these resources and the different versions of KnowNet on SemEval-2007 English Lexical Sample Task (Cuadros and Rigau, 2008a). When comparing the ranking of the different knowledge resources, the different versions of KnowNet seem to be more robust and stable across corpora changes than the rest of resources. Furthermore, we also tested the performance of KnowNet when ported to Spanish (as the Spanish WordNet is also integrated into the MCR). Starting from KnowNet-10, all KnowNet versions perform better than any other knowledge resource on Spanish derived by manual or automatic means (including the MCR) (Cuadros and Rigau, 2008b).

Table 8: P, R and F1 fine-grained results for the resources evaluated at Senseval-3, English Lexical Sample Task

KB	P	R	F1	Av. Size
TRAIN	*65.1*	*65.1*	*65.1*	450
TRAIN-MFS	*54.5*	*54.5*	*54.5*	
WN-MFS	*53.0*	*53.0*	*53.0*	
TSSEM	52.5	52.4	52.4	103
SEMCOR-MFS	*49.0*	*49.1*	*49.0*	
MCR^2	45.1	45.1	45.1	26,429
WN+XWN+KN-20	44.8	44.8	44.8	671
MCR	45.3	43.7	44.5	129
KnowNet-20	44.1	44.1	44.1	610
KnowNet-15	43.9	43.9	43.9	339
spSemCor	43.1	38.7	40.8	56
KnowNet-10	40.1	40.0	40.0	154
(WN+XWN)^2	38.5	38.0	38.3	5,730
WN+XWN	40.0	34.2	36.8	74
TSWEB	36.1	35.9	36.0	1,721
XWN	38.8	32.5	35.4	69
KnowNet-5	35.0	35.0	35.0	44
WN^3	35.0	34.7	34.8	503
WN^4	33.2	33.1	33.2	2,346
WN^2	33.1	27.5	30.0	105
spBNC	36.3	25.4	29.9	128
WN	44.9	18.4	26.1	14
RANDOM	*19.1*	*19.1*	*19.1*	

In sum, this is a preliminary step towards improved KnowNets we plan to obtain exploiting the Topic Signatures derived from monosemous words as explained in Section 3.

Acknowledgments

We want to thank Aitor Soroa for his technical support and the anonymous reviewers for their comments. This work has been supported by KNOW (TIN2006-15049-C03-01) and KYOTO (ICT-2007-211423).

References

Agirre, E., O. Ansa, D. Martinez, and E. Hovy (2000). Enriching very large ontologies with topic signatures. In *Proceedings of ECAI'00 workshop on Ontology Learning*, Berlin, Germany.

Agirre, E. and O. L. de la Calle (2004). Publicly available topic signatures for all wordnet nominal senses. In *Proceedings of LREC*, Lisbon, Portugal.

Agirre, E. and D. Martinez (2001). Learning class-to-class selectional preferences. In *Proceedings of CoNLL*, Toulouse, France.

Agirre, E. and D. Martinez (2002). Integrating selectional preferences in wordnet. In *Proceedings of GWC*, Mysore, India.

Álvez, J., J. Atserias, J. Carrera, S. Climent, A. Oliver, and G. Rigau (2008). Consistent annotation of eurowordnet with the top concept ontology. In *Proceedings of Fourth International WordNet Conference (GWC'08)*.

Atserias, J., L. Villarejo, G. Rigau, E. Agirre, J. Carroll, B. Magnini, and P. Vossen (2004). The meaning multilingual central repository. In *Proceedings of GWC*, Brno, Czech Republic.

Cuadros, M., L. Padró, and G. Rigau (2005). Comparing methods for automatic acquisition of topic signatures. In *Proceedings of RANLP*, Borovets, Bulgaria.

Cuadros, M. and G. Rigau (2006). Quality assessment of large scale knowledge resources. In *Proceedings of the EMNLP*.

Cuadros, M. and G. Rigau (2008a). KnowNet: Building a Lńarge Net of Knowledge from the Web. In *Proceedings of COLING*.

Cuadros, M. and G. Rigau (2008b). Multilingual Evaluation of KnowNet. In *Proceedings of SEPLN*.

Cuadros, M., G. Rigau, and M. Castillo (2007). Evaluating large-scale knowledge resources across languages. In *Proceedings of RANLP*.

Dorow, B. and D. Widdows (2003). Discovering corpus-specific word senses. In *EACL*, Budapest.

Fellbaum, C. (1998). *WordNet. An Electronic Lexical Database*. The MIT Press.

Leacock, C., M. Chodorow, and G. Miller (1998). Using Corpus Statistics and WordNet Relations for Sense Identification. *Computational Linguistics 24*(1), 147–166.

Lin, C. and E. Hovy (2000). The automated acquisition of topic signatures for text summarization. In *Proceedings of COLING*. Strasbourg, France.

Magnini, B. and G. Cavaglià (2000). Integrating subject field codes into wordnet. In *Proceedings of LREC*, Athens. Greece.

McCarthy, D. (2001). *Lexical Acquisition at the Syntax-Semantics Interface: Diathesis Alternations, Subcategorization Frames and Selectional Preferences*. Ph. D. thesis, University of Sussex.

Mihalcea, R. and D. Moldovan (2001). extended wordnet: Progress report. In *Proceedings of NAACL Workshop on WordNet and Other Lexical Resources*, Pittsburgh, PA.

Navigli, R. (2005). Semi-automatic extension of large-scale linguistic knowledge bases. In *Proc. of 18th FLAIRS International Conference (FLAIRS)*, Clearwater Beach, Florida.

Navigli, R. and P. Velardi (2005). Structural semantic interconnections: a knowledge-based approach to word sense disambiguation. *IEEE Transactions on Pattern Analysis and Machine Intelligence (PAMI) 27*(7), 1063–1074.

Niles, I. and A. Pease (2001). Towards a standard upper ontology. In C. Welty and B. Smith (Eds.), *Proc. of the 2nd International Conference on Formal Ontology in Information Systems (FOIS-2001)*, pp. 17–19.

Rigau, G., B. Magnini, E. Agirre, P. Vossen, and J. Carroll (2002). Meaning: A roadmap to knowledge technologies. In *Proceedings of COLING'2002 Workshop on A Roadmap for Computational Linguistics*, Taipei, Taiwan.

Snow, R., D. Jurafsky, and A. Y. Ng (2006). Semantic taxonomy induction from heterogenous evidence. In *Proceedings of COLING-ACL*.

Suchanek, F. M., G. Kasneci, and G. Weikum (2007). Yago: A Core of Semantic Knowledge. In *16th international World Wide Web conference (WWW 2007)*, New York, NY, USA. ACM Press.

Vossen, P. (1998). *EuroWordNet: A Multilingual Database with Lexical Semantic Networks*. Kluwer Academic Publishers.

Combining Word Sense and Usage for Modeling Frame Semantics

Diego De Cao[1]
Danilo Croce[1]
Marco Pennacchiotti[2]
Roberto Basili[1]

[1]University of Rome Tor Vergata (Italy)
[2]University of the Saarland (Germany)

email: decao@info.uniroma2.it

Abstract

Models of lexical semantics are core paradigms in most NLP applications, such as dialogue, information extraction and document understanding. Unfortunately, the coverage of currently available resources (e.g. FrameNet) is still unsatisfactory. This paper presents a largely applicable approach for extending frame semantic resources, combining word sense information derived from WordNet and corpus-based distributional information. We report a large scale evaluation over the English FrameNet, and results on extending FrameNet to the Italian language, as the basis of the development of a full FrameNet for Italian.

1 Introduction and Related Work

Models of lexical meaning are explicit or implicit basic components of any text processing system devoted to information extraction, question answering or dialogue. Several paradigms proposed for a variety of notions, such as word sense (Miller et al., 1990) or frame semantics (Baker et al., 1998), have given rise to large scale resources, respectively WordNet and FrameNet. Recent studies (e.g. Shen and Lapata (2007)) show that the use of FrameNet can potentially improve the performance of Question Answering systems. Yet, Shen and Lapata (2007) also point out that the low coverage of the current version of FrameNet significantly limits the expected boost in performance. Other studies have shown similar evidences for Recognizing Textual Entailment (RTE) (Clark et al., 2007; Burchardt et al., 2008): most examples of the RTE challenges corpora can be solved at the predicate-argument structure level, but FrameNet coverage is still a major problem.

Approaches to (semi-)automatically acquire frame information are then today a priority to solve these problems. Despite this, not many efforts have been paid so far in this direction. Burchardt et al. (2005) presented Detour, a system for predicting frame assignment of potential lexical units not covered by FrameNet, by using the paradigmatic information enclosed in WordNet. Although the authors do not fully solve the problem related to the fuzzy relationships between senses and frames, they propose an empirical association measure for ranking frame candidates according to sense information as stored in WordNet. To our knowledge, this is the only work trying to bridge frame membership to referential properties of lexical senses. Pitel (2006) presents a preliminary study on the applicability of semantic spaces and space geometrical transformations (namely, Latent Semantic Analysis) to expand FrameNet, but the investigation is too limited in scope to draw relevant conclusions. Finally, Padó et al. (2008) propose a method to automatically label unknown semantic roles of event nominalizations in FrameNet, but their method needs a large amount of annotated verbal data.

Another important limitation of FrameNet is the limited support to multilinguality, which is becoming a critical issue in real NLP applications. In recent years, some efforts have focused on the manual adaptation of the English FrameNet to other languages (e.g., German (Burchardt et al., 2006) and Spanish (Subirats and Petruck, 2003)). Unlike PropBank, FrameNet is in fact suitable to cross-lingual induction, as frames are mostly defined at the conceptual level, thus allowing cross-lingual interpretation. Yet, all these efforts consist in manually defining frame linguistic knowledge (e.g. lexical units) in the specific language, and in annotating a large corpus, thus requiring a large human effort. While attempts to automate the annotation process are quite promising (Pado and Lapata, 2007), they require the availability of a parallel corpus, and leave open the issue of inducing the resource as a whole in a new language.

In this work, we investigate novel methods for automatically expanding the English FrameNet, and supporting the creation of new ones in other languages (namely Italian), thus tackling the abovementioned problems of coverage and multilinguality. The proposed methods are inspired by the basic hypothesis that FrameNet can be automatically modeled by a fruitful interaction between advanced distributional techniques, and paradigmatic properties derived from WordNet.

In particular, in this paper we focus on the application of such methods to study the semantics of the core elements of FrameNet, i.e. the *lexical units* (hereafter LUs). Lexical units are predicates (nouns, verbs, adjectives, etc.) that linguistically express the situation described by a frame. Lexical units of the same frame share semantic arguments. For example the frame KILLING has lexical units such as: *assassin, bloodbath, fatal, massacre, kill, suicide*. These predicates share semantic arguments such as KILLER, INSTRUMENT and VICTIM. Our goal is to combine corpus distributional evidence with WordNet information to supply three tasks: the induction of new LUs not already in FrameNet (*unknown LUs*); the reduction of LUs polysemy by mapping them to WordNet synsets; the translation of English LUs into Italian.

The paper is organized as follows. In Section 2 we describe our FrameNet *paradigmatic* and *distributional model*, and we discuss how these two models can be combined in a single framework. In Section 3 we analyze the applicability of these models to the three proposed experimental tasks, and discuss the results. Finally, in Section 4 we draw final conclusions and outline future work.

2 Paradigmatic and distributional models of frame semantics

In this section we describe our paradigmatic, distributional and combined models for representing FrameNet. The general goal of each of these three methods is to offer a computational model of FrameNet. In such a model, frames and LUs should have a specific computational representation (e.g. vectors), and allow the computation of *similarity* either among different LUs or between a frame and a LU. Such model thus offers explicit means to use FrameNet in a NLP task or to expand FrameNet, e.g. by assigning unknown LUs to its most similar frame, or by mapping a LU to its proper WordNet synset(s). A key notion for these tasks is the definition of a principled and reliable semantic similarity measure *sim* to be applied to frames and LUs.

2.1 Paradigmatic model

The basic intuition behind our paradigmatic model is that knowledge about predicates of a frame, through a (possibly limited) set of LUs, allows to detect the set of the suitable WordNet senses able to evoke the same frame. These senses are topologically related to (one or more) sub-hierarchies capturing the lexical semantics implicit in the frame. We propose a weakly-supervised approach to discover these structures. The main idea is that frames correspond to specific sub-graphs of the WordNet hyponymy hierarchy, so that these latter can be used to predict frames valid for other LUs, not yet coded in FrameNet. Figure 1 reports the WordNet sub-hierarchy covering the frame PEOPLE_BY_AGE: here, the frame's nominal LUs *{adult, adolescent, baby, boy, infant, kid, geezer, teenager, youngster, youth}* are all represented with the senses correctly referring to the frame. The correct senses (e.g. sense 1 of *youth* out of its 6 potential senses) are selected as they share most specific generalizations with the other LUs. This graph can be intended as an *"explanation"* of the lexical semantic properties characterizing the frame: future predictions about new LUs can be done on the basis of the graph as a paradigmatic model for PEOPLE_BY_AGE. We call such a graph the *WordNet model* of the frame. As WordNet organizes nouns, verbs and other parts-of-speech in different hierarchies, three independent WordNet models (one for each part-of-speech) are created for each frame.

Formally, given the set F of the LUs of a frame, a WordNet model is built around the subset S_F of WordNet synsets able to generalize the largest number of words in F[1].

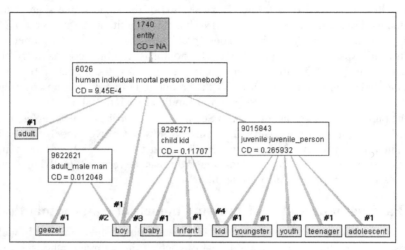

Figure 1: The WordNet model for the frame *People_by_Age* as evoked by the set of its nouns. Sense numbers #*n* refer to WordNet 2.0

The WordNet model $WN_F(\Gamma, W)$ of a frame F, is a graph

(3) $WN_F(\Gamma, W) = <W, S_F, L_F, h, sim_{WN}, m>$

where: $W \subset F$ are the subset of all LUs in F having the same part-of-speech $\Gamma \in \{verb, noun, adjective\}$, S_F is the subset of synsets in WN needed to generalize words $w \in W$; $L_F \subset S_F$ are the lexical senses of $w \in W$ subsumed by S_F; $h \subseteq S_F \times S_F$ is the projection of the hyponymy relation of WN in S_F; $m \subseteq W \times 2^{L_F}$ is the lexical relation between words $w \in W$ and synsets in L_F; $sim_{WN} : S_F \to \Re$ is a weighting function that expresses the relevance of each sense $\sigma \in S_F$ for the frame, as it is represented by its words in F.

The model exemplified in Figure 1 is

$WN_{People\_by\_Age}(noun, \{adult, ..., youth\})$, where $L_F = \{adult\#1, adolescent\#1, baby\#1, boy\#1, boy\#2, boy\#3, ..., youth\#1\}$ and the set S_F corresponds to the sub-hierarchies dominated by the synsets #6026, #9622621, #9285271 and #9015843.

The overall goal of computing the WordNet model is to determine the similarity function $sim_{WN} : S_F \to \Re$, expressing the relevance of a synset $\sigma \in S_F$ as a good representative of a frame F. This is what is hereafter referred to as the paradigmatic similarity model between words senses and frames.

Paradigmatic Similarity measures

Given the WordNet hierarchy separation on part-of-speaches, the similarity function sim_{WN} is independently defined for verbs, nouns and adjectives.

---

[1] In the following, we will use the same notation for a frame F and for the set of its known lexical units, as in our approach we use LU membership as a basic definition of a frame.

For **nouns** we adopt *conceptual density* (*cd*) (Agirre and Rigau, 1996; Basili et al., 2004), a semantic similarity measure defined for word sense disambiguation tasks. The *cd* score for a sense $\sigma \in S_F$ is the density of the WordNet sub-hierarchy rooted at σ in representing the set of nouns in F. The intuition behind this model is that the larger is the number of all and only LUs in F that are generalized by σ, the better it captures the lexical semantics intended by the frame. Coarse generalizations (i.e. synsets higher in the hierarchy) are penalized, as they give rise to bushy hierarchies, covering too many words not in the target F. The greedy algorithm proposed in Basili et al. (2004) selects the subset of synsets able to "cover" (i.e. generalize) all the input words and characterized by the highest *cd* values. The set of such synsets and their corresponding sub-hierarchies forms a graph derived from a set of LUs F. The result is the WordNet model WN_F for F, i.e. the minimal subset of WordNet that explains all (the possible) LUs in F with the maximally similar senses.

Figure 1 shows that correct senses (e.g. the sense 1 of *youth* out of the 6 potential senses) are generally detected and preserved in the model. Irrelevant senses that do not share any common hypernym with other words in F are neglected. Conceptual density scores can be used to rank individual senses as in the case of *boy*.

Given a frame F, the above model can be naturally used to compute the similarity between a noun $n \notin F$ and F. This is particularly useful in LU induction task, as described in Section 3.1. To do so, the similarity $sim_{WN}(F,n)$ between n and F is derived by computing the *cd* scores over the set $F \cup \{n\}$. The $sim_{WN}(F,n)$ is the maximal *cd* of any synset $\sigma_n \in S_F$ that is also hypernym of a lexical sense of n. In the example, the noun *boy* would receive a score of 0.117 through the hypernym $\{child, kid\}$, according to its third sense in WordNet 2.0 ("*{son, boy}*").

As conceptual density can be only applied to nouns, when **verbs** v are considered, we exploit the synonymy and co-hyponymy relations. The following similarity $sim_{WN}(F,v)$ is computed:

$$(4) \quad sim_{WN}(F,v) = \begin{cases} 1 & \textbf{iff } \exists K \subset F \text{ such that } |K| > \tau \textbf{ AND} \\ & \forall w \in K \quad w \text{ is a co-hyponym of } v \\ \varepsilon & \text{otherwise} \end{cases}$$

For **adjectives**, the similarity $sim_{WN}(F,a)$, is computed on the basis of the synonymy relation, as follows:

$$(5) \quad sim_{WN}(F,a) = \begin{cases} 1 & \textbf{iff } \exists w \in F \text{ such that} \\ & w \text{ is a synonym of } tw \\ \varepsilon & \text{otherwise} \end{cases}$$

The overall model WN_F is used to predict if a frame F is a correct situation for a given unknown LU $ul \notin F$ (a noun, a verb or an adjective), whenever $sim_{WN}(F,ul) > \varepsilon$. This can be used as a frame predictor for a ul currently not foreseen in the Berkley database but possibly very frequent in a specific corpus, as described in Section 3.1.

2.2 Distributional model

The distributional model is based on the intuition that FrameNet frames and LUs can be modelled in a semantic space, where they are represented as distributional co-occurrence vectors computed over a corpus. Such framework, it is possible to compute the similarity between a LU and a frame, by evaluating the distance of their vectors in the space.

Semantic spaces have been widely applied in several NLP tasks, ranging from information retrieval to paraphrase rules extraction (Lin and Pantel, 2001). The intuition is that the meaning of a word can be described by the set of textual contexts in which it appears (*Distributional Hypothesis* (Harris, 1964)), and that words with similar vectors are semantically related. This distributional approach has been often claimed to support the *language in use* view on meaning. Word space models (Schütze, 1993) have been shown to emphasize different aspects of lexical semantics: associative (i.e. topical) information between words, as well as paradigmatic information (i.e. *in absentia*) or syntagmatic information (i.e. *in presentia*).

In our setting, the goal is to leverage semantic spaces to capture the notion of *frame* — i.e. the property of *"being characteristic of a frame"*. To do so, we model a lexical unit l as a vector $\vec{l}$, whose dimensions represent the set of contexts of the semantic space. In our space, contexts are words appearing in a n-window of the lexical unit: such a space models a generic notion of *semantic relatedness* — i.e. two LUs close in the space are likely to be either in paradigmatic or syntagmatic relation (Pado, 2007; Sahlgren, 2006). The overall semantic space is then represented by a matrix M, whose rows describe LUs and whose columns describe contexts.

We reduce in dimensionality the matrix M by applying Singular Value Decomposition (SVD) (Landauer and Dumais, 1997), a decomposition process that creates an approximation of the original matrix, aiming to capture semantic dependencies between source vectors, i.e. contexts. The original space is replaced by a lower dimensional space M_k, called k-space in which each dimension is a derived concept. The matrix M is transformed in the product of three new matrices: U, S, and V such that $M = USV^T$. Truncating M to its first k dimensions means neglecting the least meaningful dimensions according to the original distribution. M_k captures the same statistical information in a new k-dimensional space, where each dimension is a linear combination of some original features. These newly derived features may be thought of as artificial concepts, each one representing an emerging meaning component as a linear combination of many different words (or contexts).

The SVD reduction has two main advantages. First, the overall computational cost of the model is reduced, as similarities are computed on a space with much fewer dimensions. Secondly, it allows to capture second-order relations among LUs, thus improving the quality of the similarity measure.

Once the vectors $\vec{l}$ for all FrameNet LUs are available in the reduced space, it is also possible to derive a vectorial representation $\vec{F}$ of a whole frame F. Intuitively, $\vec{F}$ should be computed as the geometric centroid of the vectors of its lexical units. Unfortunately, such a simple approach is prone to errors due to the semantic nature of frames. Indeed, even if the LUs of a given frame describe the same particular situation, they can typically do that in different type of contexts. For example, the LUs *assassinate* and *holocaust* evoke the KILLING frame, but are likely to appear in very different linguistic contexts. Then, the vectors of the two words are likely to be distant in the space. Consequently, different regions of the semantic space may act as good representations for the same frame: these regions corresponds to clusters of LUs which appear in similar contexts (e.g. {*holocaust, extermination, genocide*} and {*suicide,euthanasia*}).

We then adopt a clustering approach to model frames: each frame is represented by the set of clusters C_F of its lexical units. Clusters C_F are composed by lexical units close in the space and can have different size. They are computed by using an adaptive (unsupervised) algorithm, based on k-means (Heyer et al., 1999; Basili et al., 2007), applied to all known LUs of F. Each cluster $c \in C_F$ is represented in the space by a vector $\vec{c}$, computed as the geometric centroid of all its lexical units.

In this framework, it is then possible to compute the similarity between an unknown LU ul and a frame F, as the the cosine distance between the vector $\vec{ul}$ and the closest centroid $c \in C_F$:

(6) $sim_{LSF}(F,ul) = argmax_{c \in C_F} sim_{cos}(\vec{ul}, \vec{C_F})$

Given this measure, it is finally possible to assign an unknown ul to one or more of the most similar frames.

2.3   Combining paradigmatic and distributional models

In order to be effective in a NLP task, a model of lexical meaning should typically account for both the paradigmatic and distributional similarity. The following definition thus hold:

(7) $\mu(F,w) = \Psi(D(w,F), P(w,F))$

where $\mu(F,w)$ is the association between a word w and a frame F, Ψ is a composition operator applied to the corpus-driven distributional measure $D(F,w)$ and to the paradigmatic similarity $P(F,w)$. Notice that in this work $sim_{LSF}(F,w)$ and $sim_{WN}(F,w)$ are used as models of $D(F,w)$ and $P(F,W)$, respectively. Different combinations Ψ are here possible, from simple algebraic operations (e.g. linear combinations) to more complex algorithmics. We will explore this latter issue in section 3.1 where the evaluation of a combined model for LU induction is reported.

3   Experiments

In this section we experiment our proposed models on three different tasks: induction of new LUs (Section 3.1), mapping LUs to WordNet synsets (Section 3.2), and automatic acquisition of LUs in Italian (Section 3.3). In all the experiments we use FrameNet 1.3, consisting of 795 frames and about 10,196 LUs (7,522 unique LUs), as source information and as a gold standard. As regards WordNet, we adopt version 2.0, with all mappings from 1.6 applied through the Italian component of MultiWordNet (Pianta et al., 2008)[2]

For computing vectors in the distributional model, we use the TREC-2002 Vol.2 corpus, consisting of about 110 million words for English. The contexts for the description of LUs are obtained as ± 5 windows around each individual LU occurrence: each word occurring in this windows is retained as a potential context [3]. A resulting set of about 30,000 contexts (i.e. individual words) has been obtained. The vector $\vec{l}$

---

[2] http://www.lsi.upc.es/~nlp/tools/download-map.php

[3] For all occurrences of feature words, the POS tag has been neglected in order to verify the applicability of the model even with a shallow preprocessing. Words occurring less than 10 times in all windows are neglected in our experiments.

representing an individual LU is derived by computing pointwise mutual information between the LU and each context. The SVD reduction has been run over the resulting $7.522 \times 30,000$ matrix, with a dimension cut of $k = 50$, other values resulting in non-statistically different outcomes.

Experiments for Italian are run against the italian component of the Europarliament corpus (Koehn, 2002), made of about 1 million sentences for about 36 millions tokens, for which about 87,000 contexts are used for the targeted LUs. Also for Italian a dimension cut of $k = 50$ has been applied.

3.1 Lexical Unit induction

The goal of this experiment is to tackle the FrameNet low coverage problem, by checking if our models are good in expanding FrameNet with new LUs. Formally, we define *LU induction* as the task of assigning a generic unknown lexical unit *ul* not yet present in the FrameNet database to the correct frame(s). As the number of frames is very large, the task is intuitively hard to solve. A further complexity regards multiple assignments. Lexical units are sometimes ambiguous and can then be mapped to more than one frame (for example the word *tea* could map both to FOOD and SO-CIAL_EVENT). Also, even unambiguous words can be assigned to more than one frame — e.g. *child* maps to both KINSHIP and PEOPLE_BY_AGE.

In the experiment, we simulate the induction task by executing a leave-one-out procedure over the set of existing FrameNet LUs, as follows. First, we remove a LU from all its original frames. Then, we ask our model to reassign it to the most similar frame(s), according to its similarity measure. We repeat this procedure for all lexical units and compute the accuracy in the assignment.

We experiment all three models: distributional, paradigmatic and the combined one. In particular, the combined model is applied as follows. First, for each frame F we create its cluster set C_F in the LSA space. Then, at each iteration of the leave-one-out a different LU *ul* is removed from FrameNet, and the following steps are performed:

- We recompute the clusters for all frames F_{ul} which contain *ul*, by neglecting ul.[4]

- We compute the similarity $sim_{LFS}(F, ul)$ between *ul* and all frames. During the computation we empirically impose a threshold: if a cluster $c \in C$ has a similarity $cos(c, ul) < 0.1$ (i.e. poorly similar to *ul*), it is neglected. Finally, all suggested frames are ranked according to $sim_{LFS}(F, ul)$.

- For each frame F we also compute the similarity $sim_{WN}(F, ul)$ according to the paradigmatic model, by neglecting *ul* in the computation of the WordNet model of each frame.

- We combine the distributional and paradigmatic similarities following the general Equation 7, by applying the following specific equation:

$$(8) \quad sim(F, ul) = sim_{LFS}(F, ul) \cdot sim_{WN}(F, ul)$$

---

[4]Note that *all* appearances of *ul* in the database are neglected (irrespectively from its POS tag, e.g. *march* as a verb vs. *march* as a noun)

Table 1: The Gold Standard for the test over English and Italian

English	Number of frames: 220
	Number of LUs: 5042
	Most likely frames: *Self_Motion* (p=0.015), *Clothing* (p=0.014)
Italian	Number of frames: 10
	Number of LUs: 112
	Frames: *Buildings, Clothing, Killing, Kinship, Make_noise*
	Medical_conditions, Natural_Features, Possession, Self_Motion, Text

Note, that in practice $sim(F, ul)$ acts as a re-ranking function of the previously obtained clusters C_F

- We execute LU induction, by mapping ul to the most similar k frames according to $sim(F, ul)$.

Evaluation

We evaluate the model by computing the accuracy over the FrameNet gold standard. *Accuracy* is defined as the fraction of LUs that are correctly re-assigned to the original frame during the leave-one-out. Accuracy is computed at different levels k: a LU is correctly assigned if its gold standard frame appears among the best-k frames ranked by the model. We experimented both on English (using FrameNet version 1.3), and on Italian. Since an Italian FrameNet is not available, we manually created a gold standard of 11 frames. Overall statistics on the data are reported in Table 1: the number of frames and LUs analysed is slightly reduced wrt FrameNet as we ignored the predicate words absent from the targeted corpus (e.g. *moo* in MAKE_NOISE) and multiwords expressions as it was not possible to locate them unambiguously in the corpus (e.g. *shell out* in COMMERCE_PAY). Also, in order to get reliable distributional statistics, we filter out LUs occurring less than 50 times in the corpus, and frames with less than 10 LUs.

For all the experiments, the parameter τ in the Equation 4 of the paradigmatic model has been set to 2. As a baseline, we adopt a model predicting as best-k frames the most likely ones in FrameNet — i.e. those containing the highest number of LUs.

Results for English are reported in Figure 2.

As shown, all methods improve significantly the baseline whereas accuracy values naturally improve along increasing values for k. The performance of the paradigmatic model are significantly high even for very small k. The best model is given by the combination of distributional and paradigmatic similarity, producing significant improvements wrt the paradigmatic model alone.

Results for Italian are reported in Figure 3. The leave-one-out test has been applied as for English, but over a manually compiled set of 527 LUs for the 11 frames used as gold standard. These LUs have been obtained via direct translation of the English Framenet LUs. In order to evaluate LUs for which a consistent distributional model was available, only those occurring at least 50 times in the Europarliament corpus have been selected: this amounts to a total number of 112 Italian LUs. The paradigmatic

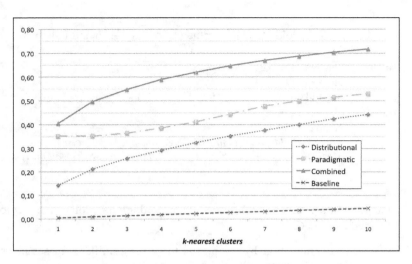

Figure 2: Accuracy of the leave-one-out over the English FrameNet 1.3

model for the test has been obtained using as source the LUs in the English FrameNet. As the computation of the $sim_{WN}(F,w)$ depends only on the hyponymy hierarchy, for each Italian noun n the conceptual density computation over the set $\{n\} \cup F$ is applied, where F is given by the LUs in English. The interlingual index is here used to map every n to its lexical senses (i.e. synsets) in the English WN. Then, the computation of the greedy algorithm is applied exactly as in the monolingual process. The same approach has been used for verbs (Equation 4) and adjectives (Equation 5).

Although the limited scale of the experiment (only 11 frames are targeted), the evidence are similar as for the test over English: the combined model is always superior to the individual ones. High levels of accuracy are achieved, although the "most likely frame" baseline is much higher than for the English test. Similar trends are also observed for the paradigmatic model, reaching a plateau for smaller values of k. Overall results indicate that reliable predictions can be obtained for unknown LUs also when a whole Italian FrameNet is not yet available. Our method can then be used to support lexicographers in the task of building a new FrameNet, in the specific stage of adding LUs to frames.

Results suggest that the WordNet models derived from the English LUs are valid predictors also for Italian words, as confirmed by the experiments in the next sections.

3.2 Assessing WordNet models of Frames

The goal of the experiment is to validate the notion of WordNet model of a frame as derived through the method discussed in Section 2.1. Formally, given the set of all possible WordNet senses S_l of a given LU l, we aim at mapping each sense $s \in S_l$ to the correct frame $f \in F_l$, where F_l is the set of frames in which l appears. If a frame cannot be found for a given sense, the sense is simply neglected.

For example, the LU *burn* has 15 senses in WordNet and it belongs to 3 frames: EMOTION_HEAT, EXPERIENCE_BODILY_HARM and PERCEPTION_BODY. Figure 2

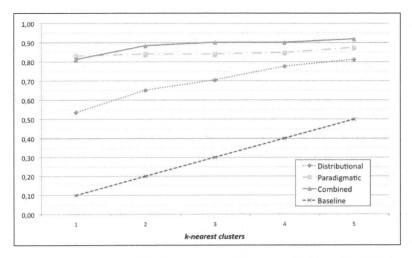

Figure 3: Accuracy of the leave-one-out tests over 11 frames in Italian

reports some of the possible correct mapping between senses and frames. Other senses, such as "*destroy by fire*" cannot be mapped to any existing frame.

By creating such an automatic mapping we achieve three goals. First, we disambiguate FrameNet lexical units. Second, we enrich WordNet synsets with new information — i.e. a computational description of the situations they refer to, as represented in FrameNet. Third, we derive a language independent model of frames based on WordNet synsets.

The mapping targeted by the experiment is carried out according to the discussion in Section 2.1. The WordNet model of a frame F for nouns is the outcome of the greedy cd computation over the set F of all frame's LUs: given a LU, a sense is accepted if it is a member of the set L_F in the model. For verbs and adjectives all co-hyponyms and synonyms used in Equations 4 and 5 are included in L_F. The procedure for developing a WordNet model is completely automatic, this avoiding the costs of manual annotation.[5]

Note that our approach is easily portable to languages different from English. Indeed, the WordNet hierarchy is the backbone of sense repositories in other languages (as for example in MultiWordNet (Pianta et al., 2008)). The English models WN_F can be then interpreted in a different language, by applying the interlingual indexes to all synsets L_F in WN_F. The corresponding sets of synonyms are natural candidates as LUs in the target language.

Evaluation

In this experiment, in order to account for data sparseness we reduce the dataset in two ways. First, we neglect low frequency lexical units: LUs occurring less than 50 times in the corpus are not considered. Second, we exclude frames that have less than

---

[5] In this experiment we focus on verbs and nouns, since they are core predicates expressing the targeted situation in sentences.

Table 2: Mapping between WordNet senses and frames for verb *burn*, as induced by the paradigmatic method

Synset	Evoked FRAME	Co-Hyponyms	WordNet Definition
1775952	EMOTION_HEAT	*chafe, fume, smolder*	Feel strong emotion, especially anger or passion; *"She was burning with anger"*; *"He was burning to try out his new skies"*
189569	EXPERIENCE_BODILY_HARM	*break, bruise, hurt, injure*	Burn with heat, fire, or radiation; *"The iron burnt a hole in my dress"*
2059143	PERCEPTION_BODY	*itch, sting*	Cause a sharp or stinging pain or discomfort; *"The sun burned his face"*

10 LUs. This leaves us with 220 frames, involving 2,200 nominal LUs and 2,180 verbal LUs. Table 3 reports overall statistics. Over the 2,200 nouns and 2,180 verbs examined, the vast majority is covered by WordNet (fourth row). For these words, a large set of lexical senses exist in WordNet giving an average polysemy between 3 and 6 senses per word (sixth row). Our paradigmatic method is able to significantly reduce the average polysemy: only 1.79 senses per verb survive among the initial 5.29, while only 1.29 among the 3.62 are retained for nouns. Moreover, the number of senses used to entirely represent a frame in a paradigmatic model (i.e. S_F) is about 3,512 and 2,718 respectively for nouns and verbs, as averaged across all frames. An example of the mapping produced by our method is reported in Table 2.

The above statistics suggest that a consistent reduction in average polysemy can be obtained when the context of a frame is used to model semantic similarity among LUs in WordNet.

Table 3: Statistics on nominal and verbal senses in the paradigmatic model of the English FrameNet

	Nouns	Verbs
Targeted Frames	220	220
Involved LUs	2,200	2,180
Average LUs per frame	10.0	9.91
LUs covered by WordNet	2,187	2,169
Number of Evoked Senses	7,443	11,489
Average Polysemy	3.62	5.97
Represented words (i.e. $\sum_F W_F$)	2,145	1,270
Average represented LUs	9.94	9.85
Active Lexical Senses (L_F)	3,095	2,282
Average Active Lexical Senses ($|L_F|/|W_F|$) per word over frames	1.27	1.79
Active synsets (S_F)	3,512	2,718
Average Active synsets ($|S_F|/|W_F|$) per word over frames	1.51	2.19

We evaluated the quality of the above process through manual validation. Given a frame, for each LU we provided two annotators with the list of all its WordNet senses, and asked to select those that correctly map to FrameNet. Then, we evaluated our automatic mapping method by computing standard Precision and Recall. In all, we analysed all 786 senses of 306 LUs in 4 frames (i.e. KILLING, PEOPLE_BY_AGE, STATEMENT and CLOTHING). The Cohen's kappa, computed over two frames (i.e. KILLING and PEOPLE_BY_AGE for 192 senses of 77 words) results in a 0.90 inter-annotator agreement: this indicates that senses and frames are highly correlated and their mapping is consistent and motivated, as Table 2 suggests.

The system is considered to accept a sense σ for a given frame F iff the conceptual density score characterizing such a sense is positive, i.e. the $\sigma \in L_F$. Our method obtained a Precision of 0.803 and a Recall of 0.79 (F-measure=0.796). Among the 786 senses tested, 85 false positives and 92 false negatives have been found: 346 senses have been correctly accepted and 263 true negatives have been rejected by the sytem. It must be also noticed that the conceptual density scores obtained are well correlated with correct senses. If senses of a word with significantly lower *cd* scores than others are removed from the set L_F of a frame, a significant improvement in precision can be obtained. For example, *tie* in CLOTHING has 9 senses, of which 3 are proposed by the system, corresponding to 1 true positives, 2 false positives and 6 true negatives. It is interesting to note that the true positive sense (i.e. *{necktie, tie}* as "*a neckwear consisting of a long narrow piece of material worn ...*") has a *cd* score of 0.492, while 0.018 is the score of all the three false positives (i.e. sense #5 *{link,linkup tie, tie-in}* as "*a fastener that serves to join or link*"; sense #8 *{tie, railroad tie, crosstie, sleeper}* as "*one of the cross braces that support the rails on a railway track*"; sense #9 *{tie}* as "*a cord with which something is tied*"). A careful selection policy can be thus easily devised to deal with such skewed preference distributions and achieve higher values of precision by neglecting lower preferences.

These results show that the proposed frame WordNet model is not only effective in reducing the average lexical polysemy (as shown in Table 3), but it is also a rather accurate method to capture the lexical semantics implied by frames. The achieved level of accuracy justifies the adoption of the model defined in (3) for the development of FrameNets in languages other than English.

3.3   Development of an Italian FrameNet

In this section we explore the use of our English paradigmatic model to automatically support the building process of a FrameNet in a different language, namely Italian. In particular, we leverage the model WN_F for the English language to induce new LUs for F in the new language. To do so, we proceed as follows.

For each frame F in FrameNet we first generate the WordNet model for English WN_F using all the LUs available in the database, as discussed in Section 2.1. Then, we use an interlingual index (e.g. MultiWordNet) to obtain words in the new language corresponding to lexical senses L_F in the model WN_F. Each of these *translated LU* l is a cross-lingual synonym of at least a sense in S_F and is a candidate LUs for the frame in the new language, since it satisfies $sim_{WN}(F, l) > \varepsilon$.

Evaluation

In the experiment we focus on Italian, for which a full FrameNet is not yet available, though a manual building process is currently underway (Tonelli and Pianta, 2008). As interlingual index we adopt the Italian component of MultiWordNet (Pianta et al., 2008). As shown in Table 4, the WordNet model allows to generate approximately 15,000 Italian LUs, partitioned in 6,600 nouns, 8,300 verbs and 130 adjectives.

Table 4: Number of generated Lexical Units

	Number of LUs
Nouns	6611
Verbs	8332
Adjectives	129
Total	15072

To evaluate the quality of the translated LUs we performed two different tests. In the first test, we collected the 776 most frequent words in the Europarliament corpus, including many generic nouns and verbs, such as *produrre* (*to_produce/make*), *fare* (*to_make/fabricate*), *avere* (*to_have*). Then we manually validated all the 1,500 system decisions regarding these words. A decision is accepted if the frame suggested for the word is correct for at least one of its senses. *Accuracy* is computed as the percentage of the correct system decisions over the number of validated cases. For some words no frame was predicted, as they were not in Wordnet or as no Wordnet model was able to correctly generalize them. The percentage of words receiving at least one correct prediction, i.e. assigned to at least one frame accepted by the annotators, is here called *Coverage*, and reported with the accuracy scores in the second line of Table 5. The above test was repeated also for more specific words, with a number of occurrences in the corpus ranging from 100 to 200. Results are reported in the third line of Table 5. These outcomes are surprisingly good especially considering that the computation of the individual $sim_{WN}(F, l)$ scores is fully automatic.

Table 5: Manual validation of the italian LUs generated through WordNet

Frequency Range	Numb. of Test pairs	Numb. of Words	Acc.	Cov.
[722;55,000]	1,500	776	0.79	93.0%
[100;200]	558	357	0.87	94.3%

In a second test, the results generated by our method were compared against the words of the oracle manually developed for the experiment in Section 3.1. In this case, the predictions of the method about frames and words are compared with the oracle. As no filter has been here applied with respect to the corpus, all the 527 $< LU, Frame >$ pairs in the manually created oracle have been used[6], although only 437 pairs were represented through the MultiWordNet resources. The system was not able to decide for 71 words, and produced wrong guesses for 49 words: 317 correct guesses are thus produced. The results is a Precision of 0.87 and a Recall of 0.72. The recall value, lower than the coverage observed in the previous test, is also by a significant generative effect: the method *discovers* a number of new entries not accounted for in the oracle.

---

[6]Notice that no LU was multiply assigned to different frames in the oracle, so that the number of predicate words here is exactly the number of different pairs.

Table 6: Excerpt of the Italian LUs in four different frames

FRAME	FRAME definition	Italian LUs
BUILDINGS	Words which name permanent fixed structures forming an enclosure and providing protection from the elements	*autorimessa, cuccia, casolare, casotto, dependance, masseria, palazzina, ...*
CLOTHING	Anything that people conventionally wear	*cappotto, calzetta, camicia_da_notte, duepezzi, ...*
SELF_MOTION	The *Self mover*, a living being, moves under its own power in a directed fashion	*annaspare, arrancare, buttarsi, claudicare, giro, ...*
TEXT	An entity that contains linguistic, symbolic information on a *Topic*, created by an *Author* at the *Time of creation*	*arringa, articolo_di_fondo, canzonetta, conto, polizza, vademecum, ...*

Typical new LUs introduced in the oracle are words not accounted for in the English Framenet, as reported in Table 6. The table shows that most of the new guesses of the system are indeed highly plausible. They represent widely used dialectal forms (e.g. *masseria* in the frame BUILDING), jargon (e.g. *duepezzi* in CLOTHING), technical terms (e.g. *polizza* in TEXT) and specific nouns (e.g. *autorimessa* in BUILDINGS). Although it is certainly questionable if words like *articolo_di_fondo* (i.e. *main article* in a newspaper) are worth to be considering as LUs for the frame TEXT, it is clear that if the application domain requires frame-like information, the presented model (even only the paradigmatic association here discussed) provides an effective tool for fast and robust prototyping. Notice that the low Recall (only 0.60 of the oracle words are correctly addressed), can be compensated by combining paradigmatic and distributional similarity (Equation 8), as experiments reported in Figure 3 suggest. We leave this last point as a future work.

4   Conclusions

We presented a combined model for representing frame semantics through paradigmatic and distributional evidence. We reported three experiments, which indicate possible application scenarios of these models. First, the combination of the presented models has been applied to extend FrameNet in a LU induction task, for English and Italian. In both cases the evaluation has shown that the combination of the two models achieves better performance against their independent uses, and that the level of accuracy is high enough to support lexicographers in the task of building FrameNets. In a second experiment, we showed that a strong association exists between lexical senses, as defined by WordNet, and the frame's lexical units in FrameNet. Its automatic detection, as proposed in this paper, results in a significant reduction of the polysemy of LUs and in a highly accurate selection of those lexical senses semantically related to the situations represented by a frame. Finally, we demonstrated that this paradigmatic information can be used to develop a FrameNet resource in another language. For

Italian, we automatically generated a very large and accurate set of 15,000 LUs.

The overall framework has encouraged us to develop a robust toolbox for the large scale acquisition of FrameNet-like lexicons in different domains and languages. The tool will be made publicly available for research studies in this area. Future work is on going on the adoption of richer models for Framenet, able to take into account more evidence than LUs, such as frame elements and syntagmatic information. Moreover, the use of the derived space as a model for the recognition of frames in free-texts is expected to speed-up the development of a large collection of annotated sentences for the Italian language.

References

Agirre, E. and G. Rigau (1996). Word sense disambiguation using conceptual density. In *Proceedings of COLING-96*, Copenhagen, Denmark.

Baker, C. F., C. J. Fillmore, and J. B. Lowe (1998). The Berkeley FrameNet project. In *Proceedings of COLING-ACL*, Montreal, Canada.

Basili, R., M. Cammisa, and F. Zanzotto (2004). A semantic similarity measure for unsupervised semantic disambiguation. In *Proceedings of LREC-04*, Lisbon, Portugal.

Basili, R., D. D. Cao, P. Marocco, and M. Pennacchiotti (2007). Learning selectional preferences for entailment or paraphrasing rules. In *Proceedings of RANLP 07*.

Burchardt, A., K. Erk, and A. Frank (2005). A wordnet detour to framenet. In *Proceedings of the GLDV 2005 GermaNet II Workshop*, Bonn, Germany.

Burchardt, A., K. Erk, A. Frank, A. Kowalski, S. Pado, and M. Pinkal (2006). The salsa corpus: a german corpus resource for lexical semantics. In *Proceedings of the 5th International Conference on Language Resources and Evaluation*, Genova, Italy.

Burchardt, A., M. Pennacchiotti, S. Thater, and M. Pinkal (2008). Assessing the impact of frame semantics on textual entailment. Journal of Natural Language Engineering (to appear).

Clark, P., P. Harrison, J. Thompson, W. Murray, J. Hobbs, and C. Fellbaum (2007, June). On the Role of Lexical and World Knowledge in RTE3. In *Proceedings of the ACL-PASCAL Workshop on Textual Entailment and Paraphrasing*, Prague, pp. 54–59. Association for Computational Linguistics.

Harris, Z. (1964). Distributional structure. In J. J. Katz and J. A. Fodor (Eds.), *The Philosophy of Linguistics*, New York. Oxford University Press.

Heyer, L., S. Kruglyak, and S. Yooseph (1999). Exploring expression data: Identification and analysis of coexpressed genes. *Genome Research 9*, 1106–1115.

Koehn, P. (2002). Europarl: A multilingual corpus for evaluation of machine translation. *Draft*.

Landauer, T. and S. Dumais (1997). A solution to plato's problem: The latent semantic analysis theory of acquisition, induction and representation of knowledge. *Psychological Review 104*, 211–240.

Lin, D. and P. Pantel (2001). DIRT-discovery of inference rules from text. In *Proceedings of the ACM Conference on Knowledge Discovery and Data Mining (KDD-01)*, San Francisco, CA.

Miller, G., R. Beckwith, C. Fellbaum, D. Gross, and K. Miller. (1990). An on-line lexical database. *International Journal of Lexicography 13*(4), 235–312.

Pado, S. (2007). *Cross-Lingual Annotation Projection Models for Role-Semantic Information*, Volume 21 of *Saarbrücken Dissertations in Computational Linguistics and Language Technology*. Saarland University.

Pado, S. and M. Lapata (2007). Dependency-based construction of semantic space models. *Computational Linguistics 33*(2), 161–199.

Padó, S., M. Pennacchiotti, and C. Sporleder (2008). Semantic role assignment for event nominalisations by leveraging verbal data. In *Proceedings of COLING 2008*, Manchester, UK.

Pianta, E., L. Bentivogli, and C. Girardi (2008). MultiWordNet: Developing an aligned multilingual database. In *Proceedings of the 1st International Global WordNet Conference*, Marrakech, Morocco, pp. 293–302.

Pitel, G. (2006). Using bilingual lsa for framenet annotation of french text from generic resources. In *Workshop on Multilingual Semantic Annotation: Theory and Applications*, SaarbrÃijcken, Germany.

Sahlgren, M. (2006). *The Word-Space Model*. Ph. D. thesis, Department of Linguistics, Stockholm University.

Schütze, H. (1993). Word space. In S. Hanson, J. Cowan, and C. Giles (Eds.), *Advances in Neural Information Processing Systems 5*. Morgan Kaufmann Publishers.

Shen, D. and M. Lapata (2007). Using semantic roles to improve question answering. In *Proceedings of the Conference on Empirical Methods in Natural Language Processing and on Computational Natural Language Learning*, Prague, pp. 12–21.

Subirats, C. and M. Petruck (2003). Surprise! Spanish FrameNet! In *Proceedings of the Workshop on Frame Semantics at the XVII. International Congress of Linguists*, Prague.

Tonelli, S. and E. Pianta (2008). Frame Information Transfer from English to Italian. In *Proceedings of LREC 2008*, Marrakech, Morocco.

Answering Why-Questions in Closed Domains from a Discourse Model

Rodolfo Delmonte

University of Venice "Ca' Foscari" (Italy)

email: delmont@unive.it

Emanuele Pianta

Fondazione Bruno Kessler – FBK (Italy)

email: pianta@fbk.eu

Abstract

In this paper we will present a system for Question Answering called GETARUNS, in its deep version applicable to closed domains, that is to say domains for which the lexical semantics is fully specified and does not have to be induced. In addition, no ontology is needed: semantic relations are derived from linguistic relations encoded in the syntax. The main tenet of the system is that it is possible to produce consistent semantic representations using a strict linguistic approach without resorting to extralinguistic knowledge sources. The paper will briefly present the low level component which is responsible for pronominal binding, quantifier raising and temporal interpretation. Then it will discuss in more detail the high level component where a Discourse Model is created from text. The system has been evaluated on a wide variety of texts from closed domains, producing full and accurate parsing, semantics and anaphora resolution for all sentences.

1   Introduction

In this paper we will present the system for Question Answering called GETARUNS, in its deep version applicable to closed domains, that is to say domains for which the lexical semantic is fully specified and does not have to be induced. GETARUNS is a GEneral multilingual Text And Reference UNderstander which follows a linguistically based approach to text understanding and embodies a number of general strategies on how to implement linguistic principles in a running system. The system addresses one main issue: how to restrict access to extralinguistic knowledge of the world by contextual reasoning, i.e. reasoning from linguistically available cues.

Another important issue addressed by the system is multilinguality. In GETARUNS the user may switch from one language to another by simply unloading the current lexicon and uploading the lexicon for the new language: at present Italian, German and English are implemented. Multilinguality has been implemented to support the theoretical linguistic subdivision of Universal Grammar into a Core and a Peripheral set of rules. The system is organized around another fundamental assumption: the architecture of such a system must be modular thus requiring a pipeline of sequential feeding processes of information, each module providing one chunk of knowledge, backtracking being allowed only within each single module. The architecture of the system is organized in such a way as to allow for feedback into the parser from Anaphoric Binding: however, when pronominals have been finally bound or left free, no more changes are allowed on the f-structure output of the parser.

Thus, we can think of the system as being subdivided into two main meta-modules or levels: Low Level System, containing all modules that operate at Sentence Level; High Level System, containing all the modules that operate at Discourse and Text Level by updating the Discourse Model. The deep and complete version of the system that we present here can be used with strictly closed domains and does not need any supporting ontology. However, it has also been used in one such context with a different architecture, which had OWL and RDFs as final external knowledge representation formalisms. Ontologies and Knowledge Sources should be used as Word Sense Disambiguation tools (we have not produced results on this however).

Texts belonging to what we define as closed domains are characterized by the fact that the system has all the semantic information which is needed process then; and most importantly, sentences making up the texts can be fully parsed without failures. In practice, these texts are relatively short and the length of sentences is below a certain threshold, typically 25 words. They are used for text understanding practice in a language learning environment. In this context, question answering is used to validate the appropriateness of the user's answer. Some such texts will be presented below. One will be the text used by Mitre in 2000 to organize the Workshop on Reading Comprehension Tests as Evaluation for Computer-Based Language Understanding Systems (Brill et al., 2000). The system has been evaluated on a wide variety of such texts and has parsed fully and accurately all sentences with the appropriate Semantics and Anaphora Resolution (Delmonte, 2007).

2   The Low Level System

Even though we assume that the output of the Low Level System is mandatory for the creation of the semantic representation needed to create a consistent Discourse Model we will not be able comment it in depth for lack of space. We will simply show the internal components or modules it encompasses and add a few comments. However we stress the paramount importance of a deep linguistic analysis of the input text.

When each sentence is parsed, tense, aspect and temporal adjuncts are used to build the basic temporal interpretation to be used by the temporal reasoner. Every constituent is checked for semantic consistency and semantic features are added to each semantic head in the form of generic concepts taken from WordNet and other similar semantic lexical resources.

Eventually two important modules are implemented: Quantifier Raising and Pronominal Binding. Quantifier Raising is computed on f-structure which is represented internally as a DAG (Direct Acyclic Graph). It may introduce a pair of functional components: an operator where the quantifier can be raised, and a pool containing the associated variable where the quantifier is actually placed in the f-structure representation. This information may then be used by the following Higher System to inspect quantifier scope.

Pronominal Binding is carried out at first at sentence internal level. DAGs will be searched for binding domains and antecedents matched to the pronouns if any to produce a list of possible bindings. Best candidates will then be chosen.

3   The Discourse Model

Informally, a Discourse Model (DM) may be described as the set of entities "specified" in a discourse, linked together by the relations they participate in. They are called discourse entities, but may also be regarded as discourse referents or cognitive elements. A discourse entity (DE) inhabits a speaker's discourse model and represents something the speaker has referred to. A speaker refers to something by utterances that either evoke (if first reference) or access (if subsequent reference) its corresponding discourse entity.

As soon as a DE is evoked, it gets a description. The initial description ID that tags a newly evoked DE might have a special status, because it is the only information about an entity that can be assumed to be shared (though not necessarily believed) by both speaker and listener alike. However certain types of DE must be derived from other ones inferentially.

Definite descriptions can be used like definite pronouns to access entities which are presumably in the listener's DM, or they can be used to evoke new entities into that model.

Building a DM is clearly only a part of the overall process of understanding which makes heavy use of background mutual knowledge on the side of the addressee in order to carry out the complex inferences required. In order to build an adequate Discourse Model we rely on a version of Situation Semantics which takes perspectives or point of view as the higher node in a hierarchical scheme in which there is a bifurcation between factual and non-factual situations. Partially following Burke (1991) we assume that the notion of perspectives is significant in situation theory insofar as the very same situations can be viewed by an agent (or by different agents) from different perspectives, hence situations may support different and perhaps conflicting kinds of information (ibid., p.134). Situations are characterized in terms of infons, or better the infons that they support. In turn we distinguish between **facts** and **concepts** where the former have to do with concrete ostensive entities which yield information that is referential, in that they explicitly involve objects in the world relative to a given perspective. On the contrary **concepts** constitutes a piece of general information about the world relative to a given perspective, which does not directly refer to any particular entity or object, nor is it specific to particular ostensive entities.

Infons are built according to situation theory: a basic infon consists of a relation, its argument roles , a polarity, and a couple of indices anchoring the event/state/processe to a given spatiotemporal location.

In our system, **facts** may describe information relative to a **subjective** or an **objective** discourse domain: subjective facts are thus computable as situations viewed from the perspective of a given agent's mind, in our case also corresponding to the Main Topic of discourse. On the contrary, objective facts are reported from the perspective of the text's author. However, to highlight the difference existing between subjective and objective information in the model, we decided to call **facts** only objective infons; subjective infons are called **sit**. Also generic facts are treated as **sits**.

These main constituents of situations are further described by taking as primitives individuals, relations and locations and by using as logical notation set theory. Thus, individuals and inferences on individuals are wrought out in set theory notation: we use **ind** for a unique individual, **set** for a collection of individuals which can be individuated by means of membership, **card** for the cardinality of any set with a numerical or indefinite quantified value, **in** to indicate membership, **class** for generic sets which can be made up of an indefinite quantity however big enough to encompass sets, subsets, classes or individuals. Each entity is assigned a constant value or **id** and an **infon** which are uniquely individuated by a number.

Infons may express or contain a main relation: relations may be properties, social or relational roles, events or states, locational modifiers or specifiers — that is attributes, etc.. Simplex properties predicate some property of a semantic identifier; complex properties take individuals and propositions as their arguments and in this case individuals are usually associated to a semantic role. Semantic roles are inherited from the lexical form associated to a given predicate in the lexicon and transferred into the f-structure of the utterance under analysis. Semantic roles are paramount in the choice and construction of questions and answers.

Inferences are produced every time a given property is reintroduced in the story in order to ascertain whether the same property was already present in the model and should not be reasserted, or whether it should be added to it. Properties may be anchored to a given location or be universally anchored: a name, is a rigid designator in that it is computed as a property associated to a given individual and has a universal locational anchoring, meaning that the same individual will always be individuated by that name in the story. The same would apply to permanent properties like the substance or matter constituting an object, like a house, or other such properties. Persistence may then be computed both for entities, properties, relations and locations; also, a **Relevance Score** is computed by a separate module that analyzes information structure for each simplex utterance.

4 Semantic Rules

After collecting all modifier heads, if any, of the current predicate, the rule for the creation of semantic individuals separates previously resolved pronouns/nouns from non resolved ones. In both cases it uses some sort of equational reasoning in order to ascribe properties to already asserted semantic identifiers, by taking advantage of linguistic information encoded in Function/Role, according to a linguistically well-defined hierarchy which treats arguments and adjuncts as semantically different. New semantic individuals are added when needed.

The module handling semantic individuals treats new individuals to be asserted in the DM separately from already asserted ones — in which case, the semantic index should be inherited from properties belonging to previously asserted individuals. In addition, quantified expressions should be treated differently from individuals or sets, be they singleton sets, or sets with a given cardinality.

Semantic attributes are collected in the f-structure representation and come from the SPEC subsidiary function. We use the following attributes to separate semantic types: definiteness, partitivity and class. *Definiteness* applies to nominal expressions: these may be definite (+def), indefinite (-def), or zero definite (def0), which applies both to bare NPs and to proper nouns; *partitivity* is an attribute which gets a value only in case of quantified NPs. Finally the *class* attribute is used to differentiate proper nouns (-class) from common nouns (+class) which may undergo quantification, and quantified pronouns (+me).

5 Question Answering from a Discourse Model

In order to show how the system behaves we report and focus only on one small text. New texts are usually fully parsed: some intervention may be required to introduce contextual classes for tag disambiguation purposes. Here below is the text and the questions proposed for the Workshop on Text Understanding quoted above:

> **How Maple Syrup is Made**
> Maple syrup comes from sugar maple trees. At one time, maple syrup was used to make sugar. This is why the tree is called a "sugar" maple tree. Sugar maple trees make sap. Farmers collect the sap. The best time to collect sap is in February and March. The nights must be cold and the days warm. The farmer drills a few small holes in each tree. He puts a spout in each hole. Then he hangs a bucket on the end of each spout. The bucket has a cover to keep rain and snow out. The sap drips into the bucket. About 10 gallons of sap come from each hole.
> 1. Who collects maple sap? (Farmers)
> 2. What does the farmer hang from a spout? (A bucket)
> 3. When is sap collected? (February and March)
> 4. Where does the maple sap come from? (Sugar maple trees)
> 5. Why is the bucket covered? (to keep rain and snow out)

As far as we gathered from the proceedings of the conference, none of the participants was able to answer all the questions (Brill et al., 2000).

This is how we organize the system. We first compute the DM of the target question (hereafter QDM), the whole process is carried out on the basis of the facts contained in the question ad text DMs. Questions are classified into three types: partial or wh-questions, why questions and complete or yes/no questions.

Recovering the answer from the DM is essentially done in four steps:

- extracting question word or question type for yes/no questions

- extracting the main predicates from the question, which are then used to

- search for identical/similar predicates in the text DM

- extraction of the argument matching the answer

As commented in the sections above, the semantic representation contained in a DM can be basically defined as Predicate-Argument Structures or PAS, with a polarity and pair of spatiotemporal indices. Given a short text and a question about the text, the QA system will build a semantic model of the text where each distinct entity is assigned a unique semantic identifier, and is represented as a pool of properties, relations and attributes. Whenever possible, the system will also draw the necessary inferences to assign relation and attributes of sets to the individuals composing those sets.

Then it will completely parse the input question and produce a QDM for it, where facts are represented as **q_fact** terms. Afterwards, the first move consists in recovering the question word in the QDM by the following conjunction of queries

```
q_fact(K,focus,[arg:Id],1,_,_),
q_fact(_,isa,[_:Id,_:Focus],1,A,B)
```

where the variable Id, associated to the property "focus", is used to recover the actual Focus in the associated "isa" fact. This Focus is constituted by the question word used to formulate the query. This is used by the system to activate specialized procedures that will address specific semantic structures. As said above, *why* questions are processed separately from other *wh-* questions. The next query fired is

```
get_focus_arg(Focus,Pred,Args,Answer,True-NewFact),
```

which will give back the contents of the answer in the variable *Answer* and the governing predicate in *Pred*. These are then used to generate the actual surface form of the answer. *Args* and *True-NewFact* are used in case the question is a complete or yes/no question. In order to generate the answer, tense and mood are searched in the DM; then a logical form is build as required by the generator, and the build_reply procedure is fired:

```
get_focus_tense(T,M), Form=[Pred,T,M,P,[D]],
build_reply(Out,Focus,Form), !.
```

We will present general *wh-* questions at first. They include all types of factoid questions and also *how* questions. The main predicate looks for an appropriate linguistic description to substitute the wh- word argument position in the appropriate PAS. Here follows the full definition of the get_focus_arg procedure for the "who" case.

```
get_focus_arg(who,Pred,Ind,D1,NewP):-
    q_getevents(A,Pred),
    q_fact(X,Pred,Args,1,_,L),
    q_role(Y,X,Z,Role),
    answer_buildarg(Role,Pred,[Idx:Z],D,Facts),
    select_from_pred1(Pred,Role,Facts,NewP,D1), !.
```

We use a different procedure in case the question governing predicate is a copulative verb, because we have to search for the associated property in the QDM, as follows:

```
copulative(Pred),
q_fact(X,Pred,[prop:Y],1,_,_),
q_fact(Y,Prop,[_:K,Role:Type],1,_,_)
q_fact(_,inst_of,[_:K,_:Z],P,T,S),
q_get_ind_des(K,Propp,Ty),
```

Copulative predicates have a proposition as their argument and the verb itself is not useful, being semantically empty. The predicate corresponding to the proposition is searched through the infon *Y* identifying the fact. When we have recovered the *Role* and the linguistic description of the property *Propp* indicated by the wh- question, we pass them to the following predicate and search the associated individual in the DM:

```
answer_buildarg(Role,Pred,[Idx:Propp],Answer,Facts)
```

Suppose the wh-question is a *where* question with a copulative verb; then the role will be a location and the *Propp* will be "in". *How* copulative questions will search for **class** properties, i.e. not for names or individuals:

```
q_fact(X,how,[_:Y],1,_,_),
q_fact(Q,isa,[_:K,class:Pred],1,_,_),
q_fact(_,inst_of,[_:K,_:Z],P,T,S)
```

Semantic roles are irrelevant in this latter case: the only indication we use for the search is a dummy *prop* role. On the contrary, when lexical verbs are governing predicates, we need to use the PAS and the semantic role associated to the missing argument to recover the appropriate answer in all other cases. Here we should also use a different semantic strategy in case an argument is questioned and there is another argument expressed in the question — what, whom, who. Or else an adjunct is questioned — where, when, how, etc. — or the predicate is intransitive, an argument is questioned and there is no additional information available.

Now consider a typical search for the answer argument:

```
answer_buildarg(Role,Pred,Tops,Answer,Facts):-
    on(Ind:Prop,Tops),
    entity(Type,Id,Score,facts(Facts)),
    extract_properties(Type,Ind,Facts,Def,Num,NProp,Cat),
    select_allrole_facts(Role,Ind,Facts,Pred,PropLoc),
    Answer=[Def,nil,Num,NProp,Cat,PropLoc], !.
```

Here, *extract_properties* checks for the appropriate semantic type and property by picking one entity and its properties at the time. When it succeeds, the choice is further checked and completed by the call to *select_allrole_facts*. This is what *extract_properties* does:

```
extract_properties(Type, Ind, Facts, Def, Num, NProp, Gend):-
  ( Sclass=prop,
    extrfacts(Facts,Ind,Gend,Sclass,Prop), Num=sing
  ; Sclass=class,
    extrfacts(Facts,Ind,CGend,Sclass,Prop),
    select_gend(Prop,CGend,Gend) ),
  topichood_stack(Prop,Def),
  ( Type=ind, Num=sing
  ; Type=set, Num=plur ),
  set_def(Sclass, Ind, Prop, Role, Def),
  confirm_head(Def, Gend, Prop, NProp), !.
```

The procedure searches for individuals or sets filling a given semantic role in the predicate-argument structure associated to the governing predicate. In addition, it has the important task of setting functional and semantic features for the generator, like gender and number. This is paramount when a pronoun has to be generated instead of the actual basic linguistic description associated to a given semantic identifier. In particular, gender may be already explicitly associated in the DM to the linguistic description of a given entity or it may be derived from WordNet or other linguistic resources handling derivational morphology. The call *topichood_stack* looks for static definiteness information associated to the linguistic description in the DM. Proper names are always "definite". On the contrary, common nouns may be used in definite or indefinite ways. This information may be modified by the dialogue intervening between user and system and be recorded in the user model. The decision is ultimately taken by the *set_def* procedure which looks into the question-answering user model knowledge base where previous mentions of the same entity might have been recorded. Or else it does it — by means of *update_user_model* — to be used in further user-system interactions. If the entity semantic identifier is already present Def will be set to "definite", otherwise it will remain as it has been originally set in the DM.

```
set_def(Def,Id,Prop,Role,Def1):-
  ( tknow(Id,Role1), swap_def(Def,Def1)
  ; tknow(Prop,Role1), swap_def(Def,Def1)
  ; update_user_model(Id,Role), assign_def(Def,Def1) ).
```

6   Computing Answers to WHY questions

Why question are usually answered by events, i.e. complete propositions. They would in general constitute cases of rhetorical clause pairs labelled either as a Motivation-Effect or a Cause-Result. In Delmonte et al. (2007), causal relations are further decomposed into the following finer-grained subprocesses:

- Cause-Result

- Rationale-Effect

- Purpose-Outcome

- Circumstance-Outcome

- Means-Outcome

Furthermore, rationale clauses have been shown to be constituted structurally by untensed Infinitival Adjuncts: on the contrary, Cause-Result pairs are usually constituted by tensed propositions.

Consider now the pieces of knowledge needed to build the appropriate answer to the question "Why is the tree called sugar maple tree?". Sentences involved to reconstruct the answer are:

> Maple syrup comes from sugar maple trees.
> At one time, maple syrup was used to make sugar.
> This is why the tree is called a "sugar" maple tree.

In other words, in order to build the appropriate answer, the system should be able to build an adequate semantic representation for the discourse anaphora "This", which is used to essentially relate the current sentence to the event chain of the previous sentence. This is a fairly common way of expressing this kind of causal relation, that we then would like to assume as a paradigmatic one. Eventually, the correct answer would be:

> Because maple syrup was used to make sugar

which as can be easily gathered is the content of the previous complex sentence. Here below is the portion of the DM representation needed to reconstruct the answer:

```
ind(infon19, id8)
fact(infon20,inst_of,[ind:id8,class:edible_animal],1,univ, univ)
fact(infon21, isa,[ind:id8,class:[maple_syrup]],1, id1, id7)
set(infon23, id9)
card(infon24, id9, 5)
fact(infon25, sugar_maple, [ind:id10], 1, id1, id7)
fact(infon26, of, [arg:id10, specif:id9], 1, univ, univ)
fact(infon27,inst_of,[ind:id9,class:plant_life],1,univ, univ)
fact(infon28, isa, [ind:id9, class:tree], 1, id1, id7)


class(infon43, id13)
fact(infon44,inst_of,[ind:id13,class:substance],1,univ, univ)
fact(infon45, isa, [ind:id13, class:sugar], 1, id1, id7)
fact(id14,make,[agent:id8,theme_aff:id13],1,tes(finf_m3), id7)
fact(infon48,isa,[arg:id14,arg:ev],1,tes(finf_m3), id7)
fact(infon49, isa, [arg:id15, arg:tloc], 1, tes(finf_m3), id7)
fact(infon50, pres, [arg:id15], 1, tes(finf_m3), id7)
fact(infon51,time,[arg:id14,arg:id15], 1, tes(finf_m3), id7)
fact(id16,use, [theme_unaff:id8,prop:id14], 1, tes(sn5_m3), id7)


fact(id21,call,[actor:id9, theme_bound:id9], 1, tes(f1_m4), id7)
ent(infon61, id18)
fact(infon62,prop,[arg:id18,
              disc_set:[id16:use:[theme_unaff:id8, prop:id14]]],
              1, id1, id7)
ind(infon63, id19)
fact(infon66, inst_of, [ind:id19, class:abstract], 1, univ, univ)
fact(infon67, isa, [ind:id19, class:reason], 1, id1, id7)
fact(infon81, in, [arg:id21, nil:id19], 1, tes(f1_m4), id7)
fact(infon83, reason, [nil:id18, arg:id19], 1, id1, id7)
fact(id23, be, [prop:infon83], 1, tes(sn10_m4), id7)
```

These three pieces of knowledge representation are built respectively when the three sentences above are processed. When the second sentence is processed, the semantic identifier *id8* is simply inherited. Also, notice that it is transferred from USE predicate to MAKE by means of controlling equations which are part of LFG syntactic representations.

The system will at first look for a REASON semantic predicate associated to a CALL predicate, as derived from the question semantic representation, which we report here below:

```
q_loc(infon3, id1, [arg:main_tloc, arg:tr(f2_q6)])
q_ind(infon4, id2)
q_fact(infon5, tree, [nil:id2], 1, id1, univ)
q_fact(infon6, maple, [ind:id2], 1, id1, univ)
q_fact(infon7, sugar, [ind:id2], 1, id1, univ)
q_fact(infon8, of, [arg:id2, specif:id2], 1, univ, univ)
q_fact(infon9, why, [ind:id2], 1, id1, univ)
q_fact(infon10, inst_of, [ind:id2, class:plant_life], 1, univ, univ)
q_fact(infon11, isa, [ind:id2, class:tree], 1, id1, univ)
q_class(infon12, id3)
q_fact(infon13, inst_of, [ind:id3, class:substance], 1, univ, univ)
q_fact(infon14, isa, [ind:id3, class:sugar], 1, id1, univ)
q_class(infon15, id4)
q_fact(infon16, inst_of, [ind:id4, class:plant_life], 1, univ, univ)
q_fact(infon17, isa, [ind:id4, class:maple], 1, id1, univ)
q_fact(infon22, tree, [nil:id2, arg:id2], 1, id1, univ)
q_fact(id5, call, [prop:infon22], 1, tes(f2_q6), univ)
q_fact(infon23, isa, [arg:id5, arg:ev], 1, tes(f2_q6), univ)
q_fact(infon24, isa, [arg:id6, arg:tloc], 1, tes(f2_q6), univ)
q_fact(infon25, pres, [arg:id6], 1, tes(f2_q6), univ)
q_fact(infon26, time, [arg:id5, arg:id6], 1, tes(f2_q6), univ)
q_fact(infon27, focus, [arg:id7], 1, tes(f2_q6), univ)
q_fact(infon28, isa, [arg:id7, arg:why], 1, tes(f2_q6), univ)
q_fact(infon29, for, [arg:id5, motiv:id7], 1, tes(f2_q6), univ)
q_fact(infon35, perf, [arg:id8, ask:id5], 1, id1, univ)
```

The final part of the answer building process is constituted by the search of the actual linguistic description to associate to the original predicate. This is done in the pool of facts associated to the current entity which has been chosen from the inventory of entities of the world associated to the original text.

```
answer_buildarg(Role,Pred,Tops,Answer,Facts,[]):-
    on(Ind:Prop,Tops),
    entity(Type,Id,Score,facts(Facts)),
    extract_properties(Type,Ind,Facts,Def,Num,NProp,Cat),
    select_allrole_facts(Role,Ind,Facts,Pred,PropLoc),
    Answer=[Def,nil,Num,NProp,Cat,PropLoc],!.

select_allrole_facts(Role,Ind,Facts,Pred,PropLoc):-
    selarf(Pred,Fact,Args,Pol,Id),
    on(Fact,Facts),
    isa_role_fatto(Args),
    ind_role(Args,Inds),
    on(Prop-Role1,Inds),
    belongsrole(Role,Role1), !.
```

For instance, when searching the answer to the question "who collects the sap?", the answer is searched in the following pool associated to the entity FARMER:

```
entity(set,id32,28,facts([
   card(infon117,id32,5),
   fact(infon118,inst_of,[ind:id32,class:man],1,univ,univ),
   fact(infon119,isa,[ind:id32,class:farmer],1,id31,id8),
   fact(id33,collect,[agent:id32,theme_aff:id28],1,tes(f1_m6),id8),
   fact(id58,drill,[agent:id32,theme_aff:id56],1,tes(f1_m9),id8),
   fact(id63,put,[agent:id32,theme_aff:id61,loc_direct:id56],1,tes(f1_m10),id8),
   fact(id69,hang,[agent:id32,theme_aff:id66,loc_direct:id67],1,tes(f1_m11),id8)])).
```

This is reached from the COLLECT and SAP entities pools, which are cross-checked to verify that the same predicates are available.

```
entity(class,id28,7,facts([
   fact(infon102,inst_of,[ind:id28,class:substance],1,univ,univ),
   fact(infon103,isa,[ind:id28,class:sap],1,id27,id8),
   fact(id29,make,[actor:id9,theme_aff:id28],1,tes(f1_m5),id8),
   fact(id33,collect,[agent:id32,theme_aff:id28],1,tes(f1_m6),id8),
   fact(id41,collect,[agent:id39,theme_aff:id28],1,tes(finf_m7),id8),
   fact(id82,drip,[agent:id28, modal:id66],1,tes(f1_m13),id8),
   fact(infon343,has,[arg:id88,theme:id28],1,id84,id85)])).
```

Then *belongsrole* checks to verify that the *Role* belongs to the appropriate set of roles adequate for that slot in the PAS. In the "why" case it has to search recursively for events. This is the case represented by discourse anaphora of the type "this is why/that is why", where the reason is a complex event structure:

```
extract_properties(Role,Ind,Facts,NewProp):-
   Fact =.. [fact,Id,Pred,Args,Pol,Time,Place],
   on(Fact,Fa),
   on(_:Ind,Args),
   on(disc_set:Disc,Args),
   Disc=[Ind1:Pre:[Ro1:Id1, Ro2:Id2]],
   buildarg2(Ro2,NewP,[Id1:Prop],FirstProp,Facts,MDs),
   FirstProp=[Def1,nil,Num,NProp,Cat,PropLoc],
   Fact1 =.. [fact,Id2,NewP,Args1,Pol1,Time1,Place1],
   on(Fact1,Facts),
   on(Ro3:Ind2,Args1),
   Ind2$\backslash$=Id1,
   buildarg2(Ro3,What,[Ind2:Prop],SecProp,Facts1,MDs),
   SecondProp=[Def2,nil,Num2, NProp2,Cat2,PropLoc2],
   Prop_Why=[to,What,NProp2],
   NewProp=[Pre,[Def1,nil,Num,NProp,Cat,Prop_Why]], !.
```

Here below is the relevant DM representation of the other WHY question, the one requesting for a Motivation through Rational clauses: "why is the bucket covered?"

```
loc(infon288, id73, [arg:main_tloc, arg:tes(sn7_m11)])
ind(infon289, id74)
fact(infon290, inst_of, [ind:id74, class:event], 1, univ, univ)
fact(infon291, isa, [ind:id74, class:rain], 1, univ, univ)
ind(infon292, id75)
fact(infon293, inst_of, [ind:id75, class:event], 1, univ, univ)
fact(infon294, isa, [ind:id75, class:snow], 1, univ, univ)
ind(infon295, id76)
fact(infon296, isa, [ind:id76, class:cover], 1, id73, id8)
fact(infon297, inst_of, [ind:id76, class:legal], 1, univ, univ)
fact(infon301, cover, [nil:id69, arg:id76], 1, id73, id8)
fact(id77,have, [owner:id69, prop:infon301],1,tes(sn10_m12),id8)
```

```
fact(infon302, isa, [arg:id77, arg:st], 1, tes(sn10_m12), id8)
fact(infon303, isa, [arg:id78, arg:tloc], 1, tes(sn10_m12), id8)
fact(infon304, pres, [arg:id78], 1, tes(sn10_m12), id8)
fact(infon305, time, [arg:id77, arg:id78], 1, tes(sn10_m12), id8)
in(infon322, id74, id79)
in(infon323, id75, id79)
fact(id80,keep_out,[actor:id69,theme_aff:id79],1,tes(finf1_m12), id8)
fact(infon308, isa, [arg:id80, arg:pr], 1, tes(finf1_m12), id8)
fact(infon309, isa, [arg:id81, arg:tloc], 1, tes(finf1_m12), id8)
fact(infon310, pres, [arg:id81], 1, tes(finf1_m12), id8)
fact(infon311, time, [arg:id80, arg:id81], 1, tes(finf1_m12), id8)
fact(infon312, result, [arg:id77, arg:id80], 1, tes(sn10_m12), id8)
during(tes(sn10_m12), tes(sn7_m11))
includes(tr(sn10_m12), id73)
```

The relevant information is expressed as a semantic role RESULT, and is the one connecting the two predicates, HAVE/KEEP_OUT. This is the piece of information that will be used to answer the question.

7 Conclusions

In the paper we have shows that one can actually implement systems using deep linguistic and semantic analysis to answer hard questions. Our systems employs representations derived from Situation Semantics paradigm (Burke, 1991) and LFG syntactic theory (Bresnan, 2001). We have exemplified its performance on a series of factoid questions and we also added "why" questions. GETARUNS has been able to answer all questions proposed in the Mitre Workshop and also the additional semantically and syntactically hard discourse bound Why question based on the recurrent formulaic copulative expression "this/that is why". For a complete presentation of the system please refer to Delmonte (2007).

References

Bresnan, J. (2001). *Lexical-Functional Syntax*. Oxford: Blackwell.

Brill, E., E. Charniak, M. Harper, M. Light, E. Riloff, and E. Voorhees (Eds.) (2000, May). *Reading Comprehension Tests as Evaluation for Computer-Based Language Understanding Sytems*, Seattle, Washington. ANLP-NAACL.

Burke, T. (1991). Peirce on truth and partiality. In J. Barwise, J. M. Gawron, G. Plotkin, and S. Tutiya (Eds.), *Situation Theory and its Applications*. Stanford: CSLI Publications.

Delmonte, R. (2007). *Computational Linguistic Text Processing: Logical Form, Semantic Interpretation, Discourse Relations and Question Answering*. New York: Nova Science Publishers.

Delmonte, R., G. Nicolae, S. Harabagiu, and C. Nicolae (2007). A linguistically-based approach to discourse relations recognition. In B. Sharp and M. Zock (Eds.), *Natural Language Processing and Cognitive Science: Proc. of 4th NLPCS (Funchal, Portugal)*, pp. 81–91. INSTICC PRESS.

Analyzing the Explanation Structure of Procedural Texts: Dealing with Advice and Warnings

Lionel Fontan
Patrick Saint-Dizier
IRIT, Toulouse (France)
email: stdizier@irit.fr

Abstract

We present the explanation structure of procedural texts, focusing on the analysis of argumentation, in particular advice and warnings. Their role is to support and motivate the goal-instruction structure, which is the skeleton of procedural texts. Procedural texts consist of a sequence of instructions, designed with some accuracy in order to reach a goal (e.g. assemble a computer). Procedural texts may also include subgoals. Goals and subgoals are most of the time realized by means of titles and subtitles. The user must carefully follow step by step the given instructions in order to reach the goal. We introduce the notion of *instructional compound*, which is a complex structure that articulates instructions with various discourse elements. We then show how arguments can be extracted with the help of patterns. We finally investigate their contribution to the structure and the understanding of procedural texts.

1 Introduction

The main goal of our project is to analyze the structure of procedural texts in order to efficiently and accurately respond to How-to-do-X? questions. This means identifying titles (which convey the main goals of the procedure), sequences of instructions serving these goals, and a number of additional structures such as prerequisites, warnings, advice, illustrations, etc. (Takechi et al. 2003, Adam, 2001). A response to an How-to question is then the well-formed text portion within the scope of the title that matches the question.

In our perspective, procedural texts range from apparently simple cooking recipes to large maintenance manuals. They also include documents as diverse as teaching texts, medical notices, social behavior recommendations, directions for use, assembly notices, do-it-yourself notices, itinerary guides, advice texts, savoir-faire guides etc. (Aouladomar et al., 2005). Procedural texts follow a number of structural criteria, whose realization may depend on the author's writing abilities, on the target user, and on traditions associated with a given domain. Procedural texts can be regulatory, procedural, programmatory, prescriptive or injunctive. The work we report here was carried out on a development corpus of 1,700 French texts taken from the Web from most of the areas cited above, and extracted randomly from our more global corpus of 8,000 texts.

We have developed a detailed analysis of procedural texts from a manual corpus analysis, identifying their main basic components as well as their global structure. For that purpose, we have defined two levels: a segmentation level that basically identifies structures considered as terminal structures (titles, instructions, prerequisites, connectors, etc.) and a grammar level that binds these terminal structures to give a global structure to procedural texts (Delpech et al. 2008). This structure is textual and dedicated only to elements relevant to procedurality. To design the grammar, we have borrowed a few considerations from Minimalist syntax, in particular recent developments of X-bar syntax and notions like merge. This point will not be developed here (but see Delpech et al. 2007). Note that text grammars are generally in a relatively early development stage (Webber 2004, Gardent 1997).

Procedural texts are complex structures, they often exhibit a quite complex rational (the instructions) and 'irrational' structure which is mainly composed out of pieces of advice, conditions, preferences, evaluations, user stimulations, etc. They form what we call the explanation structure, which motivates and justifies the goal-instructions structure, viewed as the backbone of procedural texts. A number of these elements are forms of argumentation, they appear to be very useful, sometimes as important as instructions, they provide a strong and essential internal cohesion and coherence to procedural texts.

An important aspect of this project is the accurate identification of the explanation structure as found in procedural texts in order to better understand explanation strategies deployed by humans in precise, concrete and operational situations and to transpose it to the generation of explanations in general and in cooperative question-answering systems in particular. We have already studied the instructional aspects of procedural texts and implemented a quite efficient prototype within the TextCoop project (Delpech et al. 2008) that tags titles and instructions with dedicated XML tags. In this paper, after a categorization of explanation structure as found in our corpus of procedural texts, and the presentation of instructional compounds, we focus on the recognition of warnings and advice. The work is realized for French, examples in English are just glosses.

2 The explanation structure in procedural texts

We will introduce two independent structures: the general organization of the explanation structure, and the notion of instructional compound.

2.1 A global view of the explanation structure

Procedural texts have a very rich semantic structure, with a large number of facets. From our development corpus (1,700 web texts of 1–3 pages), we established a classification of the different forms explanations may take. The explanation structure is meant to guide the user in two ways: (1) by making sure that he will effectively realize actions as they are specified, via arguments (Amgoud et al. 2001, 2005) such as threats, rewards, advice and warnings which are 'coercitive' in a certain sense, and (2) help considerations such as evaluation of work realized so far and encouragements of different kinds.

The main structures we have identified in this type of text are facilitation and argumentation structures. They are either global (adjoined to goals, and having scope over the whole procedure) or local, included into instructional compounds, with a scope local to the instructional compound (see next section). The latter is by far the most frequently encountered case.

Explanation structures can be organized as follows (the terminology is borrowed from existing work on rhetorical relations or introduced by ourselves):

- **facilitation structures**, which are rhetorical in essence (Kosseim et al. 2000, Vander Linden 1993), correspond to *How to do X?* questions, these include two subcategories:

  1. user help, with: hints, evaluations and encouragements;
  2. controls on instruction realization, with two cases:
     (a) controls on actions: guidance, focusing, expected result and elaboration;
     (b) controls on user interpretations: definitions, reformulations, illustrations and also elaborations.

- **argumentation structures**, corresponding to *Why do X?* questions. These have either:

  1. positive orientation with the author involvement (promises) or not (advice and justifications), or
  2. negative orientation with the author involvement (threats) or not (warnings).

In what follows, we will mainly concentrate on this second point, and in particular on warnings and advice which are the most frequently encountered arguments (since there are rarely involvements from the author). Roughly, we have about 25%

of instructions which have arguments in do-it-yourself texts, and up to 60% in social procedural texts. Argumentation structures are relatively general to an application domain, while facilitation structures are much more specific to the text and the targeted audiences.

2.2   From instructions to instructional compounds

In most types of texts, we do not just find sequences of simple instructions but more complex compounds composed of clusters of instructions, that exhibit a number of semantic contextual dependencies between each other, that we call **instructional compounds**. These compounds are organized around a few main instructions, to which a number of subordinate instructions, warnings, arguments, and explanations of various sorts may possibly be adjoined. All these elements are, in fact, essential in a compound for a good understanding of the procedure at stake.

An instructional compound has a very rich, but relatively well organized, discourse structure, composed of several layers, which correspond to the different aspects instructions may have. The structure is the following:

- The **goal and justification** level, which has in general wider scope over the remainder of the compound. It indicates motivations for doing actions that follow in the compound (e.g. *You must regularly clean the curtains of your bedroom: to do this ...; To change your mother card, you must...*, which here motivates actions to undertake). It gives the fundamental motivation of the compound. Compared to titles, these introduce very local goals. These are not considered in the goal hierarchy introduced by titles, and they will not be considered for question answering.

- The **instruction core (or kernel) structure**, which contains the main instructions. These are more or less explicitly temporally organized (see below). In general simple sequentiality prevails, the goal being to limit the intellectual load imposed to the user. Actions are identified most frequently via the presence of action verbs (in relation to the domain) in the imperative form, or in the infinitive form introduced by a modal (Delpech et al. 2008). We observed also a number of subordinated instructions forms adjoined to the main instructions. These are in general organized within the compound by means of rhetorical relations, as the examples below will illustrate.

- The **deontic and illocutionary force structures**: consist of marks that operate over instructions, outlining different parameters. These linguistic structures play a major role in argumentation:

  - deontic: obligatory, optional, forbidden or impossible, alternates (or),

  - illocutionary and related aspects: stresses the importance of actions: necessary, advised, recommended, to be avoided, etc. These marks are crucial to identify the weight of an argument.

- a **temporal structure** that organizes sequences of instructions (and, at a higher level, instructional compounds). In general, the temporal structure is simple, sequentiality prevails. In some cases, parallel actions are specified, which partially overlap. Action verbs may indicate some form of parallelism of actions (*incorporate and stir*). In other cases it is the user's experience that determines the exact temporal interpretation.

- The **conditional structure**: introduces conditions over instructions within the compound or even over the whole instructional compound. We encounter quite a lot of structures organizing mutually exclusive cases *If you are pregant, take medicine X ..., if you are not pregnant and between 19 and 65, it is advised that you take medecine Y, ...*

- The **rhetorical structure** whose goal is to enrich the core instructions by means of a number of subordinated aspects (realized as propositions, possibly instructions) among which, most notably: enablement, basic forms of motivation, circumstance, elaboration, instrument, precaution, manner. A group of relations of particular interest in this paper are arguments, developed hereafter.

- The **causal structure** indicating the goal of an action. We identified in procedural texts four types of causal relations, following (Talmy 2001): intend-to (direct objective of an action: *push the button to start the engine*), Instrumented (*use a 2 inch key to dismount the door*), Facilitation (*enlarge the hole to better empty the tank*) and Continue (*keep the liquid warm till its color changes*). These are local to a single instruction, with no a priori interaction with the goal or justification level advocated above.

Explanations and arguments help the reader understand why an instruction must be followed and what are the risks or the drawbacks if he does not do it properly. We will illustrate this with two instructional compound examples. In the first example, we have three main instructions, and an elaboration is adjoined to the second one. The temporal relations are simple (realized by *then, and*) and are not represented:

[*instructional−compound*
  [*instruction* The first step consists in opening the computer box,]
  [*instruction* then to place it on a large, clean surface,
    [*elaboration or precaution* where you make sure there is no risk to
        damage electronic components,]]
  [*instruction* and then to withdraw all the caches at the PC front.]]

In the second example, an argument of type advice is introduced; it is composed of two instructions (later called conclusions) and a conjunction of three supports which motivate the two instructions.

[*instructional−compound*
  [*goal* To clean leather armchairs,]
  [*argument:advice*
    [*instruction* choose specialized products dedicated to furniture],
    [*instruction* and prefer them colorless,]
    [*support* they will play a protection role, add beauty, and repair
        some small damages.]]]

Identifying rhetorical relations in this type of text is not straightforward. Some relations have a few marks associated whereas others are largely pragmatic and need some knowledge of the domain to be identified by a reader. We observed a few, partial, hierarchical relations between the items that build up an instructional compound. Scope priorities come in three groups. The first group is composed of goals and conditions, then, at a second level come causal, deontic and illucotionary elements operating over instructions. At the lower level, we have subordinated instructions, attached to the core instructions.

2.3   Implementation of instructional compounds

The actual schema for recognizing instructional compounds is quite simple at the moment, but results are quite satisfactory. Basically, such a compound contains at least one instruction. It is then delimited as follows:

- any element in an enumeration (typographically marked) is an instructional compound,

- in a paragraph which is not an enumeration, an instructional compound is delimited by expressions which induce an idea of strong break (even though this term is quite fuzzy). Such marks are for example: goal or conditional expression, end of paragraph, strong temporal mark (after two hours, when this is over, at the end of, and so on).

We have manually annotated 160 procedural texts. This is not an easy task due to the complexity of the structures at stake. Then these were compared with results obtained automatically. These will be used fully or in part to test the system. We selected texts we understand so that the risk of errors is limited as much as possible. This is presented in detail in (Delpech et al. 2008) where Kappa tests are realized to evaluate the homogeneity of human judgements.

For instructional compounds, for the three domains with best title and instruction recognition rate (do it yourself, cooking, and social life), we obtained the following results, based on a small corpus of data (60 texts):

Domain	Recall	Precision
cooking receipes	0.95	1.00
do it Yourself	0.89	0.98
social life	0.88	0.98

We have not yet attempted to implement an efficient system, but we are able to fully tag about 500 million web pages per hour, on a Pentium 4 3GhZ dual core machine with 4 Gigabyte RAM. This process includes cleaning web pages, running TreeTagger, and tagging titles, instructions and instructional compounds.

3   Identifying arguments in procedures

In this section let us first give a quite informal definition of what an argument is, and how it interacts with the goal-instructions structure. Let us then focus on warnings and advice which are, by far, the most frequently encountered structures. Most warnings and advice are included into instructional compounds.

3.1 Argumentation and Action theories

Roughly, argumentation is a process that allows speakers to construct statements for or against another statement called the conclusion. These former statements are called supports. The general form of an argument is: **Conclusion 'because' Support** (noted as *C because S*). In natural language, conclusions usually appear before the support, but they may also appear after, to stress the support. A conclusion may receive several supports, possibly of different natures (advice and warnings): *don't add natural fertilizer, this may attract insects, which will damage your young plants*. Arguments may be more or less strong, they bear in general a certain weight, mostly induced from the words they contain or from their syntactic construction (Anscombre et al. 1981, Moeschler 1985, Amgoud et al. 2001). In natural contexts, this weight is somewhat vague.

In the case of procedural texts, the representation and the role of arguments in a text can be modeled roughly as follows. Let G be a goal which can be reached by the sequence of instructions A_i, $i \in [1,n]$, whatever their exact temporal structure is. Any instruction A_i is associated with a pair (g_i, p_i) where g_i is the gain associated with A_i (there is a gain only in case where A_i is a piece of advice, improving G) and p_i is the penalty in case where the user (partly of fully) fails to realize A_i.

A subset of A_i are interpreted as explicit arguments (A_i, is a conclusion) when they are explicitly paired with a support S_i that stresses the importance of A_i (*Carefully plug in your mother card vertically, otherwise you will damage the connectors*) or when advice is given. Their general form is: A_j *because* S_j (we use here the term 'because' which is more vague than the implication symbol used in formal argumentation, because natural language is not so radical). Supports S_k which are negatively oriented are warnings whereas those which are positively oriented are pieces of advice. Neutral supports simply introduce explanations which are not arguments. For the other instructions, the support is just implicit (do the action otherwise you will run into problems).

Similarly to the principles of argumentation theory, but within the framework of action theory (e.g. Davidson 1963), it is a priori possible to evaluate for a given realization of the instructions, the gains w.r.t. the goal G (when advice is followed, improving G) and the penalties (when actions are not well performed, with or without warnings). In an abstract model, we can assign each instruction a gain and a penalty, however in practice this is a little bit difficult. At the moment, let's say that gains are a priori null, except when we have an instruction of type advice which is realized, in that case the gain is greater or equal to 1. Penalties are numbers greater than 0, high penalties corresponding to very crucial instructions. If an instruction is correctly realized, penalty is 0, if there is a complete failure, penalty is the assigned number, which may be infinite if the instruction is absolutely crucial.

Given a certain realization by a user, the success of a goal G is the sum of the gains on the one hand, and the sum of the penalties on the other. Gains and penalties do not compensate each other but operate at different levels. Since any A_i is in fact realized successfully to a certain degree by the user, gains and penalties (which are values given a priori) need to be weighted, i.e. paired with a success measure, respectively μ and τ, each of these weights being included in $[0,1]$. Then, for a given execution of the goal G, we have:

$$\text{gain}(G) = \sum_{i=1}^{n} g_i \times \mu_i \qquad\qquad \text{penalty}(G) = \sum_{i=1}^{n} p_i \times \tau_i$$

As can be noted, our definitions include terms which are gradual: 'more difficult', 'easier', because in practice, failing to realize an instruction properly does not necessarily means that the goal cannot be reached, but the user will just be less successful, for various reasons. In the natural language expressions of conclusions (the A_j) as well as of supports, there are many modals or classes of verbs (like risk verbs) that modulate the consequences on G, contrast for example:

> *use professional products to clean your leathers, they will give them a brighter aspect.*

with:

> *carefully plug in your mother card vertically, otherwise you will most likely damage its connectors.*

In the latter case, the goal 'mounting your own PC' is likely to fail (the instruction at stake will be assigned a high penalty), whereas in the former, the goal 'cleaning your leathers' will just be less successful, but there is a gain g_i associated.

3.2 Processing arguments

From the above observations, we have investigated the different forms arguments may take and how they are realized in French. We noted that, in a very large number of cases, arguments in procedural texts can be identified by means of specific terms, i.e. there is no need to make complex parses or inferences. For most of them, they are embedded into instructional compounds, it is therefore quite easy to delimit them. Their scope is in general the compound, and their delimitation is quite simple. Most of the time, arguments are introduced by a goal or a cause connector. They are quite often either a complete, independent sentence following an instruction, or a subordinated clause ending a sentence. As a result, their recognition is relatively well portable from one procedural domain to another, with only mainly generic vocabulary involved.

We have defined a set of patterns that recognize instructions which are conclusions and their related supports. We defined those patterns from a development corpus of about 1,700 texts from various domains (cooking, do it yourself, gardening, video games, social advice, etc.). The study is made on French, English glosses are given here for ease of reading. The recognition problem is twofold: identifying propositions as conclusions or supports by means of specific linguistic marks and a few typographic marks, and then delimiting these elements. In general, boundaries are either sentences or, by default, instructional compound boundaries. In procedural texts, roughly, the proportion of advice and warnings is almost equivalent.

Processing warnings

Warnings are basically organized around a unique structure composed of an 'avoid expression' combined with a proposition. The variations in the 'avoid expressions' capture the illocutionary force of the argument via several devices, ordered here by increasing force:

1. 'prevention verbs like avoid' NP / to VP (*avoid hot water*)

2. do not / never / ... VP(infinitive) ... (*never put this cloth in the sun*)

3. it is essential, vital, ... to never VP(infinitive).

In cases where the conclusion is relatively weak in terms of consequences, it may not have any specific mark, its recognition is then based on the observation that it is the instruction that immediately precedes an already identified support.

Supports are propositions which are identified from various marks: (a) via connectors such as: *otherwise, under the risk of,* etc., in French: *sinon, car, sous peine de, au risque de* or via verbs expressing consequence; (b) via negative expressions: *in order not to, in order to avoid, etc.*; (c) via specific verbs such as risk verbs introducing events (*you risk to break*) — in general the embedded verb has a negative polarity; (d) via the presence of very negative terms, such as: nouns: *death, disease, etc.*, adjectives, and some verbs and adverbs. We have a lexicon of ca. 200 negative terms found in our corpora.

Some supports have a more neutral formulation: they may be a portion of a sentence where a conclusion has been identified. For example, a proposition in the future tense or conditional following a conclusion is identified as a support. However, some supports may be empty, because they can easily be inferred by the reader. In that case, the argument is said to be truncated.

Patterns are implemented in Perl and are included into the global system (the TextCoop software). From the above observations, with some generalizations and the construction of lexicons of marks, we have summarized the extraction process in only eight patterns for supports and three patterns for conclusions. Arguments are tagged by XML tags. We carried out an indicative evaluation (e.g. to get improvement directions) on a corpus of 66 texts over various domains, containing 262 arguments. We get the following results for warnings: (supports well delimited are with respect to warnings correctly identified):

Conclusion recognition	Support recognition	Conclusions well delimited	Supports well delimited
88%	91%	95%	95%

Processing advice

Conclusions of type advice are identified essentially by means of two types of pattern (in French):

1. advice or preference expression followed by an instruction. The preference expression may be a verb or a more complex expression: *is advised to, prefer, it is better, preferable to, etc.*;

2. expression of optionality or of preference followed by an instruction: *our suggestions: ...,* or expression of optionality within the instruction (*use preferably a sharp knife*).

In addition, as for warnings, any instruction preceding a support of type advice is a conclusion. Supports of type advice are identified on the basis of 3 distinct types of pattern:

1. Goal exp + (adverb) + positively oriented term. Goal expressions are e.g.: *in order to, for*, whereas adverb includes: *better, more* (in French: *mieux, plus, davantage*), and positively oriented term includes: nouns (*savings, perfection, gain*, etc.), adjectives (*efficient, easy, useful*, etc.), or adverbs (*well, simply*, etc.). For this latter class of positively oriented terms we constructed a lexicon that contains about 50 terms.

2. Goal expressions with a positive consequence verb (*favor, encourage, save*, etc.), or a facilitation verb (*improve, optimize, facilitate, embellish, help, contribute*, etc.),

3. The goal expression in (1) and (2) above can be replaced by the verb 'to be' in the future: *it will be easier to locate your keys.*

A short example of an annotated text is given in Figure 1 below. Similarly as above, we carried out an indicative evaluation on the same corpus with 68 texts containing 240 manually identified pieces of advice (again, delimitation results are calculated with respect to advice correctly identified):

Conclusion recognition	Support recognition	Conclusions well delimited	Supports well delimited	Support/Conclusion correctly related
79%	84%	92%	91%	91%

As the reader may note, results are less satisfactory than for warnings. This is mainly due to the fact that advice is expressed in a much 'softer' way than warnings, with less emphasis and strength, therefore, terms typical of advice are not necessarily strongly marked, when present.

[*procedure*
[*title* How to embellish your balcony
[*Prerequisites* 1 lattice, window boxes, etc.] ...
[*instructional−compound* In order to train a plant to grow up a wall, select first a sunny area, clean the floor and make sure it is flat...
   [*Argument* [*Conclusion:Advice* You should better let a 10 cm interval between the wall and the lattice.]
   [*Support:Advice* This space will allow the air to move around, which is beneficial for the health of your plant.] ...]]]]

Figure 1: An annotated procedure

The terms involved in advice as well as warning patterns are mostly domain independent, they are also quite limited in number. Their variations are mainly due to the author's style and the target audience. Finally, it seems that our extraction mechanism can be used to extract arguments in a large number of non-procedural texts such as news. This is very tentative but a few tests on French news indicates an accuracy of about 75%, but these also contain a few rewards and threats. We get really good results with teaching texts, which may be felt to be at the boarder line of procedural texts, but which contain quite a lot of reward expressions since interactions are more prominent (with the teacher). In terms of multilinguality, we are at the moment developing the same approach for Thai (at Kasetsart univ., Bangkok) applied to the treatment of rice.

> [*instructional—compound* En decembre-janvier, effectuer la taille d'équilibrage et de net-
>   toyage de vos arbres.
>   [*Argument* [*Conclusion:warning* La première année de fructification, éliminer tous les
>   fruits au moment où ils se développent,]
>   [*Support:warning* Cela évite d'épuiser l'arbre.] ...]]

Figure 2: Annotated warning (gloss: *In December-January, make the first pruning and cleaning of your trees. The first year with fruits, eliminate all fruits, this avoids the tree to run out.*)

> [*instructional—compound* [*goal* Les étagères de votre meuble doivent être lisses.
>   [*Argument* [*Conclusion:advice* Utilisez si possible une ponceuse électrique,]
>   [*Support:advice* Ce sera beaucoup plus rapide et vraiment moins fatigant.] ...]]

Figure 3: Anotated advice (gloss: *The shelves of your furniture must be very smooth. Use if possible an electric sander, this will be faster and less tiring.*)

3.3 Dealing with empty supports

Considering do-it-yourself and gardening texts, we noted that about 2/3 of the arguments are not supported. This very large number of unsupported arguments, in such typically procedural texts, can be explained by several factors: (1) procedural texts are more oriented towards action than control, (2) some supports, possibly complex, could in fact introduce doubts or confusions, (3) some explanations (supports) may be too complex to be understood by a casual user, and (4) supports are sometimes sufficiently explicit in the conclusions (*do not scatter seeds by high winds!* = *they won't go where you want them to go*). In socially-oriented procedural texts, supports are often much more explicit, but this may differ depending on the author's style.

We noted that realized supports correspond to two main trends: (1) supports that express general requirements such as: efficiency of actions, security, ease of execution, adequate execution, speed, aesthetics, lower cost, etc. and (2) supports that cover more precise, domain dependent situations (*avoid pruning trees when temperature drops below zero*).

Reconstructing empty support is still under research, let us note here the still very tentative directions we are investigating, which require different forms of inference. For empty supports corresponding to general requirements, we infer a generic support based on those requirements, e.g.: *mounting your computer: use a flat and clean surface.* induced support: 'for a better ease of execution'. From our observations (which need further confirmation), generic supports are in general triggered by adjectives or by general purpose verbs used in the conclusion.

The second situation (empty support in a domain dependent situation) is more delicate and requires domain or lexical knowledge. We are investigating the use of principles of the Generative Lexicon (Pustejovsky 1991) for that purpose. Very briefly, *wind* has in its telic role several predicates like *push, take away, scatter, disperse, break, damage, ...* When applied e.g. to gardening, such as planting new flowers, since these are not so mobile when planted, a predicate like *break* or *damage* can be selected (selection principles in the Generative lexicon remain however an open and very delicate problem). Then, from a statement such as: *avoid planting flowers by high winds* the support: *because wind will damage or break flowers* can be inferred.

4 Perspectives

The work presented here complements the tagging of titles and instructional compounds in procedural texts of various domains, as reported in (Delpech et al. 2007, 2008). It allows us to have a quite comprehensive analysis of procedural texts, which turn out to have a very rich structure. Annotated corpus is available on request. We plan to include in our system the treatment of conditional expressions realized in (Bouffier et al. 2007), since we have not studied this phenomenon (and the associated scoping problems). We will then examine how illocutionary force is expressed. Finally, we plan to investigate the main lines of the facilitation structure.

We analyzed the forms arguments of type advice and warning may take, and have implemented and tested a system that tags those structures and attempts at reconstructing empty supports. At this level, there is still linguistic and formal work to be carried out, for example to evaluate the illocutionary force of arguments and to better settle this work within action theory. We believe we have a very useful corpus of examples of arguments, of much interest for research in argumentation theory. An important result is that arguments can be recognized on the basis of relatively simple parameterized patterns. The terms involved in those patterns are mostly domain independent. They may just vary depending on the author's style and the target audience. Finally, it seems that our extraction mechanism can be used to extract arguments in a large number of non-procedural texts such as news.

Besides studying the textual structure of procedural texts and responding to How-to questions from the analysis of these texts, a major application of this work is the construction of **domain know-how knowledge base**, quite basic but which could be subject to interesting generalizations. Obviously, to make this knowledge optimal, it would be useful to associate with every statement a formal representation that supports inference, data fusion, etc. This domain know-how knowledge base of advice, hints and warnings is of much importance for different types of users who have a procedure to realize a task but who want to know more before starting. Some psychological experiments have shown that, besides instructions given in procedural texts, users are very much interested in what remains implicit in those texts: what you are supposed to know or care about (but have no means to ask). Although there are already available, but manually constructed, such bases of advice, it is of much interest to construct it automatically, using the instructional compound as an advice unit.

Acknowledgements This paper relates work realized within the French ANR project TextCoop. We thank its partners for stimulating discussions. We also thank Leila Amgoud and Daniel Kayser for very useful discussions on this work. Finally, we are very grateful to three reviewers for their detailed comments which helped improve and clarify this paper.

References

Adam, J.M., *Types de Textes ou genres de Discours? Comment Classer les Textes qui Disent De et Comment Faire*, Langages, 141, pp. 10–27, 2001.

Amgoud, L., Bonnefon, J.F., Prade, H., *An Argumentation-based Approach to Multiple Criteria Decision*, in 8th European Conference on Symbolic and Quantitative Approaches to Reasoning with Uncertainty, ECSQARU'2005, Barcelona, 2005.

Amgoud, L., Parsons, S., Maudet, N., *Arguments, Dialogue, and Negotiation*, in: 14th European Conference on Artificial Intelligence, Berlin, 2001.

Anscombre, J.-Cl. Ducrot, O., *Interrogation et Argumentation*, in Langue francaise, no 52, L'interrogation, 5 - 22, 1981.

Aouladomar, F., Saint-Dizier, P., *An Exploration of the Diversity of Natural Argumentation in Instructional Texts*, 5th International Workshop on Computational Models of Natural Argument, IJCAI, Edinburgh, 2005.

Bouffier, A., Poibeau, T., *Re-engineering free texts to obtain XML documents: a discourse based approach*, RANLP 2007.

Delin, J., Hartley, A., Paris, C., Scott, D., Vander Linden, K., *Expressing Procedural Relationships in Multilingual Instructions*, Proceedings of the Seventh International Workshop on Natural Language Generation, pp. 61-70, Maine, USA, 1994.

Davidson, D., *Actions, Reasons, and Causes*, Journal of Philosophy, 60, 1963

Delpech, E., Murguia, E., Saint-Dizier, P., *A Two-Level Strategy for Parsing Procedural Texts*, VSST07, Marrakech, October 2007.

Delpech, E., Saint-Dizier, P., Anonymous, Investigating the Structure of Procedural Texts for Answering How-to Questions, LREC 2008, Marrakech.

Gardent, C., Discourse tree adjoining grammars, report nb. 89, Univ. Saarlandes, Saarbrucken, 1997.

Kosseim, L., Lapalme, G., *Choosing Rhetorical Structures to Plan Instructional Texts*, Computational Intelligence, Blackwell, Boston, 2000.

Moeschler, J., *Argumentation et Conversation, Eléments pour une Analyse Pragmatique du Discours*, Hatier - Crédif, 1985.

Pustejovsky, J., *The Generative Lexicon*, Computational Linguistics, 17(4), 1991.

Takechi, M., Tokunaga, T., Matsumoto, Y., Tanaka, H., *Feature Selection in Categorizing Procedural Expressions*, The Sixth International Workshop on Information Retrieval with Asian Languages (IRAL2003), pp. 49–56, 2003.

Talmy, L., Towards a Cognitive Semantics, vol. 1 and 2, MIT Press, 2001.

Vander Linden, K., *Speaking of Actions Choosing Rhetorical Status and Grammatical Form in Instructional Text Generation* Thesis, University of Colorado, 1993.

Webber, B., D-LTAG: extending lexicalized TAGs to Discourse, Cognitive Science 28, pp. 751–779, Elsevier, 2004.

From Predicting Predominant Senses to Local Context for Word Sense Disambiguation

Rob Koeling
Diana McCarthy
University of Sussex (UK)
email: robk@sussex.ac.uk

Abstract

Recent work on automatically predicting the predominant sense of a word has proven to be promising (McCarthy et al., 2004). It can be applied (as a first sense heuristic) to Word Sense Disambiguation (WSD) tasks, without needing expensive hand-annotated data sets. Due to the big skew in the sense distribution of many words (Yarowsky and Florian, 2002), the First Sense heuristic for WSD is often hard to beat. However, the local context of an ambiguous word can give important clues to which of its senses was intended. The sense ranking method proposed by McCarthy et al. (2004) uses a distributional similarity thesaurus. The k nearest neighbours in the thesaurus are used to establish the predominant sense of a word. In this paper we report on a first investigation on how to use the grammatical relations the target word is involved with, in order to select a subset of the neighbours from the automatically created thesaurus, to take the local context into account. This unsupervised method is quantitatively evaluated on SemCor. We found a slight improvement in precision over using the predicted first sense. Finally, we discuss strengths and weaknesses of the method and suggest ways to improve the results in the future.

1   Introduction

In recent years, a lot of research was done on establishing the predominant sense of ambiguous words automatically using untagged texts (McCarthy et al., 2004, 2007). The motivation for that work is twofold: on the one hand it builds on the strength of the *first sense heuristic* in Word Sense Disambiguation (WSD) (i.e. the heuristic of choosing the most commonly used sense of a word, irrespective of the context in which the word occurs) and on the other hand it recognizes that manually created resources for establishing word sense distributions are expensive to create and therefore hard to find. The one resource that is used most widely, SemCor (Miller et al., 1993), is only available for English and only representative for 'general' (non domain specific) text. McCarthy et al's method was successfully applied to a corpus of modern English text (the BNC (Leech, 1992)) and the predicted predominant senses compared well with the gold standard given by SemCor. Other experiments showed that the method can successfully be adapted to domain specific text (Koeling et al., 2005) and other languages (for example, Japanese (Iida et al., 2008)).

Even though the first sense heuristic is powerful, it would be preferable to only use it for WSD, when either the sense distribution is so skewed that the most commonly used sense is by far the most dominant, or as a back-off when few other clues are available to decide otherwise. The use of local context is ultimately necessary to find evidence for the intended sense of an ambiguous word. In this paper we investigate how we can exploit results from intermediate steps taken when calculating the predominant senses to this end.

The work on automatically finding predominant senses[1] was partly inspired by the observation that you can identify word senses by looking at the nearest neighbours of a target word in a distributional thesaurus. For example, consider the following (simplified) entry for the word *plant* in such a thesaurus (omitting the scores for distributional similarity):

(9)   plant : factory, industry, facility, business, company, species, tree, crop, engine, flower, farm, leaf, market, garden, field, seed, shrub...

Just by looking at the neighbours you can identify two main groups of neighbours, each pointing at separate senses of the word. First there is the set of words consisting of *factory, industry, facility, business, company, engine* that hint at the 'industrial plant' sense of the word and then there is the set consisting of *tree, crop, flower, leaf, species, garden, field, seed, shrub* that are more closely related to the 'flora' sense of the word. A few words, like *farm* and possibly *market* could be associated equally strongly with either sense. The idea behind 'sense ranking' is, that the right mix of

1. number of neighbours with a strong associations with one or more of the senses,

2. the strength of the association (semantic similarity) between neighbour and sense and

---

[1] McCarthy et al. (2004) concentrates on evaluating the predominant sense, but the method does in fact rank all the senses in order of frequency of use.

3. the strength of the distributional similarity of the contributing neighbour and the target word, will allow us to estimate the relative importance (i.e. frequency of use) of each sense.

What we want to explore here, is how we can use the local context of an occurrence of the target word, to select a subset of these neighbours. This subset should consist of words that are related more strongly to the sense of the word in the target sentence. For example, consider the word *plant* in a sentence like:

(10)   The gardener grows plants from vegetable seeds.

Plant is used in this sentence as the 'subject of grow'. A simple way of zooming in on potentially relevant neighbours is by using the most informative contexts shared between neighbours and the word in the target sentence. This is implemented by selecting just those words that occur in *the same grammatical context* (i.e. as subject of the verb 'grow') in a reference corpus[2]. If we apply that to the example in 9, we end up with the following subset: *business, industry, species, tree, crop, flower, seed, shrub*. Even though the first two words are still associated with the 'industrial plant' sense, we can see that the majority of the words in this subset is strongly associated with the intended sense.

In the next section we first give a quick introduction to the sense ranking algorithm introduced in McCarthy et al. (2004). Then we explain how we can use the database of grammatical relations that we used for creating the thesaurus, for selecting a subset of neighbours in the thesaurus. The following section describes an evaluation performed on the SemCor data. In the last two sections we discuss the results and especially why both recall and precision are lower than we had hoped and what can be done to improve the results.

2   Predominant Senses and Local Context

For a full review of McCarthy et al's ranking method, we refer to McCarthy et al. (2004) or McCarthy et al. (2007). Here we give a short description of the method. Since we need the grammatical relations used for building the thesaurus, for selecting a subset of the neighbours, we explain the procedure for building the thesaurus in 2.2. In the last part of this section we explain how we exploit local context for SD.

2.1   Finding Predominant Senses

We use the method described in McCarthy et al. (2004) for finding predominant senses from raw text. It can be applied to all parts of speech, but the experiments in this paper all focus on nouns only. The method uses a thesaurus obtained from the text by parsing, extracting grammatical relations and then listing each word (w) with its top k nearest neighbours, where k is a constant. Like McCarthy et al. (2004) we use $k = 50$ and obtain our thesaurus using the distributional similarity metric described by Lin (1998). We use WordNet (WN) as our sense inventory. The senses of a word w are each assigned a ranking score which sums over the distributional similarity scores of

---

[2]We use the same corpus used for generating the thesaurus as for the reference corpus (in all our experiments).

the neighbours and weights each neighbour's score by a WN Similarity score (Patwardhan and Pedersen, 2003) between the sense of w and the sense of the neighbour that maximises the WN Similarity score. This weight is normalised by the sum of such WN similarity scores between all senses of w and and the senses of the neighbour that maximises this score. We use the WN Similarity **jcn** score on nouns (Jiang and Conrath, 1997) since this gave reasonable results for McCarthy et al. and it is efficient at run time given precompilation of frequency information. The **jcn** measure needs word frequency information, which we obtained from the British National Corpus (BNC) (Leech, 1992). The distributional thesaurus was constructed using subject, direct object adjective modifier and noun modifier relations.

Thus we rank each sense $ws_i \in WS_w$ using Prevalence Score $ws_i =$

$$(11) \quad \sum_{n_j \in N_w} dss_{n_j} \times \frac{wnss(ws_i, n_j)}{\sum_{ws_{i'} \in WS_w} wnss(ws_{i'}, n_j)}$$

where the WordNet similarity score ($wnss$) is defined as:

$$wnss(ws_i, n_j) = \max_{ns_x \in NS_{n_j}} (wnss(ws_i, ns_x))$$

2.2 Building the Thesaurus

The thesaurus was acquired using the method described by Lin (1998). For input we used grammatical relation data extracted using an automatic parser (Briscoe and Carroll, 2002). For the experiments in this paper we used the 90 million words of written English from the BNC. For each noun we considered the co-occurring verbs in the direct object and subject relation, the modifying nouns in noun-noun relations and the modifying adjectives in adjective-noun relations. This limited set of grammatical relations was chosen since accuracy of the parser is particularly high for these 4 relations. We could easily extend the set of relations to more in the future. A noun, w, is thus described by a set of co-occurrence triples $< w, r, x >$ and associated frequencies, where r is a grammatical relation and x is a possible co-occurrence with w in that relation. For every pair of nouns, where each noun had a total frequency in the triple data of 10 or more, we computed their distributional similarity using the measure given by Lin (1998). If $T(w)$ is the set of co-occurrence types (r, x) such that $I(w, r, x)$ is positive then the similarity between two nouns, w and n, can be computed as:

$$(12) \quad \frac{\sum_{(r,x) \in T(w) \cap T(n)} (I(w, r, x) + I(n, r, x))}{\sum_{(r,x) \in T(w)} I(w, r, x) + \sum_{(r,x) \in T(n)} I(n, r, x)} \quad \text{where } I(w, r, x) = \log \frac{P(x|w \cap r)}{P(x|r)}$$

A thesaurus entry of size k for a target noun w can then be defined as the k most similar nouns to noun w.

2.3 Local Context

The basis for building the distributional similarity thesaurus, is the set of grammatical relations that the target word shares with other words. For example, if we look at the thesaurus entry for the noun *bike*, then we see that the closest neighbours are (the synonym) *bicycle* and the closely related *motorbike* (and *motorcycle*). The next 10 closest neighbours are all other vehicles (*car, van, boat, bus*, etc.). This is something we would expect to see, since all these words do occur in similar grammatical contexts. We *travel* by *bike*, as well as by *motorcycle*, *car* and *bus*. We *park* them, *drive_off* with them, *hire* them, *abandon* them and *repair* them. Many of these relations can be applied to a wide range of vehicles (or even a wider range of objects). However, some relations are more specific to two-wheeled vehicles. For example, it is quite common to *mount* a bike or a motorbike, whereas it is less common to *mount* a *car* or a *van*. *(Motor)bikes* are *chained* to stop people from stealing them and it is probably more common to *ride* a *(motor)bike* as opposed to *driving* a *car* or *truck*. Of course there are many other more general things you can do with these vehicles: *buy, sell, steal* them; there are *yellow bikes, cars* and *boats*, just like other objects. Therefore, we can see many other types of objects lower in the list of neighbours that share these more general grammatical relations, but not those that are specific to, say, vehicles or even the sub-category of two-wheeled vehicles.

Consider the following sentence containing the ambiguous noun *body*:

(13) *'Regular exercise keeps the body healthy.'*

(14) *'The funding body approved the final report.'*

We would like our algorithm to be able to recognize that Wordnet's first sense of the word body (*the entire physical structure of an organism (especially an animal or human being)*) is the most appropriate for sentence 13 and the third sense (*a group of persons associated by some common tie or occupation and regarded as an entity*) for sentence 14. If we calculate the most likely sense using all of the first 50 nearest neighbours in the thesaurus, we predict that sense 4 is the most frequently used sense (*the body excluding the head and neck and limbs*).

However, the two uses of the target word in 13 and 14 appear each in a very specific grammatical context. How can we exploit this local context to single out a certain subset of the 50 nearest neighbours, containing those words that are particularly relevant for (or more closely related to) the grammatical relation that the target word is involved in this particular sentence. The idea we pursue here is to look at those neighbours in the thesaurus that occur in the same grammatical relation as our target word and share a high mutual information (i.e. word and grammatical relation do not only occur frequently together, but also when you see one, there is a high probability that you see the other).

While creating the thesaurus we consider all the words that co-occur with a certain target word (where co-occur means that it appears in the same grammatical relation). We also calculate the mutual information of both the target word and the co-occurring word and the grammatical relation. Instead of throwing this information away after finishing an entry in the thesaurus, we now store this information in the grammatical relation database.

Since this database grows to enormous proportions (in the order of 200GB for the one built up while processing the BNC), we need to reduce its size to be able to work with it. If we only keep those entries in the database that involve the words in the thesaurus and their 50 neighbours, we can reduce the database to manageable proportions. We experimented with reducing the number of entries in the database even further by limiting the number of entries per grammatical relations to the ones with the highest mutual information scores, but this only had a negative effect on the recall, without improving the precision. As we will see later, data sparseness is a serious issue and it is therefore not advisable to cut-out any usable information that we have at our disposal. The word sense disambiguation procedure that uses the local context is then straightforward:

1. Parse the sentence with the target word (the word to be disambiguated).

2. If the target word is not involved with any of the 4 grammatical relations we considered for building up the thesaurus, local context can not be used.

3. Otherwise, consult the database to retrieve the co-occurring words:

   - Let *GR* be the set of triples $< w, r, x >$ from equation 12 in Section 2.2 for target word w.

   - Let *NGR* be the set of triples $< n_j, r, x >$ from equation 12 for any neighbour $n_j \in N_w$

   - For all $w \in T$ and all top 50 $n \in N_w$, keep entries with $< *, r, x >$ in database.

   - Let *SGR* be the set of relations $< r, x >$ in the target sentence, where $I < w, r, x >$ and $I < n, r, x >$ are both positive (i.e. r, x are both in the target sentence and have high MI in BNC for both w and n.)

4. Compute the ranking score for each sense by applying to a modified version of the ranking equation (15) (compared to the original given in (11)), where the k nearest neighbours are replaced by the subset found in the step 3.

(15) Prevalence Score $ws\_lc_i = \sum_{n_j \in N_w} MI \times dss_{n_j} \times \frac{wnss(ws_i, n_j)}{\sum_{ws_{i'} \in WS_w} wnss(ws_{i'}, n_j)}$

where the WordNet similarity score (*wnss*) is defined as before and let MI be $I < n, r, x >$, i.e. the Mutual Information given by the events of seeing the grammatical relation in question and seeing the neighbour.

2.4 An example

The fact that a subset of the neighbours in the thesaurus share some specific relations with the target word in a particular sentence is something that we wish to exploit for Word Sense Disambiguation. Let us have a closer look at the two example sentences 13 and 14 that we introduced in the previous section.

The grammatical relations that our target word *body* is involved with are (from sentences 13 and 14 respectively):[3]

(16) 'body' object of 'keep' for sentence 13 and

(17) 'body' subject of 'approved' and 'body' modified by the noun 'funding' for sentence 14

---

[3]At the moment we only take 4 grammatical relations into account: Verb-Subject, Verb-Object, Adj-Noun and Noun-Noun modifier.

Table 1: Results of evaluation on the nouns in SemCor

Method	Attempted	Correct	Wrong	Precision	Recall
Local Context	23,235	11,904	11,331	0.512	0.161
First sense	23,235	11,795	11,440	0.508	–

Since *keep* is a fairly general verb, it is not surprising that quite a few of the neighbours occur as object of *keep*. As a matter of fact, 28 of the first 50 neighbours share this relation. However, the good news is, that pretty much all the words associated with body-parts (such as *arm*, *hand*, *leg*, *face* and *head*) are among them.

The two grammatical relations that *body* is involved with in sentence 14, are more specific. There are just 6 neighbours that share the 'subject of approve' relation with *body* and another 5 that are used to modify the noun *body*. Among these words are the highly relevant words *organisation*, *institution* and *board*.

3   Evaluation on SemCor

The example in the last section shows that in certain cases the method performs the way we envisaged. However, we need a quantitative evaluation to get a proper picture of the method's usefulness. We performed a full evaluation on SemCor. In this experiment we limited our attention to *nouns* only. We further eliminated Proper Names and multi-word units from the test set. Since the nouns in both these categories are mostly monosemous, they are less interesting as test material and apart from that, they introduce problems (mostly parser related) that have little to do with the proposed method. A total of 73,918 words were left to evaluate. Table 1 summarizes the results. The figure for recall for the 'First Sense' method is not given, because we want to contrast the local context method with the first sense method. Whilst the first sense method will return an answer in most cases, the local context method proposed in this paper will not. Here we want to focus on how we can improve on using the first sense heuristic by taking local context into account, rather than give complete results for a WSD task.

There are several things to say about these results. First of all, even though the results for 'local context' are slightly better than for 'first sense', we expected more from it. We had identified quite a few cases like 13 and 14 above, where the local context seemed to be able to help to identify the right neigbours in order to make the difference. Below, we will discuss a few cases where the grammatical relations involved are so general, that the subset of neighbours is large and most importantly, not discriminative enough. It seems to be reasonable to expect that the latter cases will not influence the precision too much (i.e. a smaller group of neighbours will often give a different result, but some better, some worse).

The recall is also lower than expected. The first thought was that data sparseness was the main problem here, but additional experiments showed us that that is unlike to be the case. In one experiment we took a part of the GigaWord corpus (Graff, 2003), similar in size to the written part of the BNC (used in our original experiment) and built our grammatical relation database using the combined corpus. The recall went up a little, but at the price of a slightly lower precision.

4   Discussion

The main problem causing the low recall seems to be the small number of grammatical relations that we use for building the thesaurus. The four relations used (verb-subject, verb-object, noun–noun-modifier and adjective-noun-modifier) were chosen because of the parsers' high accuracy for these. For building the thesaurus, these grammatical relations suffice, since every word will occur in one of these relations sooner or later. However, whenever in a sentence the target word occurs outside these four relations, we are not able to look it up in our database. Nouns within prepositional phrases seem to be a major victim here. It should be straightforward to experiment with including prepositional phrase related grammatical relations. We will have to evaluate the influence of the introduced noise on creating the thesaurus. Alternatively, it is possible to use the four relations as before for creating the thesaurus and store the extra relations in our database just for look-up.

A second cause for missing target words is parser errors. Even though RASP will produce partial parses whenever a full parse of a sentence is not available, some loss is inevitable. This is a harder problem to solve. One way of solving this problem might be by using a *proximity thesaurus* instead of a thesaurus build using grammatical relatons. McCarthy et al. (2007) reported promising results for using proximity based thesaurus for predicting predominant senses, with accuracy figures closely behind those achieved with a dependency based thesaurus.

One plausible reason why the method is not working in many cases, is the fact that the word to be disambiguated in the target sentence often occurs in a very general grammatical relation. For example, 'subject of' or 'direct object of' a verb like *have*. In these cases, most of the neighbors in the thesaurus will be selected. Even though it is clear that that would minimize the *positive* effect, it is not immediately obvious that this would have a *negative* effect. It might therefore be the case that the number of cases where the grammatical relation is a good selection criterion, is just lower than we thought (although this is not the impression that you get when you look at the data). We will need to establish a way of quantitatively evaluating this.

The Mutual Information score gives us a measure of the dependence between the grammatical relation and the word (neighbour of the target word) we are interested it. It gives us a handle on 'generality' of the combination of seeing both events. This means that for a very common grammatical relation, many words will be expected to co-occur with a frequency comparable to their general frequency in texts. The contrast with relation/word combinations for which this is not the case might be usable for identifying the cases that we want to exclude here.

5   Conclusions

In this paper we propose a completely unsupervised method for Word Sense Disambiguation that takes the local context of the target word into account. The starting point for this method is a method for automatically predicting the predominant senses of words. The grammatical relations that were used to create the distributional similarity thesaurus is exploited to select a subset of the k neighbours in the thesaurus, to focus on those neighbours that are used in the same grammatical context as the word we want to disambiguate in the target sentence.

Even though the precision of our proposed method is slightly higher than for the predominant sense method, we are disappointed by the current results. We do believe that there is more mileage to be had from the method we suggest. Improvement of both recall and precision is on the agenda for future research. As we stated in the previous section, we believe that the lower than expected recall can be addressed fairly easily, by considering more grammatical relations. This is straightforward to implement and results can be expected in the near future.

A second approach, involving a thesaurus built on proximity, rather than grammatical relations will also be investigated. Considering the expected lower precision for this approach, we plan to use the proximity-based thesaurus as a 'back off' solution in case we fail to produce an answer with the dependency-based thesaurus. When the proximity-based thesaurus is in place, we plan to perform a full evaluation of the dependency versus the proximity approach.

Before we can deal with improving the local context method's precision, we need to have a better idea of the circumstances in which the method gets it wrong. We have identified a large group of examples, where it is unlikely that the method will be successful. A first step will be to develop a method to identify these cases automatically and eliminate those from the targets that we are attempting to try. In the previous section, we sketched how we think that we can achieve this by applying a Pointwise Mutual Information threshold. If we are successful, this will at least give us the opportunity to focus on the strengths and weaknesses of the method. At the moment, the virtues of the method seem to be obscured too much by dealing with cases that should not be considered.

More insight in the method can also be gained from trying to identify in which situations the method is more likely to get it right. At the moment we haven't broken down the results yet in terms of the target word's polysemy and/or frequency of use. Some grammatical relations might be more useful for identifying the intended sense than other. A detailed analysis could give us these insights.

We do believe there is a strong case to be made for using unsupervised methods for Word Sense Disambiguation (apart from McCarthy et al. (2004)'s predominant sense method, other approaches include e.g. Basili et al. (2006)). The predominant sense method has proven to be successful. However, applying the first sense heuristic should be limited to certain cases. We can think of the cases where the dominance of the predominant sense is so strong, that there is little to gain from doing a proper attempt to disambiguation or to the cases where 'everything else fails'. Ultimately, our goal is to find a balance between the dominance of the predominant sense and the strength of the evidence from the supporting context. If we are able to recognize the correct clues from the local context and use these clues to focus on those words with a high distributional similarity to the target word in the context in which the word is actually used, we can build on work on predicting predominant senses, to rely less on the first sense heuristic. This would be a good step forward for unsupervised WSD.

Acknowledgments This work was funded by UK EPSRC project EP/C537262 "Ranking Word Senses for Disambiguation: Models and Applications", and by a UK Royal Society Dorothy Hodgkin Fellowship to the second author. We would like to thank Siddharth Patwardhan and Ted Pedersen for making the WN Similarity package available and Julie Weeds for the thesaurus software.

References

Basili, R., M. Cammisa, and A. Gliozzo (2006). Integrating domain and paradigmatic similarity for unsupervised sense tagging. In *Proceedings of 7th European Conference on Artificial Intelligence (ECAI06)*.

Briscoe, E. and J. Carroll (2002). Robust accurate statistical annotation of general text. In *Proceedings of the Third International Conference on Language Resources and Evaluation (LREC)*, Las Palmas, Canary Islands, Spain, pp. 1499–1504.

Graff, D. (2003). English gigaword. Linguistic Data Consortium, Philadelphia.

Iida, R., D. McCarthy, and R. Koeling (2008). Gloss-based semantic similarity metrics for predominant sense acquisition. In *Proceedings of the Third International Joint Conference on Natural Language Processing*, Hyderabad, India, pp. 561–568.

Jiang, J. and D. Conrath (1997). Semantic similarity based on corpus statistics and lexical taxonomy. In *10th International Conference on Research in Computational Linguistics*, Taiwan, pp. 19–33.

Koeling, R., D. McCarthy, , and J. Carroll (2005). Domain-specific sense distributions and predominant sense acquisition. In *Proceedings of the Human Language Technology Conference and EMNLP*, Vancouver, Canada, pp. 419–426.

Leech, G. (1992). 100 million words of English: the British National Corpus. *Language Research 28*(1), 1–13.

Lin, D. (1998). Automatic retrieval and clustering of similar words. In *Proceedings of COLING-ACL'98*, Montreal, Canada, pp. 768–774.

McCarthy, D., R. Koeling, J. Weeds, and J. Carroll (2004). Finding predominant senses in untagged text. In *Proceedings of the 42nd Annual Meeting of the Association for Computational Linguistics*, Barcelona, Spain, pp. 280–287.

McCarthy, D., R. Koeling, J. Weeds, and J. Carroll (2007). Unsupervised acquisition of predominant word senses. *Computational Linguistics 33*(4), 553–590.

Miller, G. A., C. Leacock, R. Tengi, and R. T. Bunker (1993). A semantic concordance. In *Proceedings of the ARPA Workshop on Human Language Technology*, pp. 303–308. Morgan Kaufman.

Patwardhan, S. and T. Pedersen (2003). The CPAN WordNet::Similarity Package. http://search.cpan.org/~sid/ WordNet-Similarity-0.05/.

Yarowsky, D. and R. Florian (2002). Evaluating sense disambiguation performance across diverse parameter spaces. *Natural Language Engineering 8*(4), 293–310.

Automatic Fine-Grained Semantic Classification for Domain Adaptation

Maria Liakata

University of Wales, Aberystwyth (UK)

email: mal@aber.ac.uk

Stephen Pulman

University of Oxford (UK)

email: sgp@clg.ox.ac.uk

Abstract

Assigning arguments of verbs to different semantic classes ('semantic typing'), or alternatively, checking the 'selectional restrictions' of predicates, is a fundamental component of many natural language processing tasks. However, a common experience has been that general purpose semantic classes, such as those encoded in resources like WordNet, or hand-crafted subject-specific ontologies, are seldom quite right when it comes to analysing texts from a particular domain. In this paper we describe a method of automatically deriving fine-grained, domain-specific semantic classes of arguments while simultaneously clustering verbs into semantically meaningful groups: the first step in verb sense induction. We show that in a small pilot study on new examples from the same domain we are able to achieve almost perfect recall and reasonably high precision in the semantic typing of verb arguments in these texts.

1   Introduction

Since the earliest days of computational linguistics the semantic properties of verbal arguments have played an important role in processing. Many classic types of ambiguity, and hence their resolution, depend on this: 'flying planes can be dangerous' is ambiguous because 'flying planes' can describe an activity or a plural entity, either of which can be a semantically appropriate subject of 'be dangerous', whereas 'swallowing apples can be dangerous' does not display this ambiguity. Both 'fly' and 'swallow' can be transitive or intransitive, but whereas 'planes' is both a semantically appropriate subject for intransitive 'fly' and an appropriate object for transitive 'fly', 'apples' is not a semantically appropiate subject for intransitive 'swallow'. Semantic (mis)typing rules out this syntactically valid combination. Similarly, an important component of reference resolution is the knowledge of what semantic category an entity falls under. For example, in 'The crop can be used to produce ethanol. This can be used to power trucks or cars', knowledge that ethanol is the kind of thing that can be subject of 'power', whereas 'crop' is not, is required to successfully resolve the reference of 'this'.

When considering division into semantic categories one's immediate thought would be to take advantage of existing semantic resources (such as WordNet (Miller, 1995)) or FrameNet (Baker et al., 1998). For example, Clark and Weir (2002) calculate the probability of a noun sense appearing as a particular argument by using WordNet to generalise over the noun sense. However, even though WordNet has been extremely useful in numerous applications, many researchers have found that the fact that it is largely developed via the intuitions of lexicographers, rather than being empirically based, means that the semantic information often is poorly matched with word usage in a particular domain. Pantel and Lin (2002) and Phillips and Riloff (2002) have pointed out that WordNet often includes many rare senses while missing out domain-specific senses and terminology. Some authors, Kilgariff (1997) and Hanks and Pustejovsky (2004), among others, reject the basic idea shared by WordNet and FrameNet (as well as traditional dictionaries) that there is a fixed list of senses for many verbs, arguing that individual senses will often be domain specific and should be discovered empirically by examining the syntactic and semantic contexts they occur in. We are highly sympathetic to this view and in this work we assume, as Hanks and Pustejovsky do, that rather than relying on the intuitions of a lexicographer, it is better to try to induce verb senses and semantic types automatically from data drawn from the domain of interest.

In this paper we report on some experiments in learning semantic classes. We carry out prior syntactic and semantic analysis of a relevant corpus so that verb+argument pairs can be identified. Since we are interested in domain specific semantic classification we make the 'one sense per corpus' hypothesis and ignore word sense disambiguation. For a given verb, we find the head nouns occurring in the subject, object and indirect object noun phrases (where they exist) occurring frequently within the corpus. Now that we have information about nouns co-occurring in different argument slots of verbs we cluster the verbs according to shared argument slots: verbs which have an argument slot (not necessarily the same one) occupied by members of the same cluster are in turn clustered together. The effect of this is to derive noun clusters characterising the semantic types of the argument slots for individual verbs (learning selectional restrictions) while simultaneously clustering verbs which have similar argument slots. In the case where the same argument slot is involved across verbs, the effect of this is to induce a fine-grained semantic classification of verbs (the first step in learning verb senses). Where different argument slots are involved the effect is to suggest more complex causal or inferential relations between groups of verbs.

To give a simple illustration, if *admit, deny, suspect* all take the word 'wrongdoing' as their object, then *admit_arg2, deny_arg2, suspect_arg2*[1] are clustered together into one group *A*. If we also find that words like 'oversight' also appear frequently in the same argument position with roughly the same set of verbs, then 'oversight' will be clustered with the other fillers of group *A*.

A side-effect of the process is a classification of the verbs as well: if *admit_arg1, deny_arg1* and *admit_arg2, deny_arg2* respectively take the same values, 'deny' and 'admit' are clustered together. We may also note that the same classes occur in different argument slots of different verbs: in Liakata and Pulman (2004) we showed how this could lead to the discovery of causal relations specific to a domain: for example (in company succession events), that A succeeds B if B resigns from position C and A is appointed to C.

In the remainder of the paper we describe this clustering process in more detail. We also describe a simple pilot evaluation, by taking two unseen texts from the same domain, and observing to what extent the semantic groupings arrived at can be used to assign semantic types to arguments of verbs. We were pleasantly surprised to find almost perfect recall, and respectable precision figures.

2 Method

The method of clustering together verb argument slots for obtaining domain specific verb senses (either in terms of verb classes or through the assignment of semantic types to the verb arguments) is applied as a proof of concept to the domain of financial news. We chose this domain since the WSJ section of the Penn Treebank II is already available in the form of predicate-argument structures, obtained according to the method described in Liakata and Pulman (2002). However, the same approach can apply to predicate-arg structures from non-treebank data such as the QLFs derived from LFG structures in Cahill et al. (2003) or semantic representations such as in Bos et al. (2004).

The WSJ corpus consists of 2,454 articles with a total of 2,798 distinct verb predicates, 62 prepositional predicates and 221 copular predicates containing the verb to 'be'. Here we are only dealing with the non-prepositional predicates. The latter follow an uneven distribution of occurrences; there is a minority of very frequent verbs whereas the majority are rather sparse. The problem with infrequent predicates is that the number of instances is often too small to allow for meaningful clustering of the verb-argument slots. To circumvent this, we pre-process predicates with low frequencies (freq < 5) by looking them up in WordNet to find the conceptual group (synset) to which they belong and assigning to them the frequency of the member of the synset with the greatest count of occurrences in the corpus. Thus, words featuring as arguments of the most frequent synset member are counted as arguments of the

---

[1] arg1 is subject; arg2 is direct object; arg3 is indirect object, roughly

less frequent semantically related predicate, so that the latter receives a count boost. For example, the words that appear as subjects of the verb 'hit' are also considered subjects of the verb 'clobber', which belongs to the same synset as 'hit' but is under-represented in the corpus. This is making use of the knowledge that semantically similar verbs are similar in terms of subcategorisation (Korhonen and Preiss, 2003) and is in agreement with the approach in Briscoe and Carroll (1997) where the subcat-egorisation frames (SCFs) of representative verbs are merged together to form SCFs of the rest of the verbs belonging to the same semantic class. We understand that the above process may be indirectly adding false positives to the verb senses. It would be interesting in the future to examine the trade-off between boosting the counts of infrequent verbs and the addition of false positives.

A second pre-processing stage was applied to the arguments of the 2,798 verb pred-icates. The idea underlying this process was to create a version of the predicates where obvious semantic grouping would have already taken place. This involved merging to-gether the instances of 'named entity' classes: person names, companies, locations, propositions, money expressions, and percentage and numeric expressions. Company names and suffixes, locations and people's first names are contained in a gazetteer list collected from internet resources.

Since the similarity of argument slots of predicates is to be determined by how many common fillers they share, it is natural to use the Vector Space Model (VSM) originally from Information Retrieval to define similarities. In IR documents contain-ing the same words are considered to be similar. Argument slots of predicates can be characterised by their filler words in the same way that a document is characterised by the words it contains. This means a predicate argument slot can be modelled in terms of a vector of filler-word frequencies.

In order to apply clustering methods to the predicate-arguments, we combined them into a matrix, where each row corresponds to a verb-argument slot (verb-subj/arg1, verb-obj/arg2 or verb-iobj/arg3) and the columns correspond to words-fillers of the verb-argument slots. Each cell 'w_{ij}' in the matrix represents the frequency of word 'j' as a filler of predicate argument slot 'i'. However, even after the first step of group-ing together named entities of the same type (as described above) there were 32,990 distinct possible fillers of the three argument positions of the 2,798 verb predicates. By including all possible word fillers as columns, we would end up with a very sparse matrix of $2,798 * 3 = 8,394$ rows and 32,990 columns.

To reduce the size of the matrix it was essential to select a small number of words as representatives of the argument fillers. Even though the literature for feature selection is vast when it comes to supervised machine learning methods, there is very little on feature selection for clustering. Principal Component Analysis (PCA) would be one alternative here as it reduces dimensionality while preserving as much of the variance in the high dimensionality space as possible. However, since PCA does not consider class separability information there is no guarantee that the direction of maximum variance will contain good features for discrimination. In this preliminary experiment we decided simply to use the 100 most frequent words as features. Thus the new matrix is of the order $8,394 * 100$.

2.1 Clustering method

To perform the clustering we chose a probabilistic clustering method which allows instances to belong to more than one class with different probabilities, as this gives a better indication of the quality of each class and agrees more with the intuition that there is more than one possibility for defining the groups. In addition to this, we do not know what the expected number of classes is so ideally we would like the clustering algorithm to predict the optimal number of classes. For the previous reasons we decided to use Autoclass (Cheeseman and Stutz, 1995) which is a system for unsupervised classification, consisting of a classical mixture model enhanced by a Bayesian method for determining the optimal classes.

Autoclass is an extension of the mixture model as each instance can be characterised by multiple attributes instead of just one, so that the dataset is represented as a matrix of attribute values. One need not specify the exact number of clusters since the system first performs a random classification which it then improves through local changes. Autoclass adopts a fully Bayesian approach by assuming a prior probability distribution for each parameter. In the current experiment the instances in each class (verb argument slots) were assumed to follow a log normal distribution.

2.2 The verb argument clusters

Autoclass performed over 500 trials to converge to various solutions with differing numbers of clusters. The most probable clustering, i.e. the one with the highest log posterior, corresponds to 32 classes and was obtained after 200 trials. The high number of classes[2] returned may be due to overfitting of the model or may be a sign that there is not a clear structure in the data itself.

A class obtained from Autoclass is characterized by its class weight, the number of verb-argument slots that constitute its members, as well as its class strength and class cross entropy. There are very heavy, populous classes (e.g. class 0 with 5,571 members) and lightweight, scantily populated classes (e.g. class 31 with 34 members). Class strengths are defined by the mean probability that any instance belonging to a class would have been generated by its probabilistic model. The higher the class strength the more meaningful the class. The strongest class is class 0 followed by class 2, the third most populous class. Admittedly, the class strength for the rest of the classes is very small casting some doubt over the model's predictive power with respect to the data set. Almost every instance is assigned to a class with probability 1, which means that the classes are clearly separated. Class cross entropy, how strongly the model helps differentiate each class from the whole dataset, ranges from zero, for identical distributions, to infinite for distributions that make a complete separation between differing values of the same attribute. A class is more meaningful if its distribution is distinct from the global distribution. In this case class cross entropy has a value of over 118 for every class, suggesting that classes are distinct from the distribution of the data set. Attributes with the most overall influence in classification are the ones corresponding to precise concepts associated with specific contexts such as 'spokeswoman', 'reporter', 'source'. The least useful features for the classification are the ones with the most scattered frequencies across predicates such as 'person'. Thus, one should employ frequent features with counts concentrated in a subset of

---

[2]From here onwards we shall be using the terms 'class' and 'cluster' interchangeably

predicates and penalise the significance of words with counts distributed evenly in all predicates. This suggests that it would be more reliable to use freq*idf[3] as a criterion for feature selection.

2.3 Interpretation of the clusters

In order to be able to interpret classes, class membership was inspected by processing the class report showing which cases belong to a particular class. Class 0 contains nearly all of the third arguments (indirect objects) of all verbs, which are usually propositions functioning as verb complements. The interpretation of the resulting classes is not straightforward, though about half have some intuitive basis once outliers are ignored. For example, class 9 (below) seems to hold first arguments (subjects) of verbs denoting sudden movement and numeric change such as:

```
class(9,['add_arg1','add_up_arg1',
'back_arg1','balloon_arg1','base_arg2',
'base_arg1','bear_arg1','begin_arg1',
'bestow_arg1','block_arg1','blossom_arg1',
'blow_arg1','blow_up_arg1','come_up_arg1',
'boost_arg2','bother_arg1','break_arg1',
'break_arg2','breathe_arg1','bring_in_arg1',
'bud_arg1','build_up_arg1','bump_up_arg1',
'clean_up_arg1','clear_arg1','climb_arg1',
'come_along_arg1','come_back_arg1','cut_arg2',
'come_down_arg2','come_on_arg1','boom_arg1',
'continue_arg1','contract_arg1','deal_arg1',
'contribute_arg1','count_arg1','count_arg2',
'crack_arg1','crash_arg1','come_down_arg1'
'cut_arg1','cut_down_arg1','contrast_arg2',
'decline_arg1','deduct_arg1','defend_arg2',
'deflate_arg1', 'deflate_arg2','settle_arg1',
'set_off_arg1','shape_up_arg1','shine_arg1',
'shoot_arg1','shorten_arg1','sink_arg1',
'sit_arg1','sit_down_arg1','slip_arg1',
'slip_in_arg1','slump_arg1','soar_arg1']).
```

A closer look at the filler words of the above verbs show that most of them are 'financial indicators' of some sort such as the following:

CLIMB_arg1: share, asset, imports, exports, fund, price, rate, percentage, stock, wages, dollar, dividend, income, volume, market, capital, interest, trading, demand, maker, cost, index, new_bank_index.

SINK_arg1: percentage, yield, stake, wages, stock, index, share, dollar, georgia_gulf_stock, money, company, bank, income, investment, dividend, payout, payroll.

SOAR_arg1: earnings, asset, yield, location, exports, imports, purchase, fund, price, rate, number, wages, share, stock, rating, bid, dollar, interest, dividend, profit, income, volume, risk, holder.

DROP_arg1: borrowing, imports, increase, market, share, investor, surge, capital, money, company, auction, firm, price, bank, limit, scale, holder, profit, dollar, performance, asset, stoc, rate, index, bid, earnings, volatility.

---

[3]idf here is defined as $idf_i = \dfrac{|\text{All pred-arg slots}|}{|\text{pred-arg slots filled by i}|}$

Some other classes containing verb arguments with a clear semantic relationship to each other can be found in the following:

Class 1 consists among others of the first arguments of:

think, rethink, believe, know, consider, reconsider, understand, remember, respect, underestimate, value, view, visualize, respect

Class 4 contains objects of verbs related to financial transactions and consumption such as: buy, sell, calculate, acquire, afford, auction, buy_up, buy_out, cut_down, exchange, lose, begin, continue, feed, keep, maintain, market, obtain, regain, retain, trade, use.

Class 4 also contains subjects of verbs such as:

diminish, decrease, descend, crush, double, eat, eat_up, end, extend, fail, discharge, dismiss, dispatch, dissolve, distort, exhaust, launch, multiply, pay, plunge, profit, quadruple, shrink, spend, yield, triple.

2.4 Semantic typing of verb arguments

Clustering verb argument slots as described above leads both to the semantic grouping of verbs as well as the indirect semantic typing of the words that feature as arguments to the verbs. For the latter, details regarding membership of the 32 classes of verb argument positions were combined with information about which words appear in which slots, so that each term was assigned to the corresponding classes. This inevitably resulted in a word belonging to more than one class. For example, the term "spokeswoman" is a filler of verb argument slots in classes 6, 9, 7 and therefore belongs to the homonymous classes. However, its frequency in each class will differ so that combined with the ipf[4], the respective tf-ipfs give a better idea of how meaningful class membership is. For example, the tf-ipfs for the term "spokeswoman" are 0.0075, 0.00275 and 0.0005 for classes 6, 9 and 7 respectively, making class 6 the most representative class for this word.

By looking at the 15 highest ranking terms in each class, where rank is determined by descending tf-ipf, we attempted to give labels to the 32 classes of verb arguments. The labels originated from the 3–4 terms with the highest frequency among the top 15 words and are shown below:

```
class label
0  proposition
1  company_organisation
2  unspecified_someone
3  proposition_truth_profit_patient_impact
4  percentage_money_income_revenue_stock_share_asset
5  percentage_mony_numXpression
6  spokesman_company_person_analyst
7  income_revenue_net_rate_cost_stock
8  place_step_effect_loss_action
9  proposition_company_spokesman_revenue_analyst
10 proposition_stake_rate_percentage
11 proposition_percentage_sure_decision_bid
12 year_percentage_quarter_index
13 reporter_dividend_money_percentage_analyst
14 percentage_proposition_numXpression
```

---

[4]ipf (inverse predicate frequency) is defined in the same way as idf

```
15 proposition
16 percentage_stake_demand_money_rate_cash_capital
17 proposition_projection_rate
18 proposition_trading_pressure
19 proposition_table_corner_board_tide
20 proposition_percentage_public_private_high_low_numXpression
21 government_civilian_unspecified
22 proposition_unspecified_game_role_cash_company_agreement
23 percentage_proposition_numXpression
24 percentage_proposition_date_profit
25 director_court_partner_company
26 proposition_contract_profit_demand_requirement_proposal
27 demand_problem_leak
28 year_month_time
29 proposition_money_percentage_share_stock
30 year_time
31 fund_proposal_investor
```

As can be seen from the above, obtaining a clean-cut label reflecting the meaning of the contents in each argument class is a non-trivial process; there seems to be a significant amount of sense variance within a class and overlap between classes.

2.5   Adding hierarchy to the semantic typing

In order to obtain a sense of the extent of overlap and similarity between classes, we computed a similarity matrix consisting of the pairwise similarities between each of the 32 classes where similarity between classes was defined in terms of the **overlap coefficient**:

$$sim(A,B) = \frac{|A \cap B|}{min(|A|,|B|)}$$

Where $|A \cap B|$ is the number of words in both A,B and $|A|,|B|$ are the number of words in classes A,B respectively.

The overlap coefficient considers classes to be similar when one subsumes or nearly subsumes the other. Hierarchical clustering was performed on the the basis of the overlap similarity matrix, using euclidean distance as the distance metric. The result is the cluster dendrogram below, which illustrates the relation between classes a lot more clearly than a set of flat labels can and allows for a generalisation hierarchy of the senses reflected by the classes' semantic types.

Even though it is difficult to designate human-friendly labels to the classes that represent their meaning in a straightforward manner, we will show that these classes can be used reliably to automatically assign semantic types to the arguments of verbs.

First, we combined the information about class membership of verb argument slots to create patterns of the form:

ARG1 VERB1 (ARG2) (ARG3)

As verb-argument slots were assigned to each class with probability 1 (see Section 2.2) and we made the "one sense per corpus" assumption, there is just one pattern for each verb. Thus, for example, the pattern for the verb 'report' is the following:

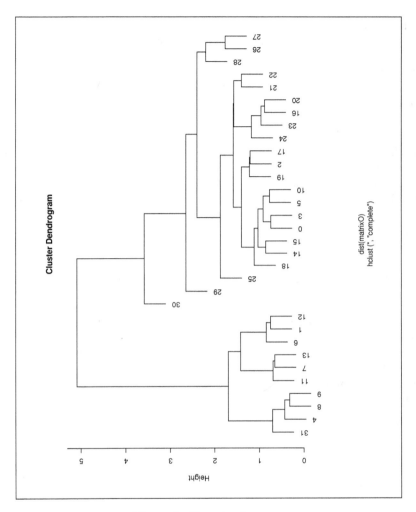

Figure 1: Class dendrogram

[1 report 4 (10)], which takes the following form when replacing class IDs with tentative semantic labels:

[*company_organisation*] report
[*percentage_money_income_revenue_stock_share_asset*]
[*proposition_stake_rate_percentage*]

However, this does not mean that a person cannot be the 1st argument of report; there is overlap between classes 1 and 6 (the major person class) and Figure 1 shows they are closely linked. Such proximity of classes is considered during pattern evaluation (Section 3).

The patterns were stored in a MySQL database. They are partly modelled on the 'Corpus Pattern Analysis' model described in Pustejovsky et al. (2004). These are syntagmatic patterns representing a selection context for the predicate they include, which determines the sense of the latter although CPA Patterns as defined by Pustejovsky et al. (2004) and Rumshisky and Pustejovsky (2006) are in fact rather more detailed than our patterns.

3   Results and Evaluation

To evaluate the semantic types assigned by the automatically derived classes as well as the transferability of the derived CPA-like patterns to unseen instances, we performed a pilot study where we applied the patterns to two randomly selected articles from the on-line versions of the WSJ and the FT from March 2008. We believe this to be a useful test for the validity of the patterns since the new articles are guaranteed to be distinct from the training WSJ data of the 90s, while still belonging to the same domain. We parsed the article using the CCG parser (Clark and Curran, 2007) and concentrated on its RASP option (Briscoe et al., 1997) output, consisting of dependency relations. Since our patterns concern the semantic typing of verb arguments, we focussed on the relations ncsubj (non-clausal subject), dobj (direct obj) and iobj (indirect obj) between a verb and the respective argument position. We ignored erroneous parses[5] as well as copular predicates with the verb to 'be', since the CCG parser's dependency relations did not maintain the connection between 'be' and the adjective or participle, making it clumsy to automatically link arguments in the way we need to.

We then followed the evaluation procedure below, where for each verb-argument pair token in the evaluation set:

1. We looked for a pattern in the database matching the verb-argument relation and augmented the count for recall if a match was found for the right verb.

2. We obtained the type (that is, the class ID) that the pattern assigns to the argument filler word. We then checked the latter in the database, to see which classes it belongs to as well as its freq, tf-idf for each class. Determining which should be the correct, gold standard class of a word given the 32 classes is very difficult considering the class overlap. Therefore, the three highest ranking classes were taken as describing the correct semantic type for the word. Here rank is defined by looking at the 10 first classes where the term has the highest tf-Idf and returning the 3 of these with the highest frequency.

3. If the type assigned to the argument filler matches any of the 3 classes-semantic types, we assumed the type assignment is correct.

4. If the type returned was not among the 3 correct semantic types, we looked at the cluster dendrogram from the previous section and counted the distance between the correct and returned types. If the correct type and the returned type are in the same cluster at the same level, we count the distance as 1. If we need

---

[5]This can be justified by the fact that we are evaluating the patterns, not the system for producing the dependency relations for evaluation

to go up a level from the returned type for them to be in the same cluster the distance is 2, if two levels, the distance is 3.

5. Proceeded to the next verb-argument pair.

To illustrate the assignment of semantic types through the application of the patterns and the ensuing evaluation procedure, we consider two example verb argument relations from the WSJ text, namely 'dobj shows declines' and 'ncsubj dropped indexes'. In the first case, we looked in the database for a pattern of the verb 'show'. The matching pattern is ' 6 show 4 14', which assigns semantic type 4 to the object of the verb, 'declines'. When looking up the noun 'decline' in the database, the 3 types constituting its correct semantic type are 9, 8, 4. Since 4, the type allocated by the pattern is among them, we consider this to have been the correct assignment of semantic type. For the second example, the pattern available in the database of the verb 'drop' is '9 drop 8 28', which means that the pattern assigns type 9 to the word 'index'. However, when we look up the word 'index' in the database, the correct semantic types for it are 7,12,4. We check in the cluster dendrogram to calculate the closest distance between type 9 and types 7,12,4 which is 2 steps, between classes 9 and 4. The semantic type assignment is therefore considered once more correct.

There were 46 distinct verbs and 78 distinct verb-argument relations that met the criteria for evaluation (out of 119 extracted predicate argument relations) in the WSJ article. For the FT article the corresponding numbers were 25 and 53 respectively (the latter out of 129 predicate-argument relations). The difference in these figures can be due to the size of the articles (6,002 words for the WSJ as opposed to only 2,702 for the FT one) as well as the preference for nominal predicates and nominalisations in the FT article.

A verb pattern existed for each of the verb-argument relations, which gave a perfect recall, 78/78, 53/53 (100%). This is gratifying since the patterns seem to cover adequately the financial domain, given that the test data come from two different newspapers. When allowing a distance of up to 3 between the assigned and correct classes precision was 60/78 (76.9%) for the WSJ and 33/53 (62.2%) for the FT article. For example, in the predicate 'oversees Mac', 'Mac', which is a company, was allocated to class 13 by the patterns whereas the correct class should have been one of 6, 9, 1. The distance between classes 13 and 6 is 3 steps, whereas 'company' features in both classes with tf 0.0008 and 0.011 respectively. The precision was reduced to 55/68 (70.5%) and 30/53 (56.6%) if we only allowed up to 2 steps (e.g. in 'index fell' 'index' was assigned to class 9 where its tf is 0.0014, as opposed to 4 where its tf is 0.0016). Precision fell further to 41/68 (53%) and 26/33 (49%) respectively for up to 1 steps (e.g. where in 'reported at 75' the iobj '75' was classified as being in class 10 (tf 0.0004) as opposed to 5 (tf 0.004). For strictly exact matches, precision was 33/78 (43%) for the WSJ and 21/53 (39.6%) for the FT (e.g. 'director' in 'director said' being assigned to class 6 where the correct type is defined by classes 25,12,6).

The results between the two articles are definitely comparable. However, it is difficult to tell whether the observed difference at the upper end is indeed statistically significant and to what extend the difference between British English and US English plays a role here. Nevertheless, even though the evaluation was only performed on a small scale, we consider the results to be at the very least, encouraging, since the texts we tested the patterns on were picked at random from the domain of financial news. The perfect recall would suggest that the verb patterns provide reasonably full coverage of the domain, while we can assign informative fine-grained semantic types to arguments with a reasonable degree of precision. Of course, a larger evaluation would be desirable, as would some task-related measure of how much this semantic typing helps in accurate processing. We hope to do this in future work.

4 Related Work

The literature on acquiring semantic classes of words is very extensive. It is mostly motivated by WSD and WSI where the aim is to discover or be able to differentiate between different senses of a target word. Pereira et al. (1993) describes a method for clustering words according to their distributions in particular syntactic contexts. Nouns for instance are classified according to their distribution as direct objects of verbs, where it is assumed that the classification of verbs and nouns co-varies. In our approach we also make this assumption and nouns are clustered indirectly by first grouping together the verb argument slots they fill. Clustering in both cases is probabilistic with the assumptions that members of the same cluster follow similar distributions or in our case a joint distribution.

Phillips and Riloff (2002) and Pantel and Lin (2002) also describe work on clustering nouns to derive semantic classes. Work more directly comparable to ours includes Schulte im Walde (2003, 2006) who presents a method for clustering German verbs by linguistically motivated feature selection. Evaluation against a manually annotated gold standard showed that syntactic subcategorisation features were most informative whereas selectional preferences added noise to the clustering. However, the author concludes that there is no perfect choice of verb features and that some verbs can be distinguished on a coarse feature level while others require fine-grained information. Korhonen et al. (2006) also use syntactically motivated features to cluster together verbs from the biomedical domain and in more recent work (Sun et al., 2008) showed that rich syntactic information about both arguments and adjuncts of verbs constitute the best performing feature set for verb clustering.

Gamallo et al. (2007) follow a similar approach to Pantel and Lin (2002) where an initial set of specific clusters, containing manually chosen terms representative of the domain as well as their lexicosyntactic contexts, are aggregated to form intermediate clusters to which hierarchical clustering is applied for further generalisation. A very interesting aspect of this work is that concept-clusters have a dual nature, consisting both of words-terms (extension) and their lexico-syntactic contexts (intension). As is the case in our approach, cluster formation is twofold, by grouping together words according to the contexts they appear in but also by clustering contexts based on the words they share though this is mentioned as future work in Gamallo et al. (2007). However, in earlier work Gamallo et al. (2005) cluster together similar syntactic positions in Portuguese derived automatically and each cluster represents a semantic condition. Words-fillers of the common position are used to extensionally define the particular condition. Clusters are formed in two stages, where first the similarity between any two positions is calculated in terms of their common word fillers, the 20 most similar ones for each position are aggreggated and the intersection of common words kept as features. Next, basic clusters are agglomerated according to the amount of shared features. The result is a lexicon of words with syntactico-semantic requirements applied successfully to PP-attachment.

The current work has a different agenda in that it aims to obtain semantic classes of nouns that feature as verb arguments. This information is combined to form selection contexts for verbs, similar to CPA patterns (Pustejovsky et al., 2004), which are then evaluated on the assignment of semantic types. However, whereas our patterns are obtained in a fully automated way, CPA patterns are acquired semi-automatically after the initial manual construction of core verb subcategorisation frames.

5 Summary and Future Work

We have presented a method for automatically acquiring domain-specific selectional restrictions for verbs in terms of semantic typing of their arguments. This was achieved by clustering together verb argument slots sharing the same filler words after obtaining all predicate-argument relations in the corpus. This also resulted in the semantic grouping of nouns, which instantiate the verb arguments. The clustering method used was Autoclass, an extension of the mixture model. We combined the information from the clusters of nouns and verb-argument slots to create contextual verb patterns. The latter were evaluated on a text chosen at random from the same domain and achieved perfect recall and reasonably high precision.

As this pilot study showed that fine-grained domain-specific semantic patterns for verbs can be obtained automatically, we would like to port the approach to a domain where fine-grained typing is of paramount importance. This is the case with the biomedical domain, where for instance verbs of biological interaction, such as inhibit or activate are semantically underspecified (Rumshisky et al., 2006; Korhonen et al., 2006). However, the specific biological interactions come only through the details of the actual arguments participating in the interaction (Rumshisky et al., 2006). We would also like to experiment with different clustering methods and use more sophisticated linguistically motivated filters for feature selection.

Acknowledgements

We would like to thank Rachele de Felice for her assistance and Stephen Clark & Rada Mihalcea for their useful comments. This work was partially funded by the Companions project (http://www.companions-project.org) sponsored by the European Commission as part of the Information Society Technologies (IST) programme under EC grant number IST-FP6-034434 and the ART Project (http://www.aber.ac.uk/compsci/Research/bio/art/) funded by the Joint Information Systems Committee (JISC).

References

Baker, C. F., C. J. Fillmore, and J. B. Lowe (1998). The Berkeley Framenet project. In *Proceedings of the COLING-ACL*, Montreal, Canada.

Bos, J., S. Clark, M. Steedman, J. Curran, and J. Hockenmaier (2004). Wide-Coverage Semantic Representations from a CCG parser. In *Proceedings of the 20th International Conference on Computational Linguistics (COLING-04)*, Geneva,Switzerland, pp. 1240–1246.

Briscoe, E. and J. Carroll (1997). Automatic extraction of subcategorisation from corpora. In *Proceedings of ACL ANLP 97*, pp. 356–363.

Briscoe, E., J. Carroll, and R. Watson (1997). The Second Release of the RASP System. In *Proceedings of the COLING/ACL 2006 Interactive Presentation Sessions*, Sydney, Australia.

Cahill, A., M. McCarthy, J. van Genabith, and A. Way (2003). Quasi-Logical Forms for the Penn Treebank. In I. v. d. S. Harry Bunt and R. Morante (Eds.), *Proceedings of the Fifth International Workshop on Computational Semantics, IWCS-05*, Tilburg, The Netherlands, pp. 55–71.

Cheeseman, P. and J. Stutz (1995). Bayesian classification (Autoclass): Theory and results. In P. S. U. Fayyad, G. Piatesky-Shapiro and R. Uthurusamy (Eds.), *Advances in Knowledge Discovery and Data Mining*, pp. 153–180. Menlo Park, CA: AAAI Press.

Clark, S. and J. Curran (2007). Wide-Coverage Efficient Statistical Parsing with CCG and Log-Linear Models. *Computational Linguistics 33(4)*, 493–552.

Clark, S. and D. Weir (2002). Class-Based Probability Estimation Using a Semantic Hierarchy. *Computational Linguistics 28(2)*, 145–186.

Gamallo, P., A. Agustini, and G. Lopes (2005). Clustering Syntactic Positions with Similar Semantic Requirements. *Computational Linguistics 31(1)*, 107–146.

Gamallo, P., G. Lopes, and A. Agustini (2007). Inducing Classes of Terms from Text. In *Proceedings of TSD 2007*, pp. 31–38.

Hanks, P. and J. Pustejovsky (2004). Common Sense About Word Meaning: Sense in Context. In *TSD 2004*, pp. 15–18.

Kilgariff, A. (1997). I don't believe in word senses. *Computers and the Humanities 31*, 91–113.

Korhonen, A., Y. Krymolowski, and N. Collier (2006). Automatic Classification of Verbs in Biomedical Texts. In *Proceedings of AC-COLING 2006*, Sydney, Australia.

Korhonen, A. and J. Preiss (2003). Improving Subcategorization Acquisition using Word Sense Disambiguation. In *Proceedings of ACL 2003*, Sapporo, Japan, pp. 48–55.

Liakata, M. and S. Pulman (2002). From Trees to Predicate-Argument Structures. In *Proceedings of the 19th International Conference on Computational Linguistics (COLING 2002)*, Taipei, Taiwan, pp. 563–569.

Liakata, M. and S. Pulman (2004). Learning Theories from Text. In *Proceedings of the 20th International Conference on Computational Linguistics (COLING 2004)*, Geneva, Switzerland.

Miller, G. A. (1995). "Wordnet: a lexical database for English.". In *Communications of the ACM*, Volume 38 (11), pp. 39 –41.

Pantel, P. and D. Lin (2002). Concept Discovery from Text. In *In Proceedings of COLING 2002*, Taipei, Taiwan.

Pereira, F., N. Tishby, and L. Lee (1993). "Distributional clustering of English words.". In *Proceedings of the 31th Annual Meeting of the Association of Computational Linguistics(ACL 93')*, Columbus, Ohio.

Phillips, W. and E. Riloff (2002). Exploiting Strong Syntactic Heuristics and Co-Training to Learn Semantic Lexicons. In *Proceedings of EMNLP 2002*.

Pustejovsky, J., P. Hanks, and A. Rumshisky (2004). Automated Induction of Sense in Context. In *COLING 2004 5th International Workshop on Linguistically Interpreted Corpora*, Geneva, Switzerland, pp. 55–58.

Rumshisky, A., P. Hanks, C. Havasi, and J. Pustejovsky (2006). Constructing a Corpus-based Ontology using Model Bias. In *FLAIRS 2006*, Melbourne Beach, Florida.

Rumshisky, A. and J. Pustejovsky (2006). Inducing Sense-Discriminating Context Patterns from Sense-Tagged Corpora. In *LREC 2006*, Genoa, Italy.

Schulte im Walde, S. (2003). Experiments on the Choice of Features for Learning Verb Classes. In *Proceedings of EACL 2003*, Budapest, Ungarn.

Schulte im Walde, S. (2006). Experiments on the Automatic Induction of German Semantic Verb Classes. *Computational Linguistics 32(2)*, 159–194.

Sun, L., A. Korhonen, and Y. Krymolowski (2008). Verb Class Discovery from Rich Syntactic Data. In *Proceedings of the 9th International Conference on Intelligent Text Processing and Computational Linguistics*, Haifa, Israel.

Analysis of ASL Motion Capture Data towards Identification of Verb Type

Evguenia Malaia
John Borneman
Ronnie B. Wilbur
Purdue University (USA)
email: emalaya@purdue.edu

Abstract

This paper provides a preliminary analysis of American Sign Language predicate motion signatures, obtained using a motion capture system, toward identification of a predicate's event structure as telic or atelic. The pilot data demonstrates that production differences between signed predicates can be used to model the probabilities of a predicate belonging to telic or atelic classes based on their motion signature in 3D, using either maximal velocity achieved within the sign, or maximal velocity and minimal acceleration data from each predicate. The solution to the problem of computationally identifying predicate types in ASL video data could significantly simplify the task of identifying verbal complements, arguments and modifiers, which compose the rest of the sentence, and ultimately contribute to solving the problem of automatic ASL recognition.

1 Introduction

In recent work, we have provided preliminary data indicating that there is a significant difference in the motion signatures of lexical predicate signs that denote telic and atelic events (Wilbur and Malaia, 2008b,c,a; Malaia et al., 2008). These results are empirical evidence for direct mapping between sign language (ASL) phonology/kinematics, and semantic decomposition of predicates (the Event Visibility Hypothesis, or EVH (Wilbur, 2003, 2009)). The present paper reviews this analysis of ASL predicate 3D motion signatures and considers further application of such data for computational processing of ASL video streams, and automatic recognition of predicate type based on 2D motion signatures. Particular attention is paid to the contribution of the slope of deceleration at the end of signs, and to the values of the maximum velocity and minimum acceleration achieved during the sign motion. The focus of the study on predicates is determined by the fact that each sentence or clause in natural languages is built around a predicate. Thus, a solution to the problem of identifying predicate types could significantly simplify the task of identifying verbal complements, arguments and modifiers, which compose the rest of the sentence.

2 Modeling events in ASL

Linguistic theory of verbal types has long observed universal correspondences between verbal meaning and syntactic behavior, including adverbial modification (Tenny, 2000), aspectual coercion (Smith, 1991), and argument structure alternations (Levin, 1993; Ramchand, 2008). Vendler (1967) proposed a system of four basic syntactically relevant semantic types of predicates: atelic States and Activities, and telic Achievements and Accomplishments. The telic/atelic distinction is most clearly analyzed in terms of the internal structure of events. 'Telic' is understood as the property of linguistic predicates (events) containing a conceptual (semantic) endpoint. In contrast, 'atelic' events do not contain such a point and have the potential to continue indefinitely. Atelic events are homogenous, in that they may be divided into identical intervals, each of which is an instance of the event itself, i.e. 'walking' as an instance of 'walking'. Telic events are composed of at least two sub-events, one of which is the final state, and are therefore heterogeneous (cannot be divided into identical intervals). The model was further developed by Pustejovsky (1991), with the primary distinction between static sub-event type S(tate) and dynamic sub-event type P(rocess). Telic events with transitions to the final state were modeled as combinations of non-identical sub-events (Table 1).

Table 1: Pustejovsky's predicate typology

Predicate type	Definition
Activity	P
State	S
Accomplishment	P → S
Achievement	S → S

Most recently, Ramchand (2008) has taken an event as the basis for hierarchical composition of phrases that replace the traditional notion of Verb Phrase, thereby simplifying the interaction between the lexicon and the syntax, at least for dynamic events. This simplification has the potential to be very useful for automatic recognition of predicate signs. Ramchand divides events into a maximum of three hierarchical phrases: an initiation phrase (InitP), a process phrase (ProcP), and a result phrase (ResP). Each of these has an associated participant: InitP: Initiator; ProcP: Undergoer; and ResP: Resultee. This eliminates traditional problems associated with determining argument structure and thematic role assignment. One or more of these phrases may be identified by a single morpheme/word/sign. As a result, the same event could be represented by one word or an entire phrase, depending on the morphology of a particular language. Ramchand further demonstrate that expression of degrees of causation (direct or indirect) is related to whether a single morpheme identifies both [init] and [proc] (yielding interpretation as direct causation) or separate morphemes are needed (yielding indirect causation). Similar effects with resultatives are found with single morpheme identification of [proc] and [res] as compared to separate morphemes.

From this perspective we can analyze ASL signs in terms of the phrases they identify. In this paper we compare signs which identify at least [ResP] (telic events) with those that do not (atelic events).[1] The notion of event-based analysis of sentential semantics and syntax was supported in general for ASL in Rathmann (2005), and for Austrian Sign Language (Schalber, 2004, 2006). Semantics of event type has been shown to have a direct effect on available morphological modifications as well: Brentari (1998) notes that [delayed completive] aspect marking only applies to telic stems. Wilbur (2009) demonstrates that some types of aspectual marking (continuative, durative) can only apply to atelic predicates. Wilbur (2003) argued that the phonological structure of predicate signs in ASL shows event composition, and that the components are grammaticalized from universally available physics of motion and geometry of space. This Event Visibility Hypothesis (EVH) was formalized as 'movement which stops at points (p) in space maps semantically to the final State of telic events (en) and its individual argument semantic variable (x)'. In Ramchand's terms, ResP can be seen in lexical predicates representing telic events by the way the movement comes to a stop. This hypothesis was tested in the motion capture experiment described below.

3   Materials and methods

A group of 29 telic and 21 atelic ASL signs were randomized, and presented as a list via Powerpoint five times through. A native bilingual right-handed ASL signer wore a Gypsy 3.0 wired motion capture suit (Figure 2).

The signer viewed the powerpoint slides with stimuli and produced the list twice with each sign in isolation, once with each sign in the carrier phrase 'SIGN X AGAIN', and once sentence- medially 'SHE X TODAY'. For each production the hands began at rest, were raised for signing, and were returned to rest. We report the data from the marker on the right wrist, as the dominant right hand carries most of the meaningful motion information in ASL (the non- dominant typically serves as ground or repeats the movement of the dominant hand). All signs selected for the experiment

---

[1] As Ramchand notes, it is possible to get telic readings without ResP from bounded path complements. However this study uses lexical items, for which bounded path analyses have not yet been demonstrated, thus we treat them all as ResP items for expository purposes.

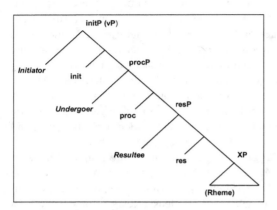

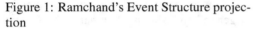

Figure 1: Ramchand's Event Structure projection   Figure 2: Signer in motion capture suit

included motion of the wrist. The data from the motion capture suit was recorded into Motionbuilder software and exported as text data for further analysis. The data included frame numbers, and marker positions along the 3D axis in millimeters for all recorded frames. Acquisition rates were 50 fps for kinematic data, and 30 fps for video data; the video also included an audio marker for alignment of the beginning of motion capture recording with the separate video recording. The time course of predicate signing in the video was annotated using ELAN software (Max Planck Institute for Psycholinguistics). The beginning of each predicate was marked once the dominant hand assumed appropriate handshape, and the end of each movement was marked at the final point of contact or maximal displacement in the lexical form of the sign. All start/stop times were determined by a single coder with over two decades experience measuring sign movement, with +/– 1 video frame precision. The vectors for the 3D location of the wrist marker were then imported into ELAN and aligned with video data using the audio marker. In addition to raw displacement data, derivatives of speed (in m/s) and acceleration (in m/s^2) were calculated in MATLAB and imported into ELAN. To minimize the difference in acquisition rates for video and kinematic data, velocity and acceleration vectors were imported into ELAN, and peak changes corresponding to the actual motion capture data points were compared to the annotations. This alignment was used to ensure the proper extraction of the motion capture data corresponding to the target sign between the marked start and end locations. Additionally, the error of measurement for each predicate was considered, evaluated as ratio of frame duration vs. predicate duration expressed in percentage. Consequently, predicates which spanned fewer than three video frames were discarded because of high error margin. For the rest of the predicates, the following metrics were calculated:

- the maximal velocity (maxV);

- the local minimum velocity following maxV (minV);

- the slope of the drop from maxV to minV (slope);

- the minimum acceleration (minA) following the maximum velocity;

- duration of the predicate (in frames);

- the frame location of maxV, minV, and minA.

These metrics were chosen to allow for maximal homogeneity in predicate comparison. The metrics related to the start of the sign were avoided as linguistically unreliable, while using the local velocity minima mitigated the effect of data interpolation in ELAN resulting from the frame difference between video recording and motion capture recording. The data were submitted to SPSS multivariate ANOVA to determine the effect of telicity value (Telic vs. Atelic).

4   Linguistic results and observations

The data from the right wrist marker indicate that in all environments, the deceleration of telic signs is steeper than that of atelic signs (Table 2).

Table 2: Deceleration slope for telic and atelic signs (* $p < 0.05$; ** $p < 0.001$)

Deceleration (mm/s2)	Atelic mean (tokens used)	Telic mean (tokens used)	Telic/Atelic Ratio and effect size
Isolation 1	−0.093 (13)	−0.136 (22)	1.46* F(1)= 4.528
Isolation 2	−0.123 (17)	−0.179 (23)	1.46* F(1)= 5.709
Carrier Phrase	−0.118 (14)	−0.233 (22)	1.97** F(1)= 15.258
Sentence	−0.14 (13)	−0.23 (18)	1.62* F(1)= 7.400

The data support the Event Visibility Hypothesis in ASL, indicating that there is a production difference reflecting the semantic distinction of event type in predicates. It appears that ASL takes advantage of available perceptual distinctions to provide cues to the viewer regarding the semantics of the predicate. Telic predicates in general have a steeper deceleration slope, marking the end-state of telic events. This deceleration may correspond to what Klima and Bellugi (1979) referred to as 'end marking'. From the perspective of syntax-semantics interface modeling theory (Ramchand, 2008; Wilbur, 2003), higher decelerations in motion signatures of telic ASL predicates also mark additional semantic arguments of the event, what Ramchand refers to as the 'Resultee'.

5   Development of metrics for computational identification of predicate types in ASL

The data from the four productions was compared in order to evaluate the consistency of production. The interval distribution of maxV and minA for all predicates, in both carrier phrases and in sentences, overlap (Figure 3), indicating that those two production conditions were not significantly different, and therefore this data could be pooled for the purposes of statistical analysis.

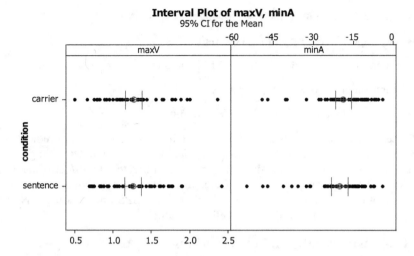

Figure 3: Interval plots of maxV and minA in carrier phrases and sentences for all predicates, displaying 95% confidence intervals for the mean values of the respective metrics

A similar comparison of maxV intervals by predicate type of those produced in isolation (Figure 4) revealed significant discrepancies between the two instances of production for atelic signs, possibly related to the attempt by the signer to reproduce the vocabulary form of the predicate. Thus, isolation data was not used for the following analysis.

A binary logistic regression was performed on the pooled data from both carrier phrase and sentence sign production, in order to search for the minimum number of variables that could be used to predict whether the signed predicate is telic or atelic. For this analysis the logit function was selected to calculate the predicted probabilities. Regression was first run with all of the measured variables from Section 3 included in the model. The variables with p-values above 0.05 threshold were rejected one at a time, and the regression calculation re-run; the process was repeated until all predictive variables in the model were below p=0.05. The model was reduced to two significant predictors: maxV and minA (maximum velocity and deceleration). The final regression model is shown in equation (1) using the variable dependence shown in equation (2).

$$P_T = \frac{e^\beta}{1+e^\beta} \qquad (1)$$

$$\beta = -4.46 + 2.63\,(\mathrm{maxV}) - 0.097\,(\mathrm{minA}) \qquad (2)$$

P_T is the probability of a predicate being telic, based on measured values for maxV and minA. Applying the above equation on the pooled data for carrier phrase and sentence production conditions (setting a 50% threshold so that $P_T > 0.5$ predicts telic, and $P_T < 0.5$ predicts atelic) ensures that 46 out of 56 telic predicates, and 32 out of

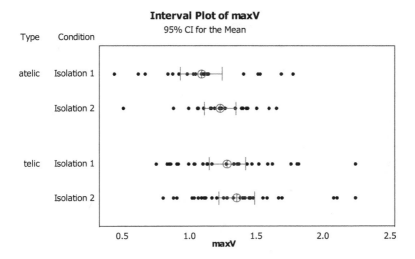

Figure 4: Interval plots of maxV in isolation productions 1 and 2 by predicate type

44 atelic predicates can be identified correctly using only maxV and minA measures (Figure 5).

However, comparing the coefficients of maxV (2.63) and minA (−0.097) in equation (2) makes it apparent that the effect of the deceleration (minA) on the output of the model is low. A regression analysis using only the maxV measurement to determine the predicate type yields a revised beta value as shown in equation (3).

$$\beta = -4.19 + 3.71 \, (\text{maxV}) \tag{3}$$

Using this simplified equation on the pooled data ensures that 47 out of 56 telic predicates, and 27 out of 44 atelic predicates can be identified correctly with a 50% probability threshold based only on maxV (Figure 6).

Direct analysis of the maximum velocity (maxV) data supports both the original model (eqn. 3) and the simplified model (eqn. 4). Telic predicates have a significantly higher maxV mean and distribution than atelic predicates, as shown in Figure 7. It is this difference in the velocity distribution that allows for telic/atelic predictions based on maxV measurements.

6   Conclusion

The above pilot data analysis indicates that there exists a production difference in maximal velocity and deceleration slope of ASL predicate signs reflecting semantic distinction of event type in ASL predicates. From the linguistic standpoint, the overt difference in sign production maps onto an event-structural representation for the syntax-semantics interface, which has implications for modeling the syntax-semantics interface in both signed and spoken languages. Empirical evidence for Event Visibility in signed languages demonstrated that individual meaningful features in signs (such as rapid deceleration to a stop) can combine to create patterns which merge the syntactic

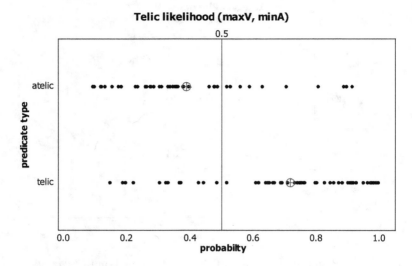

Figure 5: Probabilities of correct predicate type identification based on maxV and minA data. Data points represent the telic and atelic predicates, presented according to the probablility of their correct identification using equation (1) and variable dependence in equation (2)

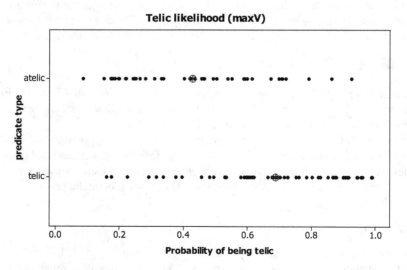

Figure 6: Probabilities of correct predicate type identification based on only maxV data. Data points represent telic and atelic predicates, presented according to the probability of their correct identification using revised beta value in equation (3). The crosshairs represent the mean probability of correct predicate type identification for atelic (0.429) and telic (0.689) predicates

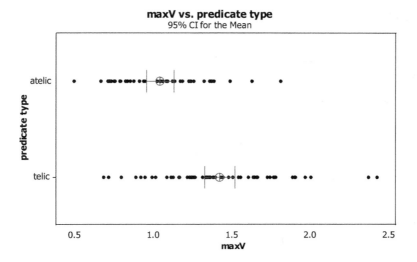

Figure 7: MaxV distribution for telic and atelic predicates in carrier phrases and sentences (pooled), displaying the mean values and 95% confidence intervals

level of a sign with its phonological level — the phenomenon which can be utilized for machine translation of signed languages.

For the purposes of computational approaches to sign recognition, the pilot data demonstrates that production differences between predicate types can be used to model the probabilities of specific predicate types occurring within the motion signature, based on either maximal velocity achieved within the sign, or maximal velocity and minimal acceleration data from each predicate. However, as pilot data analysis shows, higher acquisition rates for video and motion capture data would be beneficial to take full advantage of production differences in velocity and deceleration of different types of ASL predicates. Further research is needed to determine inter-signer variability in production differences between telic and atelic predicate signs, the reliability of maximal velocity and minimal acceleration metrics, and development of additional metrics (possibly similar to ones used for spoken language phonology (Adams et al., 1993)) which could rely on higher temporal resolution in data acquisition.

Acknowledgments Motion capture was conducted at the Envision Center for Data Perceptualization at Purdue University. We are grateful to Robin Shay, Gabriel Masters, Nicoletta Adamo-Villani, and the Purdue and Indianapolis sign language communities for their ongoing support of the Purdue Sign Language Linguistics Lab research. This work was supported by NSF Research in Disabilities Education grant #0622900 and by NIH grant DC00524 to R.B. Wilbur.

References

Adams, S., G. Weismer, and R. Kent (1993). Speaking rate and speech movement velocity profiles. *Journal of Speech and Hearing Research 36*, 41–54.

Brentari, D. (1998). *A prosodic model of sign language phonology.* Cambridge, MA: MIT Press.

Klima, E. and U. Bellugi (1979). *The Signs of Language.* Cambridge, MA: Harvard University Press.

Levin, B. (1993). *English Verb classes and alternations.* The Univ. of Chicago Press.

Malaia, E., R. Wilbur, and T. Talavage (2008). Experimental evidence of event structure effects on asl predicate production and neural processing. In *Proceedings of the 44th meeting of Chicago Linguistic Society*, Chicago, IL.

Pustejovsky, J. (1991). The syntax of event structure. *Cognition 41(1-3)*, 47–81.

Ramchand, G. (2008). *Verb Meaning and the Lexicon: A First Phase Syntax.* Cambridge: Cambridge University Press.

Rathmann, C. (2005). *Event Structure in American Sign Language.* Ph. D. thesis, University of Texas at Austin.

Schalber, K. (2004). Phonological visibility of event structure in Austrian Sign Language: A comparison of ASL and ÖGS. Master's thesis, Purdue University.

Schalber, K. (2006). Event visibility in Austrian Sign Language (ÖGS). *Sign Language & Linguistics 9*, 207–231.

Smith, C. (1991). *The Parameter of Aspect.* Dordrecht: Kluwer Academic Publishers.

Tenny, C. (2000). Core events and adverbial modification. In Tenny and Pustejovsky (Eds.), *Events as grammatical objects.* Stanford, CA: CSLA Publications.

Vendler, Z. (1967). *Linguistics in Philosophy.* Cornell University Press, New York.

Wilbur, R. (2003). Representations of telicity in ASL. *Chicago Linguistic Society 39(1)*, 354–368.

Wilbur, R. (2009). Productive reduplication in ASL, a fundamentally monosyllabic language. to appear in Language Sciences.

Wilbur, R. and E. Malaia (2008a). Contributions of sign language research to gesture understanding: What can multimodal computational systems learn from sign language research. *International Journal of Semantic Computing 2(1)*, 1–15.

Wilbur, R. and E. Malaia (2008b). Event Visibility Hypothesis: motion capture evidence for overt marking of telicity in ASL. In *Linguistic Society of America Annual Meeting.* Chicago: LSA.

Wilbur, R. and E. Malaia (2008c). From Encyclopedic Semantics to Grammatical Aspects: Converging Evidence from ASL and Co-Speech Gestures. In *DGfS annual meeting (AG 11, Gestures: A comparison of signed and spoken languages).* Bamberg, Germany: DGfS.

The Idiom–Reference Connection

Marjorie McShane
Sergei Nirenburg
University of Maryland Baltimore County (USA)
email: marge@umbc.edu

Abstract

Idiom processing and reference resolution are two complex aspects of text processing that are commonly treated in isolation. However, closer study of the reference needs of some idioms suggests that these two phenomena will need to be treated together to support high-end NLP applications. Using evidence from Russian and English, this article describes a number of classes of idioms according to their reference needs and suggests a method of lexical encoding which, supplemented by procedural semantic routines, can adequately support the full semantic and referential interpretation of these idioms.

1   Introduction

Reference resolution and idiom processing have received much attention in natural language processing (NLP), but these phenomena are commonly treated in isolation of each other, and most treatments address only a single aspect of the respective overall problems. For example, much of the work on practical reference resolution has concentrated on establishing textual coreference relations for a subset of pronouns (e.g. Mitkov et al., 2002), and the most widely pursued aspect of idiom processing has been the automatic extraction of multi-word expressions (of which idioms are a subtype) from corpora (e.g. Baldwin and Villavicencio, 2002). Of course, some contributions in both of these subfields have ventured much wider;[1] however, we have found few practical approaches that explore the interaction of idiomaticity and reference resolution and its implications for NLP.

One might ask, why treat these phenomena together? Perhaps the best reason is to highlight the indispensability for real progress in NLP of semantic analysis that goes beyond what the most researchers are currently pursuing in practical system building. Another reason to integrate the study of reference and idioms is to address the difficulties that automatic text analyzers will encounter in detecting and processing idioms when some of their components are elided. Ellipsis, a means of expressing reference, thus, becomes an important component of this study. The approach suggested here should, we believe, alleviate some of the inherent difficulties of these complex tasks. Note that similar kinds of problems are discussed in Pulman (1993), which suggests the need for "contextual reasoning" applied to idioms, which is "the process of taking the information that can be derived linguistically from a sentence and fleshing it out with information supplied by the local context or general background knowledge" (Pulman, 1993, p. 251).

The proposed analysis delineates several categories of idioms according to their reference needs and shows how the encoding of idioms in a semantically oriented lexicon can support both basic semantic analysis and reference resolution. Although the analysis is theory- and system-neutral, the exposition follows a specific, implemented theory of natural language processing. This theory, called Ontological Semantics (Nirenburg and Raskin, 2004), colors our understanding of the nature of meaning-oriented NLP, including our treatment of reference and idioms.

Ontological Semantics seeks to achieve full semantic and pragmatic analysis of texts such that interpreted structures, rather than textual strings, serve as the input to automatic reasoners. Ontological Semantics relies on knowledge obtained through many layers of processing: preprocessing followed by morphological, syntactic, semantic and discourse analysis. The static knowledge resources, which are interconnected and all use the same metalanguage of description, are a lexicon and onomasticon for each language processed, a language-independent ontology (a knowledge base of concept types), and a language-independent fact repository (a knowledge base of concept instances). Static resources are compiled manually, using sophisticated editing environments, to ensure high quality, though we are experimenting with machine learning to speed the acquisition process. Text analysis involves the automatic

---

[1] See, for example, the contributions to recent workshops (e.g., ACL 2004 "Reference Resolution and its Applications" and "Multi-word Expression: Integrating Processing"; EACL 2006 "Multi-word Expressions in a Multilingual Context") and Stanford's Multi-Word Expression Project (http://mwe.stanford.edu/).

evaluation of semantic preferences recorded in the lexicon and ontology, as well as preferences based on stochastically trained measures of semantic distance among ontological concepts.

Within this semantically-oriented, knowledge-based environment we define reference resolution rather differently than in most NLP applications, where resolving reference is understood as linking coreferring text strings. In fact, our conceptualization of reference resolution strongly influences how we approach resolving reference in idioms and therefore must be clarified from the outset.

2   What is Reference Resolution?

We define reference resolution as the anchoring of referring expressions in the episodic memory of an intelligent text processing agent. This knowledge base of stored memories, called the fact repository, differs from the ontology in that it contains indexed *instances* of ontological concepts and their property-based interconnections. Anchoring entities in the fact repository is the culmination of semantic analysis and reference resolution.

When presented with a new text, the system must first **semantically analyze every sentence**, creating an unambiguous text meaning representation (TMR); reference is then resolved for the correct meaning of each string. The TMR contains the crucial clues for **determining which entities are referring expressions**: numbered instances of ontological concepts are referring expressions whereas properties, literal property fillers, and so on, are not. As an example, consider the following context which, although contrived, illustrates many relevant phenomena at one go.

(1)   At 4:48 it became clear that the programmers couldn't finish debugging the system before the 5:00 deadline. **All hell broke loose, the boss was fit to be tied — almost strangled his project manager!**

Let us concentrate on the second sentence. In the tables below, each string or idiomatic group of strings from that sentence (top row) is associated with its corresponding semantic structure (bottom row). The concept instances set in italics must be resolved. The important thing to notice is that the system must orient around semantic structures rather than strings in order to create the correct inventory of referring expressions.

all hell	broke loose	the boss	was	fit	to be	tied		almost	strangled	his project manager
CHAOS-1	*MANAGER-1*					ANGER (RANGE 1)	*HUMAN-1*	(MODALITY-2 (TYPE EPISTEMIC) (VALUE .9) (SCOPE STRANGLE-1))	*STRANGLE-1*	*ASSISTANT-1*

Highlights of the analysis are as follows:

- Whereas *all hell* and *broke loose* could individually be referring expressions in some other context, when the are used in this idiom they together represent a single meaning, CHAOS, this instance of which is called CHAOS-1 — the first instance of the concept CHAOS encountered while processing the given text or corpus. This event, like all instances of OBJECTs and EVENTs in TMRs, requires reference resolution: it must be determined whether this is a new event to be added to the fact repository or a reference to an event that is already recorded there. In this case, it is a new event, since the algorithm used to detect event coreference requires either (a) that there be an ample overlap of properties associated with a candidate fact repository "anchor" or (b) that the new event be referred to using a definite description (e.g., *the strike*), with the definite description triggering the search for a coreferent in the context or fact repository.

- Whereas *the boss* and *his project manager* can either be descriptors (as in *This man is a boss and that man is a project manager*) or referring expressions, here they are referring expressions and must be resolved.

- Whereas *fit* and *tied* can be referring expressions in isolation, in this idiom they are not referring expressions, nor is the idiom on the whole a referring expression: it indicates the highest value of the property ANGER.

- Although the second half of the sentence has no overt subject, *he* is the understood subject. The reference resolver must detect this missing entity and create a coreference link between it and MANAGER-1.

- *Almost* is never a referring expression: it indicates a value of less than 1 for epistemic modality scoping over the given event (here, STRANGLE-1). However, some other adverbs are referring expressions (e.g., *here, yesterday*) and must be resolved.

- STRANGLE-1, like all EVENTs, must undergo reference resolution.

Once all referring expressions have been detected, the system must **resolve them against the fact repository**. There are several possible scenarios: (a) the entity has a textual antecedent, in which case the new entity is linked to the same fact repository anchor as that antecedent; (b) the entity does not have a textual antecedent but is already a known entity (like *the earth* or *Plato*) and is linked to the existing anchor in the fact repository; (c) the entity is determined to be new and a new anchor is established for it in the fact repository. This, in a nutshell, is how reference is resolved in our semantic analysis environment, OntoSem.

Our reference resolver for English is implemented and covers all the eventualities posed by this sentence. It has not yet undergone formal evaluation. We will now describe how idioms are encoded to support this process.

The examples used for illustration are not from English, they are from Russian, a language that is not currently supported in OntoSem. The reason for using Russian examples even though the implemented system does not yet cover Russian is that Russian presents a superset of challenges for reference resolution — namely, a much wider use of ellipsis, or the null referring expression; therefore, showing that the scope of phenomena presented by Russian can be handled *a fortiori* shows that the same phenomena can be handled in English. Indeed, the OntoSem environment supports multilingual text processing, using a language-independent ontology and fact repository, and using the same types of lexicon entries regardless of the language processed (see McShane et al., 2005).

3 Encoding Idioms to Support their Full Analysis

A cornerstone of theoretical, descriptive, computational and psycholinguistc work on idioms is the attempt to understand to what extent idioms are fixed and to what extent they are flexible (see, e.g., Cacciari and Tabossi (1993), whose component articles include extensive overviews of the literature). The competing classifications can derive from both theoretical considerations, like psycholinguistic evidence, and practical considerations, like whether an NLP system attempts to analyze only those idioms that are recorded or whether it attempts to analyze new coinages as well. The scope of the current analysis is idioms that *are* recorded as well as certain types of free modifications of them. Completely new idioms will need to be processed as "unexpected input", in a similar way as the system attempts to process metaphor and metonymy. Like Stock et al. (1993) (in Cacciari and Tabossi (1993)), we integrate idioms into the lexicon as "more information about particular words" (Stock et al., 1993, p. 238) rather than treat them using special lists and idiosyncratic procedures. In the discussion below, we look at some examples of idioms that highlight noteworthy reference resolution needs and show how our all-purpose lexical encoding mechanisms and reference resolution routines cover idiomatic input as readily as compositional input. A more detailed description of how we encode idioms and other multi-word expressions, as well as many additional examples, can be found in McShane et al. (2008).

3.1 Productive Syntactic Processes in Idioms

Each of the examples below contains an idiom in the second half, and each of those idioms shows at least one productive use of ellipsis. In the examples, the elided category, [e], and its antecedent, if syntactically available, are in boldface. Grammatical information is provided sparingly for reasons of space.[2]

(2) Nado   zashchishchat' **svoix**   **sotrudnikov**   a   ne
it-is-necessary to-defend   **self's**$_{ACC.PL}$ **coworkers**$_{ACC.PL}$ and not
prinosit'   [e]   v zhertvu   .
deliver$_{INFIN}$ [e]$_{ACC}$ as sacrifice$_{ACC.SG.FEM}$ ·

You should defend **your coworkers**, not sacrifice **them**.

(3) Ja ne   xochu preduprezhdat' **ego,**   [e]   xochu
I   don't want   to-forewarn   **him**$_{ACC}$ [e]$_{1.SG}$ want$_{1.SG.}$
zastat'[e]   vrasplox   .
to-catch[e]$_{3.SG.ACC.MASC}$ unawares .

I don't want to forewarn **him**, I want to catch **him** unawares.

These examples represent configurations in which ellipsis is highly promoted in non-idiomatic *and* idiomatic contexts.[3] Example (2) shows VP conjunction with the latter of two coreferential direct objects elided. Example (3) shows subject and direct object

---

[2] Most of the Russian examples here are from Lubensky (1995), which is a bilingual learner's dictionary of Russian idioms that provides grammatical descriptions but no special treatment of ellipsis.

[3] See McShane (2005) for discussion and extensive examples of ellipsis-promoting configurations using non-idiomatic examples. Idiomatic examples of many of the phenomena have also been found but are not presented here for reasons of space.

ellipsis in an "assertion + elaboration" strategy (see McShane (2005)), in which the topic of discourse is asserted then either restated or elaborated upon subsequently.

The above idioms are idiomatic VPs that are recorded in the OntoSem lexicon in a similar way as typical verbs, with just a few special features. Let us take the example of *v grob vgonjat'* 'to kill' (literally: to drive to the grave) as an example.

```
(vgonjat'-v1
   (def "idiom: v grob vgonjat' - to kill (drive to the grave)")
   (ex "Ja v grob vgonju tebja! I'll kill you!")
   (syn-struc
      ((subject ((root $var1) (cat n)))
       (root $var0) (cat v)
       (directobject ((root $var2) (cat n)))
       (pp ((root $var3) (cat prep) (root v)
            (obj ((root $var4) (cat n) (root grob)))))))
   (sem-struc
      (KILL
          (AGENT (value ^$var1))
          (THEME (value ^$var2)))
      (^$var3 (null-sem +)) (^$var4 (null-sem +))))
```

This lexical sense is headed by the verb, *vgonjat'* *'drive'*. The syntactic zone (syn-struc) says that the verb takes a subject, direct object and prepositional phrase with no unusual syntactic constraints, meaning that the structure is open to the same sorts of variability — like different verbal tenses and aspects, free word order, syntactic transformations and ellipsis — as is typical of non-idiomatic Russian. The only special syntactic feature is that the roots of the lexical components of the prepositional phrase are explicitly listed: *v* (into) and *grob* (grave). The semantic zone (sem-struc) records the semantic interpretation: it is headed by a KILL event whose AGENT and THEME are productively analyzed as the meaning of the subject and direct object, respectively. The meanings of *v* (into) and *grob* (grave), which are — under this analysis — non-compositional, are attributed null semantics.

Two aspects of semantic interpretation require comment. First, in most contexts this idiom is not used to threaten actual killing; however, the same can be said for the lexeme *kill* used in the threat *I'll kill you!*; this aspect of interpretation is clearly extra-lexical. Second, although it is likely that a person who did not know this idiom would be able to interpret its meaning using the meanings of the component elements, most NLP systems would struggle. Once we decide to record a phrase as idiomatic to ease processing, the level of transparency of the components becomes unimportant.

Analysis of a clause that uses *vgonjat' v grob* 'kill' will generate three referring expressions that must be resolved: the AGENT of the killing, the THEME of the killing (we will not quibble here about which case role to choose for the person killed), and the act of killing. These referring expressions might be realized, for example, as HUMAN-23, HUMAN-24 and KILL-4 in a given text meaning representation. Once the system has arrived at these analyses, reference resolution proceeds as it would for any referring expressions, whether or not they were part of an idiom: textual coreferents — recorded as semantic entities in TMR — are sought and, whether or not they are found, the referring expression is anchored in the fact repository. If we look at what is special about processing the reference in idioms, then, there are only two aspects: (1) ensuring that productive syntactic processes are permitted only if applicable, and (2) ensuring that the correct inventory of referring expressions — understood as semantic structures — is generated.

Let us compare this treatment of idioms to the one proposed by Villavicencio et al. (2004). They treat the potential variability of idioms using the notion of semantic decomposition. If an idiom can be paraphrased in a syntactically parallel way, it is decomposable (*spill the beans* → *reveal a secret*), even though non-standard meanings need to be assigned to each component. The fundamental differences between their approach and ours relate to semantic encoding and reference resolution. For Villavicencio et al., the semantics of idioms is conveyed by paraphrases with other linguistic elements (*spill* → *reveal, beans* → *secret*). For us, semantics is formulated using the ontologically grounded metalanguage of OntoSem. As regards the initial syntactic parse, both approaches seem to offer the same coverage of syntactic variability, and resources could be shared with seemingly minimal work devoted to format conversion.

3.2 Essentially Frozen Idioms

We have just shown how syntactic processes — specifically, various types of ellipsis — can apply to idioms in a language, and how the lexical encoding of such idioms allows for syntactic variability. Other idioms, by contrast, are syntactically frozen. Such idioms are commonly treated as strings with spaces, but this only works if absolutely no modifiers or other entities (e.g., "ahem") can intervene. If intervening material is possible, it is preferable to encode the idiom using separate syntactic constituents. However, if one records the components individually, the analysis system must understand that diathesis transformations, ellipsis, pronominalization, etc., are not applicable. In OntoSem we label frozen syntactic constituents using immediate constituents, like NP, rather than grammatical function labels, like subject. Since transformations apply only to grammatical functions, they become automatically inapplicable if immediate constituents are used. However, since all constituents are still listed individually, intervening material and free modification are permitted in the usual way, as in *He kicked the bloody bucket!*

Of course, treating free modifications of non-compositional parts of an idiom or other multi-word expression (MWE) is not trivial, as described in some depth in Mc-Shane et al. (2008). To summarize that discussion, our basic approach to treating modifiers within MWEs is to analyze the MWE as indicated in the sem-struc, then attempt to attach the meaning of "orphan" modifiers to the meaning of the entire structure using generalized processes for meaning composition. In the case of *He kicked the bloody bucket*, the basic meaning will be rendered in the text meaning representation as (DIE-1 (EXPERIENCER HUMAN-1)). The modifier *bloody* has two senses in our lexicon, semantically described as (RELATION BLOOD) and (EMPHASIS .7). We have a rule that prefers the stylistic interpretation in the case of non-compositional idioms. So the final text meaning representation will be (DIE-1 (EXPERIENCER HUMAN-1) (EMPHASIS .7)). ((emphasis .7) indicates a high value for the property EMPHASIS on the abstract scale $\{0, 1\}$.)

Such meaning composition is not specific to multi-word expressions: our semantic analyzer carries out the same process in all cases when meaning must be recovered from an incomplete parse. The latter may be due to insufficient coverage of the syntactic parser, lexical lacunae that confound the parser, or unexpected (ungrammatical, highly elliptical, etc.) input.

Returning to our main point about how to encode essentially frozen idioms, encoding their components as separate entities provides the best of both worlds: frozen components, fixed word order, and the possibility of intervening strings that typically act as modifiers. One Russian idiom that fits this description is shown below.

(4)   Ishchi-svishchi   vetra v pole .
      Look-for-whistle-for$_{IMPER}$ wind in field .
      'You'll never find him/her/it/etc.'

```
(ishchi-svishchi'-v1
    (def "idiom: ishchi-svishchi vetra v pole
               'you will never find him/her/it/etc.'")
    (syn-struc
       ((root $var0) (cat v) (form imperative)
        (np ((root $var1) (cat np) (root vetra)))
        (pp ((root $var2) (cat prep) (root v)))
        (np ((root $var3) (cat np) (root pole)))))
    (sem-struc
       (modality
          ((type potential)
           (value 0)
           (attributed-to (sem HUMAN))
           (scope (value refsem1))))
       (refsem1
          (FIND
             (AGENT (sem human))
             (THEME (sem all))
             (time (> (find-anchor-time)))))
       (^$var1 (null-sem +))
       (^$var2 (null-sem +))
       (^$var3 (null-sem )))
    (meaning-procedure
       (seek-specification
          ((value find.modality.attributed-to)
           (resolve-1st-sing)))
       (seek-specification
          ((value find.agent) (resolve-2nd-sing)))
       (seek-specification
          ((value find.theme) (resolve-3rd)))))
```

The syntactic description should be self-evident based on the examples and description above, but the semantic structure requires commentary.

The variables $var1, $var2 and $var3 are attributed null semantics because they do not contribute to compositional meaning — that is, this idiom ("look for whistle for wind in the field") is completely semantically opaque.

The sem-struc is headed by a modality statement: *it is impossible* introduces modality of the type 'potential' with a value of 0. This modality is attributed, by default, to the speaker. It scopes over a proposition headed by FIND, and the latter is ontologically defined as taking an AGENT and a THEME case role.

The semantic representation includes four referring expressions that must be resolved: (1) the speaker, to whom the modality is attributed; (2) the FIND event itself, which will be a new anchor in the fact repository; (3) the AGENT of finding, which is the interlocutor; and (4) the THEME of finding, which must be contextually computed.

The OntoSem analyzer would resolve the reference of the instance of FIND in the usual way; this requires no further comment. What does require further comment, however, is the way in which we guide the analyzer's efforts to resolve the underspecified instances of HUMAN, HUMAN and ALL that represent the speaker, the interlocutor and the object of the FIND event, respectively. We provide this guidance in the *meaning-procedures* zone of the lexicon entry, which contains calls to procedural semantic routines that are launched at run time. For example, we need to know who the speaker is so that the modality can be attributed to the correct real-world person. This is done using the "seek-specification" meaning procedure. The first argument of this procedure is what we are seeking the specification of (i.e., to whom the modality is attributed), and the second argument is the function that will let us determine this — i.e., "resolve-1st-sing", which is, incidentally, the same routine used to seek the referent of the pronoun *I*. The latter meaning procedure includes ordered routines testing for many cases including:

- the pronoun *I* being used in a context in which another pronoun *I* (which itself should have been resolved earlier) can serve as an antecedent: **I** like chocolate ice cream and always choose it if **I** have the option.

- the pronoun *I* being used within a quotation, and that quotation being the THEME of a SPEECH-ACT of which the coreferent of *I* is the AGENT: **I/Mary** said, "But **I** don't *want* strawberry ice cream!"

- the pronoun *I* being used outside of a quotation and the writer of the text being available in metadata: `<title>Understanding Your Finances</title>` `<author>Mary Smith</author>` ...**I** believe that the only way to understand your finances is to consult a financial advisor.

In short, using the combination of the information in the *sem-struc* and *meaning-procedures* zones we arm the analyzer with the types of the information a person would use to both understand the idiom and to resolve all implied references. (For a more detailed description of meaning procedures in OntoSem, see McShane et al. (2004).)

3.3 Subjectless Constructions

We conclude our example-based discussion with one category of phenomena in which idiom processing is actually much simpler than the processing of structurally similar compositional language since it permits preemptive disambiguation. The disambiguation in question regards subjects, which in Russian can be overt, elided or completely missing. Completely missing (uninsertable) subjects occur in the following constructions:

- In the *indefinite personal construction* a 3rd person plural verb form is used without a subject to indicate an unspecified person or people. It is used in contexts like the Russian equivalent of *They say it will rain today*.

- In the *non-agentive impersonal construction* a 3rd person singular verb is used without a subject to show that the event is non-agentive. It is used in contexts like the Russian equivalent of *He's attracted to girls like that*, whose structure-preserving paraphrase would be "[some unnamed force] attracts him to girls like that."

The difficulty in processing *productive* subjectless sentences is determining whether the verb *has* a specific subject that has been elided and must be recovered, or does *not* have a specific subject, in which case the generalized personal or non-agentive interpretation should be used. However, when it comes to *idioms* that employ these constructions, the syntax can be encoded to explicitly block a subject, and the semantics can explicitly indicate the interpretation added by the missing subject.

An idiom that employs the indefinite personal construction is shown in (5), along with the lexical sense of *bit'* 'hit' that records it.

(5) Lezhachego   ne b'jut   . [L-45]
     Lying-down-person$_{ACC.SG.MASC.}$ not beat$_{3.PL.PRES.}$.

     You don't/shouldn't kick a man/person/guy when he's down.

```
(bit'-v10
  (def "phrasal: Lezhachego ne b'jut - you shouldn't do
       something bad to someone who is in a bad position already")
  (ex "You don't/shouldn't kick a guy when he's down")

(syn-struc
  ((np ((root $var1) (cat n) (root lezhachij)
        (case acc) (gender masc) (number sing)))
   (verb-neg ((root $var2) (cat verb-neg)))
   (root $var0) (cat v) (tense present) (person third) (number pl))))

(sem-struc
  (modality ,                      ; ``should''
      (type obligative)
      (scope (value refsem1))
      (value 1)
      (attributed-to *speaker*))
   (refsem1
      (modality                    ; ``not''
         (type epistemic)
         (scope (value refsem2))
         (value 0)
         (attributed-to *speaker*)))
   (refsem2
      (ABUSE
         (AGENT (value refsem3))
```

```
                  (THEME (value refsem4))))
      (refsem3
        (set
           (member-type human)
           (cardinality 1)
           (complete yes)))
      (refsem4 (HUMAN (EXPERIENCER-OF MISFORTUNE)))
      (^$var1 (null-sem +)) (^$var2 (null-sem +))
    (output-syntax (cl)))
```

The syn-struc should be clear based on previous examples; the only new element is *verb-neg*, which indicates a negating particle.

The sem-struc looks more complex than it actually is because many of the slot fillers require reified structures, each of which must be pointed to using numbered variables called refsems.The sem-struc is headed by obligative modality, which scopes over an epistemic modality, which scopes over an ABUSE event. The obligative modality has the value 1 (absolute obligation), whereas the epistemic modality has the value 0 (negation). Put plainly, "it is necessary not to abuse". The AGENT of the ABUSE event is the set of all people, described just as we describe the word *everyone*. The THEME of the ABUSE event is a HUMAN who is the EXPERIENCER-OF a MISFOR-TUNE. One might ask, why not record this idiom as a fully fixed entity with white spaces in between, rather than as a multi-part syntactic structure? For the same reason as discussed earlier: there is an outside chance of modification, so the component elements must be kept separate.

Example (6) shows an idiomatic example of the second type of obligatorily subjectless sentence: the non-agentive impersonal construction.

(6) Kakim   vetrom   vas
     what*INSTR.SG.MASC.* wind*INSTR.SG.MASC.* you*ACC.PL/POLITE*
     zaneslo   sjuda   ?
     brought*3.SG.NEUT.PFV* here*DIRECTIONAL* ?
     What brings you here?/What are you doing here?

This idiom will be recorded under the headword *zanesti* 'bring'. The core meaning of the idiom — COME — heads the sem-struc. There are two variables in this multi-word expression: the direct object, mapped to the AGENT of COME, and the spatial adverbial, mapped to the DESTINATION of COME. These are productively analyzed at run-time. The meaning of 'what wind' is, of course, attributed null semantics.

To summarize this section: recording obligatorily subjectless idioms not only provides for their semantic interpretation, it also removes ambiguity in analysis, since the "elided subject" reading is explicitly blocked.

4 Final Thoughts

This paper has presented an analysis of phenomena that extends past what any given system currently uses or requires. However, the utility of this analysis reaches well beyond the traditional goals of descriptive and theoretical linguistics. Ideally, system building in NLP should centrally involve the objective of incrementally overcoming successively more difficult challenges and thus lead to more sophisticated systems in the future. Looking forward to the next stage can help us to develop methodological, architectural and knowledge infrastructures to facilitate progress toward future goals. The OntoSem environment does not currently work on Russian, though it has been applied, at least partially, to several languages apart from English in the past — including such different languages as Turkish, Spanish, Korean and Georgian. The reason for exploring the idiom-reference connection in Russian was to judge how well our approach, which is implemented for and works well in English, holds up cross-linguistically. Having worked the examples presented in this paper and many others, we are convinced that when the time comes, a Russian OntoSem will be configurable without the need to expand the theory and methodology that support our treatment of idioms, ellipsis and reference overall.

A reasonable question would be, why not evaluate the approach on English, since an English system already exists? The reason is purely practical: it is far more difficult and expensive to run evaluations of knowledge-based systems that treat complex phenomena than it is to run evaluations of systems that treat less complex phenomena. That being said, we are just completing a new version of our DEKADE knowledge acquisition and evaluation environment which will make it much easier than before to evaluate the results of text analysis. We expect regular evaluations to become part of our development work in the near future.

References

Baldwin, T. and A. Villavicencio (2002). A case study on verb-particles. In *Proceedings of the Sixth Conference on Computational Natural Language Learning (CoNLL 2002)*, pp. 98–104.

Cacciari, C. and P. Tabossi (1993). *Idioms: Processing, Structure and Interpretation*. Lawrence Erlbaum and Associates, Inc.

Lubensky, S. (1995). *Russian-English Dictionary of Idioms*. Random House.

McShane, M. (2005). *A Theory of Ellipsis*. Oxford University Press.

McShane, M., S. Beale, and S. Nirenburg (2004). Some meaning procedures of Ontological Semantics. In *Proceedings of LREC-2004*.

McShane, M., S. Nirenburg, and S. Beale (2005). An NLP lexicon as a largely language independent resource. *Machine Translation 19*(2), 139–173.

McShane, M., S. Nirenburg, and S. Beale (2008). Achieving adequacy of description of multiword entities in semantically-oriented computational lexicons. Submitted.

Mitkov, R., R. Evans, and C. Orasan (2002). A new, fully automatic version of mitkov's knowledge-poor pronoun resolution method. In *Proceedings of CICLing-2000*.

Nirenburg, S. and V. Raskin (2004). *Ontological Semantics*. MIT Press.

Pulman, S. (1993). The recognition and interpretation of idioms. In C. Cacciari and P. Tabossi (Eds.), *Idioms: Processing, Structure and Interpretation*, pp. 249–270. Lawrence Erlbaum and Associates, Inc.

Stock, O., J. Slack, and A. Ortony (1993). Building castles in the air: Some computational and theoretical issues in idiom comprehension. In C. Cacciari (Ed.), *Idioms: Processing, Structure and Interpretation*, pp. 229–248. Lawrence Erlbaum and Associates, Inc.

Villavicencio, A., A. Copestake, B. Waldron, and F. Lambeau (2004). The lexical encoding of MWEs. In *Proceedings of the ACL 2004 Workshop on Multiword Expressions: Integrating processing*.

Resolving Paraphrases to Support Modeling Language Perception in an Intelligent Agent

Sergei Nirenburg
Marjorie McShane
Stephen Beale
Universtity of Maryland Baltimore County (USA)
email: sergei@umbc.edu

Abstract

When interacting with humans, intelligent agents must be able not only to understand natural language inputs but also to remember them and link their content with the contents of their memory of event and object instances. As inputs can come in a variety of forms, linking to memory can be successful only when paraphrasing relations are established between the meaning of new input and the content of the agent's memory. This paper discusses a variety of types of paraphrases relevant to this task and describes the way we implement this capability in a virtual patient application.

1   Overview of and Rationale for Studying Paraphrase

Paraphrase, under any of its many definitions, is ubiquitous in language use. It could be likened to reference, both in function and in the complexity of its detection and resolution. Indeed, there are many ways to express a given idea in language: one can use a canonical word/phrase (*dog*), a synonymous terse locution (*mutt, pooch, canine, man's best friend*), or an explanatory description that can be of any length and include one or more specific salient features (*a pet that barks*; *one of the two most common four-legged domesticated mammals in the USA that is not a cat*). Although these locutions are not semantically identical, they are *functionally* equivalent in many contexts, meaning that they can permit a person or intelligent agent to carry out the same types of reasoning.

No matter which of the above locutions is used to express the idea of *dog*, a person or an artificial intelligent agent should be able resolve it to the concept DOG in his/its world model. Such resolution, or "anchoring", permits other knowledge about the entity to be leveraged for reasoning: for example, the sentence *Our pooch has a long tail* should be construed as perfectly normal, whereas *Our pooch wrote a grocery list* should be understood as impossible in its direct sense since dogs cannot be agents of writing. Such incongruence should, in turn, suggest either a non-real world or the use of *pooch* as a nickname for some person or intelligent agent, like an automatic grocery list writing system.

1.1   Work by Others

Paraphrase is a difficult problem: at its deepest, it centrally involves semantics, which, due to its inherent complexity, can be addressed only in limited ways in current NLP work. As a result, most contributions devoted to paraphrase can be described as syntactic or "light semantic." In some contributions, processing semantics is constrained to finding synonyms, hyponyms, etc., in a manually constructed word net, like Word-Net or any of its progeny. Some others do not rely on a manually constructed knowledge resource but, rather, aim to determine distributional clustering of similar words in corpora (see, e.g. Pereira et al. (1993) or Lin (2001)). A few approaches to dealing with paraphrase actually go beyond the detection and use of synonyms. For example, Lapata (2001) seeks to interpret the meanings of contextually elastic adjectives (such as *fast*, which means different things in *fast highway* and *fast eater*) by semi-automatically constructing paraphrases for phrases that include such adjectives. These paraphrases use the original noun and the adjective (or any of its synonyms, taken from a hand-constructed list) in its adverbial form and add a corpus-derived candidate verb intended to explain the meaning of the adjective. Results are evaluated by human judgments of whether a paraphrase (e.g., *highway travel quickly*) is appropriate as an explanation of the meaning of *fast* in *fast highway*.

Ibrahim et al. (2003) pursue the more immediate goal of supporting a question-answering system. Creating paraphrases for questions helps to expand the queries to the textual resources that are mined for answers. In an early version of this system, such paraphrase rules — which included a combination of lexical and syntactic transformations — were created by hand (Katz and Levin, 1988). The new approach follows the methodology of Lin and Pantel (2001) for dynamically determining paraphrases in a corpus by measuring the similarity of paths between nodes in syntactic dependency trees. This method was applied to pairs of sentences from different English translations of the same text. (The idea of using a monolingual "sentence-aligned" corpus is due to Barzilay and McKeown (2001).) Ibrahim et al. (2003) then suggest a set of heuristics for the subsentential-level matching of nouns and pronouns which leads to the specification of paraphrases in terms of rules such as *X became a state in Y ↔ X was admitted to the Union in Y*. The reported precision of the process is about 41%, while the upper bound is given at about 65%.[1] Ibrahim et al. state that "question answering should be performed at the level of 'key relations' in addition to keywords." We believe that it is even better to use key *word senses* rather than key *words,* and to include key relations of a semantic and pragmatic nature — though syntactic information should be retained as a valuable source of heuristics for specifying semantic relations. We believe that we have developed enabling technologies and resources that allow us, at this time, to process paraphrase by relying on meaning representations rather than just syntactic dependencies and text-level relations.

One system that has an application area similar to ours is the one developed by Boonthum (2004). Boonthum is developing an automatic tutoring application that will be enhanced by paraphrase recognition. To process paraphrase, she automatically converts natural language sentences into Conceptual Graphs (Sowa, 1983) and compares the graphs of two candidate paraphrases using various metrics. This system, unlike ours, works at the level of strings (not concepts), does not automatically carry out disambiguation, and cannot handle complex sentences or long spans of text.

Since paraphrase recognition, when viewed broadly, is a very challenging task, some developers choose to focus on a narrow application area. One such system, reported in Brun and Hagège (2003), detects paraphrases in texts about toxic products. Developers hand create rules using lexical and structural information, and system output is logical structures like PHYS_FORM(acetone,liquid), which means that the physical form of acetone is liquid. The approach taken in this work seems very appropriate for this narrow domain of interest.

1.2 Our research methodology

The research methodology we adopt has the following features, which will serve to orient it in the landscape of work by others. This methodology:

- addresses paraphrase within an application;

- takes into account the needs of question answering and — more broadly speaking — dialog processing;

- integrates paraphrasing due to different types of agent perception: the perception of language and the perception of non-linguistic inputs, like interoception (sensitivity to stimuli originating in the body, e.g., symptoms of a disease);

- uses an agent's memories as both the source of paraphrase detection and as the target to which new memories are linked; and

---

[1]We believe that the low upper bound is due to the way the problem was framed. In cases where the semantic differences among candidate paraphrases are important (not "benign"), the inter-respondent agreement, we believe, will be higher.

- has provisions for including conceptual paraphrases, which are different ways of describing the same object or event that must be interpreted using the ontological knowledge available to specific agents.

The initial experimentation that we are reporting covers a relatively narrow domain but we hypothesize that the same methodology can be used in other domains, with certain modifications related to ontological and lexical coverage.

1.3   Maryland Virtual Patient (MVP)

The application that drives our current research is Maryland Virtual Patient (MVP), which is an agent-oriented simulation and tutoring system. In MVP, a human user plays the role of a physician in training who must diagnose and treat open-ended simulations of patients, with or without the help of a virtual mentor agent (e.g. McShane et al., 2007). The virtual patient is, itself, a "double" agent, comprised of: (a) a physiological agent that lives over time and responds in realistic ways to disease progression and interventions, and (b) a cognitive agent that experiences symptoms, decides when to consult a physician, makes decisions about its lifestyle, treatment options, etc., and communicates with a human user using natural language. The system currently covers six diseases of the esophagus, so many of our examples will come from this subdomain of medicine.

As should be clear even from this brief overview, MVP is a reasoning-intensive application. Both physiological simulation and NLP are supported by hand-crafted, ontologically grounded knowledge that includes:

1. a general purpose ontology with broad and deep coverage of medical concepts, including ontological scripts describing disease progression and treatment, the plans and goals of patients and physicians, clinical best practices, medical interviews and dialog in general

2. a lexicon whose entries include a syntactic structure, a semantic structure (linked to the ontology), and calls to procedural semantic routines (e.g., to provide for the reference resolution of pronouns and other deictics)

3. a fact repository, which is a memory of assertions, as contrasted with the ontology, which covers knowledge of types.

All knowledge in the MVP environment is recorded using the metalanguage of description of Ontological Semantics (Nirenburg and Raskin, 2004). The MVP application will serve as a concrete example for the discussion of paraphrase processing in applications that include intelligent agents. However, the analysis is readily generalizable and could be applied to any system that would benefit from paraphrase understanding.

This paper will not discuss all types of paraphrase and how OntoSem (the implementation of the theory of Ontological Semantics) handles them, even though one of the core contributions of OntoSem is the robust handling of lexical and syntactic paraphrase by automatically deriving identical meaning representations for inputs that contain such paraphrases (for discussion see Nirenburg and Raskin, 2004, Chapter 8). Here we focus on just a few of the more "compositional-semantic" types of paraphrase and our theoretical and implementation-oriented solutions to treating them.

2   Paraphrase-Oriented Eventualities

Each agent in MVP is supplied with its own ontology, lexicon and fact repository (i.e., memory), which can be enriched on the fly in various ways based on the agent's activities — be they linguistic, interoceptive, or other. In order for the language-endowed agents (on whom we focus here) to operate intelligently — as when answering questions posed by the human user or learning new facts he presents to them — they must be able to **interpret** language input, **remember** the content of that input, and attempt to **match/link** that content with memories already stored in their fact repository. Linking new information to old memories is a standing goal of all intelligent agents, and in MVP it is triggered automatically for each new input. A core capability enabling such linking is the recognition and resolution of paraphrase.

We will show how various types of paraphrase are handled as part of agent memory management in the OntoSem environment. More specifically, we focus on *creating* and *linking* new knowledge from linguistic input, not on the use of this knowledge for reasoning. Memory management (e.g., modeling forgetting and generalizing) is also a key enabling technology, but one whose description lies outside of the scope of this paper.

Having generated a meaning representation (MR) for a textual input, the intelligent agent must consider the following eventualities in deciding on how to remember the content of this input. The eventualities in boldface (numbers 5, 6 and 7) are those that we will be discussing in some detail below.

1. The newly input MR is identical to a stored memory

2. The newly input MR is identical to a stored memory except for metadata values: the identity of the speaker, the time stamp, etc. This can be viewed as type coreference. For example, in the MVP environment, if the agent coughs every day, is every cough a new instance or is it better remembered as a generalized action with a given periodicity? The answer here depends in a large part on the event generalization capabilities of an agent (a component of its memory management capabilities): indeed, even in real life one cannot be immune from the failure to realize that a certain sequence of events is actually better viewed as a single periodic event.

3. The newly input MR contains a subset or a superset of properties of a stored memory. For example, the new input can describe only the location of a symptom but not its severity, whereas remembered instances of this same symptom may overtly list its severity and various other properties. Note that the information about which properties are applicable to a particular concept is stored in the ontology; the memory (fact repository) contains information about those of the properties that were overtly perceived by the agent.

4. The new input is similar to a stored memory but one or more properties has a different value. For example, an input could specify one level of symptom severity while stored instances of the symptom may specify different values of this property.

5. **The newly input MR (or a component of it) is related to a stored memory via ontological subsumption, meronymy or location.**

6. **The newly input MR is related to a stored memory as the latter's precondition or effect.**

7. **The newly input MR is related to a stored memory via "ontological paraphrase."**

8. The new input is not related to any stored memory because different concepts are used, there are conflicting property values, etc. For example, a symptom experienced by somebody other than the given agent may be known to the agent, but the agent will certainly not interpret it as coreferential with knowledge about its own symptoms.

For case 1, the new information is interpreted as confirmation of the existing memory, it is not stored as a separate memory. For case 2, the choice of storing instances individually or grouping them into a recurring event is determined by the agent's memory management activities. For cases 3-8 reasoning must be carried out to determine if there is a match or not. In our current implementation, if a stored MR unifies with the newly input MR, the two MRs are judged to be paraphrases. With respect to case 4, this is a simplification because significant differences in values of properties in the two MRs under comparison should be used as heuristics voting against declaring the two MRs paraphrases. However, this level of analysis requires the establishment of a scale of relevancy on all the properties of a given concept, a task that we defer to future system releases. For case 8, the new information should be stored as a new memory. Let us consider eventualities 5-7 in more detail.

2.1 The newly input MR (or a component of it) is related to a stored memory via ontological subsumption, meronymy or location

There is much variability in the use of language, which can result from lack of knowledge of more precise terminology or from a person's understanding that certain kinds of underspecificity are entirely acceptable. For example, one can say *Let's eat at your place* rather than specifying whether we mean a house, a condominium or a studio apartment; and one can say *Does your arm hurt?* rather than asking *Does the broken bone in your arm hurt* or, even more specifically, *Does your ulna hurt?*

When attempting to match new textual input with a stored memory, the question is, how close do the compared MRs have to be in order to be considered a match? An important consideration when making this judgment is the application. In the dialog application we are developing, the notion of **sincerity conditions** plays an important role. That is, the VP expects the physician to ask it questions that it can answer; therefore, it should try hard — and search broadly, if necessary — to come up with the closest memories that will permit it to generate a response. In McShane et al. (2008) we suggest an algorithm that determines when two closely related MRs are close enough to be considered identical. The algorithm involves following three types of ontological links — subsumption, meronymy and location; if a match is found within the "lower" (i.e., domain-specific) ontology, then the related elements are considered a paraphrase. Let us show how this paraphrase processing works using a concrete example.

The physician asks the virtual patient, *Do you have any discomfort in your esophagus?* The MR for that question is as follows.

```
(REQUEST-INFO-1
    (THEME MODALITY-1.VALUE))
(MODALITY-1
    (TYPE EPISTEMIC)
    (SCOPE DISCOMFORT-1))
(DISCOMFORT-1
    (EXPERIENCER HUMAN-1)
    (LOCATION ESOPHAGUS-1))
(ESOPHAGUS-1
    (PART-OF-OBJECT HUMAN-1))
```

The interrogative mood gives rise to the instance of request-info, whose theme is the value of epistemic modality that scopes over the proposition headed by DISCOMFORT-1. (If the event actually happened, then the value of epistemic modality is 1; if it did not happen, then the value is 0).

The event DISCOMFORT is experienced by HUMAN-1, which will be linked to a specific human (the interlocutor) via reference resolution (reference resolution is carried out on every referring expression in OntoSem). The LOCATION of the DISCOMFORT is the ESOPHAGUS of that HUMAN.

If we extract the core meaning of this question, abstracting away from the interrogative elements, we have:

```
(DISCOMFORT-1
    (EXPERIENCER HUMAN-1)
    (LOCATION ESOPHAGUS-1))
(ESOPHAGUS-1
    (PART-OF-OBJECT HUMAN-1))
```

Let us assume that the patient has stored memories about its discomfort in a different way, as an undifferentiated symptom in its chest:

```
(SYMPTOM-1
    (EXPERIENCER HUMAN-1)
    (LOCATION CHEST-1))
(CHEST-1
    (PART-OF-OBJECT HUMAN-1))
```

Note that the patient stores memories of interoception directly, translating the output of its physiological agent into a memory that is in keeping with its own ontology. This translation is necessary because the agent's own ontology is a "lay" ontology — one lacking highly specified medical subtrees. The ontology available to the physiological agent, by contrast, is an "expert" ontology that is rich enough in medical knowledge to support disease simulation and treatment (see McShane et al., 2008).

The MR components in boldface are the ones that must be matched. DISCOMFORT is a child of SYMPTOM, forming a subsumption link of only one jump. ESOPHAGUS has a LOCATION of CHEST, and they are both PART-OF-OBJECT the human in question. Therefore, according to our matching algorithm — in conjunction with the fact that the VP assumes sincerity conditions in its conversations with the physician — the VP's memory of this event sufficiently matches the physician's question and the VP can respond affirmatively to the question: i.e., the VP has a memory of the symptom the physician is asking about.

In discussing the next two paraphrase-oriented phenomena we will shift to a different application area not because the medical domain lacks examples, but because understanding them would require too much background knowledge. The application area we will posit is an agent that is a personal companion, with the agent's job being to uphold its end of an open-ended conversation.

2.2   The newly input MR is related to a stored memory as the latter's precondition or effect

Consider the following dialog snippet between an elderly woman, Anne, and an intelligent agent that serves as her "conversational companion":

> Anne: You know, my husband and I went to Rome for our honeymoon.
> Agent: Is that so?
> Anne: Yes. We ate such great artichokes in Trastevere!

As the agent participates in this conversation, it creates and stores memories of the meaning of Anne's utterances. In analyzing Anne's final utterance, the agent should create a link between Anne and her husband being in Trastevere, and Anne and her husband traveling to Rome.

OntoSem produces the following core meaning representation for the statement about traveling to Rome:

```
(TRAVEL-EVENT-1
    (AGENT SET-1)
    (DESTINATION ROME)
    (TIME (< find-anchor-time)))
(SET-1
    (MEMBERS HUMAN-1 HUMAN-2))
```

Some details are omitted in the above structure, as they are not relevant to our exposition here. Find-anchor-time is a meaning procedure that triggers a search in the metadata or in the text itself for the time of the event, which is before the time of speech. The above meaning representation will be stored by the agent in its memory.

The meaning representation (again, omitting some details) for the statement about eating in Trastevere will be:

```
(INGEST
    (AGENT SET-1) ; coreferential with SET-1 above
    (THEME ARTICHOKE-1)
    (LOCATION TRASTEVERE)
```

(TIME (< find-anchor-time)))
(MODALITY-1
  (TYPE EVALUATIVE)
  (SCOPE ARTICHOKE-1)
  (VALUE 1)
  (ATTRIBUTED-TO HUMAN-1))

At this point the agent must check whether the above MR should be linked in the agent's memory to the memory of the travel event processed earlier. In this case, a match is found — that is, the agent can establish that a precondition of the second event is among the effects of the first one. Specifically, the linking occurs because:

1. the agent's ontology contains the description of a complex event (a script) TRAVEL-EVENT, where it is listed that an *effect* of traveling to X is being in X;

2. the agent's ontology contains the knowledge that a *precondition* for an INGEST event taking place at LOCATION Y with AGENT X is that X is at LOCATION Y;

3. the agent's fact repository contains the knowledge that Trastevere is a neighborhood in Rome.

2.3 The newly input MR is related to a stored memory via ontological paraphrase

The third source of paraphrase we will discuss is what we call ontological paraphrase. This occurs when more than one metalanguage representation means the same thing. In an environment with only artificial agents, where communication can be carried out without resorting to natural language, such paraphrase should be excluded to the extent possible. However, in environments (like MVP) where meaning representations can be generated from natural language, this eventuality is more difficult to avoid. This is because a) basic meaning representations are produced on the basis of lexicon entries for words and phrases appearing in the sentence; and b) a word or phrase can be used in a particular sentence to render a narrower or broader meaning than it has in general. Now, in creating basic meaning representations, OntoSem uses concepts that are listed in the lexicon entries for the appropriate senses of the input words (in this paper we do not describe OntoSem's approach to word sense disambiguation and determination of semantic dependencies), and these concepts cannot reflect broadening or narrowing usages of the word. A good example of this phenomenon is the following: One can say (a) *go to London by plane* or (b) *fly to London*, and these inputs will generate different MRs:

(a) (MOTION-EVENT-7 (DESTINATION London) (INSTRUMENT AIRPLANE))
(b) (AERIAL-MOTION-EVENT-19 (DESTINATION London)).

This is because the semantics of the appropriate sense of *go* is explained using the concept MOTION-EVENT, while the semantics of the appropriate sense of *fly* uses AERIAL-MOTION-EVENT. In the former structure, the head event instance is more general than in the latter. In fact, the corresponding ontological concepts stand in a

direct subsumption relation. If one chooses to use a concept that is higher in the ontological hierarchy, one may have to add further overt constraints to the meaning representation (like the one about the INSTRUMENT of the MOTION-EVENT above). If one
chooses the lower-level, narrower ontological concept to start with, such constraints
may be inherent in its definition (as is the case with AERIAL-MOTION-EVENT). This
preference is the inverse of the lexical choice in text generation off of text meaning
representations (for details see Nirenburg and Nirenburg, 1988).

OntoSem can yield either of the above basic text meaning representations. In many
applications — for example, in interlingua-based machine translation — this would
be quite benign. However, it is possible to create extended meaning representations
such that the above variability is eliminated. The method we use for this purpose relies
on the dynamic tightening or relaxation of selectional restrictions and is described in
detail in Mahesh et al. (1997). Note that different paraphrases will still be produced
for inputs that, while referring to the same event instance, describe it with a different
degree of vagueness or underspecificity (see Section 2.1 above).

The fact that the two meaning representations above are paraphrases of one another can be automatically detected using a fairly simple heuristic: the ontological
description of AERIAL-MOTION-EVENT includes the following property-value pairs:

```
AERIAL-MOTION-EVENT
    IS-A MOTION-EVENT
    INSTRUMENT AIRPLANE HELICOPTER BALLOON
```

Since the head of one of the MRs is an ancestor of the other, and the property-value
pairs in the ancestor-based MR unify with the ontological definition of the descendant
(the head of the other MR), these two structures are deemed to be paraphrases.

As we see from this example, world knowledge stored in the ontology is leveraged
to carry out the reasoning needed to detect that the abovementioned formal structures
are paraphrases. Such situations are somewhat similar to "bridging references" in the
literature devoted to reference resolution (e.g. Poesio et al., 2004) because a knowledge bridge is needed to aid in the reference resolution of the entity.

A common source of this type of paraphrase derives from decisions about how to
build the ontology. Ontology building is a complex task with "the lesser of the evils"
decisions to be made at every turn. Two ontologies can be equally valid and yet look
quite different. One of the most difficult aspects of ontology building is deciding when
a new concept is needed. Let us continue with the example of taking a trip. A small
excerpt from the MOTION-EVENT subtree of our ontology is as follows:

```
MOTION-EVENT
    AERIAL-MOTION
    LIQUID-CONTACT-MOTION
    SURFACE-CONTACT-MOTION
    TRAVEL-EVENT

    . . .
```

As we can see, rather than having a single MOTION-EVENT lexically supplemented
by property-value pairs that distinguish between types of motion, we have various

types of motion being represented as different ontological concepts. This means that when different kinds of motion are referred to — even if they describe the same real-world event — they will instantiate different concepts in MR and we will be faced with the problem of matching at the level of MR. Whereas this matching problem can be seen as a vote for constraining the number of ontological concepts, there are practical reasons for not wanting to overdo this: for example, MRs are much harder to read and evaluate when lexical senses are described using property-value pairs rather than simply pointing to an iconic ontological concept that holds the description. Of course, the use of iconic concepts results in lower expressive power of an ontology, which affects the reasoning capabilities of agents in memory management, goal- and plan-based reasoning and the more complex cases of language understanding.

2.4 Theoretical Notes

This work derives from the theoretical assumption that in order for agents to show truly intelligent behavior their memory must be well managed. What is actually stored as a memory, however, is a complex question. For example, if someone were to describe a trip to New York and never referred to it as "trip to NY" but rather said that he "was in NY" (and the interlocutor knows that he doesn't live there), the interlocutor might still save the memory as

(TRAVEL-EVENT-1
  (AGENT HUMAN-1)
  (DESTINATION New York)).

So the "grain size" of memories is a compelling and complex problem. However, we must deflect a deep study of the question *What is memory*, agreeing with Minsky (2006) that lingering over definitions that might never be truly precise does not support practical progress.

Describing this work in broad terms risks conveying the impression that it is trivial, either conceptually or in terms of implementation. In fact, both of these facets of the work are quite complex, involving extensive theoretical and practical decision-making at every step — one of the reasons, perhaps, why it is not being broadly pursued. The standard counterargument that resource development for such an approach is too expensive does not hold up when one considers the cost of semantically annotating corpora and then building machine learning engines to exploit such corpora. Another criticism of knowledge-based approaches is that they are too narrow in coverage. Indeed, one cannot cover broad corpora at a deep level all at once; however, the insights gained in carrying out this kind of work, and its potential to significantly enhance the current state of the art in NLP, are really quite exciting. And, of course, there are no a priori preferences for starting with breadth and striving for depth over the opposite strategy of starting with depth and striving for breadth.

One final point must be mentioned. The OntoSem environment that forms the substrate for the work described here is used for applications that are much broader than MVP. Recent applications include question-answering and information extraction. Thus, the ongoing development of the ontology, lexicon, fact repository and semantic analyzer benefits a range of application areas.

3   State of Development

We have developed a complete simulated physiological agent that covers diseases of the esophagus and is capable of realistic physiological responses to even unexpected interventions. We have developed a tool for the fast creation of large libraries of physiological agents that feature different diseases, different genetic and behavioral predispositions and different realistic disease progressions. We have implemented a cognitive agent capable of interoception, perception through language, goal- and plan-based reasoning (within the domain of doctor-patient interaction), memory management, (simulated) physical action and (real) verbal action. With respect to interoception, we have developed a simulation of how the cognitive agent (the cognitive side of the "double" agent) perceives signals (symptoms) from its physiological agent counterpart. Even though a single knowledge representation substrate is used for modeling both agents, the interoception simulation process involves paraphrase.

We have developed a set of knowledge resources covering relevant knowledge about the world (the ontology), past events remembered by the agent (the fact repository) and knowledge about language (represented, largely, in the agent's lexicon).

The operational OntoSem semantic analyzer is used as the basic tool for creating meaning representations from language inputs. The latter already reflect results of the resolution of many kinds of paraphrase as a matter of course.

Content specification for the agent's dialog turns is addressed in the implemented goal- and plan-based reasoning module of the cognitive agent. Surface generation of agent dialog turns has, at this point, been implemented in a limited fashion, on the basis of prefabricated open textual patterns linked to types of text meaning representations that are output by the content specification module. In the next release of MVP we intend to incorporate a text realizer such as YAG (McRoy et al., 2003).

Upcoming evaluations will continue to help to debug the system and the underlying knowledge; and, more importantly for the topic of this paper, data will be collected for an evaluation of the dialog component of the system.

The quality of the system's treatment of paraphrase will be judged at two levels. First, the appropriateness of the agent's dialog responses will provide a practical, application-based measure of the quality of paraphrase processing, though blame assignment for any miscues will pose a complication. Second, we will be able to directly inspect the agent's memory for traces of the resolution of paraphrase against remembered concept instances and judge the appropriateness of these results against human decisions. To facilitate this, we will provide textual glosses to meaning representations comprising the agent's memory. The above regimen is the most economical way to evaluate our approach because an important prerequisite for evaluating the performance of paraphrase resolution algorithms in our environment is the creation of the fact repository (i.e., the agent's memory), against which the comparisons and linking occur. In the proposed testing regimen, this memory will be augmented and managed as a result of the operation of the system itself, so that there will be no need for creating it just for the purposes of evaluation.

References

Barzilay, R. and K. McKeown (2001). Extracting paraphrases from a parallel corpus. In *Proceedings of the 39th Annual Meeting of the Association for Computational Linguistics (ACL-2001)*.

Boonthum, C. (2004). iSTART: Paraphrase recognition. In *Proceedings of the Student Research Workshop at ACL 2004*, pp. 31–36.

Brun, C. and C. Hagège (2003). Normalization and paraphrasing using symbolic methods. In *Proceedings of the Second International Workshop on Paraphrasing (IWP 2003)*.

Ibrahim, A., B. Katz, and J. Lin (2003). Extracting structural paraphrases from aligned monolingual corpora. In *Proceedings of the Second International Workshop on Paraphrasing (IWP 2003)*.

Katz, B. and B. Levin (1988). Exploiting lexical regularities in designing natural language systems. In *Proceedings of the 12th International Conference on Computational Linguistics (COLING-1988)*.

Lapata, M. (2001). A corpus-based account of regular polysemy: The case of context-sensitive adjectives. In *Proceedings of the Second Meeting of the North American Chapter of the Association for Computational Linguistics (NAACL-2001)*.

Lin, D. (2001). Extracting collocations from text corpora. In *Proceedings of the First Workshop on Computational Terminology*.

Lin, D. and P. Pantel (2001). DIRT - discovery of inference rules from text. In *Proceedings of the ACM SIGKDD Conference Conference on Knowledge Discovery and Data Mining*.

Mahesh, K., S. Nirenburg, and S. Beale (1997). If you have it, flaunt it: Using full ontological knowledge for word sense disambiguation. In *Proceedings of TMI-97*.

McRoy, S. W., S. Channarukul, and S. S. Ali (2003). An augmented template-based approach to text realization. *Natural Language Engineering 9*(4), 381–420.

McShane, M., S. Nirenburg, and S. Beale (2008). Two kinds of paraphrase in modeling embodied cognitive agents. In *Proceedings of the Naturally-Inspired Artificial Intelligence AAAI Fall Symposium*.

McShane, M., S. Nirenburg, S. Beale, B. Jarrell, and G. Fantry (2007). Knowledge-based modeling and simulation of diseases with highly differentiated clinical manifestations. In *Proceedings of the 11th Conference on Artificial Intelligence in Medicine (AIME 07)*.

Minsky, M. L. (2006). *The Emotion Machine*. Simon & Schuster.

Nirenburg, S. and I. Nirenburg (1988). A framework for lexical selection in natural language generation. In *Proceedings of COLING-88*.

Nirenburg, S. and V. Raskin (2004). *Ontological Semantics*. MIT Press.

Pereira, F., N. Tishby, and L. Lee (1993). Distributional clustering of English words. In *Proceedings of the 30th Annual Meeting of the Association for Computational Linguistics (ACL-1991)*.

Poesio, M., R. Mehta, A. Maroudas, and J. Hitzeman (2004). Learning to resolve bridging references. In *Proceedings of the 42nd Annual Meeting on Association for Computational Linguistics*.

Sowa, J. F. (1983). *Conceptual Structures: Information Processing in Mind and Machine*. Addison-Wesley.

Everyday Language is Highly Intensional

Allan Ramsay
University of Manchester (UK)
email: allan.ramsay@manchester.ac.uk

Debora Field
University of Sheffield (UK)
email: D.Field@sheffield.ac.uk

Abstract

There has recently been a great deal of work aimed at trying to extract information from substantial texts for tasks such as question answering. Much of this work has dealt with texts which are reasonably large, but which are known to contain reliable relevant information, e.g. FAQ lists, on-line encyclopaedias, rather than looking at huge unorganised resources such as the web. We believe, however, that even this work underestimates the complexity and subtlety of language, and hence will inevitably be restricted in what it can cope with. In particular, everyday use of language involves considerable amounts of reasoning over intensional objects (properties and propositions). In order to respond appropriately to simple-seeming questions such as *'Is going for a walk good for me?'*, for instance, you have to be able to talk about event-types, which are intrinsically intensional. We discuss the issues involved in handling such items, and shows the kind of background knowledge that is required for drawing the appropriate conclusions about them.

1   Introduction

The work reported here aims to allow users to interact with a health information system via natural language. In this context, allowing a user to make simple statements about their condition and then ask questions about what they can or should do, as in (1), seems to be a minimal requirement.

(1)   My doctor says I am allergic to eggs. Is it safe for me to eat cake?

Understanding such utterances requires the use of a highly intensional representation language, and responding to them requires a surprising amount of background knowledge. We will consider below the problems that such everyday utterances bring for formal paraphrases of natural language, and we will look at the kind of background knowledge that is required for producing the right kinds of response. In order to produce a system that carries out the required inference we need access to an inference engine for carrying out proofs in a representation language with the required expressive power. The details of the engine we use are beyond the scope of this paper. (Ramsay, 2001; Ramsay and Field, 2008). For the purposes of the current paper we will simply show the results that can be obtained by using it.

The work reported here is complementary to work on corpus-based approaches such as textual entailment: approaches that ignore the intensionality of everyday language will inevitably fail to capture important inference patterns, but on the other hand the work reported here cannot deal with large amounts of information provided as free text. Ideally, the two approaches will be combined. The aim of the current paper is to provide a reminder of the prevalence of intensionality in everyday language, and to demonstrate that modern theorem proving techniques can cope with this kind of knowledge without introducing undue processing delays.

2   Background

The general idea behind the work reported here is that users will input statements about their health, either spontaneously or in response to prompts from the system, and will ask questions about what they can and should do, and the system will provide them with appropriate guidance. The overall architecture is completely classical:

1. The user's input is translated into a meaning representation (logical form, LF) in some suitable representation language.

2. This LF contains a specification of the illocutionary force of the input (is it a statement, or a question, or a command, or … ?).

3. If the utterance is classified as a statement, its propositional content is added to the system's view of the user's beliefs, and if it is classified as a question, the system will attempt to use its background knowledge of the domain to answer it. We are not currently attempting to make the system do anything in response to a command from the user, since users do not generally issue commands in our chosen domain, but clearly if this did happen then we would want to make the system construct a plan to carry out the required action.

This part of the system's activity requires it be able to access and exploit relevant background knowledge. This is obvious in the case of questions, but in the given domain it is also important to be able to spot situations where the user's beliefs are incomplete or are in conflict with the system's beliefs, since most people's understanding about medical topics is flawed. The ability to reason about what has been said, then, is crucial to the construction of appropriate responses.

This architecture is entirely orthodox. What is unusual about the current work is the emphasis on intensionality, so the first thing to do is examine why we believe that this is such a significant problem.

1. Doctors and patients make extensive use of generic NPs and bare plurals: *'If you follow this diet you should manage to control them without <u>drugs</u>', 'Do you normally have <u>snacks</u>?', 'When I started <u>chemotherapy</u>, on the 2nd of August, glycaemia was still rather high'* ...

   Such NPs are not, in fact, all that much more prevalent in this domain than in general language. Across the BNC, for instance, it turns out that 27% of NPs have *'the'* as their determiner, 19% are bare plurals, 29% are bare singulars, 11% have *'a'* or *'an'* as their determiner, and the remainder have a variety of other determiners[1].

   Thus bare plural and generic singular NPs occur about as frequently as *'the'* and *'a'*, and substantially more freqently than *'some'*, *'all'* and *'every'* (less than 1% each). They have, however, been much less widely discussed by formal semanticists, and there are a number of serious problems with the analyses that have been proposed (Carlson, 1989; Ramsay, 1992; Cohen, 1994).

2. Everyday language is littered with words that can be used either as nouns or verbs, and many of the apparently verbal uses of such words occur in essentially nominal contexts. Table 1 shows the pattern of usage for three common words[2], but it should be noted that about 25% of the instances that are classified as verbs are present participle forms, many of which are actually nominal or verbal gerunds and hence should be regarded as nouns.

Table 1: Uses of common words in the BNC

	Verb	Noun	Other
walk	75%	22%	3%
run	70%	24%	6%
kick	63%	35%	2%

Axiomatisation of the semantics of such words requires considerable care, since we need to ensure that all the examples in (2) have very similar consequences.

(2) a. Swimming is good for you.

---

[1] The count of bare singulars is in fact a slight overestimate, since it includes some uses of singular nouns as modifiers.

[2] The classification is taken directly from the BNC tags.

    b. Going for a swim is good for you.

    c. It is good for you to go swimming.

3. The goal of the project is to produce appropriate responses to simple statements and queries about a patient's health. To do this, we need to be able to specify a body of background knowledge in this area. We believe that for applications such as medical information provision it is important that the information provided be as accurate as possible, and hence that it may be necessary to provide the required background knowledge from scratch. This is, of course, a very time-consuming and challenging activity, and it would be nice to be able to side-step it by extracting the required information from existing texts. Unfortunately, it seems likely that any such existing text will contain gaps which will lead to the generation of partial, or wrong, answers. As noted above, ideally we would want to link special purpose knowledge of the kind outlined here with information extracted from existing texts, but for the current paper we are just looking at what is involved in providing the required knowledge from scratch.

It turns out, as will be seen below, that much of this knowledge involves quantification over situation types (of roughly the kind discussed by (Barwise and Perry, 1983)), and in particular it involves statements about whether one situation type is a subset of another, or is incompatible with it. This kind of knowledge is intrinsically intensional, but it is hard to see how it can be avoided in this domain.

3   Logical forms

The logical forms that we use are fairly orthodox.

- We assume that events are first-class objects, as suggested by Davidson Davidson (1967, 1980).

- We allow other entities to play named roles with respect to these events, where we denote that some item X is, for instance, the agent of some event E by writing $\theta(E, agent, X)$: using this notation, rather than writing $agent(E, X)$, allows us to quantify over thematic roles, which in turn allows us to state generalisations that would otherwise be awkward.

- We treat tense as a relation between speech time and 'reference time', and aspect as a relation between reference time and event time, as suggested by Reichenbach Reichenbach (1947, 1956).

- We use 'reference terms' to denote referring expressions, so that $ref(\lambda X man(X))$ is used to denote *'the man'*. Reference terms are similar to 'anchors' from (Barwise and Perry, 1983), though the treatment is essentially proof-theoretic (similar to the discussion of presupposition in (Gazdar, 1979; van der Sandt, 1992)) rather than model theoretic.

- Given that we are particularly concerned with the intensional nature of natural language, we need to use a formal language that supports intensionaly. The language we choose is a constructive version of property theory (Turner, 1987; Ramsay, 2001). We have extended the theorem prover described in (Ramsay, 2001) to cope with reasoning about knowledge and belief, and we have shown how this can be used to carry out interesting inferences in cooperative and non-cooperative situations (Ramsay and Field, 2008).

We also include the surface illocutionary force in the LF, since this is part of the meaning of the utterance and hence it seems sensible to include it in the LF. In particular, there are interactions between surface illocutionary force and other aspects of the meaning which are hard to capture if you treat them independently. This is slightly less standard than the other aspects of our LFs, but it does have the advantage that these LFs keep all the information that we can obtain by inspecting the form of the utterance in one place.

A typical example of an LF for a simple sentence is given in Figure 1[3].

(3)   The man loves a woman.

$$claim(\exists B : \{woman(B)\}$$
$$\exists C : \{past(now,C)\}$$
$$\exists D : \{aspect(C,simplePast,D)\}$$
$$\theta(D, agent, ref(\lambda E(man(E))))$$
$$\&\theta(D,object,B)$$
$$\&event(D, love))$$

Figure 1: Logical form for (3)

If you want to reason about utterances in natural language, e.g. in order to answer questions on the basis of things you have been told, then there seems to be no alternative to constructing LFs of the kind in Figure 1, axiomatising the relevant background knowledge, and then invoking your favourite theorem prover. Shallow semantic analysis simply does not provide the necessary detail, and it is very hard to link textual entailment algorithms (Dagan et al., 2005) to complex domain knowledge. The critical issue in connecting NLP systems to rich axiomatisations of domain knowledge seems likely to be that existing frameworks for constructing meaning representations are not rich enough, not that they are too rich. In the remainder of this paper we will explore three specific issues that have arisen in our attempt to use natural language as a means for accessing medical knowledge. We have beoome sensitised to these issues because of their importance for our application, but we believe that they are actually widespread, and they will need to be solved for any system which links natural language to complex domain knowledge.

4   Bare NPs

Consider (4):

---

[3]*All* the formal paraphrases in this paper are obtained from the target sentences by parsing the text and using the standard techniques of compositional semantics.

(4)   a. I am eating eggs.

       b. I eat eggs.

       c. I am allergic to eggs.

What is the status of *'eggs'* in these sentences?

It is clear that in (4a) there are some eggs that I am eating, so that (4a) means something quite like *'I am eating some eggs.'*. (4b), on the other hand, means something fairly different from *'There are some eggs that I eat'*, since it does not seem to commit the speaker to the existence of any specific set of eggs. The use of the simple aspect with a non-stative verb gives (4b) a habitual/repeated interpretation, saying that there are numerous eating events, each of which involves at least one egg.

It seems, then, that it is possible to treat *'eggs'* in (4a) and (4b) as a narrow scope existential, with the simple aspect introducing a set of eating events of the required kind.

You would not, however, want to paraphrase (4c) by saying that there are some eggs to which I am allergic. (4b) says that there is a relationship between me and situations where there is an egg present, namely that if I eat something which has been made out of some part of an egg then I am likely to have an allergic reaction. The bare plural *'eggs'* in (4c) seems to have some of the force of a universal quantifier. This is problematic: does the bare plural *'eggs'* induce an existential or a universal reading, or something entirely different?

Note that the word *'eggs'* can appear as a free-standing NP (as in (4a)) or as the head noun of an NP with an explicit determiner (as in *'He was cooking some eggs.'*). In the latter context, the meaning of *'eggs'* is normally taken be the property $\lambda X(egg(X))$, to be combined with the determiner *'some'* to produce an existentially quantified expression which can be used as part of the interpretation of the entire sentence.

It is clear that there are constructions that involve allowing prepositions to take nouns rather than NPs as their complements, in examples like *'For example, cockerels generally have more decorative plumage than hens'*, where *'example'* is evidently a noun rather than an NP. If we allow the adjective *'allergic'* to select for a PP with a noun complement rather than an NP complement, we can obtain an interpretation of (4c) which says that my allergy is a relation between me and the property of being an egg (= the set of eggs) (Figure 2).

$$
\begin{aligned}
utt(claim, \\
\exists B state(B, allergic(to, \\
\lambda C(egg(C))), \\
ref(\lambda D(speaker(D)))/0) \\
\&aspect(now, simple, B))
\end{aligned}
$$

Figure 2: Logical form for (4c)

Thus we can distinguish between cases where *'eggs'* is being used as an NP, where it introduces a narrow scope existential quantifier, and ones where it is being used as an NN, where it denotes, as usual, the property $\lambda(X, egg(X))$. We still have to work out saying that the relationship *'allergic'* holds between me and the property of being an egg, but at least we have escaped the trap of saying that it holds between me and some eggs (or indeed all eggs). We will return ton this in §6

5 Nominalisations and paraphrases

As noted above, there are often numerous ways of saying very much the same thing, and these often involve using combinations of nominal and verbal forms of the same root. To cope with these, we have to do two things: we have to construct appropriate logical forms, and we have to spot cases where we believe that there is no significant difference between the various natural language forms and introduce appropriate rules for treating one as canonical.

Gerunds and gerundives occur in very much the same places as bare NPs, and have very much the same feeling of being about types of entity.

(5) a. Exercise is good for you.

b. Swimming is good for you.

(6) a. I like watching old movies.

b. I like old movies.

It therefore seems natural to treat them in much the same way, as descriptions of event *types*, as in Figure 3

$$utt(claim,$$
$$\exists Bstate(B,$$
$$\lambda C(\exists Devent(D,swim)\ \&\ \theta(D,agent,C)),$$
$$\lambda E(good(E)))$$
$$\&for(B,ref(\lambda F(hearer(F)))!4)$$
$$\&aspect(now,simple,B))$$

Figure 3: Logical form for (5b)

The logical form in Figure 3 says that there is a state of affairs relating events where someone does some swimming and the property of being good, and that this state of affairs concerns the speaker. This does at least have the benefit of exposing the key concepts mentioned in (5b), and of doing so in such a way that it is possible to write rules that support appropriate chains of inference.

The kind of inference we are interested in concerns patterns like the ones in Figure 4

| Exercise is good for you if you are overweight |
| Swimming is a form of exercise |
| I am obese |
| Should I go swimming? |

Figure 4: A simple(!) pattern of natural reasoning

We will discuss the rules and inference engine that are required in order to support this kind of reasoning in §6 and §7. For now we are concerned with the fact that the last line in Figure 4 could have been replaced by a number of alternative forms such as *'Is swimming good for me?'* or *'Is it good for me to go swimming'* without any substantial change of meaning.

In general, we believe that determining the relationships between sentences requires inference based on background rules which describe the relationships between terms. However, when we have forms which are essentially paraphrases of one another, these rules will tend to be bi-equivalences–rules of the form $P \leftrightarrow Q$. Such rules are awkward for any theorem prover, since they potentially introduce infinite loops: in order to prove P you can try proving Q, where one of the possible ways of proving Q is by proving P, ...It is possible to catch such loops, and our inference engine does monitor for various straightforward loops of this kind, but they do introduce an extra overhead. Equivalences of this kind are, in any case, not really facts about the world so much as facts about the way natural language describes the world. It seems therefore more sensible to capture them at the point when we construct our logical forms, when they can be dealt with by straightforward pattern matching and substitution on logical forms, rather than by embodying them as bi-directional rules to be used as required by the inference engine. We use rules of the kind given in Figure 5 to canonical versions of logical forms for sentences which we regard as mutual paraphrases. These rules are matched against elements of the logical form, and the required substitutions are made. This process is applied iteratively, so that multiple rules can be applied when necessary.

$$\exists B : \{allergy(B,C)\}$$
$$\exists Devent(D,have) \ \& \ \theta(D,object,B)$$
$$\& \ \theta(D,agent,E) \ \& \ aspect(X,Y,D)$$
$$\leftrightarrow \exists F state(F,E,\lambda G(allergic(G)),to(C))$$
$$\& \ aspect(X,Y,F)$$

$$event(B,go)$$
$$\& \theta(B,event,\lambda C(event(C,D)))$$
$$\& \theta(B,agent,E)$$
$$\leftrightarrow event(B,D) \ \& \theta(B,agent,E)$$

Figure 5: Canonical form rules

The first of the rules in Figure 5 captures the equivalences between *'I have an allergy to eggs'* and *'I am allergic to eggs'*, *'having an allergy to milk is bad news'* and *'being allergic to milk is bad news'*, and so on, and the second captures the equivalences between *'I like walking'* and *'I like going walking'*, *'Swimming is good for you'* and *'Going for a swim is good for you'*, and so on. These equivalences have to be captured somewhere, and we believe that canonical forms of this kind arte a good way to do it. We will return to where the rules in Figure 5 come from in §8.

6 Intensional predicates

The material we are interested in, like all natural language, makes extensive use of intensional predicates. The adjective *'good'* in *'Going swimming is good for you'* expresses a relationship between an event type (*'going swimming'*) and an individual; the verb *'make'* in *'Eating raw meat will make you feel sick'* expresses a relationship between an event type (*'eating raw meat'*) and a state of affairs (*'you are ill'*). Constructions like these are widespread, and are inherently intensional. To draw conclusions about sentences involving them, you have to be able to reason about whether one event type or one parameterised state of affairs is a subset of another, which is the essence of intensionality.

Once you recognise that examples like these involve event types and propositions, it is fairly straightforward to construct appropriate logical forms. We simply use the notation of the λ-calculus to depict abstractions (e.g. event types), and we allow propositions to appear in argument positions, and standard techniques from comppsitional semantics do the rest.

$$
\begin{aligned}
&\exists C : \{future(now,C)\} \\
&\quad \exists Bevent(B,make) \\
&\qquad \&\theta(B, \\
&\qquad\quad scomp, \\
&\qquad\quad \lambda D(event(D,feel) \\
&\qquad\qquad \&\ \theta(D,object,\lambda E(sick(E))) \\
&\qquad\qquad \&\ \theta(D,agent,ref(\lambda F(hearer(F)))!5))) \\
&\qquad \&\theta(B, \\
&\qquad\quad cause, \\
&\qquad\quad \lambda G\ \exists Hevent(H,eat) \\
&\qquad\qquad \&\exists I : \{raw(I)\ \&\ meat(I)\}\theta(H,object,I) \\
&\qquad\qquad \&\theta(H,agent,G)) \\
&\qquad \&aspect(C,simple,B)
\end{aligned}
$$

Figure 6: Eating raw meat will make you feel sick

Figure 6 describes a relationship between situations where you eat raw meat and ones where you feel sick. This is entirely correct: what else could this sentence denote?

Constructing formal paraphrases for sentences involving intensional predicates is thus both straightforward (so long as you can parse them) and essential. Formal languages that support such paraphrases are, however, potentially problematic. The key problem is that such languages tend to permit paradoxical constructions such as the Liar Paradox and Ruessll's set which introduce sentences which are true if and only if they are false. It is difficult to provide semantics for languages which allow paradoxes to be stated, but there are a number of ways out of this dilemma, either by putting syntactic restrictions on what can be said (Whitehead and Russell, 1925; Jech, 1971) or by devising appropriate interpretations (Turner, 1987; Aczel, 1988). We choose to employ a constructive variant of property theory, because it allows us a comparatively straightforward and implemetable proof theory, but it does not really matter what you choose. What does matter is that if you choose a language with less expressive power than natural language, such as description logic, your paraphrases must fail to support some of the distinctions that are expressible in natural language, and as a consequence you will inevitably draw incorrect conclusions from the texts you are processing.

7 Inference

Consider (7):

(7)   a.   Eating eggs will make you ill if you are allergic to eggs.

     b.   I am allergic to eggs.

     c.   Will eating fried-egg sandwiches make me ill?

It is pretty obvious that the answer to (7c), given (7a) and (7b), must be *'Yes'*. The reasoning that is required to arrive at this answer turns out to be suprisingly complex.

The problem is, as noted above, that we need to reason about relationships between event types. We need to be able to spot that events where someone eats a fried-egg sandwich involve situations where they eat an egg. It is clearly quite easy, if tedious, to write rules that say that if someone eats something which contains an egg then they must eat an egg, and that fried-egg sandwiches contain eggs. The trouble is that we have to be able invoke this rule in order to determine whether the *arguments* of *'make'* are of the right kind. Because we are (correctly) allowing event types as arguments in intensional predicates, we have to be able to invoke arbitrary and unpredictable amounts of inference even to determine whether the arguments of a predicate are admissible. Roughly speaking, we have to be prepared to carry out arbitrary amounts of inference at the point where first-order theorem provers invoke unification.

There is nothing to stop us doing this. Sorted logics, for instance, use an extended notion of unification to try to ensure that items that are being considered as arguments have specific properties (Cohn, 1987). We can, indeed, do any computation we like in order to verify the suitability of arguments. The more complex the computations we perform, of course, the longer it may take to come to a decision. The key is thus to try to bound the potential costs without compromising what we can do too much. We exploit a notion of 'guarded' axioms, where we allow arbitrary amounts of reasoning to be performed to verify that some item fits a fully specified description, but we do not allow such reasoning to be used for generating candidates. We do, of course, have to put a bound on the amount of work that will be done at any point, as indeed any inference engine for a language as expressive as first-order logic must do. In general, however, using guarded intensionality in this way allows us to cover a wide range of cases which are simply inexpressible using first-order logic (or any fragment of first-order logic, such as description logic) comparatively inexpensively.

8 Conclusions

We have argued that in order to cope properly with even quite straightforward uses of language, you need large amounts of background knowledge, much of which has to be couched in some highly intensional framework, and you need inference engines which can manipulate this knowledge. In the body of the paper we have shown a number of examples which we believe illustrate this argument, and have looked at the representations and rules that we employ for dealing with these cases. The natural question that arises at this point is: that's all very well, but can the approach outlined here be extended to cover a more substantial set of cases?

There are two key issues here. How difficult is it to capture a reasonably substantial body of knowledge within the framework we have outlined, and what will happen to the inference engine when we do?

Writing rules in property theory is very hard work. Writing rules in property theory which will mesh nicely with logical forms obtained from natural language sentences is extremely hard work. If we had to hand-code the rules we want directly in property theory (or indeed in any formal language) then the approach discussed here would, clearly, be impossible to extend to cover more than a handful of cases. Fortunately, however, we have a much easier way of constructing rules. We have, after all, a mechanism for converting natural language sentences into logical forms. So if we state the rules we want in natural language we will obtain logical forms of those rules, and furthermore those paraphrases will automatically be couched in terms which mesh nicely with logical forms obtained from other natural language sentences. Thus (8) produces the rule in Figure 7

(8)   Eating Y will make X ill if X is allergic to Y.

$$\forall C \forall D \exists E state(E,C,\lambda F(allergic(F))) \,\&\, to(E,D)$$
$$\&\, aspect(now,simple,E)$$
$$\rightarrow\, \exists G : \{future(now,G)\}$$
$$\exists B event(B,make)$$
$$\&\, \theta(B,object,C)$$
$$\&\, \theta(B,object1,\lambda H(ill(H)))$$
$$\&\, \theta(B,$$
$$agent,$$
$$\lambda J\, \exists J event(J,eat)$$
$$\&\, \theta(J,object,D)$$
$$\&\, \theta(J,agent,I))$$
$$\&\, aspect(G,simple,B)$$

Figure 7: Logical form for (8)

Writing rules like (8) is clearly easier than producing formulae like Figure 7 by hand. Writing down all the knowledge you need in order to cope with a non-trivial domain is still a very substantial task, but doing it in English is at least feasible in a way that doing it directly in a formal language is not.

How will the inference engine cope when confronted with thousands of rules? Very large parts of everyday knowledge can, in fact, be expressed pretty much as Horn clauses. Our inference engine converts Horn clauses into (almost) pure Prolog, and there is certainly no problem in using very large sets of Horn clauses converted to this form (a modern Prolog system will cope comfortably with sets of several hundred thousand Horn clauses, and will carry out substantial inference chains involving such sets in small fractions of a second). The only concern here relates to non-Horn clauses (which do not tend to occur all that frequently in rules explaining the relationships between natural language terms) and intensional rules. The fact that most intensional rules are guarded has certainly meant that so far we have not encountered any problems when using them, and we are hopeful that this will remain the case.

In any case, there is an alternative question to be answered: what will happen if you *don't* take the approach outlined here? All the phenomena we have discussed are widespread–bare plurals, mutual paraphrases, intensional attitudes all occur all over the place. It is extremely hard to see that systems that rely on surface patterns (either directly, as in textual entailment, or indirectly through shallow parsing/information extraction) can support the kind of reasoning required for getting from '*I have an allergy to eggs.*' to '*It is dangerous for me to eat pancakes*', so at some point inference based on background knowledge will have to be invoked. There seems little alternative to constructing formal paraphrases that capture the subtleties of natural language in all its glory. If you don't, then you will by definition lose some of the information that was expressed in the text, and that will inevitably mean that you get things wrong. There is no way round it: either you bite the bullet, construct formal paraphrases that capture the content of the input and use them to carry out inference, or you will get some things wrong.

References

Aczel, P. (1988). *Non-Well-Founded-Sets*. Stanford: CSLI Publications.

Barwise, J. and J. Perry (1983). *Situations and Attitudes*. Cambridge, MA: Bradford Books.

Carlson, G. (1989). On the semantic composition of English generic sentences. In G. Chierchia, B. H. Partee, and R. Turner (Eds.), *Properties, Types and Meaning II: Semantic Issues*, Dordrecht, pp. 167–192. Kluwer Academic Press.

Cohen, A. (1994). Reasoning with generics. In H. C. Bunt (Ed.), *1st International Workshop on Computational Semantics*, University of Tilburg, pp. 263–270.

Cohn, A. G. (1987). A more expressive formulation of many sorted logic. *Journal of Automated Reasoning 3*, 113–200.

Dagan, I., B. Magnini, and O. Glickman (2005). The PASCAL recognising textual entailment challenge. In *Proceedings of Pascal Challenge Workshop on Recognizing Textual Entailment*.

Davidson, D. (1967). The logical form of action sentences. In N. Rescher (Ed.), *The Logic of Decision and Action*, Pittsburgh. University of Pittsburgh Press.

Davidson, D. (1980). *Essays on actions and events*. Oxford: Clarendon Press.

Gazdar, G. (1979). *Pragmatics: Implicature, Presupposition and Logical Form*. New York: Academic Press.

Jech, T. J. (1971). *Lectures in Set Theory, with Particular Emphasis on the Method of Forcing*. Berlin: Springer Verlag (Lecture Notes in Mathematics 217).

Ramsay, A. M. (1992). Bare plural NPs and habitual VPs. In *Proceedings of the 14th International Conference on Computational Linguistics (COLING-92)*, Nantes, pp. 226–231.

Ramsay, A. M. (2001). Theorem proving for untyped constructive λ-calculus: implementation and application. *Logic Journal of the Interest Group in Pure and Applied Logics 9*(1), 89–106.

Ramsay, A. M. and D. G. Field (2008). Speech acts, epistemic planning and Grice's maxims. *Journal of Logic and Computation 18*(3), 431–457.

Reichenbach, H. (1947). *Elements of Symbolic Logic*. New York: The Free Press.

Reichenbach, H. (1956). *The Direction of Time*. Berkeley: University of California Press.

Turner, R. (1987). A theory of properties. *Journal of Symbolic Logic 52(2)*, 455–472.

van der Sandt, R. (1992). Presupposition projection as anaphora resolution. *Journal of Semantics 9*, 333–377.

Whitehead, A. N. and B. Russell (1925). *Principia Mathematica*. Cambridge: Cambridge University Press.

Refining the Meaning of Sense Labels in PDTB: "Concession"

Livio Robaldo

University of Turin (Italy)

email: robaldo@di.unito.it

Eleni Miltsakaki

University of Pennsylvania (USA)

email: elenimi@linc.cis.upenn.edu

Jerry R. Hobbs

University of Southern California (USA)

email: hobbs@isi.edu

Abstract

The most recent release of PDTB 2.0 contains annotations of senses of connectives. The PDTB 2.0 manual describes the hierarchical set of senses used in the annotation and offers rough semantic descriptions of each label. In this paper, we refine the semantics of *concession* substantially and offer a formal description of concessive relations and the associated inferences drawn by the reader, utilizing basic notions from Hobbs's logic, including the distinction between causes and causal complexes (Hobbs, 2005). This work is part of a larger project on the semantics of connectives which aims at developing formal descriptions of discourse relations, useful for processing real data.

1 Introduction

As the demand for more powerful NLP applications increases, there is also an increasing need to develop algorithms for automated processing of discourse relations and models for deriving the inferences drawn by the reader. PDTB 2.0 (Prasad et al., 2008), released in January 2008, contains annotations of discourse connectives and their arguments, attribution, and sense labels giving rough semantic descriptions of the connectives. The availability of such a richly annotated corpus promises to boost our understanding of the structure and meaning of discourse and will facilitate the development of efficient algorithms for identifying discourse connectives and their arguments.

However, in order to be able to derive appropriate inferences associated with discourse relations, we need to develop useful semantic analyses of the meaning of connectives so that they will generate the same range of inferences made by humans. In this paper we take a first step in that direction, offering a simple formal analysis of concessive relations, thus refining the semantics of the concessive sense labels used in PDTB 2.0. Our analysis uses basic notions of causality developed in Hobbs (1998, 2005), capitalizing on the distinction between causes and causal complexes and on the semantics of defeasible causality. Concessive meaning involves the failure of a general defeasible causal relation in this specific instance.

The paper is organized as follows. Section 2 gives an overview of the PDTB 2.0, focusing on the annotation of the senses of connectives, especially "concession". In Section 3, we present an overview of the framework we are adopting for our formal analysis, namely, Hobbs's logic of causality, and our basic claims about how the semantics of defeasible causality contributes to the semantics of concession. Section 4 presents the semantic analysis of "concession". In Section 5, we report briefly on the distribution of concessive labels in PDTB 2.0 and conclude in Section 6.

2 Sense labels in PDTB

The Penn Discourse Treebank provides annotations of the argument structure of discourse connectives, attribution (e.g., 'ownership' of the relation by the writer or other individual), and semantic labels for all the annotated connectives (Prasad et al., 2008). This annotation of discourse connectives and their arguments draws on a lexical approach to discourse structure (Webber et al., 2003; Webber and Joshi, 2003), viewing discourse connectives as discourse-level predicates that take two *abstract objects* such as events, states, and propositions (Asher, 1993) as their arguments.

Two major types of discourse connectives are annotated in PDTB: a) explicit connectives including subordinate conjunctions, coordinate conjunctions and adverbials, and b) implicit connectives that are inserted between two adjacent sentences to capture the meaning of the inferred relation when no explicit connective is present. The PDTB 2.0 is, to date, the largest annotation effort at the discourse level, including approximately 40,000 triples in the form (`Connective`, `Arg1`, `Arg2`). Arg2 is the second argument in the text in the case of coordinating conjunctions, and is the complement of subordinating conjunctions. In the case of adverbs, `Arg2` is the element which the adverb modifies syntactically. In cases of ambiguity, sense labels indicate the intended sense in the given context. In all other cases, sense labels provide semantic descriptions of the relations conveyed by the connectives, both explicit and implicit.

The tagset of senses is organized hierarchically (Miltsakaki et al., 2008). The top level, or *class level*, has four tags representing four major semantic classes: "TEMPO-RAL", "CONTINGENCY", "COMPARISON" and "EXPANSION". For each class, a second level of *types* is defined to further refine the semantics of the class levels. For example, "CONTINGENCY" has two types "Cause" (relating two situations via a direct cause-effect relation) and "Condition" (relating a hypothetical scenario with its (possible) consequences). A third level of *subtype* specifies the semantic contribution of each argument. For "CONTINGENCY", its "Cause" type has two subtypes — "reason" (which applies when the connective indicates that the situation specified in Arg2 is interpreted as the cause of the situation specified in Arg1, as often with the connective *because*) and "result" (which is used when the connective indicates that the situation described in Arg2 is interpreted as the result of the situation presented in Arg1). That is, "reason" occurs when Arg2 causes Arg1; "result" occurs when Arg1 causes Arg2.

Connectives can also be used to relate arguments pragmatically as in *John is in the house because the lights are on* or *If you're thirsty, there's beer in the fridge*, where the relation involbes the belief in or the telling of the condition rather than the condition itself. For these *rhetorical* or *pragmatic* uses of connectives, a small set of *pragmatic* sense tags has been defined — specifically, "Pragmatic Cause", "Pragmatic Condition", "Pragmatic Contrast" and "Pragmatic Concession".

2.1 "Concession" in PDTB

"Concession" is a type of the class-level category "COMPARISON". The class tag "COMPARISON" applies when the connective indicates that a discourse relation is established between Arg1 and Arg2 in order to highlight prominent differences between the two situations. Semantically, the truth of both arguments is independent of the connective or the established relation. "COMPARISON" has two types that further specify its semantics. In some cases, Arg1 and Arg2 share a predicate or a property and the difference is highlighted with respect to the values assigned to this property. This interpretation is tagged with the type "Contrast".

There are also cases in which the highlighted differences are related to expectations raised by one argument which are then denied by the other. This intepretation is tagged with the type "Concession". According to the description in the PDTB 2.0 manual, the type "Concession" applies when the connective indicates that one of the arguments describes a situation A which normally causes C, while the other asserts (or implies) $\neg C$. Alternatively, one argument denotes a fact that triggers a set of potential consequences, while the other denies one or more of them.

Two "Concession" subtypes are defined in terms of the argument creating an expectation and the one denying it. Specifically, when Arg2 creates an expectation that Arg1 denies, it is tagged as "expectation", shown in (1.c-d). When Arg1 creates an expectation that Arg2 denies, it is tagged as "contra-expectation", shown in (1.e-f). Examples (1.a-b) are made-up sentences we use for explanation and will be discussed here and in the next section. All other examples are taken from PDTB 2.0. Each discourse fragment in (1) distinguishes between a discourse connective (underlined), and two sentence-arguments: Arg1 (italics) and Arg2 (boldface).

(1)   a.   Although **John studied hard,** *he did not pass the exam.* (expectation)

     b.   Although **running is considered healthy**, *it is not advisable for persons with heart problems.* (expectation)

     c.   Although **they represent only 2% of the population**, *they control nearly one-third of discretionary income.* (expectation)

     d.   While **acquiring a big brand-name company can be a shortcut to growth**, *it can also bring a host of unforeseen problems* (expectation)

     e.   *The Texas oilman has acquired a 26.2% stake valued at more than $1.2 billion in an automotive-lighting company, Koito Manufacturing Co.* **But he has failed to gain any influence at the company**. (contra-expectation)

     f.   *Mr. Cannell's allegations of cheating "are purely without foundation", and based on unfair inferences.* However **the state will begin keeping closer track of achievement-test preparation booklets next spring.**. (contra-expectation)

(1.a) is an example of "expectation": `Arg2` (*John studied hard*) creates the expectation that John passed the exam, which is precisely denied by `Arg1`. The same holds for (1.b-d). Note that (1.b), unlike (1.a, c-d), expresses a general concessive relation, i.e., it does not refer to particular contingent events. (1.e-f) are instances of contra-expectation, where the expectation is created by `Arg1`. In (1.e), the fact that the Texas oilman acquired the indicated stake value creates the expectation that he gained influence at the company, while, in (1.f), since Mr. Cannell's allegations of cheating are purely without foundation (in the speaker's judgement), we do not expect the state to start tracking the test preparation.

3   Toward a formal definition of "Concession"

Based on our analysis of the range of PDTB tokens tagged with a concessive label, we offer here a more detailed semantic analysis of the meaning of concessive relations. Since the direction of the concessive relation is not relevant, the argument that creates the expectation and the argument that denies it are respectively termed as Arg_{cexp} and Arg_{dexp}. We claim that a concessive relation arises from a contrast between the effects of two causal relations c_c and c_d holding in the domain. c and d stand for "creates" and "denies", respectively. The relation denoted by c_c is the causal relation that creates the expectation, and c_d the one that denies it. The effects of these causal relations, as well as their causes, are taken to be eventualities[1].

In this paper, we use the letter e for most eventualities, possibly with some subscript or superscript.[2] We make use of the subscripts $x1$ and $x2$, respectively, to distinguish between the causes and the effects in a causal relation c_x. Therefore, the causes in c_c and c_d are indicated by e_{c1} and e_{d1} respectively, and the effects by e_{c2} and e_{d2}, respectively. e_{c2} is the "created expectation"; its cause e_{c1} is conveyed by Arg_{cexp}. e_{d2} is an eventuality that denies e_{c2}, and it is explicitly described in Arg_{dexp}. The cause of

---

[1]The term "eventuality" is borrowed from (Bach, 1981). It covers both standard notions of "state" and "event".

[2]As we will see, also causal relations are eventualities; so the names c_c and c_d are an exception to this rule.

e_{d2}, i.e., e_{d1}, is usually unknown. Also e_{c2} is, in principle, unknown, but in most cases it can be taken as the negation of e_{d2}.

For instance, in the context of (1.a), the eventuality *John studied hard* (e_{c1}) creates the expectation *John passed the exam* (e_{c2}). Nevertheless, Arg$_{dexp}$ says that *John did not pass the exam* actually (e_{d2}). The reason of e_{d2} is unknown and has to be found in the context. In other words, the context, whether explicit or inferred, should include another eventuality that caused John's failure, despite his studying hard. For example, the next sentence might be *John was very tired during the exam* (e_{d1}).

In order to formalize this account of concession, we need a defeasible notion of causality. Many authors propose such an account of causality, e.g. (Achinstein, 1965; Shoham, 1990; Simon, 1991; Bell, 1999, 2003), and Giunchiglia et al. (2004). The account we use is that of Hobbs (2005). This distinguishes between the monotonic, precise notion of "causal complex" and the nonmonotonic, defeasible notion of "cause". The former gives us mathematical rigor; the latter is more useful for everyday reasoning and can be characterized in terms of the former. As Hobbs (2005) explains, when we flip a switch to turn on a light, we say that flipping the switch "caused" the light to turn on. But for this to happen, many other factors had to be in place. The bulb had to be intact, the switch had to be connected to the bulb, the power had to be on in the city, and so on. The set of all the states and events that have to hold or happen for an effect e to happen are called the "causal complex" of e. Thus, the flipping of the switch and the normal states of the bulb, the wiring, and the power supply would all be in the causal complex for the turning on of the light. In a causal complex, the majority of participating eventualities are normally true and therefore presumed to hold. In the light bulb case, unless otherwise indicated, it is normally true that the bulb is not burnt out, that the wiring is intact, that the power is on in the city, and so on. But the light switch could be on or off; neither can be presumed. Those eventualities that cannot normally be assumed to be true are identified as causes (cf. Kayser and Nouioua, 2008). They are useful in planning, because they are often the actions that the planner or some other agent must perform. They are useful in explanation and prediction because they frequently constitute the new information. They are less useful in diagnosis, where the whole causal complex has to be considered.

Note that in practice, we can never specify all the eventualities in a causal complex for an event. So while the notion of causal complex gives us a precise way of thinking about causality, it is not adequate for the kind of practical reasoning we do in planning, explaining, and predicting. For this, we need the defeasible notion of "cause".

3.1 Background on Hobbs's logic

Hobbs (1998) proposed a wide coverage logical framework for natural language based on the notion of reification. Reification is the action of making states and events first-class individuals in the logic, so they can be referred to by constants and variables. We "reify" eventualities, from the Latin word 're(s)' for 'thing': we take them to be *things*. The framework distinguishes two parallel sets of predicates: primed and unprimed. The unprimed predicates are the ordinary predicates we are used to in logical representations of language. For example, (*give a b c*) says that a gives b to c. When we assert this, we are saying that it actually takes place in the real world. The primed predicate is used to talk about the reified eventualities. The expression (*give' e a b c*) says that *e* is a giving event by *a* of *b* to *c*. Eventualities may be possible or actual. When they are actual, this is simply one of their properties. To say that a state *e* actually obtains in the real world or that an event *e* actually occurs in the real world, we write (*Rexist e*). That is, *e* really exists in the real world. If I want to fly, my wanting really exists, but my flying does not. This is represented as:[3]

$$(Rexist\ e) \wedge (want'\ e\ I\ e_1) \wedge (fly'\ e_1\ I)$$

Therefore, contrary to (*p x*), (*p' e x*) does not say that *e* actually occurs, only that if it did, it would be a "p" event. The relation between primed and unprimed predicates is then formalized by the following axiom schema:

$$(forall\ (x)\ (iff\ (p\ x)\ (exists(e)\ (and(p'\ e\ x)(Rexist\ e)))))$$

Eventualities can be treated as the objects of human thoughts. Reified eventualities are inserted as parameters of such predicates as *believe*, *think*, *want*, etc. These predicates can be applied in a recursive fashion. The fact that *John believes that Jack wants to eat an ice cream* is represented as an eventuality *e* such that[4]

$$(believe'\ e\ John\ e_1) \wedge (want'\ e_1\ Jack\ e_2) \wedge$$
$$(eat'\ e_2\ Jack\ Ic) \wedge (iceCream'\ e_3\ Ic)$$

In Hobbs's notation, every relation on eventualities, including logical operators, causal and temporal relations, and even tense and aspect, may be reified into another eventuality. For instance, by asserting (*imply' e e_1 e_2*), we reify the implication from e_1 to e_2 into an eventuality *e*. *e* has to be thought as 'the state holding between e_1 and e_2 such that whenever e_1 really exists, e_2 really exists too'. Negation is represented as (*not' e_1 e_2*): e_1 is the eventuality of the e_2's not existing. Some problems arise with negation, in that what is generally negated is an eventuality type rather than an eventuality token or instance. In order to deal with more general cases of concession, we will refer to eventualities that are *inconsistent* with other ones. Two eventualities e_1 and e_2 are said to be inconsistent iff they (respectively) imply two other eventualities e_3 and e_4 such that e_3 is the negation of e_4. The definition is as follows:

$$(forall\ (e_1\ e_3)$$
$$(iff\ (inconsistent\ e_1\ e_2)$$
$$(and\ (eventuality\ e_1)\ (eventuality\ e_2)$$
$$(exists\ (e_3\ e_4)\ (and\ (imply\ e_1\ e_3)$$
$$(imply\ e_2\ e_4)(not'\ e_3\ e_4))))))$$

3.2 Typical elements, eventuality types and tokens

Among the things we can think about are both specific eventualities, like *Fido is barking*, and general or abstract types of eventualities, like *Dogs bark*. We do not want to treat these as radically different kinds of entities. We would like both, at some level, to

---

[3]In order to increase readability, we will often make use of the symbol $\wedge$ in place of the unprimed predicate *and*.

[4]The formula expresses the de-re reading of the sentence, where e_1, e_2, e_3, *John*, *Jack*, *Ic* are first order constants.

be treated simply as eventualities that can be the content of thoughts. To this end, the logical framework includes the notion of typical element (from Hobbs (1983, 1995, 1998)). The typical element of a set is the reification of the universally quantified variable ranging over the elements of the set (cf. McCarthy (1977)). Typical elements are first-order individuals. The introduction of typical elements arises from the need to move from the standard set-theoretic notation

$$s = \{x \mid p(x)\}$$

or its logical equivalent,

$$(forall\ (x)\ (iff\ (member\ x\ s)\ (p\ x)))$$

to a simple statement that p is true of a "typical element" of s by reifying typical elements. The principal property of typical elements is that all properties of typical elements are inherited by the real members of the set.

It is important not to confuse the concept of typical element with the standard concept of "prototype", which allows defeasibility, i.e., properties that are not inherited by all of the real members of the set. Asserting a predicate on a typical element of a set is logically equivalent to the multiple assertions of that predicate on all elements of the set. Talking about typical elements of sets of eventualities leads to the distinction between eventuality types and eventuality tokens. The logic defines the following concepts, for which we omit formal details[5]: a) *Eventualities types* (aka *abstract eventualities*): eventualities that involve at least one typical element among their arguments or arguments of their arguments (we can call these "parameters"), b) *Partially instantiated eventuality types* (aka *partial instances*): a particular kind of eventuality type resulting from instantiating some of the parameters of the abstract eventuality either with real members of their sets or with typical elements of subsets, and c) *Eventuality tokens* (aka *instances*: a particular kind of partially instantiated eventuality type with no parameters. It is a consequence of universal instantiation that any property that holds of an eventuality type is true of any partial instance of it.

Hobbs's logical framework is particularly suitable to the study of the semantics of discourse connectives, in that it allows focusing on their meaning while leaving underspecified the details about the eventualities involved. In other words, we can simply assume the existence of two eventualities e_1 and e_2 coming from the two arguments Arg1 and Arg2 respectively. e_1 and e_2 may be either eventuality tokens, on atomic arguments, as in (1.a), or eventuality tokens, on collective arguments, as in (1.c), or (partially instantiated) eventuality types, as in (1.b), or any other kind of eventuality. The semantics of concession proposed below uniformly applies to all these cases.

3.3 Hobbs's Account of Causality

The account of causality described above in the introduction is represented in terms of two predicates: (*cause' c_x e_{x1} e_{x2}*) and (*causalComplex s e_{x2}*). *cause'* says that c_x is the state holding between e_{x1} and e_{x2} such that the former is a non-presumable cause

---

[5]Actually, "instance" is slightly more general, since if s is a set, x is its typical element, and y is a member of s, y is an instance of x, even though it is not an eventuality. Nevertheless, in this paper we assume "instances" and "eventuality tokens" to be synonymous.

of the latter. *causalComplex* says that s is the set of all presumable or non-presumable eventualities that are involved in causing e_{x2}. Obviously, e_{x1} belongs to s. Thus, in the light example, the predicate *cause* applies to the flipping of the switch, while the states of the bulb, the wiring, and the power supply would all be in the causal complex s. Several axioms characterize the predicates *cause* and *causalComplex*. Some of them relate causality with time[6], some relate causality with probability, and so on Hobbs (2005).

It is clear that the theory must *not* include an axiom stating that, whenever a causal relation c_x and its cause e_{x1} really exist, the corresponding effect e_{x2} really exists too. The inclusion of such an axiom would lead to a non-defeasible causality. Rather, we need an axiom stating that an effect really exists just in case all the eventualities in its causal complex really exist:

> *(forall (s e)*
>   *(if (and (causalComplex s e)*
>   *(forall (e$_1$) (if (member e$_1$ s) (Rexist e$_1$)))*
>   *(Rexist e)))*

Nevertheless, as pointed out above, we can never specify all the eventualities in a causal complex. Even in simple sentences like (1.a), the eventualities in the causal complex are not easy to list, and the real causes may not coincide with what we *think* the causes are in that context. For example, recalling our analysis of (1.a) above:

> e_{c1}="John studied hard"
> e_{c2}="John passed the exam"
> e_{d1}="John was tired during the exam"
> e_{d2}="John did not pass the exam"
> c_c="e_{c1} causes e_{c2}"; c_d="e_{d1} causes e_{d2}"

One approach at this point would be to say that both e_{c1} and the negation of e_{d1} belong to the causal complex of e_{c2}, with e_{c1} being the non-presumable cause of e_{c2}. But this would mean that *not being tired during exams* is a kind of "precondition" for *passing exams* by *studying hard*, which is obviously false in many contexts. Note, however, that there is an arbitrary quality to what we designate as being in a causal complex, because causality forms chains and we can start the chain at any point. *John was tired* caused the situation that *he did not manage to concentrate*, which caused the situation that *he made a lot of errors in the exam*, which caused the situation that *the teacher decided to fail him*. One could argue that the last of these eventualities is the real cause of e_{d2}. Similarly, one could argue that e_{c1} is not the real cause of e_{c2}: *John studied hard* causes the situation that *he makes few errors in the exam ... and the teacher decides not to fail him*. The predicate *cause* is defeasibly transitive, however, so these considerations do not affect our account of concession. Furthermore, we do not take the negation of e_{d1} as necessarily belonging to the causal complex for e_{c2}. Rather, we claim that e_{d1}, besides being the cause of e_{d2}, is the cause of another eventuality e_{dp} that is inconsistent with an element e_{cp} in the causal complex for e_{c2}.

---

[6]As argued also by Giordano and Schwind (2004), the effect caused by an eventuality can take place in the current or in a subsequent instant.

In (1.a), e_{cp} may be simply *John does not have any particular health problem that jeopardizes his passing the exam.* e_{d1} caused both John's failure and an health status that jeopardizes the passing of his exam. This is what we mean here by "denying of an expectation".

In our analysis of concession, we distinguish between abstract causalities like *hard studying causes passing exams*, and causality tokens like *John's tiredness caused John's failure.* Note that asserting *(Rexist c)* on an abstract causal relation *c* amounts to asserting *(Rexist c')* for any (partial) instance *c'* of *c*. But recall that *cause* is only defeasible. Both the abstract causal principle and its partial instance are simplified stand-ins for rules that involve entire causal complexes, not all of whose elements may obtain. Thus, just because *hard studying causes passing exams*, we cannot invariably conclude that if John really studied, he really passed the exam.

4 The meaning of concessive relations

Our basic claim is that the meaning of concessive relations is triggered by a contrast between two causal relations c_c and c_d such that one or more eventualities in the causal complex of e_{c2} (the expectation created by c_c), is denied by e_{d2} (the effect of c_d). c_c, c_d, e_{d2}, and e_{c1} (the cause in c_c) really exist in the world, or are at least believed to exist by the speaker/writer. Furthermore, all eventualities in the causal complex for e_{d2}, including the non-presumable cause e_{d1}, which is unknown in many cases, really exist too. Arg_{cexp} conveys e_{c1}, while Arg_{dexp} conveys e_{d2}.

We also claim that in all cases of concession it seems that what really creates the expectation is a causal relation c_c^a that is an abstraction of c_c. c_c really exists in the world precisely because c_c^a really exists and c_c is a partial instance of it. In other words, the real existence of c_c is inherited from c_c^a. On the other hand, there is not necessarily an abstract counterpart c_d^a for c_d that also really exists in the world. For instance, in (1.a), it seems that what creates the expectation is the assumption that the causal relation *studying hard causes passing exams* (c_c^a) really exists in the context. *John's hard studying causes John's passing exams* (c_c) is just an instance of c_c^a. This instance really exists in the world too. However, since causality is defeasible, the fact that *John really studied hard* (e_{c1}) does not entail the real existence of *John really passed the exam* (e_{c2}). In fact, this is precisely denied by Arg_{dexp}: *John did not pass the exam* (e_{d2}). The cause of John's failure, e.g., John's tiredness (e_{d1}), is (or is the cause of an eventuality e_{dp} that is) inconsistent with an element e_{cp} of the causal complex for (e_{c2}), namely, *John does not have any particural health problem that jeopardizes the passing of his exam.* Note that we do not necessarily infer that *being tired causes failing an exam*: tiredness was the cause of the failure in this particular scenario only. Therefore, we assert that c_d really exists, but we do not advocate the existence of a more abstract causal relation c_d^a that really exists too.

To summarize, the semantics of concession we propose is formalized in (2). The conjuncts *(Rexist c_c)* and *(Rexist e_{d1})* have been omitted in (2) because they may be inferred from *(Rexist c_c^a)* and *(Rexist e_{d2})*. s_c is the causal complex associated with c_c. e_{c1} and e_{d2} are given to us in Arg_{cexp} and Arg_{dexp} respectively, while all other eventualities may be inferred by abduction from the contextual knowledge; some hints about how this may be done are provided in Hobbs (2005).

(2) $(exist\ (c_c\ c^a{}_c\ e_{c1}\ e_{c2}\ c_d\ e_{d1}\ e_{d2}\ s_c\ e_{cp}\ e_{dp})$
     $(cause'\ c_c\ e_{c1}\ e_{c2}) \wedge (cause'\ c_d\ e_{d1}\ e_{d2}) \wedge (Rexist\ c^a{}_c) \wedge$
     $(partialInstance\ c_c\ c^a{}_c) \wedge (Rexist\ c_d) \wedge (Rexist\ e_{c1}) \wedge$
     $(Rexist\ e_{d2}) \wedge (cause\ e_{d1}\ e_{dp}) \wedge (Rexist\ e_{dp}) \wedge$
     $(inconsistent\ e_{c2}\ e_{d2}) \wedge (causalComplex\ s_c\ e_{c2}) \wedge$
     $(member\ e_{cp}\ s_c) \wedge (inconsistent\ e_{dp}\ e_{cp}))$

Let us now examine how the semantics given in (2) applies for corpus examples tagged as "expectation" or "contra-expectation". Let us analyze (1.b) in the light of the semantics proposed in (2). The abstract causality that creates the expectation ($c^a{}_c$) is *Something that is considered healthy for humans is advisable for them*[7]. This is partially instantiated in *Since running is considered healthy for persons with heart problems, it is advisable for them* (c_c). Nevertheless, the fact that *running is really considered healthy* in the context (e_{c1}) does not suffice to assert that *running is really advisable for persons with heart problems* (e_{c2}). There is a particular reason why *running is not advisable for persons with heart problems* (e_{d2}), e.g. *their hearts do not tolerate a heartbeat increase* (e_{d1}). Since running causes a heartbeat increase, *the heart can tolerate a heartbeat increase* (e_{cp}) is in the causal complex for e_{c2} and it is inconsistent with e_{d2}.

Similarly, in (1.c), which is taken from the PDTB, it is true that *representing a low percentage of the population causes controlling low percentage of income* (c^a_c). Therefore, *they represent 2% of population* (e_{c1}) causes *they control low percentage of income* (e_{c2}). Nevertheless, e_{c2} does not really exists in the context, in that it is inconsistent with *they control nearly one-third of income* (e_{d2}). There must be another reason for why e_{c2} does not hold. For instance, either *they are very rich*, or *they do not have as many basic expenses as other people*, or a more complex condition. This unknown cause, i.e. e_{d1}, both makes e_{d2} true and e_{c2} false in the context.

The last example highlights the point that finding the eventualities involved in (2) is strongly dependent upon contextual knowledge. 2% is not taken to be a low percentage in *any* context. For instance, 2% mercury in the water may be considered a high percentage of pollution. Analogously, one third may be considered a high percentage in that context, especially if compared with 2% of population, but it may be a low or medium percentage in many other contexts. The analysis of examples (1.d-e) in terms of the definition in (2) is analogous.

5   A survey of concessive relations in PDTB 2.0

PDTB 2.0 contains 1193 tokens of *explicit* connectives which are annotated with one sense tagged as "Concession", "contra-expectation" and "expectation". There are also another 20 tokens that have been annotated with double senses, one of which is the concessive type or subtypes. Table (1) shows the distribution of concessive labels for the 1193 tokens. Explicit connectives with a concessive label assigned to less than 10 tokens are grouped under "other". The rest of the connectives shown in Table (1) amount to 98% of all "contra-expectation" and 95% of all "expectation" tokens. The

---

[7]This is a paraphrase of *Something being considered healthy for humans causes it to be advisable for humans*.

Table 1: Concessive labels in PDTB 2.0

CONN	"contra-exp."	"exp."	"Concession"	Total
although	21	132	1	154 (13%)
but	494	12	2	508 (42.5%)
even if	3	31	1	35 (3%)
even though	15	52	5	72 (6%)
however	70	2	5	77 (6.5%)
nevertheless	19	0	0	19 (1.5%)
nonetheless	17	0	0	17 (1.5%)
still	79	2	1	82 (7%)
though	30	53	1	84 (7%)
while	3	79	1	83 (7%)
yet	32	0	0	32 (2.5%)
other	13	17	0	30 (2.5%)
Total	796	380	17	1193

most common connective annotated with the 'Concession' type or one of its two sub-types is "but" with 508 tokens (42% of all concessive labels), followed by "although" with 154 tokens (13% of all concesive labels).

We are currently evaluating the robustness of the proposed refined semantics for concessive labels in PDTB 2.0 starting with the most the most common concessive connectives. While the validation process for the entire corpus is still work in progress, preliminary results on 25% of 'but' tokens indicate that the semantics of concession based on defeasible causality applies straightforwardly to more than 60% of the data. In future work, we hope to be able to offer a more comprehensive account of all the concessive labels in PDTB 2.0 including cases of concession in which the created expectation arises from an implication rather than from a causal relation (about 23%), as in (3)

(3)   Although **working for U.S. intelligence,** *Mr. Noriega was hardly helping the U.S. exclusively.* (expectation)

In (3), it is strange to say that *working for U.S. intelligence* normally "causes" *helping U.S. exclusively.* Rather, the former seems a kind of necessary condition or job requirement for the latter: *working for U.S. intelligence* implies (among other things) *helping U.S. exclusively.* Suppose that someone discovers that Mr. Noriega is not helping the U.S. exclusively. Mr. Noriega is arguably breaking a rule or flauting an expectation. Therefore, *working for U.S. intelligence* "implies" rather than "causes" *helping U.S. exclusively.*

It is unsurprising that there are cases of concession based on implication rather than causality, because the two concepts are very close to each other. One could think of implication as a kind of abstract, informational, or "denatured" causality. Both obey a kind of (defeasible) modus ponens. When the cause or antecedent happens or holds, so does the effect or consequent. The other key property of causal complexes is that all the eventualities in it are relevant, in a sense that is made precise in Hobbs (2005). This notoriously does not hold for material implication, but as many have argued, it probably does hold for felicitous uses of our everyday notion of implication. In addition, there are easy conversions between causality and implication. If *A* causes *B*, then the fact that *A* happens (defeasibly) implies that *B* happens. If *P* implies *Q* in the everyday sense, then one's belief in *P* (defeasibly) causes one's belief in *Q*. In fact, implicational cases of concession could be viewed as instances of metonymy, where "believe" is the coercion relation, and hence really causal cases of concession.

6   Conclusion

We presented a formal description of the meaning of concession, a substantial refinement of the rough semantics given in the manual of sense annotations of connectives in PDTB 2.0. Our analysis builds on Hobbs's logic of defeasible causality enabled by the crucial distinction between causes and causal complexes. Our basic claim is that concession is triggered by the contrast between two causal relations. The causal relation between the content of one argument of the relation and some implicit eventuality (the expectation created based on the content of the argument) and the content of another causal relation, that between the eventuality described in second argument and *its* implicit cause. This second causal relation picks an element of the causal complex that we would normally assume to hold and challenges it, hence the notion of defeasible causality.

This work illustrates the mutual benefit that corpus annotation and formal analysis can provide to each other. Corpus examples constitute a forcing function on the formal analysis; definitions must accommodate the complexities one finds in the real world. On the other hand, all good annotation rests on solid theory, and formal analysis can help in the adjudication of difficult examples. The particular analysis we give in this paper for the concession relation can clarify issues that arise in annotation, and can also form the basis for recognizing these relations using a knowledge-rich inferencing system.

References

Achinstein, P. (1965). 'Defeasible' Problems. *The Journal of Philosophy 62*(21), 629–633.

Asher, N. (1993). *Reference to Abstract Objects*. Kluwer, Dordrecht.

Bach, E. (1981). On Time, Tense, and Aspect: An Essay in English Metaphysics. In P. Cole (Ed.), *Radical Pragmatics*, pp. 63–81. Academic Press, New York.

Bell, J. (1999). Primary and secondary events. In M. Thielscher (Ed.), *Proc. of the IJCAI-99 Workshop on Nonmonotonic Reasoning, Action and Change*, pp. 65–72.

Bell, J. (2003). A common sense theory of causation. In P. Blackburn, C. Ghidini, R. Turner, and F. Giunchiglia (Eds.), *Modeling and Using Context: Fourth International and Interdisciplinary Conference, Context 2003*, Berlin, pp. 40–53. Springer-Verlag.

Giordano, L. and C. Schwind (2004). Conditional logic of actions and causation. *Artificial Intelligence 157*(1–2), 239–279.

Giunchiglia, E., J. Lee, V. Lifschitz, N. McCain, and H. Turner (2004). Nonmonotonic causal theories. *Artificial Intelligence 153*(1–2), 49–104.

Hobbs, J. (1983). An Improper Treatment of Quantification in Ordinary English. In *Proc. of the 21st Annual Meeting of the Association for Computational Linguistics*, Cambridge, Massachusetts, pp. 57–63.

Hobbs, J. (1995). Monotone Decreasing Quantifiers in a Scope-Free Logical Form. In K. van Deemter and S. Peters (Eds.), *Semantic Ambiguity and Underspecification*, CSLI Lecture Notes, pp. 55–76. CSLI.

Hobbs, J. (1998). The Logical Notation: Ontological Promiscuity. In *Discourse and Inference*, Chapter 2.

Hobbs, J. (2005). Towards a Useful Notion of Causality for Lexical Semantics. *Journal of Semantics 22*(2), 181–209.

Kayser, D. and F. Nouioua (2008). From the Description of an Accident to its Causes. submitted to Artificial Intelligence.

McCarthy, J. (1977). Epistemological Problems of Artificial Intelligence. In *Proc. of International Joint Conference on Artificial Intelligence*, Cambridge, Massachusetts, pp. 1038–1044.

Miltsakaki, E., L. Robaldo, A. Lee, and A. Joshi (2008). Sense Annotation in the Penn Discourse Treebank. In *Proc. of Computational Linguistics and Intelligent Text Processing*, Volume 4919 of *LNCS*, pp. 275–286. Springer.

Prasad, R., N. Dinesh, A. Lee, E. Miltsakaki, L. Robaldo, A. Joshi, and B. Webber (2008). The Penn Discourse Treebank 2.0. In *Proc. of the 6th Int. Conf. on Language Resources and Evaluation*.

Prasad, R., E. Miltsakaki, N. Dinesh, A. Lee, A. Joshi, B. Webber, and L. Robaldo (2008). The Penn Discourse Treebank 2.0. Annotation Manual. Technical Report IRCS-06-01, IRCS Technical Report, Institute of Research in Cognitive Science, University of Pennsylvania.

Shoham, Y. (1990). Nonmonotonic reasoning and causation. *Cognitive Science 14*, 213–252.

Simon, H. (1991). Nonmonotonic reasoning and causation: Comment. *Cognitive Science 49*, 517–528.

Webber, B. and A. Joshi (2003). Anchoring a lexicalized tree-adjoining grammar for discourse. In M. Stede, L. Wanner, and E. Hovy (Eds.), *Discourse Relations and Discourse Markers: Proceedings of the Conference*, pp. 86–92.

Webber, B., A. Joshi, M. Stone, and A. Knott (2003). Anaphora and discourse structure. *Computational Linguistics 29*(4), 545–587.

Connective-based Local Coherence Analysis: A Lexicon for Recognizing Causal Relationships

Manfred Stede

University of Potsdam (Germany)

email: stede@ling.uni-potsdam.de

Abstract

Local coherence analysis is the task of deriving the (most likely) coherence relation holding between two elementary discourse units or, recursively, larger spans of text. The primary source of information for this step is the connectives provided by a language for, more or less explicitly, signaling the relations. Focusing here on causal coherence relations, we propose a lexical resource that holds both lexicographic and corpus-statistic information on German connectives. It can serve as the central repository of information needed for identifying and disambiguating connectives in text, including determining the coherence relations being signaled. We sketch a procedure performing this task, and describe a manually-annotated corpus of causal relations (also in German), which serves as reference data.

1   Introduction

"Text parsing" aims at deriving a structural description of a text, often a tree in the spirit of Rhetorical Structure Theory (Mann and Thompson, 1988). For automating this task (see, e.g., Sumita et al. (1992); Corston-Oliver (1998); Marcu (2000)), the central source of information are the *connectives* that the author employed to more or less specifically signal the type of coherence relation between adjacent spans. For illustration, consider this short text:[1].

> Because well-formed XML does not permit raw less-than signs and ampersands, if you use a character reference such as < or the entity reference < to insert the < character, the formatter will output < or perhaps <.

Supposing that we are able to identify the connectives and punctuation symbols correctly (here in particular: note that *to* is not a spatial preposition; distinguish between commas in enumerations and those finishing clauses), we can identify the "scaffold" of this short text as the following:

Because A, if B or C to D, E or F

with A to F representing the minimal units of analysis. Next, fairly simple rules will be sufficient to guess the most likely overall bracketing of this string:

(Because A, (if ((B or C) to D)), (E or F))

And finally, it happens that the connectives *because, if, to* and *or* are quite reliable signals of the coherence relations *Reason, Condition, Purpose* and *Disjunction*, respectively. Combining this information with the bracketing, we can obtain a tree structure in spirit of RST.

Texts of this level of complexity could be handled by early text parsers (see Section 2). But, obviously, not too many texts behave as nicely as our example does. In general, constructing a discourse tree is highly complicated even without trying to find semantic/pragmatic labels for the relationships; the discussion by Polanyi et al. (2004) demonstrates that just the structural decisions are often very difficult to make. Taking a different viewpoint, this author argues in Stede (2008) that constructing "the" tree structure for a text should not be regarded as such an important goal and that coherence should rather be explained as the interplay of different levels of (possibly partial) description, such as referential and thematic structure, intentional structure, and a level of *local coherence analysis* that records the clearly recognizable relationships between adjacent text spans but does not aim at constructing a complete and well-formed tree. In the present paper, this viewpoint is taken to the task of automatic analysis, which aims at identifying individual coherence relations and the spans related. We restrict ourselves here to *causal* relationships and moreover to those that are explicitly signaled by a connective. The central resource used in our approach is a lexicon that collects the information associated with individual connectives and makes it available to applications such as a coherence analysis or text generation.

The paper is organized as follows. After reviewing some earlier research on text parsing in Section 2, we turn to connectives in Section 3 and point out a number of problems that sophisticated coherence analyzers have to reckon with. Then, Section 4 explains the connective lexicon we developed, and Section 5 describes a corpus we collected and annotated manually for causal connectives and the relations they signal.

---

[1] Source: http://www.cafeconleche.org/books/bible2/chapters/ch17.html

It serves as a reference for designing the analysis procedure, which is finally sketched in Section 6. Our analysis and implementation target German text, but most of the phenomena apply equally to English.

2 Related Work

In the late 1990s. the best-known work on "text parsing" was that of Marcu, which is collected in Marcu (2000). He had used surface-based and statistical methods to identify elementary discourse units, hypothesize coherence relations between adjacent segments, and finally compute the most likely overall "rhetorical tree" for the text. Surface-based methods were highly popular at the time, but with the recent advances in robust and wide-coverage sentence parsing, it seems sensible to cast local coherence analysis as a problem of linguistic analysis, drawing on the results of syntactic parsing (or even, on top of that, semantic analysis).

An early approach in this spirit was implemented in the RASTA analyzer (Corston-Oliver, 1998). It perused the output of the 'Microsoft English Grammar' to guess the presence of coherence relations on the basis of accumulated evidence from a variety of more or less deep linguistic features. For instance, a hypotactic clause would always figure as the satellite of some nucleus-satellite relation in RST terms. For some relations (e.g., *Elaboration*), the type of referring expressions, especially in subject position, was considered a predictive feature. In general, RASTA employed a set of necessary criteria for each relation to hold in a particular context, and for those relations passing the filter, a voting scheme accumulated evidence to decide on the most likely relation. The system worked on *Encarta* articles, hence on expository text; 13 relations were being used.

While RASTA employed a relation-centric approach, the recent work by Lüngen et al. (2006) places the connectives at the center of the analysis, recording information about them in a specific lexicon (similar to our own earlier work (Stede, 2002)). In the lexicon used by Lüngen et al., an entry consists of three zones: the *identification* zone gives the textual representation of the connective, its lemma and part-of-speech tag; the *filter* zone encodes necessary conditions for particular discourse relations, in the form of context descriptions; the *allocation* zone then specifies a default relation to be assumed if no other relation can be derived on the basis of further (soft) conditions. It also encodes constraints on the size of units to be related, the nuclearity assignment, and the information whether the segment including the connective attaches to the left or to the right in the text. Each entry gives rise to a rule used by a shift-reduce parser that tries to build a complete rhetorical tree. This parser works in close cooperation with a module identifying logical document structure, and the context conditions specified in lexicon entries often refer to this level of structure, or to a syntactic dependency analysis provided by the *Connexor* parser[2].

We share with these approaches (and with that of Polanyi et al. (2004)) the desire to derive as much information about discourse relations as possible *without* resorting to non-linguistic knowledge, so that the role of local coherence analysis in effect can be seen as extending the realm of robust sentence parsing. Our approach is to represent as much of the necessary information as possible in a declarative resource: a lexicon

---

[2]http://www.connexor.com

of connectives.

3   Complications with Connectives

Connectives are closed-class lexical items that can belong to four different syntactic categories: coordinating and subordinating conjunction, adverbial, and preposition (such as *despite* or *due to*). They have in common that semantically they denote two-place relations, and the text spans they relate can at least potentially be expressed as full clauses (Pasch et al., 2003). As mentioned in the beginning, they are not always as easy to interpret as in our "well-formed XML" example. In this section, we suggest an inventory of the complications that a thorough local coherence analysis procedure needs to deal with. We group them into four categories.

Ambiguity. Here we need to distinguish two kinds: (i) ambiguity as to whether a word is used as a connective or not, and (ii) ambiguity as to the semantic reading of a connective. Certain cases of (i) correspond to the distinction between 'sentential use' and 'discourse use' that Hirschberg and Litman (1994) had proposed not for connectives but more generally for 'cue phrases' in spoken language. For example, German *denn* can be a coordinating conjunction (sentential use) or a particle often used in questions without a recognizable semantic effect (discourse use). Other cases of (i) reflect ambiguity between different 'sentential' uses. Sometimes this coincides with a syntactic difference (e.g., English *as* is a connective only when used as subordinator), but with many adverbials it does not (e.g., German *daher* can be a locative adverbial 'from there' or a causal adverbial 'therefore'). Also, sometimes the distinction coincides with semantic scope, as with the focus particle / connective *nur* ('only'):

(1)   Es war ein schöner Sommertag. Nur die Vögel sangen nicht.
      ('It was a nice summer day. Only the birds weren't singing.')

In a narrow-scope reading of 'only', the message is that everybody was singing except for the birds; in a wide-scope reading, 'only' connects the two sentences and signals a restrictive elaboration. Ambiguity of type (i) is more widespread than one might think; in Dipper and Stede (2006), we report that 42 out of 135 frequent German connectives also have a non-connective reading, and we point out that many of the problems cannot be handled with off-the-shelf part-of-speech taggers.

Concerning ambiguity (ii), some connectives can have more than one semantic reading, which we regard as a difference in the coherence relation being signaled. Sometimes, the relation can be established on different levels of linguistic description (see, e.g., Sweetser (1990)). For example, *finally* can be used to report the last one in a sequence of events, or it can be used by the author as a device for structuring the discourse ("and my last point is..."). Interestingly, the very similar German word *schließlich* in addition has a third reading: It can also be an argumentative marker conveying that a presented reason is definitive or self-evident, which in English may be signaled with 'after all': *Vertraue ihr. Sie ist schließlich die Chefin.* ('Trust her. She is the boss, after all.')

Pragmatic features. In addition to the relational differences, connectives can sometimes be distinguished by more fine-grained pragmatic features, which are usually not modeled as a difference in coherence relation. A well-known case in point is the difference between *because* and *since* (corresponding to German *weil / da*), where only the latter has a tendency to mark the following information as hearer-old (not necessarily discourse-old). The same pair of connectives serves to illustrate the feature of non-/occurrence within the scope of focus particles:

(2)   Nur weil/?da es regnet, nehme ich das Auto
       ('Only because/?since it's raining, I take the car.')

While in German, the *da* variant is hardly acceptable at all, in English there is a tendency for *since* to be interpreted in its temporal reading when used within the scope of *only*.

Also, connectives can convey largely the same information yet differ in terms of stylistic nuances, for instance in degree of formality. Thus a concessive relation in English may be signaled in a standard way with *although*, or with a rather formal, and in that sense "marked" *notwithstanding* construction.

Form. While the majority of connectives consist of a single word, some of them have two parts. Well-known instances are *either .. or* and *if .. then*. For the German version of the latter (*wenn .. dann*), a coherence analyzer must account for the possibility of its occurring in reverse order: *Dann nehme ich eben das Auto, wenn Du so bettelst.* ('Then I'll take the car, if you're begging so much'.) Further, looking at highly frequent collocations such as *even though* or *even if*, it is difficult to decide whether we are dealing with a single-word connective and a focus particle, or with a complex connective; one solution is to check in such cases whether the meaning is in fact derived compositionally and then to prefer the focus particle analysis. From "regular" two-word connectives it is only a small step to the shady area of *phrasal* connectives, which can allow for almost open-ended variation and modification: *for this reason / for these reasons / for all these very good reasons / ....*

For German, we have dealt with the issue of differentiating between types of multi-token connectives in a separate paper Stede and Irsig (2008).

Discourse structure. As is well-known, the structural description of a text can also be more complicated than in our "well-formed XML" example shown at the beginning. For one thing, discourse units can be embedded into one another, using parenthetical material or appositions. Further, connectives can occasionally link text segments that are non-adjacent — a phenomenon that has been studied intensively by Webber et al. (2003) and also by Wolf and Gibson (2005). An example from Webber et al.: *John loves Barolo. So he ordered three cases of the '97. But he had to cancel the order because then he discovered he was broke.* Here, the *then* is to be understood as linking the discovery event back to the ordering event rather than to the (adjacent) canceling. In German, many adverbial connectives have an overt anaphoric affix (e.g., *des*wegen, *da*her, trotz*dem*), and the ability to link non-adjacent segments appears to be restricted to these. Non-adjacency also leads to the issue of crossing dependencies, which is also discussed by the two teams of authors mentioned above. It correlates with the problem of two connectives occurring in the same clause, as it happens in the *Barolo* example (*because then*), which renders the parsing task significantly more complex than in the "well-formed XML" example.

A different problem is to be found in situations where a single coherence relation is signaled twice, by two different connectives, where one typically is to be read cataphorically:

(3)   Ich nehme deshalb$_i$ das Auto, weil$_i$ Du so bettelst.
      ('I take the car (for that reason)$_i$ because$_i$ you're begging so much.')

This phenomenon is difficult to reproduce in English; again, in German it is also limited to a certain class of connectives that can serve as cataphoric 'correlates'. Obviously, in such examples, a coherence analyzer will have to be very careful not to hypothesize two separate causal relationships. The same danger applies when multiple causes are enumerated for the same consequence, or multiple consequences arising from the same cause. The mere insertion of the focus particle *auch* ('also') in example 3 can fundamentally change the discourse structure to stating two reasons for taking the car:

(4)   Es regnet sehr stark. Ich nehme deshalb das Auto, auch weil Du so bettelst.
      ('It's raining heavily. I therefore take the car, also because you're begging so much.')

Finally, it is to be noted that certain connectives convey information about the discourse structure *beyond* the local relation between two segments. A case in point is the first word of this paragraph, which not only makes a 'List' or 'Enumeration' relation explicit, but also provides the information that this very list is now coming to an end. A smart coherence analyzer could thus reduce the search space for linking the subsequent text segment — it will definitely *not* be part of the same 'List' configuration.

4   A Rich Lexical Resource for Connectives

For building programs to perform local coherence analysis on texts that display the complexities discussed above, our approach is to clearly divide the labor between a declarative connective lexicon on the one hand, and a flexible analysis procedure on the other. In this section, we describe our *Discourse Marker Lexicon* (DIMLEX), whose first version was described in Stede (2002). At the time, it was used for relatively simple text parsing as outlined at the beginning of the paper, and also for a language generation application. The multi-functionality results from using a rather abstract XML encoding for the "master" lexicon, which is transformed by XSLT scripts to the format needed by a specific application — both in terms of technical format (e.g., programming language) and the amount and granularity of information needed for the application. With our current focus on causal relations, we extended the DIM-LEX entries of the causal connectives to a richer scheme, which will gradually be transferred to the remaining connectives as well.

It is not trivial to define an inventory of causal connectives, due to the grey area of words marking a semantic relationship that readers *can* also interpret causally — after all, causality is very often not explicitly signaled but being left for the reader to reconstruct. For example, in *The wind shook the shed for a few seconds, and then it collapsed* there certainly is causality involved in the relationship between the sentences, but we would not want to treat *and* or *then* as causal connectives. With the help of the 'Handbook of German Connectives' (Pasch et al., 2003), we determined a set of 66 German connectives that *primarily* convey causality.

The DIMLEX entries for these connectives consist of the following zones of information: (1) orthography, syntax, and structural features; (2) non-/connective disambiguation rules; (3) semantic and pragmatic features, including information on disambiguating different readings, and on role linking. As for the type of information, entries contain both binary features and probabilities derived from corpus analyses.

Orthography and syntax. Orthographic variants that we store in the lexicon result from the recent official German spelling reform and from frequent mistakes made by speakers/authors (as found in corpora). Also, we list both upper and lower case spellings because this difference plays a role in many disambiguation rules (see below). Each variant has a unique identifier that is being used in those rules. Also, one of the variants is marked as 'canonical' for co-reference purposes. Here is a sample excerpt from the entry for *aufgrund*, corresponding to the English *due to*:

```
<orth type="simple" canon="1" onr="k2v1">
   <part type="cont">aufgrund</part> </orth>
<orth type="complex" canon="0" onr="k2v2">
   <part type="cont">auf Grund</part> </orth>
<orth type="simple" canon="0" onr="k2v3">
   <part type="cont">Aufgrund</part> </orth>
<orth type="complex" canon="0" onr="k2v4">
   <part type="cont">Auf Grund</part> </orth>
```

Each `orth` is of type 'simple' or 'complex', depending on the number of tokens involved. For simple connectives (single tokens), the `part type` is always 'cont' (continuous), whereas for complex connectives it may also be 'discontinuous' if linguistic material can intervene between the parts (which is not the case for the two complex variants above).

Syntactically, connectives can be subordinating conjunctions; *Postponierer*; pre-, post- and circumpositions; and adverbials, some of which can occur only in specific positions (characterized in accordance with the *Feldermodell* that is often used to describe German sentence structure in terms of *Vorfeld, Mittelfeld, Nachfeld*). We encode this information following the classification by Pasch et al. (2003)), whose primary criterion is whether the connective can be *integrated* into the clause, and if so, at what positions it can occur. Here is the information for the prepositional adverb ('padv') *dadurch* ('by means of this'):

```
<padv>
  <vorfeld>1</vorfeld>
  <mittelfeld>1</mittelfeld>
  <nacherst>0</nacherst>
  <nachfeld>1</nachfeld>
  <nullstelle>0</nullstelle>
  <nachnachfeld>0</nachnachfeld>
  <satzklammer>0</satzklammer>
</padv>
```

The binary features say that the connective can be in the Vorfeld (preceding the finite verb or auxiliary: *Dadurch ist es geschehen*), Mittelfeld (between auxiliary and verb: *Es ist dadurch geschehen*), and Nachfeld (following the verb phrase: *Es ist geschehen dadurch*).

As a representation more directly usable for computational purposes, we also specify patterns of the connective being situated in a syntax tree in TIGER format (Brants et al., 2004). This format is used both in large hand-annotated German corpora as well as in an automatic parser[3]. The idea of the patterns in the lexical entry thus is to find instances of the word in a TIGER-tree, whether coming from a treebank or from a parser. For illustration, here is the pattern for the complex connective *so .. dass* ('so .. that'):

```
(#avp:[cat="AVP"] > [lemma="so"])
&
((#avp > #s:[cat="S"])
 |
 ((#avp > #cs:[cat="CS"]) &
  (#cs > #s:[cat="S"]))
)
&
(#s > [lemma=("dass")])
```

This expression looks for an adverbial phrase (AVP) that dominates both *so* and a sentence (S), or a coordination of sentences (CS) that in turn dominate *dass*. Between the *so* and *dass*, any material can intervene. An examples matched by this expression in the TIGER corpus is: *Der Kanzler hat China so gern , daß er ihm sogar die höchsten Berge der Welt zu schenken vermöchte.* ('The chancellor likes China so much, that he even wants to give the world's highest mountains as a present to the country.')

Besides the syntactic structure of individual conjuncts, we also need to represent the possibilities on linear order of the conjuncts. This is also based on the terminology of Pasch et al. (2003), who distinguish between the *internal* conjunct (the clause or phrase that the connective syntactically belongs to) and the *external* one. Sometimes, this a hard constraint: With the conjunction *denn* (causal 'for'), the internal conjunct can only follow the external one. With other connectives, e.g., *weil* ('because'), both orderings are possible, i.e., the *because*-clause giving a reason can precede or follow the clause giving the effect. In these cases we include probabilities derived from a corpus analysis, which the coherence analysis module can use for disambiguating scope when it has no other information available.

The syntactic representations become somewhat more complicated in case of *complex* connectives. For instance, there is a variant of *dadurch* that co-occurs with a subsequent (but not necessarily adjacent!) complement clause headed by *dass* ('that'). Similarly, as shown in the previous section, certain causal conjunctions and adverbials can co-occur and redundantly mark the same relation. Our lexicon entries contain features representing those possible pairings. For a more general discussion on German complex connectives, see Stede and Irsig (2008).

Finally, we include a feature stating whether the connective can be in the scope of a focus particle. This information can sometimes support non-/connective disambiguation.

---

[3] http://www.ims.uni-stuttgart.de/tcl/SOFTWARE/BitPar.html

Non-/connective disambiguation. In Dipper and Stede (2006), we reported on an approach to disambiguating non-/connective use for nine connectives by incrementally training a Brill tagger, which lead to F-measures of 81% (+connective) and 95% (–connective) in the best of four training scenarios. During this work it became clear that the part-of-speech context of the word often indeed provides enough information for making the decision. The main reason why off-the-shelf taggers, however, do not perform very well is that tagsets do not reflect the distinction — recall the syntactic heterogeneity of the "class" of connectives. From our findings we thus constructed for each connective a set of patterns over part-of-speech and lemma information, leading to regular expressions associated with probabilites (again gathered from corpus studies). These expressions become part of the *DiMLex* entries and can be used by the coherence analyzer. Starting from the Dipper/Stede results, we manually created classes of connectives with apparently-equivalent behavior, rather than studying each of the 66 connectives in detail. For illustration, here is the pattern set for *daher*, which can be a causal connective ('therefore') or a locative adverb ('from there'):

```
<conn-disambi>
   <pros>
      <pro value="90" ref="k5v2"> $. $$/PROAV </pro>
      <pro value="90" ref="k5v1"> VVFIN $$/PROAV </pro>
   </pros>
   <cons>
      <con value="99" ref="k5v1 k5v2">
         $$/PROAV $, {'dass'}/KOUS
      </con>
      <con value="95" ref="k5v2">
         $. $$/PROAV .* {'kommen' 'ruehren'} .+ $, {'dass'}/KOUS
      </con>
      <con value="99" ref="k5v1"> $$/PROAV $. </con>
   </cons>
</conn-disambi>
```

Weights range from 0 to 100, so 99 represents basically a strict rule. Notice the `ref` attribute, which restricts the rules to orthographic variants (in this case to upper and lower case ones). The first two rules support a +connective reading: *daher* tagged as pronominal adverb (PROAV) following a full stop or a finite verb, respectively. The following three rules support a –connective reading: *daher* followed by the subordinating conjunction (KOUS) *dass*; occurring in a collocation like *kommt daher, dass* ('stems from'); occurring before a full stop, i.e., sentence-final.

Semantics and Pragmatics. As stated earlier, we identify a difference in readings with a difference in *coherence relation* signaled by the connective. As for the inventory of relations, we take inspiration from Mann and Thompson (1988), Asher and Lascarides (2003), and especially for the causal relations, from the taxonomic approach of Sanders et al. (1992). Not every distinction made in the literature can be traced to connectives; so we do for instance not follow RST's distinction between 'Volitional Cause' and 'Non-volitional Cause' in DIMLEX. But we find differences in connective use for semantic versus pragmatic causal relations (Sanders et al., 1992).

For instance, the *denn* used in (4) below is quite typical for pragmatic relations (see, e.g. Pasch, 1989).

(5)   Er wird bestimmt pünktlich kommen, denn er ist doch immer so gewissenhaft.
      ('Surely he will arrive on time, for he is always so assiduous.')

Thus, in the realm of causality we use coherence relations labeled 'Argument-Claim' (pragmatic) and 'Reason-Consequence' (semantic). Further, if the consequence is a yet-unrealized intended effect, we assign the relation 'Purpose' as it has been suggested by Mann and Thompson (1988). The connectives associated with Purpose are mostly quite specific (e.g., English *in order to*; German *um .. zu*), but there can also be ambiguity between Purpose and "other" causality (e.g., English *so that*; German *damit*).

Disambiguation between the semantic and the pragmatic relation is usually very difficult and thus a matter of heuristically weighing the evidence. Similar to our handling non-/connective disambiguation (see above), we use a scheme of weight accumulation for features indicating the presence of a relation. For example, for the connective *schließlich* we found that with the main verb of the clause elided, the pragmatic reading is very unlikely; on the other hand, if the verb is in present tense and the Aktionsart is 'state', it very likely signals the pragmatic 'Claim-Argument' relation. Other evidence for this relation includes modal particles signaling the epistemic status of the proposition(s), often in conjunction with present or future tense. This is illustrated in example 4 above, where the speaker expresses her confidence that the event will materialize with *bestimmt* ('surely'), while *doch* äin the second clause marks the information has hearer-old, so that the difference between claim and argument in this case is quite transparent. Other features we modeled are inspired by the empirical work of Frohning (2007). They include position, tense and aspect of the clause, mood and modality, and lexical collocations; Frohning derived their weights from corpus analyses.

Often, however, no compelling evidence for either of the three relations can be found, and for these cases we use a neutral relation called 'Cause-Caused', which is thus meant to subsume the two others.

In addition to relation(s), a lexicon entry specifies the *role linking* for connectives: the mapping from the syntactically internal or external conjunct (see above) to its function in the relation. We label these functions in accordance with the relations: 'Argument', 'Claim', 'Reason', and so forth. Since causal relations are directed, and the mapping cannot be predicted from syntactic features, it is crucial to represent this information explictly.

Besides, we use a number of more idosyncratic features to represent information that is relevant only for certain connectives, in particular to distinguish very similar ones. An example mentioned in the previous section is the information-structural difference between *weil* ('because') and *da* ('since'). For other families of connectives, this "miscelleneous features" section is more important; with temporal connectives, for instance, we specify in addition to the coarse-grained coherence relation more fine-grained distinctions such as whether the time spans of the related events meet or not, etc.

Having discussed our treatment of syntax and semantics separately, we now have to attend to the relationship between the two, i.e., to the issues of ambiguity and polysemy. The majority of connectives has one syntactic description and can convey one or two similar coherence relations (the typical ambiguity between semantic and pragmatic reading). We do, however, also find other configurations:

- Two syntactic descriptions: *weil* used to be a subordinating conjunction, but in spoken German is now widely accepted as a coordinating conjunction as well. Since the meaning is the same, it suffices to simply list both syntactic variants in DIMLEX.

- One syntactic description, many coherence relations: When used as an adverb, the connective *damit* can signal Purpose ('so that') or Reason-Consequence ('thus'). This situation is similar to the previous one: We provide a disjunction of semantic readings (including the disambiguation information) and a single syntactic description.[4]

- Two syntactic descriptions, several coherence relations: These cases are the only serious complications, as a difference in syntax can correlate with one in semantics, so that we cannot simply specify disjunctions for the syntactic and semantic descriptions. Instead, we use multiple lexical entries, in accordance with the intuition that we are dealing with fairly unrelated items (polysemy). An example is *dann* ('then'), which on the one hand is a temporal adverbial, and on the other hand can express a Condition relation (optionally with a corresponding *wenn* ('if') in the other clause). In the latter case, it does not behave as an adverb, though, but it governs a verb-second clause. So, distributing the information across two separate lexicon entries seems to be appropriate.

Finally, to enhance the maintainability of DIMLEX, we inlcude with the entries a range of linguistic examples that illustrate the relevant distinctions, and we also citee information that is provided by standard dictionaries — especially in those cases where our formalization is not yet complete. One of the XSLT scripts for converting DIMLEX maps the base lexicon to an HTML format that allows for inspecting the entries, including the information just mentioned, which is intended for the human eye rather than for automatic parsers or generators.

5   A Corpus Annotated with Causal Relations

As a preparatory step for implementing a local coherence analyzer that aims specifically at identifying causal relations, we built a corpus with causal connectives annotated manually. We selected 200 short texts from a product review web site[5], where travelers comment on various tourist destinations. Since they often give reasons for the opinions they express, this genre offers more instances of causal connectives than, say, newspaper text. On the other hand, there is the undeniable drawback of frequent

---

[4] As a matter of fact, the situation is more difficult: *Damit* is one of the most complicated words in our lexicon, as it also has a reading as subordinator where it signals Purpose, as well as a non-connective adverbial reading ('with it/that').

[5] http://www.dooyoo.de

mistakes in grammar and orthography, which makes any automatic analyis quite hard, and also sometimes poses challenges to the human annotator.

Creating the corpus involved several steps. First, potential causal connectives were searched automatically (using the list from DIMLEX) and manually filtered. Subsequently, *identifying* causal connectives was not an issue for the annotation process, as they were already presented to annotators as "anchors" for their task. We then designed annotation guidelines with instructions for identifying causes and effects. As for the length of spans, annotators were encouraged to prefer a shorter span in cases where the boundary of a cause or effect is not quite clear. At the same time, they were asked to mark two discontinuous spans in cases where a cause/effect was interrupted by extraneous material such as authors' remarks on their own text production. Thus, in the following example, the C1 and C2 indices mark the intended cause, and E the intended effect.

(6) [The beach was not very pleasant]$_E$, as [it was,]$_{C1}$ I just have to say this here, [utterly littered with remains of picnics.]$_{C2}$

When multiple reasons are given for the same effect (or vice versa), annotators had to mark them separately, so that each cause-effect pair can be derived individually from the annotated data. Sometimes this multiplicity can involve separate connectives, as in the following example. In such cases, annotators had to choose a central connective (the one linking the adjacent cause and effect) and then add additional ones as secondary connectives, possibly forming a chain. This ensures easy retrievability of all pairs from the data.

(7)   [We reached the hotel late]$_E$ [due to]$_{Co1}$ [the flight's delay]$_{Ca}$ and also [because]$_{Co2}$ [it took so long to find a cab.]$_{Cb}$

Further, annotators had to identify possible redundant markings of the *same* cause-effect pair (as with the cataphoric correlates discussed above) as well as focus particles that modify connectives. Thus, in example (7), they would mark *also* and link it to the modified *because*.

Our first version of the annotation guidelines was subject to an informal evaluation with annotators who had not been involved in the project. On the basis of the results we clarified several aspects in the guidelines and thus wrote the final version. Furthermore, we prepared two instructional videos: one for using the annotation tool MMAX2[6], and one for our specific annotation scenario, illustrating the handling of a fairly complicated text passage. In the formal evaluation with two annotators, they received no training other than by the guidelines and the two videos. Of 78 connectives, 34 were analyzed identically. The vast majority of the mismatches (36 of 44) resulted from different span length: There was overlap between the spans chosen by the annotators, but the boundaries were not exactly identical. Other mismatches, which occurred only a few times, included different decisions on secondary connectives and the resulting chains of causes/effects.

Finally, with the guidelines having become stable, experienced annotators created the "official" annotation of the entire corpus of 200 texts (containing some 1,200

---

[6]http://mmax2.sourceforge.net

causal connectives). It is now is available as a resource for training and evaluation of automatic procedures. We also developed a web-based viewer (essentially translating the MMAX2 format to HTML and Javascript) that allows for manually browsing the corpus comfortably.[7]

6 Towards recognizing causal relations automatically

Having described DIMLEX as the central resource for local coherence analysis, and the corpus as reference and evaluation tool, we now briefly sketch a procedure for recognizing causal relations, whose implementation is currently under way in our text analysis workbench (Chiarcos et al., 2008), a standoff XML architecture for fusing linguistic annotations coming from different manual or automatic annotation tools. In this highly modular approach, the output of each individual analysis module is stored in a separate layer, using our standoff XML format PAULA (Dipper, 2005). Analysis tools can use previously computed layers for their own task, which usually involves creating one or more new layers.

In this setting, the task of local coherence analysis involves the following layers. The first four are to be built in the pre-processing phase, and the last two are the result of the coherence analyzer:

1. Token layer (including sentence boundaries)

2. Part-of-Speech

3. Logical document structure (headlines, paragraph breaks, etc.)

4. Dependency syntax analysis

5. Elementary discourse units

6. Connectives and (sets of) EDUs they relate

The procedure of coherence analysis consists of the following three sequential steps, which at various points make use of information from DIMLEX:

Connective identification. All the words listed in DIMLEX as some orthographic variant of a causal connective are identified in the text. This includes a check for complex connectives as listed in the lexicon, i.e., two corresponding words in adjacent clauses (amongst others, the *if .. then* type). It also includes a check for correlates, i.e., a connective that according to DIMLEX can be a correlate occurring in a clause immediately preceding a subordinate clause governed by a connective that according to DIMLEX can have a correlate (the *deshalb .. weil* type. For these checks, the syntax layer (4) is used to identify adjacent clauses.

Next, the single-word connective candidates are run through the disambiguation filters, i.e., the PoS/token regular expressions specified in their lexical entries are matched against the text's PoS representation on the corresponding layer (2). Those items that appear to be words in non-connective use are removed from the connective list. Finally, a new layer (6) is created, for now holding only the words that were recognized as connectives.

---

[7]All material can be found at `http://www.ling.uni-potsdam.de/~stede/kausalkorpus.html`.

Segmentation. The basic idea of our approach follows that of the module implemented by Lüngen et al. (2006) for German. We first overgenerate, guessing segment boundaries at every possible position, according to the dependency parse result; then, contextual rules remove those boundaries that appear to be wrong (e.g., commas in enumerations). We are, however, using somewhat different definitions of segments, namely a variant of Jasinskaja et al. (2007), and the corpus annotated according to those segmentation guidelines will be used to evaluate our module. One issue where we diverge from both Lüngen *et al.* and from Jasinskaja *et al.* is in our handling of prepositions: We do admit certain prepositional phrases as elementary discourse units, but only those that are headed by a preposition listed in DIMLEX, e.g., the causal markers *wegen* ('due to') or *durch* ('through'). The resulting sequence of segments is represented on a new layer of analysis (5).

Relation and scope identification. Next, the connective layer (6) is extended with information on relations and scopes: Every connective is associated with one or more attribute-value structures listing possible coherence relations along with probabilities. To this end, all relations stored with the connective in DIMLEX are recorded as hypotheses, and weights are accumulated as the result of evaluating the associated disambiguation rules, which largely operate on the syntax layer, as explained in Section 4.

Finally, for each relation we also hypothesize its scope: the thematic roles are associated with sequences of minimal units from layer (5). Given a reliable syntactic analysis, scope determination is usually straightforward for coordinating and subordinating conjunctions. For adverbials, we hypothesize different solutions and rank them according to size: The most narrow interpretation is taken as most likely. In this step, we also consider the layer of logical document structure in order to avoid segments that would stretch across paragraphs or other kinds of boundaries. Similarly, a layer with the results of "text tiling" (breakdown of the text in terms of thematic units, in the tradition of Hearst (1994)) could be used for this purpose, as well as as an 'attribution' layer that identifies those modal contexts that attribute a span of text to a particular source (as in indirect speech).

In this way, the module will generate hypotheses of coherence relations and related spans, for the time being solely on the basis of connectives occurring in the text. As explained, this information is represented in two additional analysis layers. Modules following in the processing chain may combine the various hypotheses into the most likely overall relational tree structure for the paragraph (or a set of such tree structures, see Reitter and Stede (2003)), or they may use the hypotheses directly for some application that does not rely on a spanning tree.

7   Discussion

The central idea behind the separation of the declarative DIMLEX resource and the (ongoing) implementation of an analysis procedure is to facilitate a smooth extensibility of the overall approach towards further kinds of connectives and coherence relations. When the lexicon is extended — while the underlying scheme remains unchanged — coverage of the analyzer grows without adaptations to the analysis procedure. An important benefit of the XML-based organization of the lexicon is its suitability for a variety of applications (parsing, generation, lexicography), which can each select from the master lexicon exactly those types of information that are relevant for them. On the other hand, an obvious drawback of the present "flat" XML format is a relatively high degree of redundancy. The good reasons for introducing inheritance-based representation formalisms in "standard" computational lexicons of content words largely apply to the realm of connectives (and possibly to other function words) as well. For the time being, however, the more mundane task of lexical description still offers a great many open questions for individual connectives and families thereof; the issue of more intelligent storage should become prominent later, when the groundwork has stabilized.

As with the vast majority of coherence relations, causal ones often need not be explicitly signaled at the linguistic surface by a connective. Thus the approach proposed in this paper will of course only partially solve the problem of local coherence analysis. An important challenge for future work is to identify linguistic features of discourse units *other than* connectives that can also serve to at least constrain the range of admissible coherence relations (see, e.g. Asher and Lascarides, 2003). Investigating these with empirical methods is an important next step in the overall program of partially deriving coherence relations in authentic text *without* resorting to non-linguistic knowledge.

Acknowledgments

The following people from the Potsdam Applied Computational Linguistics Group contributed to the work described in this paper (in alphabetical order): André Herzog (causality corpus); Kristin Irsig (DiMLex entries for causal connectives); Andreas Peldszus (causality corpus and annotation guidelines); Uwe Küssner (implementation of LCA module).

References

Asher, N. and A. Lascarides (2003). *Logics of Conversation*. Cambridge: Cambridge University Press.

Brants, S., S. Dipper, P. Eisenberg, S. Hansen, E. König, W. Lezius, C. Rohrer, G. Smith, and H. Uszkoreit (2004). Tiger: Linguistic interpretation of a german corpus. *Research on Language and Computation 2*(4), 597–620.

Chiarcos, C., S. Dipper, M. Götze, J. Ritz, and M. Stede (2008). A flexible framework for integrating annotations from different tools and tagsets. In *Proc. of the First International Conference on Global Interoperability for Language Resources*, Hongkong.

Corston-Oliver, S. (1998). *Computing of Representations of the Structure of Written Discourse*. Ph. D. thesis, University of California at Santa Barbara.

Dipper, S. (2005). XML-based stand-off representation and exploitation of multi-level linguistic annotation. In R. Eckstein and R. Tolksdorf (Eds.), *Proceedings of Berliner XML Tage*, pp. 39–50.

Dipper, S. and M. Stede (2006). Disambiguating potential connectives. In M. Butt (Ed.), *Proceedings of KONVENS '06*, Konstanz, pp. 167–173.

Frohning, D. (2007). *Kausalmarker zwischen Pragmatik und Kognition. Korpusbasierte Analysen zur Variation im Deutschen.* Tübingen: Niemeyer. (Im Erscheinen).

Hearst, M. A. (1994). Multi-paragraph segmentation of expository text. In *Proceedings of the 32nd Meeting of the Association for Computational Linguistics*, Las Cruces/NM.

Hirschberg, J. and D. J. Litman (1994). Empirical studies on the disambiguation of cue phrases. *Computational Linguistics 19*(3), 501–530.

Jasinskaja, K., J. Mayer, J. Boethke, A. Neumann, A. Peldszus, and K. J. Rodríguez (2007). Discourse tagging guidelines for German radio news and newspaper commentaries. Ms., Universität Potsdam.

Lüngen, H., H. Lobin, M. Bärenfänger, M. Hilbert, and C. Puskas (2006). Text parsing of a complex genre. In B. Martens and M. Dobreva (Eds.), *Proc. of the Conference on Electronic Publishing (ELPUB 2006)*, Bansko, Bulgaria.

Lüngen, H., C. Puskas, M. Bärenfänger, M. Hilbert, and H. Lobin (2006). Discourse segmentation of German written text. In T. Salakoski, F. Ginter, S. Pyysalo, and T. Phikkala (Eds.), *Proceedings of the 5th International Conference on Natural Language Processing (FinTAL 2006)*, Berlin/Heidelberg/New York. Springer.

Mann, W. and S. Thompson (1988). Rhetorical structure theory: Towards a functional theory of text organization. *TEXT 8*, 243–281.

Marcu, D. (2000). *The theory and practice of discourse parsing and summarization.* Cambridge/MA: MIT Press.

Pasch, R. (1989). Adverbialsätze – kommentarsätze – adjungierte sätze. eine hypothese zu den typen der bedeutungen von 'weil', 'da' und 'denn'. In W. Motsch (Ed.), *Wortstruktur und Satzstruktur*, Linguistische Studien des ZISW: Reihe A – Arbeitsberichte 194, pp. 141–158. Berlin: Akademie der Wissenschaften der DDR.

Pasch, R., U. Brauße, E. Breindl, and U. H. Waßner (2003). *Handbuch der deutschen Konnektoren.* Berlin/New York: Walter de Gruyter.

Polanyi, L., C. Culy, M. van den Berg, G. L. Thione, and D. Ahn (2004). A rule based approach to discourse parsing. In *Proceedings of the SIGDIAL '04 Workshop*, Cambridge/MA. Assoc. for Computational Linguistics.

Reitter, D. and M. Stede (2003). Step by step: underspecified markup in incremental rhetorical analysis. In *Proceedings of the 4th International Workshop on Linguistically Interpreted Corpora (LINC)*, Budapest.

Sanders, T., W. Spooren, and L. Noordman (1992). Toward a taxonomy of coherence relations. *Discourse Processes 15*, 1–35.

Stede, M. (2002). DiMLex: A lexical approach to discourse markers. In *Exploring the Lexicon - Theory and Computation*. Alessandria: Edizioni dell'Orso.

Stede, M. (2008). RST revisited: Disentangling nuclearity. In C. Fabricius-Hansen and W. Ramm (Eds.), *'Subordination' versus 'coordination' in sentence and text*. Amsterdam: John Benjamins.

Stede, M. and K. Irsig (2008). Identifying complex connectives: Complications for local coherence analysis. In A. Benz, P. Kühnlein, and M. Stede (Eds.), *Proceedings of the Workshop on Constraints in Discourse*, Potsdam, pp. 77–84.

Sumita, K., K. Ono, T. Chino, T. Ukita, and S. Amano (1992). A discourse structure analyzer for Japanese text. In *Proceedings of the International Conference on Fifth Generation Computer Systems*, pp. 1133–1140.

Sweetser, E. (1990). *From etymology to pragmatics*. Cambridge: Cambridge University Press.

Webber, B., M. Stone, A. Joshi, and A. Knott (2003). Anaphora and discourse structure. *Computational Linguistics 29*(4), 545–587.

Wolf, F. and E. Gibson (2005). Representing discourse coherence: a corpus-based study. *Computational Linguistics 31*(2), 249–287.

Open Knowledge Extraction through Compositional Language Processing

Benjamin Van Durme
Lenhart Schubert
University of Rochester (USA)
email: vandurme@cs.rochester.edu

Abstract

We present results for a system designed to perform *Open Knowledge Extraction*, based on a tradition of compositional language processing, as applied to a large collection of text derived from the Web. Evaluation through manual assessment shows that well-formed propositions of reasonable quality, representing general world knowledge, given in a logical form potentially usable for inference, may be extracted in high volume from arbitrary input sentences. We compare these results with those obtained in recent work on Open *Information* Extraction, indicating with some examples the quite different kinds of output obtained by the two approaches. Finally, we observe that portions of the extracted knowledge are comparable to results of recent work on *class attribute* extraction.

1   Introduction

Several early studies in large-scale text processing (Liakata and Pulman, 2002; Gildea and Palmer, 2002; Schubert, 2002) showed that having access to a sentence's syntax enabled credible, automated semantic analysis. These studies suggest that the use of increasingly sophisticated linguistic analysis tools could enable an explosion in available symbolic knowledge. Nonetheless, much of the subsequent work in extraction has remained averse to the use of the linguistic deep structure of text; this decision is typically justified by a desire to keep the extraction system as computationally lightweight as possible.

The acquisition of background knowledge is not an activity that needs to occur online; we argue that as long as the extractor will finish in a *reasonable* period of time, the speed of such a system is an issue of secondary importance. Accuracy and usefulness of knowledge should be of paramount concern, especially as the increase in available computational power makes such "heavy" processing less of an issue.

The system explored in this paper is designed for *Open Knowledge Extraction*: the conversion of arbitrary input sentences into general world knowledge represented in a logical form possibly usable for inference. Results show the feasibility of extraction via the use of sophisticated natural language processing as applied to web texts.

2   Previous Work

Given that the concern here is with *open* knowledge extraction, the myriad projects that target a few prespecified types of relations occurring in a large corpus are set aside.

Among early efforts, one might count work on deriving selectional preferences (e.g., Zernik (1992); Resnik (1993); Clark and Weir (1999)) or partial predicate-argument structure (e.g., Abney (1996)) as steps in the direction of open knowledge extraction, though typically few of the tuples obtained (often a type of subject plus a verb, or a verb plus a type of object) can be interpreted as complete items of world knowledge. Another somewhat relevant line of research was initiated by Zelle and Mooney (1996), concerned with learning to map NL database queries into formal DB queries (a kind of semantic interpretation). This was pursued further, for instance, by Zettlemoyer and Collins (2005) and Wong and Mooney (2007), aimed at learning log-linear models, or (in the latter case) synchronous CF grammars augmented with lambda operators, for mapping English queries to DB queries. However, this approach requires annotation of texts with logical forms, and extending this approach to general texts would seemingly require a massive corpus of hand-annotated text — and the logical forms would have to cover far more phenomena than are found in DB queries (e.g., attitudes, generalized quantifiers, etc.).

Another line of relevant work is that on semantic role labelling. One early example was MindNet (Richardson et al., 1998), which was based on collecting 24 semantic role relations from MRDs such as the *American Heritage Dictionary*. More recent representative efforts includes that of Gildea and Jurafsky (2002), Gildea and Palmer (2002), and Punyakanok et al. (2008). The relevance of this work comes from the fact that identifying the arguments of the verbs in a sentence is a first step towards forming predications, and these may in many cases correspond to items of world knowledge.

Liakata and Pulman (2002) built a system for recovering Davidsonian predicate-argument structures from the Penn Treebank through the application of a small set of syntactic templates targeting head nodes of verb arguments. The authors illustrate their results for the sentence "*Apple II owners, for example, had to use their television sets as screens and stored data on audiocassettes*" (along with the Treebank annotations); they obtain the following QLF, where verb stems serve as predicates, and arguments are represented by the head words of the source phrases:

```
have(e1,owner, (use(e3,owner,set), and as(e3,screen)),
          and (store(e2,owner,datum), and on(e2,audiocassette))))
```

For a test set of 100 Treebank sentences, the authors report recall figures for various aspects of such QLFs ranging from 87% to 96%. While a QLF like the one above cannot in itself be regarded as world knowledge, one can readily imagine postprocessing steps that could in many cases obtain credible propositions from such QLFs. How accurate the results would be with machine-parsed sentences is at this point unknown.

In the same year, Schubert (2002) described a project aimed directly at the extraction of general world knowledge from Treebank text, and Schubert and Tong (2003) provided the results of hand-assessment of the resulting propositions. The Brown corpus yielded about 117,000 distinct simple propositions (somewhat more than 2 per sentence, of variable quality). Like Liakata and Pulman's approach the method relied on the computation of unscoped logical forms from Treebank trees, but it abstracted propositional information along the way, typically discarding modifiers at deeper levels from LFs at higher levels, and also replacing NPs (including named entities) by their types as far as possible. Judges found about 2/3 of the output propositions (when automatically verbalized in English) acceptable as general claims about the world. The next section provides more detail on the extraction system, called KNEXT, employed in this work.

Clark et al. (2003), citing the 2002 work of Schubert, report undertaking a similar extraction effort for the 2003 Reuters corpus, based on parses produced by the Boeing parser, (see Holmback et al. (2000)), and obtained 1.1 million subject-verb-object fragments. Their goal was eventually to employ such tuples as common-sense expectations to guide the interpretation of text and the retrieval of possibly relevant knowledge in question-answering. This goal, unlike the goal of inferential use of extracted knowledge, does not necessarily require the extracted information to be in the form of logical propositions. Still, since many of their tuples were in a form that could be quite directly converted into propositional forms similar to those of Schubert, their work indicated the potential for scalability in parser-based approaches to information extraction or knowledge extraction.

A recent project aimed at large-scale, open extraction of tuples of text fragments representing verbal predicates and their arguments is TextRunner (Banko et al., 2007). This systems does part-of-speech tagging of a corpus, identifies noun phrases with a noun phrase chunker, and then uses tuples of nearby noun phrases within sentences to form apparent relations, using intervening material to represent the relation. Apparent modifiers such as prepositional phrases after a noun or adverbs are dropped. Every candidate relational tuple is classified as trustworthy (or not) by a Bayesian classifier, using such features as parts of speech, number of relevant words between the noun phrases, etc. The Bayesian classifier is obtained through training on a parsed corpus, where a set of heuristic rules determine the trustworthiness of apparent relations between noun phrases in that corpus. As a preview of an example we will discuss later, here are two relational tuples in the format extracted by TextRunner:[1]

> (the **people**) use (**force**),
> (the **people**) use (**force**) to impose (a **government**).

No attempt is made to convert text fragments such as *"the people"* or *"use _ to impose"* into logically formal terms or predicates. Thus much like semantic role-labelling systems, TextRunner is an *information* extraction system, under the terminology used here; however, it comes closer to knowledge extraction than the former, in that it often strips away much of the modifying information of complex terms (e.g., leaving just a head noun phrase).

2.1 KNEXT

KNEXT (Schubert, 2002) was originally designed for application to collections of manually annotated parse trees, such as the Brown corpus. In order to extract knowledge from larger text collections, the system has been extended for processing arbitrary text through the use of third-party parsers. In addition, numerous improvements have been made to the semantic interpretation rules, the filtering techniques, and other components of the system. The extraction procedure is as follows:

1. Parse each sentence using a Treebank-trained parser (Collins, 1997; Charniak, 1999).

2. Preprocess the parse tree, for better interpretability (e.g., distinguish different types of SBAR phrases and different types of PPs, identify temporal phrases, etc.).

3. Apply a set of 80 interpretive rules for computing unscoped logical forms (ULFs) of the sentence and all lower-level constituents in a bottom-up sweep; at the same time, *abstract* and collect phrasal logical forms that promise to yield stand-alone propositions (e.g., ULFs of clauses and of pre- or post-modified nominals are prime candidates). The ULFs are rendered in Episodic Logic (e.g., (Schubert and Hwang, 2000)), a highly expressive representation allowing for generalized quantifiers, predicate modifiers, predicate and sentence reification operators, and other devices found in NL. The abstraction process drops modifiers present in lower-level ULFs (e.g., adjectival premodifiers of nominal predicates) in constructing higher-level ULFs (e.g., for clauses). In addition, named entities are generalized as far as possible using several gazetteers (e.g., for male and female given names, US states, world cities, actors, etc.) and some morphological processing.

4. Construct complete sentential ULFs from the phrasal ULFs collected in the previous step; here some filtering is performed to exclude vacuous or ill-formed results.

---

[1] Boldface indicates items recognized as head nouns.

5. Render the propositions from the previous step in (approximate) English; again significant heuristic filtering is done here.

As an example of KNEXT output, the sentence:

> *Cock fights, however, are still legal in six of the United States, perhaps because we still eat chicken regularly, but no-longer dogs.*

yields a pair of propositions expressed logically as:

[(K (NN cock.n (PLUR fight.n))) legal.a],
[(DET (PLUR person.n)) eat.v (K chicken.n)]

and these are automatically rendered in approximate English as:

COCK FIGHTS CAN BE LEGAL.
PERSONS MAY EAT CHICKEN.

As can be seen, KNEXT output does not conform to the ⟨relation, arg1, arg2, ...⟩, *tuple* style of knowledge representation favored in information extraction (stemming from that community's roots in populating DB tables under a fixed schema). This is further exemplified by the unscoped logical form:[2]

[(DET (PLUR person.n)) want.v (Ka (rid.a (of.p (DET dictator.n))))]

which is verbalized as PERSONS MAY WANT TO BE RID OF A DICTATOR and is supported by the text fragment:

> *... and that if the Spanish people wanted to be rid of Franco, they must achieve this by ...*

Later examples will be translated into a more conventional logical form.

One larger collection we have processed since the 2002-3 work on Treebank corpora is the British National Corpus (BNC), consisting of 100 million words of mixed-genre text passages. The quality of resulting propositions has been assessed by the hand-judging methodology of Schubert and Tong (2003), yielding positive judgements almost as frequently as for the Brown Treebank corpus. The next section, concerned with the web corpus collected and used by Banko et al. (2007), contains a fuller description of the judging method. The BNC-based KB, containing 6,205,877 extracted propositions, is publicly searchable via a recently developed online knowledge browser.[3]

---

[2] Where Ka is an action/attribute reification operator.
[3] http://www.cs.rochester.edu/u/vandurme/epik

3 Experiments

The experiments reported here were aimed at a comparative assessment of linguistically based knowledge extraction (by KNEXT), and pattern-based information extraction (by TextRunner, and by another system, aimed at class attribute discovery). The goal being to show that logically formal results (i.e. *knowledge*) based on syntactic parsing may be obtained at a subjective level of accuracy similar to methods aimed exclusively at acquiring correspondences between string pairs based on shallow techniques.

Dataset Experiments were based on sampling 1% of the sentences from each document contained within a corpus of 11,684,774 web pages harvested from 1,354,123 unique top level domains. The top five contributing domains made up 30% of the documents in the collection.[4] There were 310,463,012 sentences in all, the sample containing 3,000,736. Of these, 1,373 were longer than a preset limit of 100 tokens, and were discarded.[5] Sentences containing individual tokens of length greater than 500 characters were similarly removed.[6]

As this corpus derives from the work of Banko et al. (2007), each sentence in the collection is paired with zero or more *tuples* as extracted by the TextRunner system.

Note that while websites such as `Wikipedia.org` contain large quantities of (semi-)structured information stored in lists and tables, the focus here is entirely on natural language sentences. In addition, as the extraction methods discussed in this paper do not make use of intersentential features, the lack of sentence to sentence coherence resulting from random sampling had no effect on the results.

Extraction Sentences were processed using the syntactic parser of Charniak (1999). From the resultant trees, KNEXT extracted 7,406,371 *propositions*, giving a *raw* average of 2.47 per sentence. Of these, 4,151,779 were unique, so that the average extraction frequency per sentence is 1.78 unique propositions. Post-processing left 3,975,197 items, giving a per sentence expectation of 1.32 unique, filtered propositions. Selected examples regarding knowledge about people appear in Table 1.

For the same sample, TextRunner extracted 6,053,983 *tuples*, leading to a raw average of 2.02 tuples per sentence. As described by its designers, TextRunner is an *information* extraction system; one would be mistaken in using these results to say that KNEXT "wins" in raw extraction volume, as these numbers are not in fact directly comparable (see section on *Comparison*).

Table 1: Verbalized propositions concerning the class PERSON

A PERSON MAY...			
SING TO A GIRLFRIEND	RECEIVE AN ORDER FROM A GENERAL	KNOW STUFF	PRESENT A PAPER
EXPERIENCE A FEELING	CARRY IMAGES OF A WOMAN	BUY FOOD	PICK_UP A PHONE
WALK WITH A FRIEND	CHAT WITH A MALE-INDIVIDUAL	BURN A SAWMILL	FEIGN A DISABILITY
DOWNLOAD AN ALBUM	MUSH A TEAM OF (SEASONED SLED DOGS)		RESPOND TO A QUESTION
SING TO A GIRLFRIEND	OBTAIN SOME_NUMBER_OF (PERCULA CLOWNFISH)		LIKE (POP CULTURE)

---

[4] `en.wikipedia.org`, `www.answers.com`, `www.amazon.com`, `www.imdb.com`, `www.britannica.com`

[5] Typically enumerations, e.g., *There have been 29 MET deployments in the city of Florida since the inception of the program : three in Ft. Pierce , Collier County , Opa Locka , ...*

[6] For example, *Kellnull phenotypes can occur through splice site and splice-site / frameshift mutations301,302 450039003[...]3000 premature stop codons and missense mutations.*

1.	A REASONABLE GENERAL CLAIM
	e.g., A grand-jury may say a proposition
2.	TRUE BUT TOO SPECIFIC TO BE USEFUL
	e.g., Bunker walls may be decorated with seashells
3.	TRUE BUT TOO GENERAL TO BE USEFUL
	e.g., A person can be nearest an entity
4.	SEEMS FALSE
	e.g., A square can be round
5.	SOMETHING IS OBVIOUSLY MISSING
	e.g., A person may ask
6.	HARD TO JUDGE
	e.g., Supervision can be with a company

Figure 1: Instructions for categorical judging

Evaluation Extraction quality was determined through manual assessment of verbalized propositions drawn randomly from the results. Initial evaluation was done using the method proposed in Schubert and Tong (2003), in which judges were asked to label propositions according to their category of acceptability; abbreviated instructions may be seen in Figure 1.[7] Under this framework, category one corresponds to a strict assessment of acceptability, while an assignment to any of the categories between one and three may be interpreted as a weaker level of acceptance. As seen in Table 2, average acceptability was judged to be roughly 50 to 60%, with associated Kappa scores signalling fair (0.28) to moderate (0.48) agreement.

Table 2: Percent propositions labeled under the given category(s), paired with Fleiss' Kappa scores. Results are reported both for the authors (judges one and two), along with two volunteers

Category	% Selected	Kappa	% Selected	Kappa
1	49%	0.4017	50%	0.2822
1, 2, or 3	54%	0.4766	60%	0.3360
	judges		judges w/ volunteers	

Judgement categories at this level of specificity are useful both for system analysis at the development stage, as well as for training judges to recognize the disparate ways in which a proposition may not be acceptable. However, due to the rates of agreement observed, evaluation moved to the use of a five point sliding scale (Figure 2). This scale allows for only a single axis of comparison, thus collapsing the various ways in which a proposition may or may not be flawed into a single, general notion of acceptability.

---

[7] Judges consisted of the authors and two volunteers, each with a background in linguistics and knowledge representation.

> THE STATEMENT ABOVE IS A REASONABLY
> CLEAR, ENTIRELY PLAUSIBLE GENERAL
> CLAIM AND SEEMS NEITHER TOO SPECIFIC
> NOR TOO GENERAL OR VAGUE TO BE USEFUL:
> 1.   I agree.
> 2.   I lean towards agreement.
> 3.   I'm not sure.
> 4.   I lean towards disagreement.
> 5.   I disagree.

Figure 2: Instructions for scaled judging

The authors judged 480 propositions sampled randomly from amongst bins corresponding to frequency of support (i.e., the number of times a given proposition was extracted). 60 propositions were sampled from each of 8 such ranges.[8] As seen in Figure 3, propositions that were extracted at least twice were judged to be more acceptable than those extracted only once. While this is to be expected, it is striking that as frequency of support increased further, the level of judged acceptability remained roughly the same.

4   Comparison

To highlight differences between an extraction system targeting knowledge (represented as logical statements) as compared to information (represented as segmented text fragments), the output of KNEXT is compared to that of TextRunner for two select inputs.

4.1   Basic

Consider the following sentence:

> *A defining quote from the book, "An armed society is a polite society",*
> *is very popular with those in the United States who support the personal*
> *right to bear arms.*

From this sentence TextRunner extracts the tuples:[9]

> (A defining **quote**) is a (polite **society** "),
> (the personal **right**) to bear (**arms**).

We might manually translate this into a crude sort of logical form:

> IS-A(A-DEFINING-QUOTE, POLITE-SOCIETY-"),
> TO-BEAR(THE-PERSONAL-RIGHT, ARMS).

---

[8] $(0, 2^0, 2^1, 2^3, 2^4, 2^6, 2^8, 2^{10}, 2^{12})$, i.e., (0,1], (1,2], (2,8], ...

[9] Tuple *arguments* are enclosed in parenthesis, with the items recognized as *head* given in bold. All non-enclosed, conjoining text makes up the tuple *predicate*.

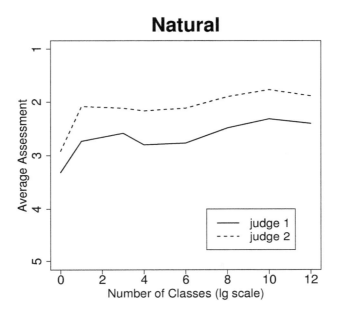

Figure 3: As a function of frequency of support, average assessment for propositions derived from *natural* sentences

Better would be to consider only those terms classified as head, and make the assumption that each tuple argument implicitly introduces its own quantified variable:

$\exists$x,y. QUOTE(x) & SOCIETY(y) & IS-A(x,y),
$\exists$x,y. RIGHT(x) & ARMS(y) & TO-BEAR(x,y).

Compare this to the output of KNEXT:[10]

$\exists$x. SOCIETY(x) & POLITE(x),
$\exists$x,y,z. THING-REFERRED-TO(x) & COUNTRY(y) & EXEMPLAR-OF(z,y) & IN(x,z),
$\exists$x. RIGHT(x) & PERSONAL(x),
$\exists$x,y. QUOTE(x) & BOOK(y) & FROM(x,y),
$\exists$x. SOCIETY(x) & ARMED(x),

which is automatically verbalized as:

A SOCIETY CAN BE POLITE,
A THING-REFERRED-TO CAN BE IN AN EXEMPLAR-OF A COUNTRY,
A RIGHT CAN BE PERSONAL,
A QUOTE CAN BE FROM A BOOK,
A SOCIETY CAN BE ARMED.

---

[10]For expository reasons, scoped, simplified versions of KNEXT's ULFs are shown. More accurately propositions are viewed as weak *generic conditionals*, with a non-zero lower bound on conditional frequency, e.g., [$\exists$x. QUOTE(x)] $\Rightarrow_{0.1}$ [$\exists$y. BOOK(y) & FROM(x,y)], where x is dynamically bound in the consequent.

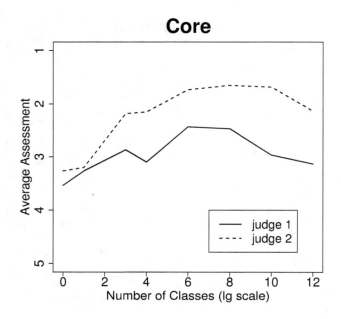

Figure 4: As a function of frequency of support, average assessment for propositions derived from *core* sentences

4.2 Extended Tuples

While KNEXT uniquely recognizes, e.g., adjectival modification and various types of possessive constructions, TextRunner more aggressively captures constructions with extended cardinality. For example, from the following:

> *James Harrington in The Commonwealth of Oceana uses the term anarchy to describe a situation where the people use force to impose a government on an economic base composed of either solitary land ownership, or land in the ownership of a few.*

TextRunner extracts 19 tuples, some with three or even four arguments, thus aiming beyond the binary relations that most current systems are limited to. That so many tuples were extracted for a single sentence is explained by the fact that for most tuples containing $N > 2$ arguments, TextRunner will also output the same tuple with $N - 1$ arguments, such as:

> (the **people**) use (**force**),
> (the **people**) use (**force**) to impose (a **government**),
> (the **people**) use (**force**) to impose (a **government**) on (an economic **base**).

In addition, tuples may overlap, without one being a proper subset of another:

(a **situation**) where (the **people**) use (**force**),
(**force**) to impose (a **government**),
(a **government**) on (an economic **base**) composed of
    (either solitary land **ownership**).

This overlap raises the question of how to accurately quantify system performance. When measuring average extraction quality, should samples be drawn randomly across tuples, or from originating sentences? If from tuples, then sample sets will be biased (for good or ill) towards fragments derived from complex syntactic constructions. If sentence based, the system fails to be rewarded for extracting as much from an input as possible, as it may conservatively target only those constructions most likely to be correct. With regards to volume, it is not clear whether adjuncts should each give rise to additional facts added to a final total; optimal would be the recognition of such optionality. Failing this, perhaps a tally may be based on unique predicate head terms?

As a point of merit according to its designers, TextRunner does not utilize a parser (though as mentioned it does part of speech tagging and noun phrase chunking). This is said to be justified in view of the known difficulties in reliably parsing open domain text as well as the additional computational costs. However, a serious consequence of ignoring syntactic structure is that incorrect bracketing across clausal boundaries becomes all too likely, as seen for instance in the following tuple:

> (**James Harrington**) uses (the term **anarchy**) to describe (a **situation**) where (the **people**),

or in the earlier example where *from the book, "An armed society* appears to have been erroneously treated as a post-nominal modifier, intervening between the first argument and the *is-a* predicate.

KNEXT extracted the following six propositions, the first of which was automatically filtered in post-processing for being overly vague:[11]

> ⋆ A MALE-INDIVIDUAL CAN BE IN A NAMED-ENTITY OF A NAMED-ENTITY,
> A MALE-INDIVIDUAL MAY USE A (TERM ANARCHY),
> PERSONS MAY USE FORCE,
> A BASE MAY BE COMPOSED IN SOME WAY,
> A BASE CAN BE ECONOMIC,
> A (LAND OWNERSHIP) CAN BE SOLITARY.

5   Extracting from Core Sentences

We have noted the common argument against the use of syntactic analysis when performing large-scale extraction viz. that it is too time consuming to be worthwhile. We are skeptical of such a view, but decided to investigate whether an argument-bracketing system such as TextRunner might be used as an extraction *preprocessor* to limit what needed to be parsed.

For each TextRunner tuple extracted from the sampled corpus, *core* sentences were constructed from the predicate and noun phrase arguments,[12] which were then used as input to KNEXT for extraction.

---

[11]The authors judge the third, fifth and sixth propositions to be both well-formed and useful.

[12]Minor automated heuristics were used to recover, e.g., missing articles dropped during tuple construction.

From 6,053,981 tuples came an equivalent number of core sentences. Note that since TextRunner tuples may overlap, use of these reconstructed sentences may lead to skewed propositional frequencies relative to "normal" text. This bias was very much in evidence in the fact that of the 10,507,573 propositions extracted from the core sentences, only 3,787,701 remained after automatic postprocessing and elimination of duplicates. This gives a per-sentence average of 0.63, as compared to 1.32 for the original text.

While the raw number of propositions extracted for each version of the underlying data look similar, 3,975,197 (natural) vs. 3,787,701 (core), the actual overlap was less than would be expected. Just 2,163,377 propositions were extracted jointly from both natural and core sentences, representing a percent overlap of 54% and 57% respectively.

Table 3: Mean judgements (lower is better) on propositions sampled from those supported either exclusively by natural or core sentences, or those supported by both

	Natural	Core	Overlap
judge 1	3.35	3.85	2.96
judge 2	2.95	3.59	2.55

Quality was evaluated by each judge assessing 240 randomly sampled propositions for each of: those extracted exclusively from natural sentences, those extracted exclusively from core sentences, those extracted from both (Table 3). Results show that propositions exclusively derived from core sentences were most likely to be judged poorly. Propositions obtained both by KNEXT alone and by KNEXT- processing of TextRunner-derived core sentences (the overlap set) were particularly likely to be judged favorably.

On the one hand, many sentential fragments ignored by TextRunner yield KNEXT propositions; on the other, TextRunner's output may be assembled to produce sentences yielding propositions that KNEXT otherwise would have missed. Ad-hoc analysis suggests these new propositions derived with the help of TextRunner are a mix of noise stemming from bad tuples (usually a result of the aforementioned incorrect clausal bracketing), along with genuinely useful propositions coming from sentences with constructions such as appositives or conjunctive enumerations where TextRunner outguessed the syntactic parser as to the correct argument layout. Future work may consider whether (syntactic) language models can be used to help prune core sentences before being given to KNEXT.

Figure 4 differs from Figure 3 at low frequency of support. This is the result of the partially redundant tuples extracted by TextRunner for complex sentences; the core verb-argument structures are those most likely to be correctly interpreted by KNEXT, while also being those most likely to be repeated across tuples for the same sentence.

6   Class Properties

While TextRunner is perhaps the extraction system most closely related to KNEXT in terms of generality, there is also significant overlap with work on *class attribute*

Table 4: By frequency, the top ten attributes a class MAY HAVE. Emphasis added to entries overlapping with those reported by Paşca and Van Durme. Results for starred classes were derived without the use of prespecified lists of instances

COUNTRY	government, war, team, history, rest, coast, census, economy, *population*, independence
DRUG*	*side effects*, influence, *uses*, doses, manufacturer, efficacy, release, graduates, plasma levels, safety
CITY*	makeup, heart, center, *population*, history, side, places, name, edge, area
PAINTER*	*works*, art, brush, skill, lives, sons, friend, order quantity, muse, eye
COMPANY	windows, products, word, page, review, film, team, award, studio, director

extraction. Paşca and Van Durme (2007) recently described this task, going on to detail an approach for collecting such attributes from search engine query logs. As an example, the search query *"president of Spain"* suggests that a *Country* may have a *president*.

If one were to consider attributes to correspond, at least in part, to things a class MAY HAVE, CAN BE, or MAY BE, then a subset of KNEXT's results may be discussed in terms of this specialized task. For example, for the five classes used in those authors' experiments, Table 4 contains the top ten most frequently extracted things each class MAY HAVE, as determined by KNEXT, without any targeted filtering or adaptation to the task.

Table 5: Mean assessed acceptability for properties occurring for a single class (1), and more than a single class (2+). Final column contains Pearson correlation scores

	1	2+	1	2+	corr.
MAY HAVE	2.80	2.35	2.50	2.28	0.68
MAY BE	3.20	2.85	2.35	2.13	0.59
CAN BE	3.78	3.58	3.28	2.75	0.76
	judge 1		judge 2		

For each of these three types of attributive categories the authors judged 80 randomly drawn propositions, constrained such that half (40 for each) were supported by a single sentence, while the other half were required only to have been extracted at least twice, but potentially many hundreds or even thousands of times. As seen in Table 5, the judges were strongly correlated in their assessments, where for MAY HAVE and MAY BE they were lukewarm (3.0) or better on the majority of those seen.

In a separate evaluation judges considered whether the number of classes sharing a given attribute was indicative of its acceptability. For each unique attributive propo-

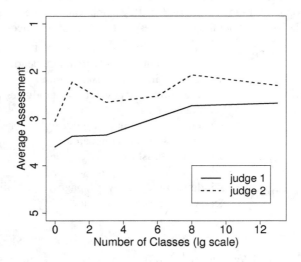

Figure 5: Mean quality of class attributes as a function of the number of classes sharing a given property

sition the class in "subject" position was removed, leaving fragments such as that bracketed: A ROBOT [CAN BE SUBHUMAN]. These attribute fragments were tallied and binned by frequency,[13] with 40 then sampled from each. For a given attribute selected, a single attributive proposition matching that fragment was randomly drawn. For example, having selected the attribute CAN BE FROM A US-CITY, the proposition SOME_NUMBER_OF SHERIFFS CAN BE FROM A US-CITY was drawn from the 390 classes sharing this property. As seen in Figure 5, acceptability rose as a property became more common.

7   Conclusions

Work such as TextRunner (Banko et al., 2007) is pushing extraction researchers to consider larger and larger datasets. This represents significant progress towards the greater community's goal of having access to large, expansive stores of general world knowledge.

   The results presented here support the position that advances made over decades of research in parsing and semantic interpretation do have a role to play in large-scale knowledge acquisition from text. The price paid for linguistic processing is not excessive, and an advantage is the logical formality of the results, and their versatility, as indicated by the application to class attribute extraction.

---

[13]Ranges: $(0, 2^0, 2^1, 2^3, 2^6, \infty)$

Acknowledgements We are especially grateful to Michele Banko and her colleagues for generously sharing results, and to Daniel Gildea for helpful feedback. This work was supported by NSF grants IIS-0328849 and IIS-0535105.

References

Abney, S. (1996). Partial Parsing via Finite-State Cascades. *Natural Language Engineering 2*(4), 337–344.

Banko, M., M. Cafarella, S. Soderland, M. Broadhead, and O. Etzioni (2007). Open Information Extraction from the Web. In *Proceedings of the 20th International Joint Conference on Artificial Intelligence (IJCAI-07)*, pp. 2670–2676.

Charniak, E. (1999). A Maximum-Entropy-Inspired Parser. In *Proceedings of the 1st Conference of the North American Chapter of the Association for Computational Linguistics (NAACL 2000)*, pp. 132–139.

Clark, P., P. Harrison, and J. Thompson (2003). A Knowledge-Driven Approach to Text Meaning Processing. In *Proceedings of the HLT-NAACL 2003 Workshop on Text Meaning*, pp. 1–6.

Clark, S. and D. Weir (1999). An iterative approach to estimating frequencies over a semantic hierarchy. In *Proceedings of the 1999 Joint SIGDAT Conference on Empirical Methods in Natural Language Processing and Very Large Corpora (EMNLP/VLC-99)*, pp. 258–265.

Collins, M. (1997). Three Generative, Lexicalised Models for Statistical Parsing. In *Proceedings of the 35th Annual Conference of the Association for Computational Linguistics (ACL-97)*, pp. 16–23.

Gildea, D. and D. Jurafsky (2002). Automatic labeling of semantic roles. *Computational Linguistics 28*(3), 245–288.

Gildea, D. and M. Palmer (2002). The necessity of syntactic parsing for predicate argument recognition. In *Proceedings of the 40th Annual Conference of the Association for Computational Linguistics (ACL-02)*, Philadelphia, PA, pp. 239–246.

Holmback, H., L. Duncan, and P. Harrison (2000). A word sense checking application for Simplified English. In *Proceedings of the 3rd International Workshop on Controlled Language Applications (CLAW00)*, pp. 120–133.

Liakata, M. and S. Pulman (2002). From Trees to Predicate Argument Structures. In *Proceedings of the 19th International Conference on Computational Linguistics (COLING-02)*, pp. 563–569.

Paşca, M. and B. Van Durme (2007). What You Seek is What You Get: Extraction of Class Attributes from Query Logs. In *Proceedings of the 20th International Joint Conference on Artificial Intelligence (IJCAI-07)*, pp. 2832–2837.

Punyakanok, V., D. Roth, and W. tau Yih (2008). The Importance of Syntactic Parsing and Inference in Semantic Role Labeling. *Computational Linguistics 34*(2), 257–287.

Resnik, P. (1993). Semantic classes and syntactic ambiguity. In *Proceedings of ARPA Workshop on Human Language Technology*, pp. 278–283.

Richardson, S. D., W. B. Dolan, and L. Vanderwende (1998). MindNet: Acquiring and Structuring Semantic Information from Text. In *Proceedings of the 17th International Conference on Computational linguistics (COLING-98)*, pp. 1098–1102.

Schubert, L. K. (2002). Can we derive general world knowledge from texts? In *Proceedings of the 2nd International Conference on Human Language Technology Research (HLT 2002)*, pp. 94–97.

Schubert, L. K. and C. H. Hwang (2000). Episodic Logic meets Little Red Riding Hood: A comprehensive, natural representation for language understanding. In L. Iwanska and S. Shapiro (Eds.), *Natural Language Processing and Knowledge Representation: Language for Knowledge and Knowledge for Language*, pp. 111–174.

Schubert, L. K. and M. H. Tong (2003). Extracting and evaluating general world knowledge from the Brown corpus. In *Proceedings of the HLT-NAACL 2003 Workshop on Text Meaning*, pp. 7–13.

Wong, Y. W. and R. J. Mooney (2007). Learning Synchronous Grammars for Semantic Parsing with Lambda Calculus. In *Proceedings of the 45th Annual Conference of the Association for Computational Linguistics (ACL-07)*, pp. 960–967.

Zelle, J. M. and R. J. Mooney (1996). Learning to Parse Database Queries using Inductive Logic Programming. In *Proceedings of the 13th National Conference on Artificial Intelligence (AAAI-96)*, pp. 1050–1055.

Zernik, U. (1992). Closed yesterday and closed minds: Asking the right questions of the corpus to distinguish thematic from sentential relations. In *Proceedings of the 19th International Conference on Computational Linguistics (COLING-02)*, pp. 1305–1311.

Zettlemoyer, L. and M. Collins (2005). Learning to Map Sentences to Logical Form: Structured Classification with Probabilistic Categorial Grammars. In *Proceedings of the 21st Conference on Uncertainty in Artificial Intelligence (UAI-05)*, pp. 658–666.

PART II

SHARED TASK

Introduction to the Shared Task on Comparing Semantic Representations

Johan Bos

University of Rome "La Sapienza" (Italy)

email: bos@di.uniroma1.it

Abstract

Seven groups participated in the STEP 2008 shared task on comparing semantic representations as output by practical wide-coverage NLP systems. Each of this groups developed their own system for producing semantic representations for texts, each in their own semantic formalism. Each group was requested to provide a short sample text, producing a shared task set of seven texts, allowing participants to challenge each other. Following this, each group was asked to provide the raw system output for all texts, which are made available on http://www.sigsem. org. Two groups were extremely inspired by the shared task and also provided gold-standard semantic representations for the seven texts, together with evaluation measures. The STEP 2008 workshop itself will continue the discussion, focusing on the feasibility of a theory-neutral gold standard for deep semantic representations.

1   Introduction

Following advances made in computational syntax in the last years, we have recently witnessed progress in computational semantics too. Thanks to the availability of wide-coverage parsers, most of them implementing statistical approaches with models trained on the Penn Treebank, we now have at our disposal tools that are able to produce formal, semantic representations on the basis of the output of the aforementioned parsers, achieving high coverage. Computational semantics isn't anymore limited to tedious paper and pencil exercise, nor to implementations of tiny fragments of natural language, and has genuinely matured to a level useful for real applications.

As a direct consequence, the question as to how to measure the quality of semantic representations output by these systems pops up. This is an important issue for the sake of the field, but difficult to answer. On the one hand one might think that the quality of semantic representations, because they are more abstract than surface and syntactic representations, should be easy to evaluate. On the other hand, however, because there are several "competing" semantic formalisms, and the depth of analysis is arbitrary, it is hard to define a universal theory-neutral gold standard for semantic representations (see, e.g. Bos, 2008a).

Partly in response to this situation in the field, a "shared task" was organised as s special event on the STEP 2008 conference. The aim of this shared task was primarily to *compare* semantic representations for texts as output by state-of-the-art NLP systems. This was seen a first step for designing evaluation methodologies in computational semantics, with a practical bottom-up strategy: rather than defining theoretical gold standard representations, we look what current systems can actually produce and start working from that.

2   Participants

In response to the call for participation seven groups were accepted to take part in the shared task. Table 1 gives an overview of the participants, the system they have developed, and the semantic formalism they adopted. This volume contains full descriptions of these systems (please follow the page numbers in Table 1).

Table 1: Overview of shared task participants at STEP 2008

	System	Type of Formalism	Authors	Pages
1	BLUE	Logical Form	Clark and Harrison	263–276
2	Boxer	Discourse Representation Theory	Bos	277–286
3	GETARUNS	Situation Semantics	Delmonte	287–298
4	LXGram	Minimal Recursion Semantics	Branco and Costa	299–314
5	OntoSem	Ontological Semantics	Nirenburg et al.	315–326
6	TextCap	Semantic Triples	Callaway	327–342
7	Trips	Logical Form	Allen et al.	343–354

All but one group have NLP systems developed to deal with the English language. One group has an NLP system for Portuguese (LXGram). This made it more difficult to organise the task (the English text had to be translated, Branco and Costa (2008)), but also more interesting. After all, it is a reasonable assumption that semantic representations ought to be independent of the source language.

Also note that basically all participants adopt different semantic formalisms (Table 1), even though they all claim to do more or less the same thing: computing semantic representations for text. These differences in (formal) background make the shared task only more interesting.

3   The Shared Task Texts

All participants were asked to submit an authentic small text, not exceeding five sentences and 120 tokens. The pool of test data for the shared task is composed out of all the texts submitted by the seven participants. This procedure allowed the participants to "challenge" each other. Below are the original texts as submitted by the participants — the numbering follows the numbering of the participants in Table 1.

Text 1
An object is thrown with a horizontal speed of 20 m/s from a cliff that is 125 m high. The object falls for the height of the cliff. If air resistance is negligible, how long does it take the object to fall to the ground? What is the duration of the fall?

Text 2
Cervical cancer is caused by a virus. That has been known for some time and it has led to a vaccine that seems to prevent it. Researchers have been looking for other cancers that may be caused by viruses.

Text 3
John went into a restaurant. There was a table in the corner. The waiter took the order. The atmosphere was warm and friendly. He began to read his book.

Text 4
The first school for the training of leader dogs in the country is going to be created in Mortagua and will train 22 leader dogs per year. In Mortagua, Joao Pedro Fonseca and Marta Gomes coordinate the project that seven people develop in this school. They visited several similar places in England and in France, and two future trainers are already doing internship in one of the French Schools. The communitarian funding ensures the operation of the school until 1999. We would like our school to work similarly to the French ones, which live from donations, from the merchandising and even from the raffles that children sell in school.

Text 5
As the 3 guns of Turret 2 were being loaded, a crewman who was operating the center gun yelled into the phone, "I have a problem here. I am not ready yet." Then the propellant exploded. When the gun crew was killed they were crouching unnaturally, which suggested that they knew that an explosion would happen. The propellant that was used was made

from nitrocellulose chunks that were produced during World War II and were repackaged in 1987 in bags that were made in 1945. Initially it was suspected that this storage might have reduced the powder's stability.

Text 6
Amid the tightly packed row houses of North Philadelphia, a pioneering urban farm is providing fresh local food for a community that often lacks it, and making money in the process. Greensgrow, a one-acre plot of raised beds and greenhouses on the site of a former steel-galvanizing factory, is turning a profit by selling its own vegetables and herbs as well as a range of produce from local growers, and by running a nursery selling plants and seedlings. The farm earned about $10,000 on revenue of $450,000 in 2007, and hopes to make a profit of 5 percent on $650,000 in revenue in this, its 10th year, so it can open another operation elsewhere in Philadelphia.

Text 7
Modern development of wind-energy technology and applications was well underway by the 1930s, when an estimated 600,000 windmills supplied rural areas with electricity and water-pumping services. Once broad-scale electricity distribution spread to farms and country towns, use of wind energy in the United States started to subside, but it picked up again after the U.S. oil shortage in the early 1970s. Over the past 30 years, research and development has fluctuated with federal government interest and tax incentives. In the mid-'80s, wind turbines had a typical maximum power rating of 150 kW. In 2006, commercial, utility-scale turbines are commonly rated at over 1 MW and are available in up to 4 MW capacity.

The first text is taken from an AP Physics exam (the fourth sentence is a simplified reformulation of the third sentence) and constitutes a multi-sentence science question (Clark and Harrison, 2008). Text 2 is taken from the *Economist*, with the third sentence slightly simplified (Bos, 2008b). Text 4 was taken from a Portuguese newspaper and translated into English (Branco and Costa, 2008). Text 6 is also a fragment of a newspaper article, namely the *New York Times* (Callaway, 2008). Text 7 is an excerpt from http://science.howstuffworks.com. The origin of Text 3 is unknown.

4   Preliminary Results

All groups produced semantic representations for the texts using their NLP systems. The results are, for obvious reasons of space, not listed here, but available at the SIGSEM website http://www.sigsem.org. The papers that follow the current article describe the individual results in detail. It should be noted that two groups created gold standard representations for all seven texts, and alrady performed a self evaluation (Nirenburg et al., 2008; Allen et al., 2008).

The workshop itself (to be held in Venice, September 2008) will feature further comparison and manual evaluation of the systems' output — the system with the most complete and accurate semantic representation will receive a special STEP award. This event should naturally lead to a discussion on the feasibility of a gold standard for deep semantic representations, and furthermore identify a set of problematic and relevant issues for semantic evaluation.

References

Allen, J. F., M. Swift, and W. de Beaumont (2008). Deep Semantic Analysis of Text. In J. Bos and R. Delmonte (Eds.), *Semantics in Text Processing. STEP 2008 Conference Proceedings*, Volume 1 of *Research in Computational Semantics*, pp. 343–354. College Publications.

Bos, J. (2008a). Let's not argue about semantics. In *Proceedings of the 6th Language Resources and Evaluation Conference (LREC 2008)*, Marrakech, Morocco.

Bos, J. (2008b). Wide-Coverage Semantic Analysis with Boxer. In J. Bos and R. Delmonte (Eds.), *Semantics in Text Processing. STEP 2008 Conference Proceedings*, Volume 1 of *Research in Computational Semantics*, pp. 277–286. College Publications.

Branco, A. and F. Costa (2008). LXGram in the Shared Task "Comparing Semantic Representations" of STEP 2008. In J. Bos and R. Delmonte (Eds.), *Semantics in Text Processing. STEP 2008 Conference Proceedings*, Volume 1 of *Research in Computational Semantics*, pp. 299–314. College Publications.

Callaway, C. B. (2008). The TextCap Semantic Interpreter. In J. Bos and R. Delmonte (Eds.), *Semantics in Text Processing. STEP 2008 Conference Proceedings*, Volume 1 of *Research in Computational Semantics*, pp. 327–342. College Publications.

Clark, P. and P. Harrison (2008). Boeing's NLP System and the Challenges of Semantic Representation. In J. Bos and R. Delmonte (Eds.), *Semantics in Text Processing. STEP 2008 Conference Proceedings*, Volume 1 of *Research in Computational Semantics*, pp. 263–276. College Publications.

Delmonte, R. (2008). Semantic and Pragmatic Computing with GETARUNS. In J. Bos and R. Delmonte (Eds.), *Semantics in Text Processing. STEP 2008 Conference Proceedings*, Volume 1 of *Research in Computational Semantics*, pp. 287–298. College Publications.

Nirenburg, S., S. Beale, and M. McShane (2008). Baseline Evaluation of WSD and Semantic Dependency in OntoSem. In J. Bos and R. Delmonte (Eds.), *Semantics in Text Processing. STEP 2008 Conference Proceedings*, Volume 1 of *Research in Computational Semantics*, pp. 315–326. College Publications.

Boeing's NLP System and the Challenges of Semantic Representation

Peter Clark
Phil Harrison
The Boeing Company (USA)
email: peter.e.clark@boeing.com

Abstract

We describe Boeing's NLP system, BLUE, comprising a pipeline of a parser, a logical form (LF) generator, an initial logic generator, and further processing modules. The initial logic generator produces logic whose structure closely mirrors the structure of the original text. The subsequent processing modules then perform, with somewhat limited scope, additional transformations to convert this into a more usable representation with respect to a specific target ontology, better able to support inference. Generating a semantic representation is challenging, due to the wide variety of semantic phenomena which can occur in text. We identify seventeen such phenomena which occurred in the STEP 2008 "shared task" texts, comment on BLUE's ability to handle them or otherwise, and discuss the more general question of what exactly constitutes a "semantic representation", arguing that a spectrum of interpretations exist.

1 System Description

1.1 Overview and Scope

As our contribution to the 2008 STEP Symposium's "shared task" of comparing semantic representations (Bos, 2008), we describe Boeing's NLP system, BLUE (Boeing Language Understanding Engine), and subsequently analyze its performance on
the task's shared texts. BLUE consists of a pipeline of a parser, logical form (LF)
generator, an initial logic generator, and subsequent processing modules. The parser
has broad coverage and is domain general. The logical form generator currently deals
with a (reasonably large) subset of linguistic phenomena, including simple sentences,
prepositional phrases, compound nouns, ordinal modifiers, proper nouns, some simple types of coordination, adverbs, negation, comparatives, and modals. The initial
logic generator performs a straightforward transformation of the LF to first-order logic
syntax. Subsequent processing modules then perform word sense disambiguation, semantic role labeling, coreference resolution, and some limited metonymic and other
transformations. The overall system currently produces output expressed in one of
two target ontologies, namely WordNet and the University of Texas at Austin's Component Library (CLib) (Barker et al., 2001). In this paper we illustrate the system's
use with WordNet's ontology. The overall system was originally developed for interpreting a controlled language called CPL (Clark et al., 2007), but also often makes
reasonable interpretations of more complex, open text sentences, as we illustrate here.

1.2 Parsing and the Logical Form Generator

Parsing is performed using SAPIR, a mature, bottom-up, broad coverage chart parser
(Harrison and Maxwell, 1986). The parser's cost function is biased by a database of
manually and corpus-derived "tuples" (good parse fragments), as well as hand-coded
preference rules. During parsing, the system also generates a logical form (LF), a
semi-formal structure between a parse and full logic. The LF is a simplified and
normalized tree structure with logic-type elements, generated by rules parallel to the
grammar rules, that contains variables (prefixed by underscores "_") and additional
expressions for other sentence constituents. Variables can represent noun phrases,
propositions, and even verb phrases (e.g., "To solve this problem is difficult").

Some disambiguation decisions are performed at this stage (e.g., structural, part of
speech), while others are deferred (e.g., word senses, semantic roles), and there is no
explicit quantifier scoping. Various syntactic properties and relationships are captured
in the LF, including: S (sentence), PP (prepositional phrase), NN (noun compound),
PN (proper name), PLUR (plural), PLUR-N (numbered plural). Tense, aspect, and
polarity are also recorded in the LF. For example:

```
;;; LF for "An object is thrown with a horizontal speed of 20 m/s
            from a cliff that is 125 m high."
(DECL
   ((VAR _X1 "an" "object")
    (VAR _X3 NIL (PLUR-N "20" "m/s"))
    (VAR _X2 "a" "horizontal speed" (PP "of" _X3))
    (VAR _X4 "a" "cliff"
       (DECL NIL (S (PRESENT) _X4 "be"
          (S-ADJ _X4 (DEGREE
                (MEASUREMENT "125" "m") "high"))))))
    (S (PRESENT) NIL "throw" _X1
 (PP "with" _X2) (PP "from" _X4)))
```

1.3   The Initial Logic Generator

The LF is then used to generate ground logical assertions of the form r(x,y), containing Skolem instances (denoting existentially quantified variables) by applying a set of simple, syntactic rewrite rules recursively to it. Verbs are reified as individuals, Davidsonian-style. At this stage of processing, the binary predicates are: subject (syntactic subject), sobject (syntactic object), mod (modifier), all the prepositions, value (for physical quantities), number-of-elements (for numbered plurals), and named (for proper names). For example, the above LF is translated into "syntactic logic" (additional predicates indicating part of speech, tense, aspect, determiners, and polarity are not shown):

```
;;; "An object is thrown with a horizontal speed
;;;     of 20 m/s from a cliff that is 125 m high."
 "object"(object01),
 value(quantity01,[20,m/s_n1]),
 "m/s"(m/s_n1),
 "speed"(speed01),
 "horizontal"(horizontal01),
 mod(speed01,horizontal01),
 "of"(speed01,quantity01),
 "cliff"(cliff01),
 "be"(be01),
 subject(be01,cliff01),
 sobject(be01,height01),
 value(height01,[125,m_n1]),
 "m"(m_n1),
 "height"(height01),
 "throw"(throw01),
 sobject(throw01,object01),
 "with"(throw01,speed01),
 "from"(throw01,cliff01).
```

1.4   Subsequent Processing Modules

While the output of the basic system is in a logic syntax, it is not coherent enough to support inference as it preserves many difficult linguistic phenomena (ambiguity, metonymy, etc.). Further semantic interpretation involves disambiguation and aligning the interpretation with the target ontology we are using. In general, this is a complex task and our system only makes limited steps in this direction using five modules: word sense disambiguation (WSD); semantic role labeling (SRL); coreference resolution (including across different parts of speech); metonymy resolution (with respect to the target ontology); and structural transformations. We describe these modules below.

Word Sense Disambiguation When using WordNet's ontology, each synset in WordNet is a target concept for WSD. BLUE currently performs naive word sense disambiguation by simply selecting the most common synset for a given word+part-of-speech using context-independent frequency statistics. When using the Component Library (CLib) ontology, BLUE exploits hand-authored mappings between WordNet synsets and CLib concepts: Given a word, e.g., "cliff", BLUE first finds WordNet synsets for the word, then climbs WordNet's taxonomy from those synsets until it finds synsets mapped to CLib concepts, and returns those CLib concepts, again using preference based on context-independent frequency statistics. Verb nominalizations map to the denominalized verb, thus "fall"(n) and "falling"(n) both map to synsets for "fall"(v).

Semantic Role Labeling With both ontologies, BLUE uses the same relational vocabulary of approximately 100 binary semantic relations, drawn from the relation set used by UT's Component Library. Semantic role labeling (SRL), for both for verb-noun and noun-noun relationships, is performed using a set of hand-authored SRL rules, e.g., "from"(x,y) is labeled as origin(x,y) if x is a movement event and y is an object. In cases where the rules are not adequate to clearly identify a semantic relation, the relation is left as a syntactic relation.

Coreference Coreference (e.g., "the ball") is computed by searching for a previous entity in the discourse with the same word and qualifiers as in the referring noun phrase. (Coreference using synonyms or types produced more errors than it removed).

Metonymy Often a sentence relates entities in a way inconsistent with the target ontology. For example, with the Component Library (CLib) ontology, movement properties (e.g., speed, acceleration) are defined as properties of the movement events, rather than of the object moving. Thus a phrase like "the initial speed of the ball" is metonymous (with respect to CLib) for "the initial speed of the movement of the ball". This module spots and corrects such metonymies using a small set of metonymy resolution rules. Note that metonymy resolution is ontology-specific, reflecting design decisions about what is and is not an allowable expression in the target ontology.

Structural Transformations Often, the structure of the syntactic and (desired) semantic representations differ, and so some structural transformations are necessary. For example, in the basic processing, verbs (e.g., "weigh") are reified as individuals with semantic roles, e.g., "weigh"(w), subject(w,x), sobject(w,y), whereas the target ontology stipulates that some particular verbs denote relations e.g., "weigh" corresponds to the CLib relation weight(x,y), not a Weigh event. (This is indicated in CLib by the relation weigh() being associated with synsets for the verb "weigh"). Similarly, nouns associated with relations will be transformed to introduce that relation into the representation, e.g., "weight"(y), "of"(y,x) will be transformed to weight(x,y). This module makes these and other transformations. The verbs "be" and "have" are similarly mapped to relations, but with the extra step that the target relation depends on the arguments. A small set of rules determines the appropriate relation to use.

2 Semantic Formalism

2.1 Form (Syntax)

Our system produces output in a subset of first-order logic, illustrated later in this paper. For the most part, it simply outputs a flat list of ground assertions containing Skolemized existential variables, and does not handle universal quantification (a significant limitation for expository rather than story-like texts). In addition, BLUE allows propositions to themselves be arguments to other propositions as a nested structure, e.g., for modals:

```
;;; "The man wanted to leave the house"
isa(leave01,leave_v1), etc, ...
agent(want01,man01),
object(want01,[
        agent(leave01,man01),
        object(leave01,house01)]).
```

2.2 Ontology (Content)

As described earlier, BLUE currently uses two alternative conceptual vocabularies, namely the concepts in WordNet (with minor extensions) or the Component Library. BLUE's relational vocabulary is approximately 100 semantic relations drawn from the Component Library.[1]

3 Example

We illustrate our system using an example from Project Halo (Clark et al., 2007), where the system is used to interpret multi-sentence science questions posed to a knowledge-based system. While BLUE produces a slightly better output for this text using the Component Library ontology, we illustrate it using WordNet's ontology for consistency with our output for the other shared task texts (we use WordNet for these as WordNet has broader coverage). We also discuss our system further in Section 4 on additional sentences.

The first three sentences are (largely) a question from an AP Physics exam, the fourth is a hand-written simplified version of the third sentence. Our system is able to create coherent representations of sentences 1, 2, and 4, i.e., sufficient for the KB to answer the question correctly, but not of sentence 3.

Shared Task Text 1:
(1.1) An object is thrown with a horizontal speed of 20 m/s from a cliff that is 125 m high.
(1.2) The object falls for the height of the cliff.
(1.3) If air resistance is negligible, how long does it take the object to fall

---

[1]http://www.cs.utexas.edu/users/mfkb/RKF/trunktree/components/specs/
slotdictionary.html

to the ground?
(1.4) What is the duration of the fall?

Semantic Representation

```
(1.1)  "An object is thrown with a horizontal speed of 20 m/s
          from a cliff that is 125 m high."
isa(object01,object_n1),
isa(speed01,velocity_n1),
isa(horizontal01,horizontal_a1),
isa(cliff01,cliff_n1),
isa(height01,height_n1),
isa(throw01,throw_v1),
height(cliff01,height01),
value(speed01,[20,m/s_n1]),
mod(speed01,horizontal01),
value(height01,[125,m_n1]),
object(throw01,object01),
"with"(throw01,speed01),
origin(throw01,cliff01).
```

Here object01 etc. denote Skolem instances, object_n1 etc. denote WordNet concepts (synsets). Note word and role disambiguation, adjective-noun transformation ("high" → height()), "be" interpretation, and handling of units of measurement ("125 m", "20 m/s"). Using WordNet's ontology, this interpretation is not perfect as two semantic roles have (undesirably) been left underspecified ("mod" and "with").

```
(1.2)  "The object falls for the height of the cliff."
isa(fall01,fall_v1),
height(cliff01,height01),
agent(fall01,object01),
distance(fall01,height01).
```

Note coreference with first sentence ("height", "cliff", "object") and semantic role labeling ("for height" → height()).

```
(1.3)  "If air resistance is negligible, how long does it
          take the object to fall to the ground?"
```

(See the STEP Shared Task Web site[2] for BLUE's semantic representation). BLUE's representation for this is largely incoherent, in particular a "take" event is created with a proposition (meaning "length of fall to the ground") as its 2nd argument.

```
(1.4)  "What is the duration of the fall?"
isa(fall01,fall_v1),
isa(duration01,duration_n1),
duration(fall01,duration01),
query-for(duration01).
```

Note noun-verb coreference ("fall"(n) → fall01) and query variable identification.

---

[2]http://www.sigsem.org

4 Performance on All Shared Texts

As part of the STEP 2008 Symposium, seven groups (including us) each submitted a paragraph of text and then all groups ran their NLP systems on all texts (Bos, 2008). We now discuss BLUE's capabilities further in the context of these shared texts. For this exercise, we made some minor bug fixes to the system but did not significantly change or extend the final output representations. In the below discussion we refer to the text and sentence numbers in the form (text#.sentence#). Sometimes text snippets have been simplified for clarity.

What constitutes a Semantic Representation?

The notion of a semantic representation can be interpreted in several ways. At one extreme, a representation which captures all the salient linguistic structure and phenomena could be considered "semantic". Such representations will have structure somewhat similar to the syntactic structure of the original text, and the task of interpreting the inferential consequences of those structures is then left to downstream processing, and considered part of commonsense reasoning rather than "language understanding". At the other extreme, one might require the full logical interpretation of the text to be explicit, in order that the representation be truely "semantic", on the grounds that if the representation does not explicitly support inference of valid consequences, the meaning has not been captured. Various positions exist between these two extremes. For example, one might represent:

(4.2) "a vaccine prevents cervical cancer"

as

a. prevents(vaccine,cervical-cancer); or

b. $\exists v$ type-of(v,vaccine) & $\forall x,y$ isa(x,v), isa(y, cervical-cancer) $\rightarrow$ prevents(x,y); or

c. the logic for, approximately, "for all people given (a specific type of) vaccine, they will not subsequently develop cervical cancer"

Similarly, one might represent "typical" in

(7.4) "turbines had a typical power rating of 150 kW."

as

a. have(turbine,power-rating), value(power-rating, 150kW), typical(power-rating); or

b. logic for (say) "the mode of the power rating of the set of turbines is (approximately) 150kW"

Clearly the more a representation is syntax-like, the more a downstream reasoning component will need have to do to identify its inferential consequences. Conversely, the more a representation makes the meaning explicit, the harder it is to generate those representations in the first place as even simple sentences can often have highly complex meanings. At what point one considers a representation "semantic" is matter for debate; what is clear is that there is often a significant journey to make to get from text to valid inferential consequences of that text. From a pragmatic point of view, like most other language systems BLUE generates representations which are more syntactically structured. This means that, whether one considers them "semantic" or not, considerable additional machinery would typically be needed for performing inference using them.

Some other examples of simple sentences with complex meanings include:

- (6.2) "selling a range of produce" meaning, approximately, "the number of types of produce sold is reasonably large";

- (6.4) "research has fluctuated with tax incentives" meaning, approximately, a qualitative relationship exists between the amount of research and the amount of tax incentives;

- (7.2) "electricity distribution spread to farms" appealing to the abstract notion of a spatial region, and meaning, approximately, that the region grows with time.

Even with a more syntactic notion of "semantic representation", there are numerous more specific issues which need to be addressed. Below we identify some which arise in the shared task texts, and comment on our system's ability to handle them.

4.1   Word Sense Disambiguation (WSD)

BLUE currently uses a naive, context-independent approach to WSD. While the naive guess is often right, there are many cases in the shared texts of unusual senses which BLUE will miss, e.g., (1.3) "how long [time] does it take", (2.2) "led to [inspired the development of] a vaccine", (6.2) "turn [generate] a profit".

An interesting phenomenon is seen with: (6.2) "Greensgrow [is] a plot of land and is selling its own vegetables". which mixes senses of "Greensgrow" as a piece of land and an institution in the same sentence, causing challenges for standard WSD. One might consider "Greensgrow" as denoting an institution and thus "Greensgrow is a plot of land" as metonymy, or "Greensgrow" as a complex concept with various facets. In either case some complex processing is required.

4.2   Semantic Role Labelling (SRL)

SRL is itself challenging. In many cases BLUE has left the relation underspecified (especially noun-noun relations), and has occasionally maked mistakes, e.g.,

```
(3.2) "A table in the corner"
is-inside(table01, corner01).

(5.1) "I have problem"
has-part(i01,problem01).
```

4.3   Coordination

BLUE will multiply out coordinates, e.g.:

```
(3.4) "The atmosphere was warm and friendly"
"be"(atmosphere01, warm01).
"be"(atmosphere01, friendly01).
```

Sometimes this multiplication is inappropriate, for example below, BLUE misinterprets each place as being in both England and France simultaneously:

```
(4.3) "They visited places in England and France"
object(visit01,place01),
is-inside(place01,England01),
is-inside(place01,France01).
```

Note that the alternative "places in Africa and South of the Equator" would not be inconsistent as these areas do overlap; domain knowledge is thus required to understand the intended semantics.

BLUE does not distribute modifiers across coordinates, and thus misses the distribution (7.1) "wind-energy technology and applications" → "wind-energy technology and wind-energy applications".

4.4 Coreference and Anaphora

BLUE performs definite reference resolution based on name, e.g., (1.2) "an object...the object...", and across part of speech, e.g., verb-noun (1.4) "falls... the fall...", and adjective-noun (1.2) "high... height...", but not across different names, e.g., (6.3) "Greenslow... The farm...". BLUE does not currently do anaphoric reference resolution, so leaves occurrences of "it" etc. unresolved.

There are some interesting complex examples of coreference also in the texts:

- (3.3) "The waiter took the order"
  The two referents are not mentioned earlier, but are understood by the reader to refer to objects in the described scene. A system should thus realize that "The waiter" is the waiter in the restaurant, and "the order" is John's order.

- (2.2) "Cervical cancer is caused by a virus. That has been known..."
  Here the anaphor ("That") refers to a proposition rather than an object in the world.

- (2.3) "other cancers"
  This refers to the set of cancers except those previously mentioned, requiring discourse analysis to fully capture the semantics.

4.5 Generics and Universal Quantification

BLUE interprets generics as statements relating individuals, thus requiring further downstream interpretation of those individuals and transformation of the representation (e.g., to universal quantification and conditionals) for correct inference. In general, generics are complex to interpret; not only are quantifications ambiguous, but also generics typically require substantial unstated information to be filled in for the interpretation to be meaningful. For example,

(2.1) "Cervical cancer is caused by a virus"

should ultimately be interpreted as (something like) "An event involving a virus can create an incidence of cervical cancer". An even fuller semantics, requiring more world knowledge, would be that the event is infection of a person and that the cancer incidence is in the same person. How far one should go to reach this degree of interpretation in a "semantic representation" is open to debate.

Adjectives and adverbs can modify the expectation of measurement results on an ensemble, again requiring special representational machinery. Examples include:

> (7.4) "turbines have a typical power rating of..."
> (7.5) "turbines are commonly rated as"
> (6.1) "the community often lacks it [fresh food]"

4.6 Time

BLUE ignores tense and aspect information (although it extracts it in the intermediate logical form), a gap for complete semantics. However, BLUE will handle some references to events situated in time and in relation to other events. In the examples below of BLUE's interpretation, note the use of temporal predicates:

```
(5.5) "...made in 1945"
time-int-during(make01,year1945)

(4.4) "ensures operation until 1999"
time-ends(ensure01, year1999).

(5.3) "...yelled. Then the propellant exploded"
next-event(yell01,explode01).

(5.4) "When they killed, they were crouching"
time-at(crouch01,kill01).
```

However BLUE does not recognize more complex time references as such, e.g.,

> (7.1) "the 1930s",
> (7.2) "the early 1970s",
> (7.4) "mid-'80s" (misparsed as an adjective), and
> (7.3) "the past 30 years"

In addition, facts or beliefs may themselves be situated in time, requiring a time-stamp or situation to be attached to an assertion (which BLUE does not do), for example (6.3) "revenue of $450,000 in 2007" A particularly complex example is (5.6) "Initially it was suspected that..." meaning, approximately, X suspected Y at the time immediately after the previously described event. Computationally disentangling the meaning of this sentence is a formidable challenge.

4.7 Plurals and Collectives

BLUE represents a numbered collective as an individual with a number-of-elements() predicate attached, for example:

```
(4.2) "seven people developed"
isa(person01, person_n1),
agent(develop01, person01),
number-of-elements(person01,7).
```

where person01 denotes the collective of 7 people. (While it is strictly incorrect to assert person01 as an instance of the class person_n1, there are pragmatic benefits for doing so.) Unnumbered plurals and generics are naively represented as single individuals at present.

4.8 "Light" nouns and verbs

Arguably, some nouns and verbs do not denote objects and events in the world in a literal sense. For example, "X occurred" can be taken to mean just "X", rather than there being a separate "occur" event. Recognizing and transforming these requires special processing machinery. BLUE handles a few examples, e.g., "X occurred" → "X", but not the following in the shared texts:

- (1.3) "how long does it [the fall] take" meaning "how [temporally] long is the fall"

- (4.3) "doing internship" meaning "interning"

- (5.4) "an explosion happened" meaning "There was an explosion"

- (7.1) "development was underway" meaning "There was development"

4.9 Adjectives and Adverbs

While an adjective or adverb can be trivially attached to a noun/verb, as BLUE does, an elaborated representation of its meaning, as required for inference, is very challenging and context-dependent. Challenging examples include:

- (6.1) "North Philadelphia"; what is the extent of this region?

- (7.1) "modern development"

- (4.3) "similar places"; other entities with properties close to some currently mentioned entity

- (4.3) "future trainer"; a non-intersective adjective (like "fake gun")

- (5.4) "crouching unnaturally"

4.10 Modals and Higher-Order Expressions

BLUE will handle some modal expressions by placing a proposition as an argument to another proposition, for example:

```
(4.5) "We would like our school to work similarly..."
agent(like01,we01).
object(like01,[agent(work01,school01),
                manner(work01,similarly01)])
```

```
(5.6) "It was suspected that this storage reduced the
      powder's stability."
object(suspect01,["of"(stability01,powder01),
                  agent(reduce01,storage01),
                  object(reduce01,stability01)]).
```

A particularly complex example (which BLUE does not handle) is (5.3) "They were crouching, which suggested that they knew that an explosion would happen." where a past event implies belief in a future event's occurrence.

4.11 Uncertainty and possibility

The phrases (2.3) "cancers may be caused by viruses" and (5.6) "the storage might have reduced stability" have a complex semantics concerning possibility. While we represent the may/might aspect in the initial logical form, BLUE ignores it in the subsequent representations.

4.12 Metonymy

The occurrence of metonymy is somewhat subjective because metonymy is relative to a target ontology. A full semantic interpretation would include metonymy resolution where present. BLUE will resolve some special cases of metonymy, in particular with respect to the Component Library ontology, but those did not occur in these texts. Some metonymy-like examples in the shared texts (which BLUE did not resolve) include:

(6.3) "The [people of the] farm hopes to make a profit"
(2.1) ".cancer is caused by a virus [infection]."
(7.3) "[The amount of] research has fluctuated"

4.13 Implicit Arguments

Sometimes a verb or noun has implicit arguments that an interpretation should make explicit. BLUE will recognize some implicit arguments for modals, e.g.: that .the farm. is the implied object making the profit in the below:

```
(6.3) "The farm hopes to make a profit"
agent(hope01,farm01),
object(hope01,[ agent(make02,farm01),  ; implicit arg found
                object(make02,profit02)])
```

but not in other cases, such as in (6.3) "revenue of $450,000" → "the revenue of the farm was $450,000".

In general, many relationships are unstated in text and need to be inferred for a full understanding. Text 3 (the restaurant story) is particularly challenging in this regard.

4.14 Special Constructs

There are some specialized grammatical constructs which are not inherently complex to handle, but require special processing. Examples include money, e.g., (6.3) "$10,000", dates, e.g., (7.4) "mid-'80s", and units of measure, e.g., (1.1) "m/s". BLUE currently only recognizes the latter, which is hard-coded as a single token. BLUE also does not handle quote characters, e.g., (5.1) ... yelled "I have a problem" ...

4.15 Proper Names

BLUE will recognize proper names and encode them with a specific named() predicate, e.g.,:

```
(4.2) "Joao Pedro Fonseca"
isa(Fonseca01, person_n1),
named(Fonseca01, ["Joao","Pedro","Fonseca"]).
```

4.16 Physical quantities

Physical quantities need special processing. BLUE represents physical quantities using a special predicate (called value()) linking the quantity to its magnitude and unit of measurement, e.g.,:

```
(1.1) "125 m"
value(height01,[125,m_n1]).
```

4.17 Questions

BLUE recognizes several question types ("what is the...", "what is a...", "how many...", "how much...", "is it true that...", "why...", "how...") and represents them using special annotations on the variable/proposition in the query, for example:

```
(1.4) "What is the duration?"
query-for(duration01).
```

5 Summary and Conclusion

Our language system, BLUE, is able to generate representational structures for many texts, capturing numerous linguistic phenomena while also missing or misinterpreting a variety of others. We have presented a small catalog of these phenomena, and comments on BLUE's ability to handle them or otherwise. As discussed, BLUE's output representation is still fairly linguistic in structure, and despite some transformations would often require substantial downstream processing to identify the explicit meaning and inferential consequences of those structures. Despite this, for cases where the gap between syntax and final logical semantics is small, in particular for the controlled language subset it was originally designed to support, it can generate useful output, and thus constitutes a small step along the way to language understanding.

References

Barker, K., B. Porter, and P. Clark (2001). A library of generic concepts for composing knowledge bases. In *Proc. 1st Int Conf on Knowledge Capture (K-Cap'01)*, pp. 14–21. ACM.

Bos, J. (2008). Introduction to the Shared Task on Comparing Semantic Representations. In J. Bos and R. Delmonte (Eds.), *Semantics in Text Processing. STEP 2008 Conference Proceedings*, Volume 1 of *Research in Computational Semantics*, pp. 257–261. College Publications.

Clark, P., J. Chaw, J. Thompson, and P. Harrison (2007). Capturing and answering questions posed to a knowledge-based system. In D. Sleeman and K. Barker (Eds.), *Proc Int Conf on Knowledge Capture (KCap'07)*, pp. 63–70.

Clark, P., P. Harrison, J. Thompson, R. Wojcik, T. Jenkins, and D. Israel (2007). Reading to learn: An investigation into language understanding. In *Proc. AAAI Spring Symposium on Machine Reading*. AAAI.

Harrison, P. and M. Maxwell (1986). A new implementation of GPSG. In *Proc. 6th Canadian Conf on AI (CSCSI-86)*, pp. 78–83.

Wide-Coverage Semantic Analysis with Boxer

Johan Bos

University of Rome "La Sapienza" (Italy)

email: bos@di.uniroma1.it

Abstract

Boxer is an open-domain software component for semantic analysis of text, based on Combinatory Categorial Grammar (CCG) and Discourse Representation Theory (DRT). Used together with the C&C tools, Boxer reaches more than 95% coverage on newswire texts. The semantic representations produced by Boxer, known as Discourse Representation Structures (DRSs), incorporate a neo-Davidsonian representations for events, using the VerbNet inventory of thematic roles. The resulting DRSs can be translated to ordinary first-order logic formulas and be processing by standard theorem provers for first-order logic. Boxer's performance on the shared task for comparing semantic represtations was promising. It was able to produce complete DRSs for all seven texts. Manually inspecting the output revealed that: (a) the computed predicate argument structure was generally of high quality, in particular dealing with hard constructions involving control or coordination; (b) discourse structure triggered by conditionals, negation or discourse adverbs was overall correctly computed; (c) some measure and time expressions are correctly analysed, others aren't; (d) several shallow analyses are given for lexical phrases that require deep analysis; (e) bridging references and pronouns are not resolved in most cases. Boxer is distributed with the C&C tools and freely available for research purposes.

1   Introduction

Boxer is an open-domain tool for computing and reasoning with semantic representations. Based on Discourse Representation Theory (Kamp and Reyle, 1993), Boxer
is able to construct Discourse Representation Structures (DRSs for short, informally
called "boxes" because of the way they are graphically displayed) for English sentences and texts. There is a translation from DRSs to first-order formulas, which
opens the way to perform inference by including automated reasoning tools such as
theorem provers and model builders (Blackburn and Bos, 2005).

2   Theory

2.1   Combinatory Categorial Grammar

As a preliminary to semantics, we need syntax. Boxer implements a syntax-semantics
interface based on Combinatory Categorial Grammar, CCG (Steedman, 2001). CCG
lends itself extremely well for this task because it is lexically driven and has only few
"grammar" rules, and not less because of its type-transparency principle, which says
that each syntactic type (a CCG category) corresponds to a unique semantic type (a
lambda-expression). Because the syntax-semantics is clearly defined, the choice of
logical form can be independent of the categorial framework underlying it. Steedman
uses simple predicate argument structures expressed via the untyped lambda calculus
to illustrate the construction of logical forms in CCG (Steedman, 2001). We instead
opt for Discourse Representation Theory, a widely accepted sophisticated formal theory of natural language meaning dealing with a large variety of semantic phenomena.

2.2   Discourse Representation Theory

DRT is a formal semantic theory originally designed by Kamp to cope with anaphoric
pronouns and temporal relations (Kamp, 1981). DRT uses an explicit intermediate
semantic representation, called DRS (Discourse Representation Structure), for dealing with anaphoric or other contextually sensitive linguistic phenomena such as ellipsis and presupposition. We choose DRT because it has established itself as a well-
documented formal theory of meaning, covering a number of semantic phenomena
ranging from pronouns, abstract anaphora, presupposition, tense and aspect, propositional attitudes, to plurals (Kamp and Reyle, 1993; Asher, 1993; Van der Sandt, 1992).

   In terms of expressive power, three different kinds of representations are distinguished in Boxer:

1. Discourse Representation Structures (DRSs)

2. Underspecified DRSs (DRSs + merge + alfa)

3. λ-DRSs (UDRSs + lambda + application)

DRSs are the representations corresponding to natural language sentences or texts.
This is the core DRT language compatible with first-order logic. The DRS language
employed by Boxer is a subset of the one found in Kamp and Reyle (1993). We define
the syntax of DRSs below with the help of Backus-Naur form, where non-terminal
symbols are enclosed in angle brackets. The non-terminal <ref> denotes a discourse
referent, and <sym$_n$> an n-place predicate symbol.

$$<exp_e> ::= <ref>$$
$$<exp_t> ::= <drs>$$

$$<drs> ::= \boxed{\begin{array}{c} <ref>* \\ \hline <condition>* \end{array}}$$

$$<condition> ::= <basic> \mid$$
$$<complex>$$
$$<basic> ::= <sym_1>(<exp_e>) \mid$$
$$<sym_2>(<exp_e>,<exp_e>) \mid$$
$$<named>(<exp_e>,<nam>,<sort>)$$
$$<complex> ::= \neg<exp_t> \mid$$
$$<exp_t> \Rightarrow <exp_t> \mid$$
$$<exp_t> \vee <exp_t> \mid$$
$$<ref>:<exp_t>$$

DRSs are structures comprising two parts: 1) a set of discourse referents; and 2) a set of conditions constraining the interpretation of the discourse referents. Conditions can be simple properties of discourse referents, express relations between them, or be complex, introducing (recursively) subordinated DRSs.

The standard version of DRT formulated in Kamp & Reyle incorporates a Davidsonian event semantics (Kamp and Reyle, 1993), where discourse referents can also stand for events and be referred to by anaphoric expressions or constrained by temporal relations. The neo-Davidsonian system, as implemented in Boxer, uses the inventory of roles proposed by VerbNet (Kipper et al., 2008), and has some attractive formal properties (Dowty, 1989). There is only one way to state that an individual is participating in an event—namely by relating it to the event using a binary relation expressing some thematic role. Furthermore, the approach clearly distinguishes the participants of an event by the semantic roles they bear. Finally, it also allows us to characterize the meaning of thematic roles independently of the meaning of the verb that describes the event.

We won't show the standard translation from DRS to FOL here (Blackburn et al., 2001; Bos, 2004; Kamp and Reyle, 1993). Intuitively, translating DRSs into first-order formulas proceeds as follows: each discourse referent is translated as a first-order quantifier, and all DRS-conditions are translated into a conjunctive formula of FOL. Discourse referents usually are translated to existential quantifiers, with the exception of those declared in antecedents of implicational DRS-conditions, that are translated as universal quantifiers. Obviously, negated DRSs are translated as negated formulas, disjunctive DRSs as disjunctive formulas, and implicational DRSs as formulas with material implication.

Boxer outputs either resolved semantic representations (in other words, completely disambiguated DRSs), or underspecified representations, where some ambiguities are left unresolved in the semantic representation. This level of representation is referred to as underspecified DRS, or UDRS for short. It is a small extension of the DRS language given in the previous section and is defined as follows:

$$<exp_t> ::= <udrs>$$
$$<udrs> ::= <drs> \mid (<exp_t>;<exp_t>) \mid (<exp_t>\alpha<exp_t>)$$

Note here that expressions of type *t* are redefined as UDRSs. UDRSs are either ordinarily DRSs, DRSs conjoined by the merge (for which we use the semicolon), or

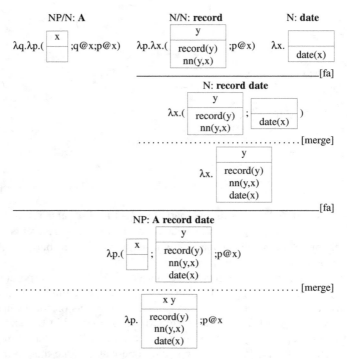

Figure 1: Derivation with λ-DRSs, including β-conversion, for "A record date". Combinatory rules are indicated by solid lines, semantic rules by dotted lines.

DRS composed by the α-operator. The merge conjoins two DRSs into a larger DRS — semantically the merge is interpreted as (dynamic) logical conjunction. Merge-reduction is the process of eliminating the merge operation by forming a new DRS resulting from the union of the domains and conditions of the argument DRSso of a merge, respectively (obeying certain constraints). Figure 1 illustrates the syntax-semantics interface (and merge-reduction) for a derivation of a simple noun phrase.

Boxer adopts Van der Sandt's view as presupposition as anaphora (Van der Sandt, 1992), in which presuppositional expressions are either resolved to previously established discourse entities or accommodated on a suitable level of discourse. Van der Sandt's proposal is cast in DRT, and therefore relatively easy to integrate in Boxer's semantic formalism. The α-operator indicates information that has to be resolved in the context, and is lexically introduced by anaphoric or presuppositional expressions. A DRS constructed with α resembles the proto-DRS of Van der Sandt's theory of presupposition (Van der Sandt, 1992) although they are syntactically defined in a slightly different way to overcome problems with free and bound variables, following Bos (2003). Note that the difference between anaphora and presupposition collapses in Van der Sandt's theory.

The types are the ingredients of a typed lambda calculus that is employed to construct DRSs in a bottom-up fashion, compositional way. The language of lambda-

DRSs is an extension of the language of (U)DRS defined before:

$$<exp_e> ::= <ref> \mid <var_e>$$
$$<exp_t> ::= <udrs> \mid <var_t>$$
$$<exp_\alpha> ::= (<exp_{\langle\beta,\alpha\rangle}> @ <var_\beta>) \mid <var_\alpha>$$
$$<exp_{\langle\alpha,\beta\rangle}> ::= \lambda<var_\alpha>.<exp_\beta> \mid <var_{\langle\alpha,\beta\rangle}>$$

Hence we define discourse referents as expressions of type e, and DRSs as expressions of type t. We use @ to indicate function application, and the λ-operator to bind free variables over which we wish to abstract.

3 Practice

3.1 Preprocessing

The input text needs to be tokenised with one sentence per line. In the context of this paper, Boxer was put into action after using a combined processing pipeline of the C&C tools consisting of POS-tagging, named entity recognition, and parsing (Curran et al., 2007). The POS tags are used to specify the lexical semantics for ambiguous CCG categories (see below); the named entity tags are transferred to the level of DRSs as well and added as sorts to named discourse referents. An example of a CCG derivation is shown in Figure 2.

```
                                                            a       virus
                                                          --[lex] --[lex]
                                        by                np:nb/n n
                                      --------------------[lex] ----------[fa]
Cervical cancer                       caused  ((s:pss\np)\(s:pss\np))/np np:nb
---[lex] --[lex]                      ---[lex] -------------------------------[fa]
n/n      n          is                s:pss\np (s:pss\np)\(s:pss\np)
-----------[fa] ---------------[lex]  -------------------------------------------[ba]
n               (s:dcl\np)/(s:pss\np) s:pss\np
-----------[tc] -----------------------------------------------------------------[fa]
np              s:dcl\np
--------------------------------------------------------------------------------[ba]
s:dcl
```

Figure 2: CCG derivation as generated by the C&C tools

3.2 Lexicon

In CCG, the syntactic lexicon comprises the set of lexical categories. CCGbank hosts more than a thousand different categories. The semantic lexicon defines a suitable mapping from categories to semantic representations. In the context of Boxer, these semantic representations are defined in the shape of lambda-DRSs. Boxer implements almost all categories employed by the C&C parser, which is a subset of the ones found in CCGbank, leaving out extremely rare cases for the sake of efficiency.

Defining the lexical semantics cannot always be done solely on the basis of the category, for one lexical category could give rise to several different semantic interpretations. So we need to take other resources into account, such as the assigned part of speech (PoS), and sometimes the wordform or named entity type associated with the category. For the majority of categories, in particular those that correspond to open-class lexical items, we also need access to the morphological root of the word that triggered the lexical category.

Although there is a one-to-one mapping between the CCG categories and semantic types — and this must be the case to ensure the semantic composition process proceeds without type clashes — the actual instantiations of a semantic type can differ even within the scope of a single CCG category. For example, the category n/n can correspond to an adjective, a cardinal expression, or even common nouns and proper names (in the compound expressions). In the latter two cases the lexical entry introduces a new discourse referent, in the former two it does not. To account for this difference we also need to look at the part of speech that is assigned to a token.

3.3 Resolution

Boxer implements various presupposition triggers introduced by noun phrases, including personal pronouns, possessive pronouns, reflexive pronouns, emphasising pronouns, demonstrative pronouns, proper names, other-anaphora, definite descriptions. In addition, some aspects of tense are implemented as presupposition triggers, too.

Anaphora and presupposition resolution takes place in a separate stage after building up the representation, following the resolution algorithm outlined in Bos (2003). The current implementation of Boxer aims at high precision in resolution: personal pronouns are only attempted to be resolved to named entities, definite descriptions and proper names are only linked to previous discourse referents if there is overlap in the DRS-conditions of the antecedent DRS and alpha-DRS. If no suitable antecedent can be found, global accommodation of the anaphoric discourse referent and conditions will take palce.

Because Boxer has the option to output unresolved DRSs too, it is possible to include external anaphora or coreference resolution components.

3.4 Example Analysis

We illustrate the capabilities of Boxer with the following example text shown below (aka as Text 2 of the shared task).[1] The text consists of three sentences, the second being a coordinated sentence. It contains a passive construction, three pronouns, relative clauses, control verbs, and a presupposition trigger *other*.

> **Text 2**
> Cervical cancer is caused by a virus. That has been known for some time and it has led to a vaccine that seems to prevent it. Researchers have been looking for other cancers that may be caused by viruses.

The output of Boxer for this text is shown in Figure 3. Only the box format is shown here — Boxer is also able to output the DRSs in Prolog or XML encodings. It was run without analysing tense and aspect and without discourse segmentation (both of these are possible in Boxer, but still undergo development, and are therefore disregarded here).

As we can see from the example and Boxer's analysis various things go right and various things go wrong. Boxer deals fine with the passive construction (assigned the

---

[1] This text was taken from the Economist Volume 387 Number 8582, page 92. The third sentence has been simplified.

appropriate semantic role), the relative clauses, and the control construction (*vaccine is the agent of the prevent event*). It also handles the presupposition trigger anaphorically linking the mention of *other cancers* in the third sentence with the phrase *cervical cancer* in the first sentence, and asserting an inequality condition in the DRS.

Boxer failed to resolve three pronouns correctly. These are all accommodated at the global level of DRS, which is the DRS on the left-hand side in Figure 3. All of the pronouns have textual antecedents: the abstract pronoun *that* in the second sentence refers to the fact declared in the first sentence. The first occurrence of *it* in the second sentence also seems to refer to this fact — the second occurrence of *it* refers to cervical cancer mentioned in the first sentence.

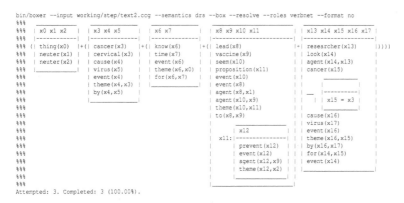

Figure 3: Boxer output for Shared Task Text 2

4 Performance on Shared Task

Here we discuss the output of Boxer on the Shared Task Texts (Bos, 2008). Boxer was able to produce semantic representation for all text without any further modifications to the software. For each text we briefly say what was good and bad about Boxer's analysis. (We won't comment on the performance on the second text, as this is the text proposed by ourselves and already discussed in the previous section.)

Text 1: An object is thrown with a horizontal speed ...

Good: The resulting predicate argument structure was fine overall, including a difficult control construction ("how long does it take the object to fall ..."). The definite description "the object" was correctly resolved. The conditional got correctly analysed.

Bad: The measure phrase "125 m high" got mis-interpreted as noun-noun comnpound. The definite description "the fall" was not linked to the falling event mentioned before.

Comments: Because there were two questions in this text we parsed it using the C&C parser with the model trained on questions.

Text 3: John went into a restaurant ...

Good: The pronouns were correctly resolved to the proper name "John" rather than "the waiter", even though this is based on the simple strategy in Boxer to link third-person pronouns to named entities of type human. The coordination construction "warm and friendly" got correctly analysed (distributively), and the control construction "began to read his book" received a proper predicate argument structure.

Bad: Boxer doesn't deal with bridging references introduced by relational nouns, so expressions "the corner" were not linked to other discourse entities.

Text 4: The first school for the training of leader dogs ...

Good: The named entities were correctly recognised and classified (locations and proper names). The VP coordination in the first and later sentences was correctly analysed. The expression "this school" got correctly linked to the schhol mentioned earlier in the text. The time expression "1999" got the right interpretation.

Bad: The adjectives/determiners "first" and "several" didn't receive a deep analysis. The complex NP "Joao Pedro Fonseca and Marta Gomes" was distributively interpreted, rather than collective. The pronoun "they" wasn't resolved. The preposition "In" starting the second sentence was incorrectly analysed by the parser.

Text 5: As the 3 guns of Turret 2 were being loaded ...

Good: The discourse structures invoked by the sentence initial adverbs "As" and "When" was correctly computed. Predicate argument structure overall good, including treatment of the relative clauses. The expression "the propellant" was correctly resolved. Time expressions in the one but last sentence got a correct analysis.

Bad: The name "Turret 2" was incorrectly analysed (not as a compound). The adverbs "yet" and "then" got a shallow analysis. The first-person pronoun "I" was not resolved to the crewman.

Comments: The quotes were removed in the tokenisation phase, because the C&C parser, being trained on a corpus without quotes, performs badly on texts containing quotes.

Text 6: Amid the tightly packed row houses of North Philadelphia ...

Good: The named entities were correctly recognised and classified as locations. The various cases of VP coordination all got properly analysed. The numerical and date expressions got correct representations.

Bad: The occurrences of the third-person neuter pronouns were not resolved. The preposition "Amid" was not correctly analysed.

Text 7: Modern development of wind-energy technology and applications ...

Good: Correct interpretation of time expressions "1930s" and "1970s". Correct predicate argument structure overall.

Bad: "Modern" was recognised as a proper name. The noun phrase "wind-energy technology and applications" was distributively analysed with "wind-energy" only applying to "technology". The sentence-initial adverb "Since" did not introduce proper discourse structure. The units of measurement in the last two sentences were not recognised as such. The tricky time expression "mid-80's" only got a shallow interpretation.

5 Conclusion

Boxer is a wide-coverage system for semantic interpretation. It takes as input a CCG derivation of a natural language expression, and produces formally interpretable semantic representations: either in the form of DRSs, or as formulas of first-order logic. The existence of CCGbank (Hockenmaier, 2003) and robust parsers trained on it (Clark and Curran, 2004; Bos et al., 2004) make Boxer a state-of-the-art open-domain tool for deep semantic analysis.

Boxer's performance on the shared task for comparing semantic represtations was promising. It was able to produce DRSs for all texts. We can't quantify the quality of Boxer's output, as we don't have gold standard representations at our disposal. Manually inspecting the output gives us the following impression:

- computed predicate argument structure is generally of good quality, including hard constructions involving control or coordination;

- discourse structure triggered by conditionals, negation or discourse adverbs is overall correctly computed;

- some measure and time expressions are correctly analysed, others aren't;

- several shallow analyses are given for lexical phrases that require deep analysis;

- bridging references and pronouns are not resolved in most cases; but when they are, they are mostly correctly resolved (high precision at the cost of recall).

Finally, a comment on availability of Boxer. All sources of Boxer are available for download and free of non-commercial use. It is distributed with the C&C tools for natural language processing (Curran et al., 2007), which are hosted on this site:

```
http://svn.ask.it.usyd.edu.au/trac/candc/wiki/boxer
```

References

Asher, N. (1993). *Reference to Abstract Objects in Discourse*. Dordrecht: Kluwer Academic Publishers.

Blackburn, P. and J. Bos (2005). *Representation and Inference for Natural Language. A First Course in Computational Semantics*. CSLI.

Blackburn, P., J. Bos, M. Kohlhase, and H. de Nivelle (2001). Inference and Computational Semantics. In H. Bunt, R. Muskens, and E. Thijsse (Eds.), *Computing Meaning Vol.2*, pp. 11–28. Kluwer.

Bos, J. (2003). Implementing the Binding and Accommodation Theory for Anaphora Resolution and Presupposition Projection. *Computational Linguistics 29*(2), 179–210.

Bos, J. (2004). Computational Semantics in Discourse: Underspecification, Resolution, and Inference. *Journal of Logic, Language and Information 13*(2), 139–157.

Bos, J. (2008). Introduction to the Shared Task on Comparing Semantic Representations. In J. Bos and R. Delmonte (Eds.), *Semantics in Text Processing. STEP 2008 Conference Proceedings*, Volume 1 of *Research in Computational Semantics*, pp. 257–261. College Publications.

Bos, J., S. Clark, M. Steedman, J. R. Curran, and J. Hockenmaier (2004). Wide-Coverage Semantic Representations from a CCG Parser. In *Proceedings of the 20th International Conference on Computational Linguistics (COLING '04)*, Geneva.

Clark, S. and J. Curran (2004). Parsing the WSJ using CCG and Log-Linear Models. In *Proceedings of the 42nd Annual Meeting of the Association for Computational Linguistics (ACL '04)*, Barcelona, Spain.

Curran, J., S. Clark, and J. Bos (2007, June). Linguistically motivated large-scale nlp with c&c and boxer. In *Proceedings of the 45th Annual Meeting of the Association for Computational Linguistics Companion Volume Proceedings of the Demo and Poster Sessions*, Prague, Czech Republic, pp. 33–36. Association for Computational Linguistics.

Dowty, D. (1989). On the semantic content of the notion thematic role. In *Properties, Types, and Meanings*, Volume 2. Kluwer.

Hockenmaier, J. (2003). *Data and Models for Statistical Parsing with Combinatory Categorial Grammar*. Ph. D. thesis, University of Edinburgh.

Kamp, H. (1981). A Theory of Truth and Semantic Representation. In J. Groenendijk, T. M. Janssen, and M. Stokhof (Eds.), *Formal Methods in the Study of Language*, pp. 277–322. Amsterdam: Mathematical Centre, Amsterdam.

Kamp, H. and U. Reyle (1993). *From Discourse to Logic; An Introduction to Modeltheoretic Semantics of Natural Language, Formal Logic and DRT*. Dordrecht: Kluwer.

Kipper, K., A. Korhonen, N. Ryant, and M. Palmer (2008). A large-scale classification of english verbs. *Language Resources and Evaluation 42*(1), 21–40.

Steedman, M. (2001). *The Syntactic Process*. The MIT Press.

Van der Sandt, R. (1992). Presupposition Projection as Anaphora Resolution. *Journal of Semantics 9*, 333–377.

Semantic and Pragmatic Computing with GETARUNS

Rodolfo Delmonte

University of Venice "Ca' Foscari" (Italy)

email: delmont@unive.it

Abstract

We present a system for text understanding called GETARUNS, in its deep version applicable only to Closed Domains. We will present the low level component organized according to LFG theory. The system also does pronominal binding, quantifier raising and temporal interpretation. Then we will introduce the high level component where the Discourse Model is created from a text. Texts belonging to closed domains are characterized by the fact that their semantics is controlled or under command of the system; and most importantly, sentences making up the texts are fully parsed without failures. In practice, these texts are short and sentences are also below a certain threshold, typically less than 25 words. For longer sentences the system switches from the topdown to the bottomup system. In case of failure it will backoff to the partial system which produces a very lean and shallow semantics with no inference rules. The small text we will present contains what is called a "psychological statement" sentence which contributes an important bias as to the linking of the free pronominal expression contained in the last sentence.

1   The System GETARUNS

GETARUNS, the system for text understanding developed at the University of Venice, is equipped with three main modules: a lower module for parsing where sentence strategies are implemented; a middle module for semantic interpretation and discourse model construction which is cast into Situation Semantics; and a higher module where reasoning and generation takes place.

The system is based on LFG theoretical framework (Bresnan, 2001) and has a highly interconnected modular structure. The Closed Domain version of the system is a top-down depth-first DCG-based parser written in Prolog Horn Clauses, which uses a strong deterministic policy by means of a lookahead mechanism with a WFST to help recovery when failure is unavoidable due to strong attachment ambiguity.

It is divided up into a pipeline of sequential but independent modules which realize the subdivision of a parsing scheme as proposed in LFG theory where a c-structure is built before the f-structure can be projected by unification into a DAG (Direct Acyclic Graph). In this sense we try to apply in a given sequence phrase-structure rules as they are ordered in the grammar: whenever a syntactic constituent is successfully built, it is checked for semantic consistency. In case the governing predicate expects obligatory arguments to be lexically realized they will be searched and checked for uniqueness and coherence as LFG grammaticality principles require.

Syntactic and semantic information is accessed and used as soon as possible: in particular, both categorial and subcategorization information attached to predicates in the lexicon is extracted as soon as the main predicate is processed, be it adjective, noun or verb, and is used to subsequently restrict the number of possible structures to be built. Adjuncts are computed by semantic compatibility tests on the basis of selectional restrictions of main predicates and adjuncts heads.

The output of grammatical modules is fed then onto the Binding Module (BM) which activates an algorithm for anaphoric binding. Antecedents for pronouns are ranked according to grammatical function, semantic role, inherent features and their position at f-structure. Eventually, this information is added into the original f-structure graph and then passed on to the Discourse Module (DM).

The grammar is equipped with a core lexicon containing most frequent 5,000 fully specified inflected word forms where each entry is followed by its lemma and a list of morphological features, organised in the form of attribute-value pairs. However, morphological analysers for English are also available with big root dictionaries (25,000 for English) which only provide for syntactic subcategorization, though. In addition to that there are all lexical form provided by a fully revised version of COMLEX, and in order to take into account phrasal and adverbial verbal compound forms, we also use lexical entries made available by UPenn and TAG encoding. Their grammatical verbal syntactic codes have then been adapted to our formalism and are used to generate a subcategorization schemes with an aspectual and semantic class associated to it — however no restrictions can reasonably be formulated on arguments of predicates. Semantic inherent features for Out of Vocabulary Words, be they nouns, verbs, adjectives or adverbs, are provided by a fully revised version of WordNet (Fellbaum, 1998) — plus EuroWordnet, with a number of additions coming from computer, economics, and advertising semantic fields — in which we used 75 semantic classes similar to those provided by CoreLex (Buitelaar, 1998).

When each sentence is parsed, tense aspect and temporal adjuncts are accessed to build the basic temporal interpretation to be used by the temporal reasoner. Eventually two important modules are fired: Quantifier Raising and Pronominal Binding. QR is computed on f-structure which is represented internally as a DAG. It may introduce a pair of functional components: an operator where the quantifier can be raised, and a pool containing the associated variable where the quantifier is actually placed in the f-structure representation. This information may then be used by the following higher system to inspect quantifier scope. Pronominal binding is carried out at first at sentence internal level. DAGs will be searched for binding domains and antecedents matched to the pronouns if any to produce a list of possible bindings. Best candidates will then be chosen.

2 The Upper Module

GETARUNS has a highly sophisticated linguistically based semantic module which is used to build up the Discourse Model. Semantic processing is strongly modularized and distributed amongst a number of different submodules which take care of Spatio-Temporal Reasoning, Discourse Level Anaphora Resolution, and other subsidiary processes like Topic Hierarchy which cooperate to find the most probable antecedent of coreferring and cospecifying referential expressions when creating semantic individuals. These are then asserted in the Discourse Model (hence the DM), which is then the sole knowledge representation used to solve nominal coreference.

The system uses two resolution submodules which work in sequence: they constitute independent modules and allow no backtracking. The first one is fired whenever a free sentence external pronoun is spotted; the second one takes the results of the first submodule and checks for nominal anaphora. They have access to all data structures contemporarily and pass the resolved pair, anaphor-antecedent to the following modules.

Semantic Mapping is performed in two steps: at first a Logical Form is produced which is a structural mapping from DAGs onto unscoped well-formed formulas. These are then turned into situational semantics informational units, infons which may become facts or sits. Each unit has a relation, a list of arguments which in our case receive their semantic roles from lower processing — a polarity, a temporal and a spatial location index.

3 The Text

The text we present for the shared task (Bos, 2008) is a "psychological statement" text, i.e. it includes a sentence (namely sentence 4) that represents a psychological statement, i.e. it expresses the feelings and is viewed from the point of view of one of the participants in the story. The relevance of the sentence is its role in the assignment of the antecedent to the pronominal expressions contained in the following sentence. Without such a sentence the anaphora resolution module would have no way of computing "John" as the legitimate antecedent of "He/his". On the contrary, in a system like ours that computes Point of View and Discourse Domain on the basis of Informational Structure and Centering information, it will be possible to make available the appropriate antecedent to the anaphora resolution module.

We will discuss mainly semantic information processing. In so doing we shall have to devote some space to LFG grammatical representation, to Logical Form and eventually the Discourse Model. However, since this is meant to be a short paper, we will only be able to show some fragments of the overall representation, highlighting the most important features and disregarding the rest. So first of all, consider the sentences making up the text:

1. John went into a restaurant.
2. There was a table in the corner.
3. The waiter took the order.
4. The atmosphere was warm and friendly.
5. He began to read his book.

We will be able to present an almost complete sequence of representations as produced by GETARUNS only for one sentence, and then we will comment on the rest.

```
1. John went into a restaurant

index:f1
pred:go
lex_form:[np/subj/agente/[human, object],
          sp/obl/locat/[to, in, into]/[object, place]]
voice:active; mood:ind; tense:pres; cat:risultato
subj/agent:index:sn4
          cat:[human]; pred:'John'
          gen:mas; num:sing; pers:3; spec:def:'0'
          tab_ref:[+ref, -pro, -ana, -class]
obl/locat:index:sn5
          cat:[place]; pred:restaurant
          num:sing; pers:3; spec:def:-
          tab_ref:[+ref, -pro, -ana, +class]; qmark:q1
aspect:achiev_tr
rel1:[td(f1_res2)=tr(f1_res2)]
rel2:[included(tr(f1_res2), tes(f1_res2))]
specificity:-; ref_int:[tr(f1_res2)]
qops:qop:q(q1, indefinite)
```

'Centering and Topic Hierarchy'
state(1, retaining)   topic(1, main, id5)   topic(1, potential, id1)

```
INFORMATIONAL STRUCTURE

CLAUSE IDENTIFIER:          2-n1
CLAUSE TYPE:                main/prop
FACTUALITY:                 factive
CHANGE IN THE WORLD:        null
RELEVANCE:                  background
TEMP_RELATION:              undef(tes(f1_res2), nil)
DISCOURSE FOCUS:            tes(f1_res2)
DISCOURSE RELATION:         narration
DISCOURSE DOMAIN:           objective
POINT OF VIEW:              narrator
```

```
LOGICAL FORM
wff(situation,
    wff(go,
        < entity : sn4 : wff(isa, sn4,  John) >,
        < indefinite : sn5 : wff(isa, sn5, restaurant) >,
        < event : f1 :
            wff(and, wff(isa,  f1,  ev),
                    wff(time, f1, < definite : t2 :
                        wff(and, wff(isa, t2, tloc),
                            wff(pres, t2)) >)) >))
```

DISCOURSE MODEL 2

```
/*** There was a table in the corner. ***/
loc(infon13, id4, [arg:main_sloc, arg:restaurant])
ind(infon14, id5)
fact(infon15, inst_of, [ind:id5, class:man], 1, univ, univ)
fact(infon16, name, ['John', id5], 1, univ, univ)
fact(id6, go, [agente:id5, locat:id1], 1, tes(f1_res2), id4)
fact(infon19, isa, [arg:id6, arg:ev], 1, tes(f1_res2), id4)
fact(infon20, isa, [arg:id7, arg:tloc], 1, tes(f1_res2), id4)
fact(infon21, pres, [arg:id7], 1, tes(f1_res2), id4)
fact(infon22, time, [arg:id6, arg:id7], 1, tes(f1_res2), id4)
includes(tr(f1_res2), univ)
```

Sentence 2, is a presentational structure, where the subject form "there" is recovered as being part of the meaning of the main predicate in the semantics. The location "in the corner" is computed as a adjunct and it is understood as a entertaining a meronimic relation with the main location, "the restaurant", again in the semantics. When building the Discourse Model it is possible to fire inferences to recover pragmatic unexpressed implicatures, as for instance, the fact that introducing a "table" with a presentational structure and an indefinite NP but accompanied by a definite location induces the reader to produce such implicit information as indicated below, i.e, the fact that the main topic and only current participant to the discourse is supposed to be sitting at the table in the corner. This inference is fired by inferential rules that look for relations intevening between main location and current location; also presentational structure contributes by introducing an indefinite "table" which is the trigger of the SITTING event.

DISCOURSE MODEL 3

```
/*** The waiter took the order. ***/
loc(infon26, id8, [arg:main_tloc, arg:tes(f1_res2)])
ent(infon27, id9)
fact(infon28, inst_of, [ind:id9, class:place], 1, univ, univ)
fact(infon29, isa, [ind:id9, class:table], 1, id8, id4)
in(infon30, id9, id4)
fact(id10, sit, [actor:id5, locat:id9], 1, tes(f5_id10), id4)
fact(infon31, isa, [arg:id10, arg:ev], 1, tes(f5_id10), id4)
fact(infon32, isa, [arg:id11, arg:tloc], 1, tes(f5_id10), id4)
fact(infon33, isa, [arg:id11], 1, tes(f5_id10), id4)
ind(infon34, id12)
fact(infon35, inst_of, [ind:id12, class:place], 1, univ, univ)
```

```
fact(infon36, isa, [ind:id12, class:corner], 1, id8, id4)
fact(infon37, part_of, [restaurant, id12, id1], 1, id8, id4)
fact(id13, there_be, [prop:id9], 1, tes(f4_res3), id4)
```

This sentence is computed as containing an idiomatic predicate "take_order" which in turn has a BENEFICIARY/GOAL of the same event. In turn the Goal is computed as if it were an obligatory semantic role like the missing Agent of passivized structures. The semantics is then responsible for checking consistency of predicate-argument structures. The Goal induces the presence of an Oblique which is filled with an "exist" dummy predicate. This predicate is then linked to the only other available participant in the topic structure organized by the Centering Algorithm, John with semantic Id = id5.

```
index:f1
pred:take
lex_form:[np/subj/agent/[human], idioms/obj/form/[order],
          pp/obl/goal/from/[human]]
voice:active; mood:ind; tense:pres; cat:activity
subj/agent:index:sn3
          cat:[human, social]; pred:waiter
          gen:mas; num:sing; pers:3; spec:def:+
          tab_ref:[+ref, -pro, -ana, +class]
ogg/form:index:sn4
          cat:[activity, event]; pred:order
          num:sing; pers:3; spec:def:+
          tab_ref:[+ref, -pro, -ana, +class]
obj2/goal:index:sn5
          cat:[human, animate]; pred:exist
          spec:def:-; part:+
          tab_ref:[+ref, -pro, -ana, +me]
aspect:activity
rel1:[td(f1_res4)=tr(f1_res4)]
rel2:[included(tr(f1_res4), tes(f1_res4))]
specificity:+; ref_int:[tr(f1_res4)]
```

'Centering and Topic Hierarchy'
state(4, continue)   topic(4, main, id5)   topic(4, potential, id16)

DISCOURSE MODEL 4

```
/*** The atmosphere was warm and friendly. ***/
loc(infon49, id15, [arg:main_tloc, arg:tes(f4_res3)])
ind(infon50, id16)
fact(infon51, inst_of, [ind:id16, class:social_role], 1, univ, univ)
fact(infon52, isa, [ind:id16, class:waiter], 1, id15, id4)
fact(infon53, role, [waiter, id4, id16], 1, id15, id4)
fact(infon55, isa, [arg:id5, arg:exist], 1, id15, id4)
fact(id18, take_order, [agent:id16, goal:id5], 1, tes(f1_res4), id4)
```

Sentence 4, is the psychological statement, where the Centering Algorithm uses the information made available by the computational called Informational Structure that we report here below.

'Centering and Topic Hierarchy'
state(4, continue)   topic(4, main, id5)   topic(4, potential, id21)

```
INFORMATIONAL STRUCTURE

CLAUSE IDENTIFIER:              5-n1
CLAUSE TYPE:                    main/prop
FACTUALITY:                     factive
CHANGE IN THE WORLD:            null
RELEVANCE:                      background
TEMP_RELATION:                  during(tes(f1_res5), tes(f1_res4))
DISCOURSE FOCUS:                tes(f1_res5)
DISCOURSE RELATION:             explanation
DISCOURSE DOMAIN:               subjective
POINT OF VIEW:                  John
```

As can be noticed, the system has computed the Discourse Domain as "subjective", and the Point of View as belonging to one of the participants, the one referred by with a proper name. In fact, it is just the use of a definite expression "the waiter" that tells the system to underrate the importance in the Topic Hierarchy automatically built by the Centering Algorithm.

DISCOURSE MODEL

```
loc(infon77, id24, [arg:main_tloc, arg:tes(f1_res5)])
fact(infon78, poss, ['John', id5, id25], 1, id24, id4)
ind(infon79, id25)
fact(infon80, inst_of, [ind:id25, class:thing], 1, univ, univ)
fact(infon81, isa, [ind:id25, class:book], 1, id24, id4)
fact(id26, read, [agent:id5, theme_aff:id25], 1, tes(finf1_res6), id4)
fact(infon85, isa, [arg:id26, arg:ev], 1, tes(finf1_res6), id4)
fact(infon86, isa, [arg:id27, arg:tloc], 1, tes(finf1_res6), id4)
fact(infon87, pres, [arg:id27], 1, tes(finf1_res6), id4)
fact(infon88, time, [arg:id26, arg:id27], 1, tes(finf1_res6), id4)
fact(id28, begin, [actor:id5, prop:id26], 1, tes(f1_res6), id4).
```

4   Performance on the Shared Task Texts

If we try to grade the seven texts of the shared task (Bos, 2008), from the point of view of their intrinsic semantic complexity we should get the following picture:

(a) Texts 6, 7 (scientific texts)
(b) Texts 4, 5 (newswire articles)
(c) Texts 1, 2, 3 (made up texts, schoolbook texts)

Overall, the system performed better with category (c). texts and worse with scientific texts, category (a). I take Text 6 and 7 to be in need of a specific domain ontology in order to have semantic inferences fired when needed. In addition, in our case, these two texts have sentences exceeding the maximum length for topdown parsing, which is the modality that better guarantees a full parse. Text 6 has sentences respectively 31, 38 and 49. In fact Text 1 represents an easy to understand scientific text and is much easier to parse — even though there are mistakes in Adjuncts attachment.

Apart from Texts 6 and 7, which lack in semantic relations due to the lack of semantic information, the remaining texts abound in semantically relevant syntactic information which can be used to assert facts in the Discourse Model which create a network of meaningful associations. PAs, that is Predicate Argument structures, together with implicit optional and obligatory arguments are mostly recovered — more on this in the following sections.

The system has failed in finding antecedents for the pronoun IT. The current version of the complete system is not equipped with an algorithm that tells expletive IT cases from referential ones. On the contrary, one such algorithm has been successfully experimented with the partial system. Other pronouns are almost all correctly bound. As for nominal expressions, problems arise with scientific texts in case a different linguistic description is used to corefer or cospecify to the same entity.

For every text we will list pieces of what we call the Discourse Model World of Entities participating in the events described in the text. This file is produced at the end of the analysis and contains all entities recorded with a semantic Identifier by the system during the analysis of the text. The file is produced by a procedure that recursively searches the dynamic database of FACTS or Infons in Situation Semantics terms, associated to each entity semantic identifier. These Infons may register properties, attributes or participation in events. Eventually, Infons may also be inherited in case one of the entity is semantically included in another entity — see the case of CANCER being included in the more general notion of CANCERS at the end of Text 2.

The procedure produces a score that is derived from the relevance in terms of topichood — being Main, Secondary or Potential Topic — as asserted by the Centering algorithm. Entities and their associated infons are thus graded according to relevance. They are listed on the basis of their ontological status: INDividuals, SETs, CLASSes.

4.1 Text One

The main topic is the OBJECT. As can be gathered from the question posed to the system at the end of the parse, the main relations are all captured throughout the text. They can also be recovered from the Inherited Discourse World of Entities:

```
entity(ind,id2,9,facts([
   fact(infon111, coincide, [arg:id24, arg:id29], 1, tes(sn59_t13), id20),
   fact(infon4, isa, [ind:id2, class:object], 1, id1, univ),
   fact(infon5, inst_of, [ind:id2, class:thing], 1, univ, univ),
   fact(id9, throw, [tema_nonaff:id2, agente:id8], 1, tes(sn42_t11), univ),
   fact(id17, fall, [actor:id2, modale:id16], 1, tes(f1_t12), univ),
   fact(id29, take, [actor:id26, theme_aff:id2], 1, tes(finf1_t13), id20)])).
```

THROW is understood as being an event that takes place from a CLIFF and with a SPEED. However the SPEED is HORIZONTAL but the CLIFF is not HIGH — this relation has been missed. The OBJECT falls from a height of the same CLIFF. The one but last sentence is only partially represented. On the contrary, the final question is perfectly understood.

4.2 Text Two

The main topic is CANCER. From the Discourse World we know that:

```
entity(class,id3,2,facts([
   fact(infon7, inst_of, [ind:id3, class:stato], 1, univ, univ),
   fact(infon8, isa, [ind:id3, class:cancer], 1, id1, univ),
```

```
        fact(id4, cause, [theme_aff:id3, agent:id2], 1, tes(f2_t21), univ),
        fact(infon81, isa, [arg:id3, arg:cancer], 1, id25, id26),
        fact(id31, look, [actor:id27, locat:id3], 1, tes(f3_t23), id26)]])).
```

CANCER is CAUSED by a VIRUS and that RESEARCHERs have been LOOKing for other CANCERs which receive a different semantic identifier but inherit all the properties:

```
    entity(class,id28,2,facts([   in(infon79, id28, id3),
        fact(infon75, cause, [ind:id28], 1, id25, id26),
        fact(infon76, of, [arg:id28, specif:id28], 1, univ, univ),
        fact(infon77, inst_of, [ind:id28, class:stato], 1, univ, univ),
        fact(infon78, isa, [ind:id28, class:cancer], 1, id25, id26),
        fact(*, inst_of, [ind:id28, class:stato], 1, univ, univ),
        fact(*, isa, [ind:id28, class:cancer], 1, id1, univ),
        fact(*, cause, [theme_aff:id28, agent:id2], 1, tes(f2_t21), univ),
        fact(*, isa, [arg:id28, arg:cancer], 1, id25, id26),
        fact(*, look, [actor:id27, locat:id28], 1, tes(f3_t23), id26)]])).
```

The VIRUS is understood as the AGENT.

```
    entity(ind,id2,11,facts([
        fact(infon4, isa, [ind:id2, class:virus], 1, id1, univ),
        fact(infon5, inst_of, [ind:id2, class:animal], 1, univ, univ),
        fact(id4, cause, [theme_aff:id3, agent:id2], 1, tes(f2_t21), univ),
        fact(infon82, isa, [arg:id2, arg:virus], 1, id25, id26),
        fact(id29, cause, [agent:id2], 1, tes(f2_t23), id26)]])).
```

The system also understands that those EVENTs, were KNOWn for some time, as shown by the ID8 which is bound in the discourse by means of THAT to the event id4 listed above,

```
    entity(ind,id8,1,facts([
        fact(infon21, prop, [arg:id8,
                    disc_set:[id4:cause:
                            [theme_aff:id3, agent:id2]]],
                    1, id6, id7),
        fact(infon31, isa, [arg:id8, arg:that], 1, id6, id7),
        fact(id12, know, [tema_nonaff:id8, actor:id11], 1, tes(f2_t22), id7)]])).
```

However the system has not bound IT to THAT so we do not know what LEADs to a vaccine, nor do we know what prevents from what. All IT are unbound.

4.3 Text Three

This is the text that we proposed for the shared task and is already completely and consistently semantically and pragmatically represented. It has already been presented above.

4.4 Text Four

The text is not completely and consistently represented but most of the relations are fully understood. In particular consider THEY in the third sentence which is rightly bound to the SET of two trainers asserted in the Discourse World. The school is always coindixed. The last sentence contains a first plural pronoun WE which is interpreted as being coindexed with the narrator, but also wrongly with the location of the text.

4.5   Text Five

The text is not completely and consistently represented but most of the relations are fully understood. We still know a lot about the main Entities, the PROPELLANT and NITROCELLULOSE which is composed in CHUNKs.

```
entity(ind,id19,8,facts([
    fact(infon42, inst_of, [ind:id19, class:sub], 1, univ, univ),
    fact(infon43, isa, [ind:id19, class:propellant], 1, id18, nil),
    fact(infon44, isa, [arg:id19, arg:propellant], 1, id18, univ),
    fact(id20, explode, [agent:id19], 1, tes(f1_t53), univ),
    fact(infon108, isa, [arg:id19, arg:propellant], 1, id30, univ),
    fact(id38, use, [theme_aff:id19, actor:id37], 1, tes(f2_t55), univ),
    fact(id41, make, [theme_aff:id19, actor:id40, loc_origin:id31],
                     1, tes(sn32_t55), univ),
    fact(id20, explode, [agent:id19], 1, tes(f1_t53), univ),
    fact(infon50, sub, [prop:id20], 1, id18, univ)])).

entity(ind,id32,1.2,facts([ in(infon91, id32, id31),
    fact(infon89, inst_of, [ind:id32, class:sub], 1, univ, univ),
    fact(infon90, isa, [ind:id32, class:nitrocellulose], 1, id30, nil),
    fact(*, nitrocellulose, [ind:id32], 1, id30, nil),
    fact(*, produce, [ind:id32], 1, id30, nil),
    fact(*, repackage, [ind:id32], 1, id30, nil),
    fact(*, of, [arg:id32, specif:id31], 1, univ, univ),
    fact(*, of, [arg:id32, specif:id31], 1, univ, univ),
    fact(*, of, [arg:id32, specif:id31], 1, univ, univ),
    fact(*, inst_of, [ind:id32, class:col], 1, univ, univ),
    fact(*, isa, [ind:id32, class:chunk], 1, id30, nil),
    fact(*, make, [theme_aff:id19, actor:id40, loc_origin:id32],
                  1, tes(sn32_t55), univ)])).

entity(set,id31,1,facts([ card(infon79, id31, 5),
    fact(infon80, nitrocellulose, [ind:id31], 1, id30, nil),
    fact(infon81, produce, [ind:id31], 1, id30, nil),
    fact(infon82, repackage, [ind:id31], 1, id30, nil),
    fact(infon83, of, [arg:id31, specif:id31], 1, univ, univ),
    fact(infon86, inst_of, [ind:id31, class:col], 1, univ, univ),
    fact(infon87, isa, [ind:id31, class:chunk], 1, id30, nil),
    fact(id41, make, [theme_aff:id19, actor:id40, loc_origin:id31],
                     1, tes(sn32_t55), univ)])).
```

The relation intervening between CHUNKS and NITROCELLULOSE endows transitivity to the EVENTS taking place so that both are involved in REPACKAGE, PRODUCE, MAKE. We also know that a CREWMAN was OPERATING at a center and that the GUN CREW was KILLed, by an unknown AGENT, id26.

```
entity(class,id23,6,facts([
    fact(infon55, of, [arg:id23, specif:id8], 1, univ, univ),
    fact(infon56, inst_of, [ind:id23, class:institution], 1, univ, univ),
    fact(infon57, isa, [ind:id23, class:crew], 1, id22, nil),
    fact(id27, kill, [theme_aff:id23, agent:id26], 1, tes(f2_t54), univ)])).
```

We know that EVENTS happened during WORLD_WAR_II. Also notice that IT SUBJect of SUSPECT is correctly computed as an expletive.

4.6 Text Six

Two of the sentences are parsed by the partial system, but the main relations are well understood. The FARM and the COMMUNITY provide FOOD and EARNs a REVENUE.

```
entity(ind,id13,3,facts([
    fact(infon30, inst_of, [ind:id13, class:informa], 1, univ, univ),
    fact(infon31, isa, [ind:id13, class:farm], 1, univ, univ),
    fact(id17, provide, [goal:id8,tema_nonaff:id7,actor:id13],1,univ,univ),
    fact(infon85, isa, [arg:id13, arg:farm], 1, id41, univ),
    fact(id43, earn, [agent:id13, theme_aff:id42], 1, tes(sn59_t63),univ)])).

entity(ind,id7,0,facts([
    fact(infon10, inst_of, [ind:id7, class:any], 1, univ, univ),
    fact(infon11, isa, [ind:id7, class:food], 1, univ, univ),
    fact(id17, provide,[goal:id8,tema_nonaff:id7,actor:id13],1,univ,univ)])).

entity(ind,id42,2,facts([
    fact(infon83, inst_of, [ind:id42, class:legal], 1, univ, univ),
    fact(infon84, isa, [ind:id42, class:revenue], 1, id41, nil),
    fact(id43, earn, [agent:id13, theme_aff:id42], 1, tes(sn59_t63), univ)])).
```

The COMMUNITY LACK the FOOD

```
entity(ind,id8,0,facts([
    fact(infon13, inst_of, [ind:id8, class:luogo], 1, univ, univ),
    fact(infon14, isa, [ind:id8, class:community], 1, univ, univ),
    fact(id17, provide, [goal:id8,tema_nonaff:id7,actor:id13],1,univ,univ),
    fact(id14, lack, [theme_aff:id9, actor:id8, purpose:cl5, result:id14],
                     1, univ, univ)])).
```

Most of the sentences are parsed by the partial system. However questions can be asked and get a reply, even though the generator does not handle uncountable nouns like MONEY properly.

4.7 Text Seven

The most difficult text is fully parsed but not satisfactorily semantically represented. We only know few things, and they are all unrelated. There is no way to related WIND to TURBINE and to ENERGY in a continuous way.

```
entity(set,id61,4,facts([ card(infon253, id61, 5),
    fact(infon254, power, [nil:id61], 1, id60, id20),
    fact(infon255, maximum, [ind:id61], 1, id60, id20),
    fact(infon256, of, [arg:id61, specif:id61], 1, univ, univ),
    fact(infon257, wind_turbine, [ind:id61], 1, id60, id20),
    fact(infon258, inst_of, [ind:id61, class:thing], 1, univ, univ),
    fact(infon259, isa, [ind:id61, class:[wind, turbine]], 1, id60, id20),
    fact(infon264, of, [arg:id63, specif:id61], 1, univ, univ),
    fact(infon267, isa, [arg:id61, arg:wind_turbine], 1, id60, id20),
    fact(infon268, isa, [arg:id61, arg:power], 1, id60, id20),
    fact(infon269, typical, [arg:id61], 1, id60, id20),
    fact(infon271, power, [nil:id61, arg:id61], 1, id60, id20)])).
```

```
entity(ind,id14,2,facts([
   fact(infon52, inst_of, [ind:id14, class:abstract_state], 1, univ, univ),
   fact(infon53, inst_of, [ind:id14, class:energy], 1, univ, univ),
   fact(infon54, isa, [ind:id14, class:energy], 1, univ, univ),
   fact(infon55, isa, [ind:id14, class:wind_energy], 1, univ, univ),
   fact(infon58, of, [arg:id15, specif:id14], 1, univ, univ)])).

entity(ind,id22,1,facts([   in(infon90, id22, id15),
   fact(infon88, inst_of, [ind:id22, class:thing], 1, univ, univ),
   fact(infon89, isa, [ind:id22, class:wind], 1, id19, id20),
   fact(*, isa, [ind:id22, class:wind], 1, univ, univ),
   fact(*, of, [arg:id22, specif:id14], 1, univ, univ)])).
```

We know that WIND and ENERGY are related, and also that there is one such technology, but is semantically set apart, due to orthography.

```
entity(class,id11,1,facts([
   fact(infon39, 'wind-energy', [ind:id11], 1, id1, univ),
   fact(infon44, of, [arg:id11, specif:id12], 1, univ, univ),
   fact(infon45, inst_of, [ind:id11, class:abstract_state], 1, univ, univ),
   fact(infon46, isa, [ind:id11, class:technology], 1, id1, univ)])).

entity(class,id12,0,facts([
   fact(infon41, inst_of, [ind:id12, class:astratto], 1, univ, univ),
   fact(infon42, isa, [ind:id12, class:energy], 1, univ, univ),
   fact(infon44, of, [arg:id11, specif:id12], 1, univ, univ),
   fact(infon103, has, [arg:id26, tema:id12], 1, id19, id20),
   fact(infon109, of, [arg:id26, specif:id12], 1, univ, univ)])).
```

I assume that scientific language requires a different setup of semantic rules of inference, which can only be appropriately specified in a domain ontology.

References

Bos, J. (2008). Introduction to the Shared Task on Comparing Semantic Representations. In J. Bos and R. Delmonte (Eds.), *Semantics in Text Processing. STEP 2008 Conference Proceedings*, Volume 1 of *Research in Computational Semantics*, pp. 257–261. College Publications.

Bresnan, J. (2001). *Lexical-Functional Syntax*. Oxford: Blackwell.

Buitelaar, P. (1998). *CoreLex: Systematic Polysemy and Underspecification*. Ph. D. thesis, Brandeis University.

Delmonte, R. (2007). *Computational Linguistic Text Processing: Logical Form, Semantic Interpretation, Discourse Relations and Question Answering*. New York: Nova Science Publishers.

Fellbaum, C. (1998). *WordNet: An Electronic Lexical Database*. Cambridge (MA): MIT Press.

LXGram in the Shared Task "Comparing Semantic Representations" of STEP 2008

António Branco
Francisco Costa
Universidade de Lisboa (Portugal)
email: Antonio.Branco@di.fc.ul.pt

Abstract

LXGram is a hand-built Portuguese computational grammar based on HPSG (syntax) and MRS (semantics). The LXGram system participated in the STEP 2008 shared task which aims at comparing semantic representations produced by NLP systems such as LXGram. Every participating team had to contribute a small text. The text that we submitted for the shared task was originally in Portuguese (an excerpt from a newspaper) and translated into English, to make a meaningful comparison at the shared task possible. Likewise, the English texts contributed by the other participating teams were translated into Portuguese. Because the LXGram generates many different analyses (mainly due to PP attachment ambiguities), the preferred analysis was selected manually. It was required to extend LXGram's lexicon and inventory of syntax rules to be able to get a reasonable performance on the shared task data. Eventually, our system was able to produce an analysis for 20 out of the 30 sentences of the shared task data.

1 Introduction

This paper describes the participation of the Portuguese grammar LXGram in the Shared Task of STEP 2008 "Comparing Semantic Representations" (Bos, 2008). This Shared Task was held in the University of Venice on 22–24 September 2008, with the purpose of comparing semantic representations produced by different natural language processing systems. This task had seven participating teams. Each team contributed with a small text (up to five sentences long) to be processed by all the systems.

LXGram is a hand-built, general purpose computational grammar for the deep linguistic processing of Portuguese. It is developed under the grammatical framework of Head-Driven Phrase Structure Grammar, HPSG (Pollard and Sag, 1987, 1994; Sag et al., 2003) and uses Minimal Recursion Semantics, MRS (Copestake et al., 2005) for the representation of meaning. This grammar implementation is undertaken with the LKB (Copestake, 2002) grammar development environment and its evaluation and regression testing is done via [incr tsdb()] (Oepen, 2001). It is also intended to be compatible with the PET parser (Callmeier, 2000).

The LinGO Grammar Matrix (version 0.9), an open-source kit for the rapid development of grammars based on HPSG and MRS, was used as the initial code upon which to build LXGram. The grammar is implemented in the LKB using the $\mathcal{TDL}$ formalism (Krieger and Schäfer, 1994), based on unification and on typed feature structures, and whose types are organized in a multiple inheritance hierarchy.

For more information, please refer to a detailed implementation report (Branco and Costa, 2008a) or on pages 31–43 of this volume (Branco and Costa, 2008b). A free version of the grammar can also be obtained at http://nlx.di.fc.ul.pt/lxgram, under an ELDA research license.

Section 2 introduces the main features of the Minimal Recursion Semantics format, which is employed in the semantic representations produced by LXGram. In Section 3, the sample text that the LXGram team submitted is described, together with an explanation of the representations derived by the grammar. Finally, Section 4 discusses the results for the full data set of the Shared Task.

2 Semantic Formalism

In LXGram, semantic information is encoded following Minimal Recursion Semantics (MRS) format for semantic representation (Copestake et al., 2005). MRS has several properties that makes it an interesting semantic representation format from the point of view of computational semantics.

Notoriously, it allows underspecification of the scope of relevant operators, which permits that a sentence with scope ambiguities can be given a single, underspecified representation. For some applications, for instance machine translation between closely related languages from the same language family, the underspecified representations may be sufficient and bring the benefit of avoiding possible combinatorial explosion into as many parses as readings.

In a nutshell, the underspecification of scope is achieved by associating every basic relation to a handle (in the feature structure for a relation, the feature LBL encodes this handle) and describing the constraints that hold between these handles (in the feature HCONS, handle constraints). These constraints can be stated in a way such that some scope resolution options are allowed while others are discarded. Nevertheless, there may applications for which it may be important to get fully specified semantic representations. In this case, MRS permits that the different scope possibilities be computed on demand from the underspecified representation.

Also worth referring in this very brief presentation of the gist of MRS, it is the representation of conjunction with the relative order of conjuncts underspecified, by giving the same handle to the different conjuncts. This avoids computing associativity and commutativity of conjunction in situations where spurious overgeneration may arise.

Please consult Branco and Costa (2008a) in this volume (pages 31–43) for an example illustrating quantifier scope ambiguities and underspecification. Due to space limitations, it is not possible to provide further details on the MRS formalism here. For the presentation of MRS, please consult Copestake et al. (2005).

3 Sample Text

The following sentences are our examples for the shared task:

(1) A primeira escola de treino de cães-guias do País vai
the first school of training of leader dogs of the country goes
nascer em Mortágua e treinará 22 cães-guias por ano.
to be born in Mortágua and will train 22 leader dogs per year

The first school for the training of leader dogs in the country is going to be created in Mortágua and will train 22 leader dogs per year.

(2) Em Mortágua, João Pedro Fonseca e Marta Gomes coordenam o
in Mortágua João Pedro Fonseca and Marta Gomes coordinate the
projecto que sete pessoas desenvolvem nesta escola.
project that seven people develop in this school

In Mortágua, João Pedro Fonseca and Marta Gomes coordinate the project that seven people develop in this school.

(3) Visitaram vários espaços semelhantes em Inglaterra e em França,
they visited several spaces similar in England and in France,
e numa das escolas francesas estão já em estágio duas
and in one of the schools French are already in internship two
futuras treinadoras.
future trainers

They visited several similar places in England and in France, and two future trainers are already doing internship in one of the French schools.

(4) Os fundos comunitários asseguram a manutenção da escola até
the funding communitarian ensure the maintenance of the school until
1999.
1999

The communitarian funding ensures the operation of the school until 1999.

(5)   Gostaríamos que a nossa escola funcionasse à   semelhança das
        we would like that the our school worked   to the similarity of the
        francesas, que   vivem de dádivas, do   merchandising e até
        French   which live   from donations from the merchandising and even
        das   rifas que as crianças vendem nas   escolas.
        from the raffles that the children sell   in the schools

> *We would like our school to work similarly to the French ones, which live*
> *from donations, from the merchandising and even from the raffles that chil-*
> *dren sell in school.*

These sentences were adapted from newspaper text. We have chosen them because they display interesting phenomena.

The semantic representations that LXGram produces for these sentences are presented at the Shared Task website http://www.sigsem.org. An example is included in Appendix B. Several analyses are obtained for these examples (e.g. one of the sentences got 540 parses), the main reason being PP attachment ambiguity. The semantic representations we present are the ones associated to the preferred analyses, which were selected manually.

Note that since the representations could not be displayed in a single page, the value of the feature RELS was split across multiple pages. To ensure readability, the values of the other features (LTOP, INDEX and HCONS) are repeated on every page pertaining to the same representation.

Some comments are in order concerning these representations:

- The morphological person, number and gender are encoded as features (PERSON, NUMBER, GENDER) of the relevant index (quantified variable) that is present there. For indices, the boolean feature DIV is also used, that shows the value + for plurals and mass nouns.

- Event variables are included for the relations introduced by verbs, adjectives, prepositions and adverbs (under their ARG0 feature). The morphological information on the verbs is also encoded as features of these events. This is the purpose of the features MOOD, TENSE and ASPECT. There is also a feature SF (sentence force) that represents whether a sentence denotes a proposition, a question or a command. The feature ELLIPTICAL-PUNCT denotes whether the sentence ends with an ellipsis (...) and is useful in order to constrain what is generated by the grammar.

- There is a *tense_rel* relation associated to each verb form. Its ARG0 feature is the same as the ARG0 of the verb it is associated with. The purpose of this extra relation is to make an event variable present in the semantic representations for the copular sentences where the relevant predicate is provided by a noun (none of these examples). In such cases this event will contain the morphological information of the copular verb.

- Note that the information about whether adjectives have intersective semantics (see "francês"—"French"—in sentence (3)) or non-intersective semantics (see "futuro"—"future"—in sentence (5)) is visible in the corresponding semantic representations.

The names of the predicates that correspond to lexical items of several classes (common nouns, verbs, adjectives, adverbs, prepositions, etc.) follow a naming convention that includes a lemma field, a part-of-speech field and an optional sense field (often reflecting subcategorization). Table 1 lists the predicates present in these representations and provides the corresponding English lemmas. There are other special relations in these representations:

- *udef_q_rel*
  the quantifier for bare NPs

- *proper_q_rel*
  the quantifier for proper names

- *tense_rel*
  associated to every verbal relation (see discussion above)

- *named_rel*
  associated to proper names

- *name-precedes_rel*
  associated to proper names

- *string-equals_rel*
  equality between strings

- *indef_q_rel*
  associated to some indefinites. In particular it is the quantifier used for NPs that are introduced by elements that can also follow determiners (e.g. cardinals and vague quantifiers like "vários"—"several")

- *cardinal_rel*
  constrains the cardinality of the set denoted by the expression linked to its ARG1 feature

- *greater-or-equal_rel*
  the integer in its ARG0 is greater than or equal to the integer in its ARG1 feature

- *plus_rel*
  the integer in its ARG0 is the result of summing the two integers in the TERM0 and TERM1 features

- *int-equals_rel*
  equality between integers

- *ellipsis-or-generic_n_1_rel*
  placeholder relation when there are missing nouns

Table 1: Correspondence of Portuguese MRS relations and English lemmas

MRS Relation	English lemma
_ano_n_rel	year
_à_semelhança_a_-de-_rel	similarly
_assegurar_v_rel	to ensure
_até_a_rel	even
_até_p_rel	until
_cão-guia_n_rel	leader dog
_comunitário_a_rel	communitarian
_coordenar_v_rel	to coordinate
_criança_n_rel	child
_dádiva_n_-de-a-_rel	donation
_de_p_rel	of, from
_desenvolver_v_rel	to develop
_e_coord_rel	and
_em_p_rel	in
_espaço_n_rel	space
_estágio_n_rel	internship
_este_a_rel	this
_escola_n_rel	school
_francês_a_rel	French
_funcionar_v_rel	to work
_fundo_n_rel	funding
_futuro_a_rel	future
_gostar_v_rel	to like
_ir_v_aux_rel	to be going to
_já_a_rel	already
_manutenção_n_-de-por-_rel	maintenance
_merchandising_n_rel	merchandising
_nascer_v_rel	to be born
_o_q_rel	the
_país_n_rel	country
_por_p_rel	per
_pessoa_n_rel	person
_primeiro_a_rel	first
_projecto_n_-de-por_rel	project
_rifa_n_rel	raffle
_semelhante_a_-a-_rel	similar
_treinador_n_-de-_rel	trainer
_treinar_v_rel	to train
_treino_n_-de-por-_rel	training
_um_q_rel	a
_vários_a_scop_rel	several
_vender_v_-a-_rel	to sell
_visitar_v_rel	to visit
_viver_v_rel	to live

Sometimes some details of the semantic representations that are possible to obtain depend on the features of the system where LXGram is developed and runs. In particular, for each feature that represents an argument of a relation (ARG0, ARG1, ARG2, CARG, . . .), it must be stated in the configuration files whether it will contain a constant (e.g. a string literal). For instance, we must say that the feature CARG always contains a value, for visualization purposes. This fact sometimes constrains the display of the semantic representations. It is the reason why the semantics for proper names and for cardinals is more copious than what would seem necessary at first.

For instance, the semantics associated to "7 pessoas" ("7 people") in sentence (2) is roughly $\lambda x.cardinal\_rel(e, \_pessoa\_n\_rel(x), j_1) \wedge greater\text{-}or\text{-}equal\_rel(j_1, j_2) \wedge int\text{-}equals(j_2, 7)$ (note that conjunction is denoted in MRS via identical labels for relations). The information conveyed by the last two predicates could be simply given by $greater\text{-}or\text{-}equal\_rel(j_1, 7)$. However, for that to display correctly we would have to configure the system to display the second argument of the $greater\text{-}or\text{-}equal\_rel$ relation as a constant. This will not always be the case: in the semantics for "22" that argument is the integer that is the result of summing "20" and "2" (number expressions receive compositional semantics), represented with the help of the *plus_rel* relation. The LKB does not allow one to compute arithmetic expressions.

These few sentences present some interesting problems for the computation of semantic representation in general.

Typically, one is not able to resolve missing nouns, as this sometimes requires access to pragmatic information. As a consequence, the semantics produced for sentences with a missing noun (see sentence (5)) includes an *ellipsis-or-generic_n_1_rel* instead of the relation corresponding to that noun.

Also, it is very hard if not impossible to recover missing arguments. See for instance the semantics for the adjective "semelhante" ("similar") in sentence (3). The missing argument is given the type r, instead of the type x of quantified variables, so that we can omit a quantifier for it in the semantics and still be able to ask the system for scoped solutions (the system would complain about free variables if these elements were given the type x).

Finally, it is worth noting that there are some limitations of the semantic representations obtained given that the empirical coverage of the grammar is still in development. Currently, the grammar does not make yet any distinction between restrictive and non-restrictive relative clauses, as we have not focused on the fully-fledged implementation of the semantics of non-restrictive relative clauses yet. This can be seen in the semantics for the last example, where both relative clauses are semantically combined with their head in the same way.

4 Performance in the Shared Task

There are seven small texts in the Shared Task. The sample text we submitted is text 4. We translated the other six texts into Portuguese before passing them to the system.

Translation of the Texts

The translations were done by the authors. We tried to make them as literal as possible in order to support comparability of the different systems taking part in the Shared Task, but some bits were not literally translated as that would have produced unnatural sentences. We also tried not to make the texts easy to parse by the system by simplifying the texts in the translations. We present the translation for the texts 1, 2, 3, 5, 6 and 7 in the Appendix A, with English glosses.

Initial Coverage

When we tried to parse the other six texts of the Shared Task, we got 0% coverage. The causes for parse failure were missing words in the lexicon and missing syntactic constructions.

Since the aim of the Shared Task is not to evaluate data coverage but rather to compare the semantic representations output by different NLP systems, we made an effort to expand LXGram by enlarging the lexicon and implementing some syntax rules, with the purpose of producing semantic representations for as many sentences in the Shared Task data as possible, within the time constraints.

During this grammar expansion, we tried not to tune the grammar to these particular sentences. We tried to make the implementation of new phenomena general. For this reason, some phenomena were not implemented deliberately, because we felt that we would not be able to produce general solutions for them within the time limit. This is the case of WH- questions (present in the first text), which are not yet supported by LXGram and whose implementation we did not want to rush.

Grammar Expansion

We added 97 lexical entries to the grammar. For some of these items, we had to create new lexical types, because they have subcategorization frames for which there was still no lexical type in the grammar. One example is the noun "pedido" (*order*), which was implemented as having two arguments realized by prepositional phrases, the first one headed "de" and the second one headed by "a". LXGram already contained lexical types for nouns with two arguments, but introduced by different prepositions. Although these two arguments of the noun were not present in the example where this noun occurs (the third sentence of text 3), we nevertheless created a new lexical type for this subcategorization frame. We could have used an existing lexical type for nouns with no complements and that particular sentence would have parsed fine, but the predicate for that noun would not be a two-place predicate in the MRS representation. We added 10 new lexical types.

The constructions that were implemented in LXGram in order to parse these sentences were:

- the progressive. In European Portuguese, the progressive is expressed via a form of the verb "estar" (*to be*) combined with an infinitive preceded by the preposition "a".

- temporal expressions headed by the verb "haver" (*there to be*). The temporal expression *for some time* (second sentence of text 2) is expressed in Portuguese as "há algum tempo" (literally: *there is some time*). The verb form cannot be analyzed as a preposition, because this sort of expression is syntactically compositional. For instance, the verb inflects for tense (it can appear in the imperfect if the main verb of the clause is in a past tense) and there can be adverbs modifying it to its right ("há já algum tempo", *there is already some time*, i.e.

for some time now). We created a unary syntax rule that takes as daughter a clause headed by this verb and produces a mother node with the syntactic characteristics of a clause introduced by a subordinating conjunction and modifying another clause. This rule adds a relation similar to a relation introduced by a subordinating conjunction, and it's called *abstract-temporal_x_rel*. We take this relation as having the meaning of "since", but with the two arguments reversed, and the Portuguese clause for *that is known for some time* gets analyzed as meaning roughly *there is some time (some time has passed) since that is known*. That is a very literal semantic representation, but it allows us to keep the semantic composition mechanism completely monotonic.

- the impersonal pronoun "se". The most naturally sounding translation of *it was suspected that* (last sentence of text 5) is "suspeitou-se que", with a verb in the active voice and its subject being realized by a clitic pronoun. This clitic has to appear adjacently to the verb, which is atypical for subjects in Portuguese.

- NP appositives. We also implemented a rule to allow NP apposition. This was because of sentences like the second sentence in text 6.

Additionally, a few preprocessor rules were expanded. For instance, sentences like the last sentence of text 7 require integer literals to be considered as proper names. We cannot create lexical entries for all integers, so we added preprocessor rules in order to contemplate the possibility of integers as proper names.

Final Results

After grammar expansion, 20 sentences out of the 30 sentences in all the texts of the Shared Task got an analysis. The sentences that could not be parsed are the following:

- Text 1: sentences (c) and (d).

- Text 5: sentences (a), (c) and (d)

- Text 6: all sentences

- Text 7: sentences (a) and (b)

The two sentences of text 1 that could not be parsed contain WH- questions, which are currently not supported by the system.

The sentence (a) of text 5 could not be parsed because it contains two sentences as the complement of a verb. LXGram cannot yet combine two independent sentences, and we chose to not implement this possibility because the combination of an n-way ambiguous sentence with another m-way ambiguous sentence would be n × m-way ambiguous.

The sentence (c) of the same text was not parsed because of a semantically vacuous clitic (not implemented yet) and a relative clause modifying another clause (also not covered). LXGram does not support sentence relatives and we chose not to implement them yet because, if the relative pronoun is filling a subject position (as in that sentence), the verb has to allow for propositional subjects. In LXGram, we currently only have subcategorization frames for verbs that take NPs as subjects, and we have to review all lexical entries for verbs before we can parse that sentence.

For the remaining sentences without a parse, the reason was efficiency. Several of the sentences in the Shared Task data translate to Portuguese sentences that are very long (over 40 words) or have a very high number of prepositions, producing many attachment possibilities. Note that we were doing exhaustive search. In many cases the parser would run out of memory. In order to alleviate this problem, we used the PET parser instead of the LKB parser for the longer sentences. PET is considerably faster, because it is implemented in C (the LKB is in Lisp), and it precompiles the grammar into a binary format. Also, the input to PET can be preprocessed by a POS tagger, in order to reduce lexical ambiguity. We did this preprocessing for some of the longer sentences.

However, PET dumps MRS representations as text, and choosing the best parse from this sort of output is not practical, especially for sentences with many readings. So we exported the results into a format that can be read by [incr tsdb()], a tool for the management of test suites and corpora. With this tool, it is possible to choose parses by choosing discriminants derived from all analyses. Choosing or rejecting a single discriminant can eliminate a large number of analyses in one step. However, [incr tsdb()] calls the LKB to reconstruct the trees based on the output of PET (which includes the names of the rules used and syntactic constituency), when one wants to choose the best parse. Even though the parse forest has already been built by the PET parser, the LKB can still run out of memory when it is reconstructing the feature structures if the number of analyses is sufficiently large (we had a sentence with over 18000 parses).

We also tried commenting out some rules that were not necessary to parse these sentences, with the purpose of reducing the search space. Examples include robustness rules, for parsing strings with no verb.

In the near future, we will be working on a stochastic disambiguation module, which PET supports, in order to constrain the parser's search space and to keep only the best *n* parses, so that we can avoid the efficiency problems that we are facing at the moment.

Analyses

The semantic representations for the sentences that LXGram parsed successfully are presented in the appendix. As mentioned before, we performed exhaustive search. We chose the best parse manually.

We used [incr tsdb()] associated to the LKB in order to choose the preferred reading. After that we exported the MRS representation. The LKB exports LaTeX directly. We edited the exported LaTeX in order to make the representations fit into the pages of the appendix. This involved manually adding newlines and page breaks. We also corrected characters with diacritics, which did not display correctly, and we removed characterization information: after the name of each predicate, there is a pair of character positions indicating the substring in the input spanned by the lexical items or rules associated to that predicate; they were removed because they are not interpretable by someone who does not know the implementation details, e.g. the semantics for null subjects span the substring of the entire VP since this piece of semantics is introduced by a unary rule that takes a VP as daughter.

Discussion of the Results

We would like to comment on some of the semantic representations obtained with LXGram.

As we have pointed out before, some details of the semantics are not completely independent of language. For an example, see the discussion above about temporal expressions headed by the verb "haver".

MRS does not directly support a treatment of intentionality. For instance, sentence (c) of text 2 contains an intentional context: it does not assert the existence of "other cancers caused by viruses". There is no standard way of representing this sort of intentionality with MRS.

Also, MRS does not support conjunction of quantifiers. There is no MRS equivalent to a lambda expression like $\lambda P.Quant_1(x, P(x)) \wedge Quant_2(y, P(y))$. The usual MRS representations associated with NP coordination have to include an explicit relation for the truth function involved (but taking referential indices as arguments), as well as an extra quantifier relation (the relation used in these cases is called *udef_q_rel*, which is also the name for the quantifier of bare NPs).

Some phenomena are difficult to analyze. An example is in sentence (c) of text 7. In the Portuguese translation, we have two coordinated NPs at the end of the sentence (the best sounding translation requires a determiner before each of the two nouns), which are followed by a PP. The Portuguese translation interprets this PP as realizing an argument of both nouns (cf. *federal government interest and federal government tax incentives*). We could not get this reading, because we do not allow PP arguments to attach higher than determiners. The analysis that we present leaves the first noun with this argument underspecified, as this PP attaches directly to the second noun in the corresponding syntax tree. This possibility of PP attachment seems to be required for cases of NP coordination like this one, but it can be a source of overgeneration for NPs that are not coordinated. This phenomenon affects other NP elements, like adjective phrases, that can also take scope over a coordination of NPs. The current implementation forces all noun dependents that have a restrictive interpretation to attach lower than determiners, as that is the place where the restrictor of the quantifier for that NP is visible in the feature structures.

References

Bos, J. (2008). Introduction to the Shared Task on Comparing Semantic Representations. In J. Bos and R. Delmonte (Eds.), *Semantics in Text Processing. STEP 2008 Conference Proceedings*, Volume 1 of *Research in Computational Semantics*, pp. 257–261. College Publications.

Branco, A. and F. Costa (2008a). A computational grammar for deep linguistic processing of Portuguese: LXGram, version A.4.1. Technical report, University of Lisbon, Department of Informatics.

Branco, A. and F. Costa (2008b). High Precision Analysis of NPs with a Deep Processing Grammar. In J. Bos and R. Delmonte (Eds.), *Semantics in Text Processing. STEP 2008 Conference Proceedings*, Volume 1 of *Research in Computational Semantics*, pp. 31–43. College Publications.

Callmeier, U. (2000). PET — A platform for experimentation with efficient HPSG processing techniques. *Natural Language Engineering* 6(1), 99–108. (Special Issue on Efficient Processing with HPSG).

Copestake, A. (2002). *Implementing Typed Feature Structure Grammars*. Stanford: CSLI Publications.

Copestake, A., D. Flickinger, I. A. Sag, and C. Pollard (2005). Minimal Recursion Semantics: An introduction. *Journal of Research on Language and Computation* 3(2–3), 281–332.

Krieger, H.-U. and U. Schäfer (1994). $\mathcal{TDL}$ — A type description language for constraint-based grammars. In *Proceedings of the 15th International Conference on Computational Linguistics*, Kyoto, Japan, pp. 893–899.

Oepen, S. (2001). [incr tsdb()] — competence and performance laboratory. User manual. Technical report, Computational Linguistics, Saarland University, Saarbrücken, Germany. In preparation.

Pollard, C. and I. Sag (1987). *Information-Based Syntax and Semantics, Vol. 1*. Number 13 in CSLI Lecture Notes. Stanford: CSLI Publications.

Pollard, C. and I. Sag (1994). *Head-Driven Phrase Structure Grammar*. Stanford: Chicago University Press and CSLI Publications.

Sag, I. A., T. Wasow, and E. M. Bender (2003). *Syntactic Theory – A Formal Introduction* (2nd ed.). Stanford: CSLI Publications.

Appendix A: Translations of the Texts for the Shared Task

Text 1

(1) Um objecto é lançado com uma velocidade horizontal de 20 m/s de   um penhasco que tem 125
an object is thrown with a   speed   horizontal of 20 m/s from a   cliff   that has 125
m de altura.
m of height

An object is thrown with a horizontal speed of 20 m/s from a cliff that is 125 m high.

(2) O objecto cai pela   altura do   penhasco.
the object falls for the height of the cliff

The object falls for the height of the cliff.

(3) Se a resistência do   ar é negligenciável, quanto   tempo demora o objecto a cair ao
if the resistance of the air is negligible   how much time   takes   the object to fall to the
chão?
ground

If air resistance is negligible, how long does it take the object to fall to the ground?

(4) Qual é a   duração da   queda?
what is the duration of the fall

What is the duration of the fall?

Text 2

(1) O cancro cervical é causado por um vírus.
the cancer cervical is caused by a   virus

Cervical cancer is caused by a virus.

(2) Isso é conhecido há   algum tempo e   levou a uma vacina que parece preveni-lo.
that is known   there is some time and led to a   vaccine that seems to prevent it

That has been known for some time and it has led to a vaccine that seems to prevent it.

(3) Os investigadores têm procurado outros cancros que possam ser causados por vírus.
the researchers   have looked   other cancers that may   be caused   by viruses

Researchers have been looking for other cancers that may be caused by viruses.

Text 3

(1) O John foi   a um restaurante.
the John went to a   restaurant

John went into a restaurant.

(2) Havia   uma mesa no   canto.
there was a   table in the corner

There was a table in the corner.

(3) O empregado anotou   o pedido.
the waiter   wrote down the order

The waiter took the order.

(4) A atmosfera era acolhedora e   simpática.
the atmosphere was warm   and friendly

The atmosphere was warm and friendly.

(5) Ele começou a ler o seu livro.
he began   to read the his book

He began to read his book.

Text 5

(1) Enquanto os 3 canhões do   torreão 2 eram carregados, um membro da   equipa que estava a
     as   the 3 guns   of the Turret 2 were loaded   a member of the crew   who was to
     operar o   canhÃčo central gritou ao   telefone "Tenho aqui um problema. Ainda não estou
     operate the gun   central yelled to the phone   I have here a   problem. Still   not I am
     preparado".
     ready

     As the 3 guns of Turret 2 were being loaded, a crewman who was operating the center gun yelled
     into the phone, "I have a problem here. I am not ready yet."

(2) Então o   explosivo rebentou.
     then   the propellant exploded

     Then the propellant exploded.

(3) Quando os membros da   equipa do   canhão morreram, estavam   agachados de forma não
     when   the members of the crew   of the gun   died   they were crouching of way not
     natural, o que sugeria   que sabiam   que se   daria   uma explosão.
     natural which suggested that they knew that DUMMY CLITIC would happen an   explosion

     When the gun crew was killed they were crouching unnaturally, which suggested that they knew that
     an explosion would happen.

(4) O   explosivo que foi usado era feito de   pedaços de nitrocelulose que foram produzidos
     the propellant that was used was made from chunks of nitrocellulose that were   produced
     durante a   Segunda Guerra Mundial e   foram reembalados em 1987 em sacos que foram feitos
     during the second   world war   and were repackaged in 1987 in bags that were made
     em 1945.
     in 1945

     The propellant that was used was made from nitrocellulose chunks that were produced during World
     War II and were repackaged in 1987 in bags that were made in 1945.

(5) Inicialmente, suspeitou-se   que este armazenamento poderia ter
     initially   suspected IMPERSONAL SUBJECT that this storage   might have
     reduzido a   estabilidade da   pólvora.
     reduced the stability   of the powder

     Initially it was suspected that this storage might have reduced the powder's stability.

Text 6

(1) Entre as filas cerradas   de casas do   norte de Filadélfia,   uma quinta urbana pioneira
     amid the rows tightly packed of houses of the north of Philadelphia a   farm urban pioneering
     está a produzir comida local fresca para uma comunidade que frequentemente não a tem, e   a
     is to produce food   local fresh for a   community that often   not it has and to
     gerar   dinheiro com isso.
     generate money   with it

     Amid the tightly packed row houses of North Philadelphia, a pioneering urban farm is providing
     fresh local food for a community that often lacks it, and making money in the process.

(2) Greensgrow, um terreno de um acre de canteiros elevados e   estufas   no   local de uma
     Greensgrow a   plot   of one acre of beds   raised   and greenhouses on the site of a
     antiga fábrica de galvanização de aço, está a ter lucro vendendo os próprios vegetais   e
     former factory of galvanization of steel is to have profit selling   the own   vegetables and
     ervas assim como uma gama de produtos de agricultores locais, e   gerindo um viveiro que
     herbs as well as a   range of products from farmers   local and managing a nursery that
     vende plantas e   plântulas.
     sells plants and seedlings

     Greensgrow, a one-acre plot of raised beds and greenhouses on the site of a former steel-galvanizing
     factory, is turning a profit by selling its own vegetables and herbs as well as a range of produce
     from local growers, and by running a nursery selling plants and seedlings.

(3)   A   quinta lucrou cerca de 10000 dólares com uma receita   de 450000 dólares em 2007, e
the farm   earned about   10000 dollars with a   revenue of 450000 dollars in   2007 and
espera ter   um lucro de 5% sobre os   650000 dólares de receitas neste ano, o   seu 10Âž ano,
hopes to have a   profit of 5% on   the 650000 dollars of revenue in this year the its   10th   year
para   poder   abrir   outra   actividade noutro   sítio   de Filadélfia.
in order to be able to open another operation   in another place of   Philadelphia

The farm earned about $10,000 on revenue of $450,000 in 2007, and hopes to make a profit of 5 percent on $650,000 in revenue in this, its 10th year, so it can open another operation elsewhere in Philadelphia.

Text 7

(1)   O   desenvolvimento moderno da   tecnologia   e   aplicações   de energia eólica
the development   modern   of the techonology and applications of energy wind.ADJECTIVE
já   estava numa fase   avançada nos   anos 30, quando por estimativa cerca de 600000
already was   in a   phase advanced by the years 30   when   by estimation about   600000
moinhos forneciam áreas rurais com electricidade e   serviços de bombeamento de água.
mills   supplied   areas rural with electricity   and services of pumping   of water

Modern development of wind-energy technology and applications was well underway by the 1930s, when an estimated 600,000 windmills supplied rural areas with electricity and water-pumping services.

(2)   Quando a   distribuição em larga escala de electricidade chegou às   quintas e   às   terras
when   the distribution in broad scale of electricity   arrived to the farms   and to the small
pequenas, o   uso de energia eólica   nos   Estados Unidos começou a   diminuir, mas
towns   the use of energy wind.ADJECTIVE in the United States   started   to subside   but
voltou   a subir depois da   falta   de petróleo nos   EUA no   começo   dos   anos
it went back to raise after   of the shortage of oil   in the US   in the beginning of the years
70.
70

Once broad-scale electricity distribution spread to farms and country towns, use of wind energy in the United States started to subside, but it picked up again after the U.S. oil shortage in the early 1970s.

(3)   Nos   últimos 30 anos, a   investigação e   o   desenvolvimento têm   oscilado   de acordo
in the last   30 years the research   and the development   have fluctuated in accordance
com o   interesse e   os benefícios fiscais do   governo   federal.
with the interest   and the benefits   fiscal   of the government federal

Over the past 30 years, research and development has fluctuated with federal government interest and tax incentives.

(4)   Em meados dos   anos   80, as   turbinas eólicas   tinham tipicamente uma potência
in   middle of the years 80   the turbines wind.ADJECTIVE had   typically   a   power rating
máxima   de 150 kW.
maximum of 150 kW

In the mid-'80s, wind turbines had a typical maximum power rating of 150 kW.

(5)   Em 2006, as   turbinas comerciais   de grande escala são comummente avaliadas em mais de   1
In   2006 the turbines commercial of large   scale   are commonly   rated   at   more than 1
MW e   estão disponíveis em no   máximo 4 MW de capacidade.
MW and are   available   in   at the most   4 MW of capacity

In 2006, commercial, utility-scale turbines are commonly rated at over 1 MW and are available in up to 4 MW capacity.

Appendix B: MRS Representation for Text 4, Sentence 1

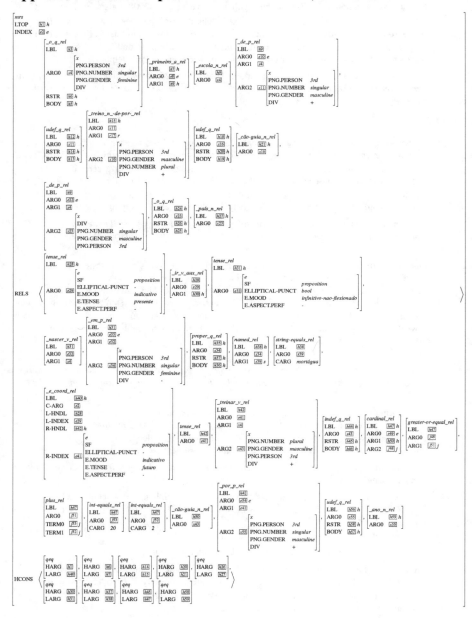

Baseline Evaluation of WSD and Semantic Dependency in OntoSem

Sergei Nirenburg
Stephen Beale
Marjorie McShane
University of Maryland Baltimore County (USA)
email: sergei@umbc.edu

Abstract

This paper presents the evaluation of a subset of the capabilities of the On-toSem semantic analyzer conducted in the framework of the Shared Task for the STEP 2008 workshop. We very briefly describe OntoSem's components and knowledge resources, describe the work preparatory to the evaluation (the creation of gold standard basic text meaning representations) and present OntoSem's performance on word sense disambiguation and determination of semantic dependencies. The paper also contains elements of a methodological discussion.

1 Overview of OntoSem

OntoSem, which is the implementation of the theory of Ontological Semantics (Nirenburg and Raskin, 2004), is a text-processing environment that takes as input unrestricted raw text and carries out preprocessing followed by morphological, syntactic, semantic, and discourse analysis, with the results of analysis represented as a formal text-meaning representation (TMR) that can then be used as the basis for various applications. Text analysis relies on several knowledge resources, briefly described in the subsections below.

1.1 The OntoSem Ontology

The OntoSem ontology is a formal, language-independent, unambiguous model of the world that provides a metalanguage for describing meaning. It is a multiple-inheritance hierarchical collection of frames that contains richly interconnected descriptions of types of OBJECTs, EVENTs and PROPERTies. It is a general purposes ontology, containing about 9,000 concepts, that has a number of especially well developed domains that reflect past and ongoing application-specific knowledge acquisition. Each OBJECT and EVENT is described by several dozen properties, some property values being locally specified and others, inherited from ancestors.

Selectional restrictions in the ontology are multivalued, with fillers being introduced by a facet. The *value* facet is rigid and is used less in the ontology than in its sister knowledge base of real-world assertions, the fact repository (see Section 1.3). The facets *default* (for strongly preferred constraints) and *sem* (for basic semantic constraints) are abductively overridable. The *relaxable-to* facet indicates possible but atypical restrictions, and *not* blocks the given type of filler.

Event-oriented scripts encode typical sequences of EVENTs and the OBJECTs that fill their case-roles. Scripts are used to reason about both language and the world and, in addition to supporting text processing, can support simulation, as in our ongoing Maryland Virtual Patient project (see, e.g. McShane et al., 2007).

The number of concepts in the ontology is far fewer than the number of words or phrases in any language due to the existence of synonyms in language; the possibility of describing lexical items using a combination of ontological and extra-ontological (e.g., temporal) descriptors; the use of a single concept for each scalar attribute that describes all words on that scale (e.g., gorgeous, pretty, ugly); and the decision not to include language-specific concepts in the ontology.

As an example of the description of an ontological concept, consider an excerpt from the description of the concept ESOPHAGUS:

```
ESOPHAGUS
    IS-A              value ANIMAL-ORGAN
    LOCATION         sem    TRUNK-OF-BODY
    DISTAL-TO        sem    PHARYNX
    PROXIMAL-TO      sem    STOMACH
    LENGTH           sem    24
                     default-measure CENTIMETER
    INSTRUMENT-OF    sem    SWALLOW
    THEME-OF         sem    ESOPHAGEAL-CANCER
                            ACHALASIA ...
```

It is the richness of the property-based descriptions that permit the OntoSem ontology to be used for high-end applications like medical simulation and tutoring.

1.2   The OntoSem Lexicon

Even though we refer to the OntoSem lexicon as a semantic lexicon, it contains more than just semantic information: it also supports morphological and syntactic analysis and generation. Semantically, it specifies what concept, concepts, property or properties of concepts defined in the ontology must be instantiated in the TMR to account for the meaning of a given lexical unit of input.

Lexical entries are written in an extended Lexical-Functional Grammar formalism using LISP-compatible format. The lexical entry — in OntoSem, it is actually called a *superentry* — can contain descriptions of several lexical senses; we call the latter *entries*. As an example, consider the 2nd sense of *take*:

```
(take-v2
   (cat v)
   (def "to begin to grasp physically")
   (ex "He took her hand as she got out of the car.")
   (syn-struc
      ((subject ((root $var1) (cat n)))
       (root $var0) (cat v)
       (directobject ((root $var2) (cat n)))))
   (sem-struc
      (HOLD
         (phase begin)
         (AGENT (value ^ $var1))
         (THEME (value ^ $var2)))))
```

The sem-struc says that the meaning of this word sense is the inceptive aspect ("phase begin") of the ontological event HOLD. The AGENT of HOLD is assigned the meaning of $var1 (the caret indicates "the meaning of") in the input text, and the THEME of HOLD is assigned the meaning of $var2. The OntoSem lexicon currently contains approximately 35,000 senses. For further information about the lexicon, see, e.g., McShane et al. (2005b).

A sister resource to the lexicon is the onomasticon, a lexicon of proper names linked to their respective ontological concepts: e.g., *IBM* is semantically described as CORPORATION.

1.3   The Fact Repository

The fact repository contains numbered remembered instances of concepts, with the numbers being used for disambiguation: e.g., HUMAN-FR88 is the 88th human stored in the fact repository — e.g., *President Clinton*. Some aspects of "general world knowledge" are part of the seed fact repository used for all applications: e.g., France is recorded as NATION-FR47, and this information is available to all intelligent agents in our environment. This seed fact repository is then dynamically augmented as a given corpus is being processed. The fact repository also supports text processing, as for reference resolution: e.g., *President Clinton* in any text will be coreferential with HUMAN-FR88.

2   Text Meaning Representations (TMRs)

Section 3 includes an example of a TMR taken from the competition texts as well as a description of it. Here we will give a brief overview of the status of TMRs in OntoSem.

TMRs represent propositions connected by discourse relations (see Nirenburg and Raskin (2004), Chapter 6 for details). Propositions are headed by instances of ontological concepts, parameterized for modality, aspect, proposition time and overall TMR time.Each proposition is related to other instantiated concepts using ontologically defined relations. Coreference links form an additional layer of linking between instantiated concepts in the TMR as well as stored concept instances in the fact repository.

3   The STEP 2008 Shared Task

This section describes the evaluation of OntoSem results for the shared task at the STEP 2008 Workshop. Individual groups were allowed to make their own decisions with respect to a number of important parameters of the task, including, among others:

1. the nature of the metalanguage of semantic description (e.g., whether it relies on uninterpreted clusters of word senses, defined either within a language or cross-linguistically; whether it is based on a language-independent "interlingual" vocabulary; whether the latter is interpreted by assigning properties to vocabulary elements and constraints on the values of these properties, etc.);

2. the breadth of the coverage of phenomena (e.g., whether to include word sense disambiguation, semantic dependency determination, reference resolution, coverage of modality, aspect, time, quantification, etc.);

3. the depth of coverage of phenomena (e.g., the grain size of the description of word senses, the size of the inventory of semantic roles and other descriptive properties);

4. whether the analyzer is tuned to produce a complete result for any input; to produce partial results for all or some inputs; to produce output only for inputs it knows it can process;

5. whether (and how) the analyzer takes into account benign ambiguities, vagueness and underspecification;

6. whether the analyzer creates a semantic and pragmatic context for the input texts, thus modeling human ability to activate relevant knowledge not expressly mentioned in the text;

7. the practical end application(s) that a particular semantic analyzer aims to support.

In working on the shared task, our group has elected to test our system's performance on word sense disambiguation (WSD) and semantic dependency determination. (For an early small-scale evaluation, see Nirenburg et al. (2004).) A prerequisite for our chosen evaluation experiment was filling the lacunae in lexical coverage. Two points are important to make here: a) we acquired what we consider a complete set of senses for each input word absent from our lexicon, not just the sense that was needed for the text — in other words, this was general-purpose acquisition; b) this was a part of routine ongoing work on resource acquisition and improvement in OntoSem. The only difference that these input texts made was with respect to the schedule of what to acquire first. Here are some basic statistics about our lexicon work. The input texts contained 270 lemmata, of which 36 (13%) were not originally in the OntoSem lexicon. 44 senses were added to the lexicon for the 36 words (these words were predominantly very specific, single-sense ones). In 12 cases, a sense was added to an existing lexicon entry (bringing the average number of senses for these 12 lemmata to 10.5). Finally, 5 word senses were added not because of any lacunae in the lexicon but just to make the life of the analyzer more difficult. In the end, the lexicon contained 1,168 senses for the 270 lemmata (an average of 4.33 senses per word).

Note that OntoSem processes more phenomena than WSD and dependency — aspect, time, speaker attitudes (called modalities in OntoSem), reference resolution and semantic ellipsis, discourse relations, unexpected input, metonymy, etc. In broad terms, the overall objective of the OntoSem analyzer, when viewed outside of the needs of this evaluation experiment, is to generate a significant amount of machine-tractable knowledge from the text, knowledge that includes not just a minimum of information gleaned from the text but also preference information obtained from the ontological and fact-repository substrate to be used in disambiguation heuristics and applications relying on the human ability to reconstruct meanings not overtly mentioned in the text for the purposes of reasoning and applications like question answering. For an overview of how TMRs produced by OntoSem can be used in lieu of traditional annotation schemes, see McShane et al. (2005a).

A standard example of using world knowledge activated in the process of text analysis is being able to infer (abductively) that once "virus" has been resolved to be the organism rather than the computer program, then if the word "operation" appears further on in the text, it is more probable that it means surgery rather than a computer operation or a military operation. The meaning extraction process also has a strong filtering ability to reject most of the senses of the words in the input as inappropriate for the particular text. This ability is not error-proof but the filtering capacity is quite strong even in the current state of the OntoSem analyzer; also note that the ratio of selected senses to those filtered away is a good measure of how much the static resources were tuned to a particular text or domain — the greater the number of senses per word, the less tuning occurred.

OntoSem distinguishes two stages of meaning representation producing, respectively, what is called basic and extended TMRs. The former covers the parts of the semantic representation that can be derived from the syntactic and lexical-semantic information and contains triggers (called "meaning procedures") for a variety of microtheories that require additional heuristics (and usually, as in the case of reference resolution, use general world knowledge from the ontology and fact repository as well as a window of text that is wider than a single sentence; for more on meaning procedures see McShane et al. (2004)). In this evaluation we constrained ourselves to the level of basic TMRs.

We will use the following relatively simple example sentence to demonstrate the scope of work of OntoSem.

Researchers have been looking for other cancers that may be caused by viruses.

The basic TMR for this sentence is as follows:

```
SEARCH-103
    AGENT        RESEARCHER-102
    THEME        CANCER-104
    textpointer  look
    word-num     3
    from-sense   look-v2
RESEARCHER-102
    AGENT-OF     SEARCH-103
    multiple     +
    textpointer  researcher
    word-num     0
    from-sense   researcher-n1
CANCER-104
    THEME-OF     SEARCH-103
    CAUSED-BY    VIRUS-DISEASE-108
    multiple     +
    textpointer  cancer
    word-num     6
    from-sense   cancer-n1
MODALITY-105
    TYPE         EPISTEMIC
    SCOPE        CAUSED-BY-109
    VALUE        0.5
    textpointer  may
    word-num     8
    from-sense   may-aux1
CAUSED-BY-109
    DOMAIN       CANCER-104
    RANGE        VIRUS-DISEASE-108
    SCOPE-OF     MODALITY-105
    textpointer  caused by
    word-num     10
    from-sense   cause-v1
VIRUS-DISEASE-108
    EFFECT       CANCER-104
    multiple     +
    textpointer  virus
    word-num     12
    from-sense   virus-n1
```

We will describe select aspects of this TMR that apply to all frames. The head of the TMR is a SEARCH event with the instance number 103. Its AGENT is RESEARCHER-102 and its THEME is CANCER-104. Both of these case-role fillers also have their own frames that show inverse relations as well as other properties: e.g., RESEARCHER-102 has the property "multiple +", which indicates a set with cardinality > 1. A textpointer is the word in the text that gives rise to the given concept; its word number is shown, as is the appropriate lexical sense. The textpointer is included for the benefit of the human users, as an aid in debugging. It does not have any bearing on the meaning representation, as used by an application. Ontological concepts are unambiguous, as can be seen by the mapping of *virus* to the concept VIRUS-DISEASE rather than COMPUTER-VIRUS. Modalities are defined for type, scope and value, with values being on the abstract scale $\{0, 1\}$. They are also defined for their attribution, which defaults to the speaker if no person is indicated explicitly in the text.

In this TMR, it so happens, there are no overt triggers for further processing — even though reference resolution is routinely triggered on all objects and events with the exception of those that are known not to require it (e.g., NPs with an indefinite article or universally known single entities, such as the sun).

The English gloss of the above TMR is as follows. There is one main event in the sentence — the searching event (represented by the word *look*). The agent of this event is a set of researchers and the theme of this event is a set of cancers, understood as diseases. This latter set is further qualified to include only those cancers that are caused by viruses, understood as organisms. The researchers are not sure at the moment of speech whether particular cancers are indeed caused — fully or partially — by viruses. It is known to the researchers and the author of the text that some cancer or cancers may, in fact, be caused by viruses (this is a contribution of the word *other* to the meaning of the sentence; another contribution of that word is posting a meaning procedure for blocking coreference of the cancer or cancers mentioned in this sentence with those mentioned in previous text). The search started before the time of speech and is still ongoing at the time of speech.

4 Creating Gold Standard TMRs

Gold standard TMRs form the basis for evaluating the results of automatic semantic analysis. To serve as useful measures, these TMRs must be created on the basis of the available static knowledge resources (in the case of OntoSem, mainly the lexicon and the ontology) and reflect the maximum of what a system could in principle do with the given resources.

Creating gold standard TMRs is similar to manually annotating texts using the metalanguage of OntoSem. Text annotation is a difficult and time-consuming (and, therefore, expensive) task. The deeper the level of annotation, the less reliable the results are. Even syntactic annotation poses problems and does not yield acceptable kappa scores measuring agreement among annotators (and, of course, agreement among annotators is not a fool-proof measure of the quality of an annotation). The annotation necessary for evaluating OntoSem TMRs is quite deep. Our experience showed that building gold standard TMRs entirely by hand is a very costly task — it requires highly skilled personnel and involves many searches in the knowledge resources for selecting appropriate TMR components.

In view of the above, we decided on semi-automatic production of gold standard TMRs as the most economical way of producing high-quality annotations. The process is, briefly, as follows. OntoSem operation is modularized into stages. Given an input, OntoSem runs the first stage and presents its results to the human validator/editor. The latter corrects any mistakes and submits the resulting structure to the next stage of OntoSem. The process repeats until OntoSem's final stage results are corrected and approved by the human validator, thus yielding a gold standard TMR.

Although "raw" TMRs can be cumbersome to read, the presentation format shown below — which is automatically generated from raw TMRs — reads rather easily as non-natural languages go. This demonstrates how our representation is actually quite NL-like, its role being not unlike the English "possibilistic" sentences of Schubert (2002). As concerns writing TMRs, people practically never do it — the most they do is check and, sometimes, correct the output of the automatic analysis system.

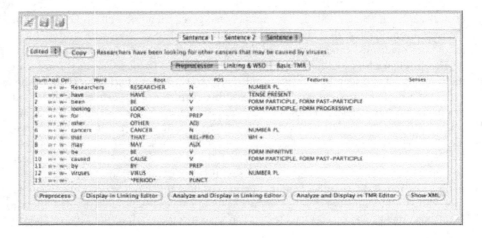

Figure 1: The preprocessor editor of DEKADE

The user interfaces supporting the production of gold standard TMRs are incorporated in DEKADE, OntoSem's Development, Evaluation, Knowledge Acquisition and Demonstration Environment. The editor for preprocessor results is illustrated in Figure 1.

The process of gold standard TMR creation has undergone modifications since the first version of DEKADE was deployed. In particular, experience showed that people find it difficult to edit the results of syntactic analysis, since it produces a densely populated chart of various options. So, instead of the syntax editor, we introduced a linking editor (see Figure 2) that helps to establish the correct linking between syntactic arguments and adjuncts on the one hand and semantic case roles and other ontological properties on the other. We will return to editing syntactic dependency structures once we devise or import an ergonomically appropriate method for this task. Figure 3 illustrates the editor of basic TMRs.

The semi-automatic methodology of creating gold standard TMRs has proved adequate. It takes a well-trained person on average less than a minute to correct preprocessing results for an average sentence of 25 words. Establishing correct linking between syntactic arguments and semantic case roles can take much longer. Together with the task of validating word sense selection (because of the peculiarities of the DEKADE editors), this task takes on average about 30 minutes per 25-word sentence. The time for final editing of the basic gold standard TMRs varies depending on how much material is present that does not relate to the "who did what to whom" component of meaning. However, the overall net time needed to create a gold standard TMR

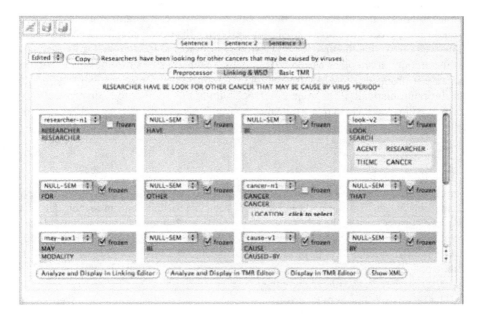

Figure 2: The linking editor of DEKADE

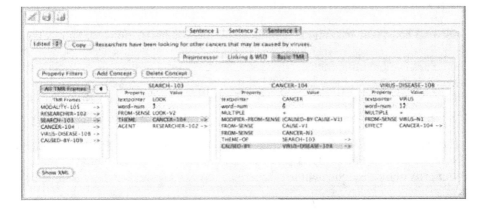

Figure 3: The TMR editor of DEKADE

for a 25-word sentence is on the order of about 40 minutes.

Our methodology of semi-automatic creation of gold standard TMRs differs from the established rules of the game in the annotation-based evaluation business. We selected this approach because it a) significantly cuts the time needed for TMR production (we believe that the task would be simply impractical if attempted fully manually — the amount of annotation required being too extensive); b) simplifies the evaluation because it produces the TMR for the one paraphrase that OntoSem will (attempt to) produce automatically. The main efficiency gain in this semi-automatic production of gold standard TMRs is in using the OntoSem analyzer as a means of quickly retrieving and easily inspecting and selecting the lexical senses for the words in the input.

5   Results

Depending on a particular setting, OntoSem can seek one result for WSD or dependency determination, n-best results or both for each case of ambiguity. We chose to create both types of output. At the level of basic TMR there can in principle be one or more correct results, the latter case may signify a situation of underspecification or vagueness, to be resolved in OntoSem by special microtheories leading to the production of an extended TMR. In producing gold standard TMRs we always selected the single correct word sense, irrespective of whether we had to consult other parts of the input text or general world knowledge.

The results of OntoSem's performance on word sense disambiguation were evaluated against the gold standard TMRs and involved four different scores. In the case of each of the scores, performance on individual instances of word sense disambiguation was averaged over each sentence and text.

Score1 is 1 if the disambiguation was correct and 0 if it was not.

Score2 is 1 if the correct result is in the set of best results returned by OntoSem for a particular disambiguation instance such that the quality score generated for them by OntoSem is within 0.03 of the single best score (on the scale from 0 to 1). This score is 0 if the correct result is not within the above set. This measure was used because the significance of a preference at this fine-grain level is minimal.

Score3 takes into account the complexity of the disambiguation task by involving the number of senses from which the choice is made. Indeed, selecting out of 13 candidates is more difficult than out of, say, just 2. Thus, returning an incorrect result when there are 2 candidates earns a 0 but if there are more than 2 candidates, instead of 0 (as in Score1), we list the score of $1 - (2/n)$, where n is the number of senses. A correct result is given a score of 1. As usual, cumulative scores were computed as simple averages over the input words.

Score4 was calculated using partially corrected results of the preprocessing and syntactic stages of the analysis process. This score did **not** take into account the complexity of the disambiguation task, as did Score3. It was, in fact, Score2 computed over partially corrected preprocessing results. The purpose of using it is to attempt to assign blame across the various components of the rather complex OntoSem system.

Semantic dependency results are scored as 1 when they are correct and 0 when they are incorrect. If an element of TMR is not a part of the semantic dependency structure but should be then we count that as an error. The results of the evaluation are summarized in the table below:

Text	WSD Score1		WSD Score2		WSD Score3		WSD Score4		Dependencies	
1	42/55	.78	43/55	.87	49.707/55	.90	48/55	.87	20/34	.59
2	30/40	.75	31/40	.78	37.030/40	.93	36/40	.90	15/20	.75
3	22/29	.76	23/29	.79	26.348/29	.91	24/29	.83	18/22	.82
4	75/114	.66	77/114	.68	96.966/114	.85	87/114	.76	44/84	.52
5	67/105	.64	67/105	.64	88.440/105	.84	85/105	.81	36/62	.58
6	82/129	.64	84/129	.65	104.807/129	.79	92/129	.71	45/99	.45
7	95/133	.71	95/133	.71	114.260/133	.86	101/133	.76	47/88	.53
Total	413/605	.68	420/605	.69	517.550/605	.86	474/605	.78	225/410	.55

6 Discussion

Our goal was not to get the best results for this particular task but rather to test some of the capabilities of the "raw" OntoSem analyzer. We have always advocated hybridization of methods, a direct consequence of our group's belief in task- rather than method-oriented approaches to system building. We fully expect to take that route when we are putting together the next end application. However, from the scientific point of view, it is important to assess the quality and promise of a particular method, even if it is known beforehand that it will be used in practical applications together with other methods.

Some practical limitations influenced our results. This is why we included the word "baseline" in the title of this paper. We intend to eliminate these limitations over time. The syntactic support for the system has been recently fully revamped to incorporate the Stanford parser. The work on deriving full syntactic dependency structures compatible with the requirements and coverage of the OntoSem syntax-to-semantics linking module from the results provided by the Stanford parser was not completed by the time of the evaluation. This means, among other things, that not all the diathesis transformations needed have been included.

In the current version of DEKADE, the automatic validator of lexicon acquisition does not yet indicate to acquirers when a new lexical sense has the same or very similar syntactic and semantic constraints. As a result, some of the word senses cannot currently be disambiguated using the standard selectional restriction-based method.

In addition to the above general limitations, there were some challenges specific to the particular input corpus. For example, the microtheory of measure has not yet been fully implemented in OntoSem.

We have not yet done enough to determine the contribution of preprocessing, syntax and the various semantic microtheories to the final result. We intend to pay more attention to this blame assignment task.

We restricted ourselves to evaluating just WSD and dependency determination because of time and resource limitations. It is clear that the quality of OntoSem's output for the other microtheories mentioned in Section 3 above, among others, must also be evaluated.

In addition to the above, we also plan to run an evaluation of OntoSem's performance on treating unexpected input, using the version of the lexicon existing before the shared task started.

We will also work on modifying the relative importance of heuristics from different sources. In particular, we will work toward reducing the influence of syntactic clues and thereby moving the center of gravity of the analysis process toward semantics proper.

The process of evaluating TMRs has benefits beyond assessing our progress. It facilitates debugging and enhancing the knowledge resources and processing modules of the system. Finally, we believe that the gold standard TMRs required for evaluation can also be used as an annotated training corpus for machine learning experiments in semantic analysis. We believe that the annotation task is quite feasible. If we estimate the time to create a gold standard basic TMR for a 25-word sentence takes one person-hour, counting the estimated time for acquiring the missing lexicon and ontology information, then it should be possible to create a 100,000-word corpus of gold standard basic TMRs in about two person-years.

References

McShane, M., S. Beale, and S. Nirenburg (2004). Some meaning procedures of ontological semantics. In *Proceedings of LREC-2004*.

McShane, M., S. Nirenburg, and S. Beale (2005a). An NLP lexicon as a largely language independent resource. *Machine Translation 19*(2), 139–173.

McShane, M., S. Nirenburg, and S. Beale (2005b). Text-meaning representations as repositories of structured knowledge. In *Proceedings of the Fourth Workshop on Treebanks and Linguistic Theories (TLT 2005)*.

McShane, M., S. Nirenburg, S. Beale, B. Jarrell, and G. Fantry (2007). Knowledge-based modeling and simulation of diseases with highly differentiated clinical manifestations. In *Proceedings of the 11th Conference on Artificial Intelligence in Medicine (AIME 07)*.

Nirenburg, S., S. Beale, and M. McShane (2004). Evaluating the performance of the OntoSem semantic analyzer. In *Proceedings of the ACL Workshop on Text Meaning Representation*.

Nirenburg, S. and V. Raskin (2004). *Ontological Semantics*. MIT Press.

Schubert, L. (2002). Can we derive general world knowledge from texts? In *Proceedings of the HLT Conference*.

The TEXTCAP Semantic Interpreter

Charles B. Callaway

University of Edinburgh (UK)

email: ccallawa@inf.ed.ac.uk

Abstract

The lack of large amounts of readily available, explicitly represented knowledge has long been recognized as a barrier to applications requiring semantic knowledge such as machine translation and question answering. This problem is analogous to that facing machine translation decades ago, where one proposed solution was to use human translators to post-edit automatically produced, low quality translations rather than expect a computer to independently create high-quality translations. This paper describes an attempt at implementing a semantic parser that takes unrestricted English text, uses publically available computational linguistics tools and lexical resources and as output produces semantic triples which can be used in a variety of tasks such as generating knowledge bases, providing raw material for question answering systems, or creating RDF structures. We describe the TEXTCAP system, detail the semantic triple representation it produces, illustrate step by step how TEXTCAP processes a short text, and use its results on unseen texts to discuss the amount of post-editing that might be realistically required.

1 Introduction

A number of applications depend on explicitly represented knowledge to perform basic tasks or add customization to existing tasks. Improving the quantity and quality of the knowledge contained in knowledge bases could lead to the improved performance of many applications that depend on knowledge and inference such as:

- Generating scientific or educational explanations of natural or mechanical systems and phenomena (Lester and Porter, 1997),

- Question answering systems (Clark et al., 2001) that use reasoning to solve problems rather than looking up answers,

- Multimodal information presentation systems that depend on specific real world knowledge in order to describe or refer to it for audiences (Callaway et al., 2005; Stock et al., 2007).

These systems have typically relied on hand-built and domain specific knowledge bases requiring years of effort to produce. The need to speed up this process as well as make the resulting representations more consistent are well-known problems that have yielded a number of potential solutions (Blythe et al., 2001; Reiter et al., 2003; Carenini et al., 2005; Barker et al., 2007), but large scale, domain independent, and fully automatic knowledge acquisition on unrestricted text is still in its infancy.

Over the last decade research in applied computational linguistics has extended the various components necessary for semantic parsing, but have tended to focus on increasing the measurable performance of individual subtask in isolation (e.g., parsing, anaphora resolution, semantic role labelling, and word sense disambiguation) rather than on an entire end-to-end system. Meanwhile, theoretical CL research has examined issues such as underspecification, scoping and reference resolution in discourse contexts, but has set aside issues such as large-scale robustness, ontology integration and evaluation which are vital for applied uses of semantic parsing.

In this paper we discuss an implementation to automatically extract explicitly coded conceptual and ontological knowledge from unrestricted text using a pipeline of NLP components, as part of the STEP shared task (Bos, 2008). The TEXTCAP system performs the basic steps towards this task by gluing together an off-the-shelf parser with semantic interpretation methods. It is intended to be a test case for (1) establishing baseline performance measures for semantic parsing and (2) determining what degree of post-editing might be necessary in real-world environments.

Because major components of such a system would not be tailored towards the semantic parsing task, we would rightly expect its output to be imperfect. This problem is analogous to that facing machine translation decades ago, where one proposed solution was to use human translators to post-edit automatically produced, low quality translations rather than expect a computer to independently create high-quality translations. One aspect of this research is thus to investigate how much post-editing would be required to convert the system's output to usable semantic triples.

Finally, this paper presents the results of TEXTCAP on the 2008 STEP shared task corpus, giving specific comments about the difficulties in encountered. Although not a formal evaluation, we were satisfied with its performance in terms of accuracy and efficiency for helping humans post-edit semantic triples.

2 System Description

TEXTCAP performs basic steps towards the task of converting free text into semantic triples by gluing together an off-the-shelf parser with ad-hoc semantic interpretation methods. TEXTCAP parses a document into Penn TreeBank form and then traverses each syntactic parse tree performing a series of step-by-step tasks such as discourse parsing, clause separation, word sense disambiguation, anaphora resolution and semantic role labelling. Ad hoc rules then create a set of triples from the resulting semantically-enhanced parse tree.

TEXTCAP first uses the domain-independent Charniak parser (Charniak, 2000) to convert sentences in the source document into a sequence of syntactic parses. It then applies syntax-based discourse parsing rules (such as Soricut and Marcu (2003)) to reduce coordinate, subordinate, and relative clauses into coindexed, simpler sentence parses headed by single verbal relations.

It then marks for grammatical roles (subject, object, etc.) and syntactic features (e.g., passivity) before using a simple anaphora resolution algorithm based on those features and a word sense disambiguation algorithm grounded in WordNet (Fellbaum, 1998) senses that helps determine additional features such as animacy. A two-pass method is applied where first monosemous words are assigned senses, and then remaining senses are selected together with verb types (TEXTCAP uses ad hoc rules rather than current verb taxonomies like FrameNet). Selectional restrictions from the verb type then allows for labelling of peripheral grammatical roles as semantic roles. Finally, entities representing specific objects are marked with ontological relations and discourse relations are realized between individual verbal relations.

The end product of TEXTCAP is thus a list of coindexed semantic triples representing the explicitly recoverable semantic content of the input text.

3 Text Processing Components

Corpus methods underlie many of the recent improvements in a wide array of generic NLP tools. For instance, the introduction of large-scale lexical and syntactic resources like the Penn TreeBank (Marcus et al., 1993) have led to highly accurate, domain independent parsers (Collins, 1999; Charniak, 2000). Wide-coverage anaphora resolution systems process references across multiple sentences, and recent work on anaphora resolution by Poesio and Kabadjov (2004) describes itself as the first such system which can be used off-the-shelf.

Word sense disambiguation (Gliozzo et al., 2005), often based on term frequency analyses of large annotated corpora, can help localize search in a particular area of a knowledge base to find the most related concepts and instances. Semantic role labelers (Gildea and Jurafsky, 2002; Yeh et al., 2006) annotate what role each entity has in relation to its local man verb, and can provide additional clues for disambiguating words and locating them in an ontological space.

In addition to lexical and semantic tasks, multi-sentence linguistic analysis such as discourse segmentation and parsing is needed to semantically label the roles of verb phrases in relation to one other. Soricut and Marcu (2003) presented a statistical system that automatically produces an analysis of the rhetorical structure that holds between sets of sentences or clauses at the paragraph level.

As a generalization, NLP research has been conducted separately and few attempts have been made to connect each of them into the longer chains and pipelines needed for more complete and deeper text processing such as is needed for tasks like knowledge acquisition. Additionally, most of these tools are intended to iteratively examine each sentence individually within a larger document. But often important linguistic phenomena cross sentence boundaries, yet are just as necessary to properly understand the semantic content of a document.

4 Knowledge Representation in TEXTCAP

A common method of representing semantic knowledge in the Knowledge Base community (Brachman and Schmolze, 1985; Clark and Porter, 1998) is through three-place predicates, or triples, of the form (CONCEPT RELATION CONCEPT). A concept can signify either a generic entity or class, like "houses", or a particular instance, such as "my house at 35 Lincoln Avenue"; instances are coindexed to indicate they are the same entity in multiple predicates. Relations are typed according to domain, range and cardinality, and can also be marked as instances to indicate that they refer to specific events or properties that hold at a particular time place, etc.

Databases and knowledge bases can both be represented as large collections of triples. Knowledge bases differ from databases in that they are generally organized around a hierarchical taxonomy, or ontology, of both entities and relations, allowing for subsumption as inference and for knowledge to be separated into subgroups. Knowledge bases differ from ontologies in that, like databases, they also contain a larger set of specific knowledge (instances) that describes non-taxonomic relationships between members and instances of the ontology's concepts.

For instance, the sentence "My dog chases rabbits." talks about a specific instance of the class dog and its relationship to the generic class representing rabbits, perhaps represented as the triple (DOG492 CHASING RABBIT-ANIMAL). To know that this dog really is a member of what we consider as the class of all dogs, we would need to add an ontological triple such as (DOG492 INSTANCE-OF DOG). To represent the possessive grammatical relation in "my dog" we would need to agree on some particular person (an instance) to represent the speaker of the utterance (PERSON142 INSTANCE-OF PERSON) and then also add a relation to indicate possession (DOG492 OWNED-BY PERSON142). Because language is ambiguous compared to semantic triples, we wouldn't want the word "my" to always be mapped to the same relation, for instance, obtaining (PERSON366 OWNED-BY PERSON142) from the phrase "my friend".

Like concepts, relations can also have instances since they can refer to particular events with particular modifiers. For instance, in the sentence "My dog quickly chased rabbits yesterday." we would need to change the relation CHASING from the triple above to (DOG492 CHASING141 RABBIT-ANIMAL) to indicate its modifiers, perhaps with (CHASING141 SPEED QUICKLY) and (CHASING141 EVENT-TIME YESTERDAY). We would also need to indicate the taxonomic relationship between the two relations, (CHASING141 INSTANCE-OF CHASING).

Because over the years different research groups have created differing ontologies, it is important to have a common ontology (and arguably, mapping of lexical items to classes in that ontology) for purposes such as evaluative comparison, even if implementations that acquire semantic triples can use any available ontology.

In keeping with the practice of much recent large-scale NLP, TEXTCAP uses Word-Net (Fellbaum, 1998) as an underlying ontology and sense repository for generic classes, giving it the ability to leverage recent NLP tools that rely on it, such as for word sense disambiguation (Gliozzo et al., 2005). Thus given the sentence in Figure 1(a), we are interested in producing the semantic triples in (b) where generic entities and relations are grounded in WordNet.

5   Processing The Text

To illustrate how TEXTCAP works, we follow how it processes the following paragraph of newspaper text from the New York Times:

> Amid the tightly packed row houses of North Philadelphia, a pioneering urban farm is providing fresh local food for a community that often lacks it, and making money in the process. Greensgrow, a one-acre plot of raised beds and greenhouses on the site of a former steel-galvanizing factory, is turning a profit by selling its own vegetables and herbs as well as a range of produce from local growers, and by running a nursery selling plants and seedlings. The farm earned about $10,000 on revenue of $450,000 in 2007, and hopes to make a profit of 5 percent on $650,000 in revenue in this, its 10th year, so it can open another operation elsewhere in Philadelphia.

The first sentence as parsed by Charniak and converted into Lisp notation is:

```
(S (PP (IN "Amid")
       (NP (NP (DT "the") (ADJP (RB "tightly") (VBN "packed"))
               (NN "row") (NNS "houses"))
           (PP (IN "of") (NP (NNP "North") (NNP "Philadelphia")))))
   (PUNCTUATION COMMA)
   (NP (DT "a") (JJ "pioneering") (JJ "urban") (NN "farm"))
   (VP (AUX "is")
       (VP (VP (VBG "providing")
               (NP (JJ "fresh") (JJ "local") (NN "food"))
               (PP (IN "for")
                   (NP (NP (DT "a") (NN "community"))
                       (SBAR (WHNP (WDT "that"))
                             (S (ADVP (RB "often"))
                                (VP (VBZ "lacks") (NP (PRP "it")))))))))
           (PUNCTUATION COMMA)
           (CC "and")
           (VP (VBG "making")
               (NP (NN "money"))
               (PP (IN "in") (NP (DT "the") (NN "process")))))))
```

(a)   "My dog quickly chased rabbits yesterday."

(b)   (DOG492 INSTANCE-OF DOG#n1)
       (PERSON142 INSTANCE-OF PERSON#n1)
       (CHASING141 INSTANCE-OF CHASING#v1)
       (DOG492 CHASING141 RABBIT#n1)
       (CHASING141 SPEED QUICKLY#adv1)
       (CHASING141 EVENT-TIME YESTERDAY#adv1)

Figure 1: WordNet senses as generic entities and relations

We first normalize this from the form used by the Charniak and Collins parsers (which do no semantic role labelling and introduce some simplifications) into a corrected version following the original Penn TreeBank format. In the above parse, the following lines are normalized to mark grammatical subject and correctly mark the auxiliary verb:

```
       . . .
    (NP-SBJ (DT "a") (JJ "pioneering") (JJ "urban") (NN "farm"))
    (VP (VBZ "is")
       (VP (VP (VBG "providing")
              . . .
```

We then apply a customized discourse parser which converts full syntactic parses into subparses headed by single verb relations. This is done using purely syntactic information to break up coordinate, subordinate and relative clauses while adding coindexed traces at the appropriate parse level and introducing a new tree-level tag DR for discourse relations marked according to Rhetorical Structure Theory (Mann and Thompson, 1987). All three sentences in the paragraph above are thus converted into the following 13 discourse parses:

```
(S (PP (IN "Amid")
       (NP (NP (DT "the") (ADJP (RB "tightly") (VBN "packed"))
          (NN "row") (NNS "houses"))
          (PP (IN "of") (NP (NNP "North") (NNP "Philadelphia")))))
   (PUNCTUATION COMMA)
   (NP-SBJ (DT "a") (JJ "pioneering") (JJ "urban") (NN "farm") (TRACE 1))
   (VP (VBZ "is")
       (VP (VP (VBG "providing")
              (NP (JJ "fresh") (JJ "local") (NN "food"))
              (PP (IN "for")
                 (NP (DT "a") (NN "community") (TRACE 2)))))))

(S (NP-SBJ (DT "a") (NN "community") (TRACE 2))
   (ADVP (RB "often"))
   (VP (VBZ "lacks") (NP (PRP "it"))))

(S (NP-SBJ (DT "a") (JJ "pioneering") (JJ "urban") (NN "farm") (TRACE 1))
   (VP (VBZ "is")
       (VP (VBG "making")
          (NP (NN "money"))
          (PP (IN "in") (NP (DT "the") (NN "process"))))))

(S (NP-SBJ (NNP "Greensgrow") (TRACE 3))
   (VP (VBZ "is")
       (NP (NP (DT "a") (JJ "one-acre") (NN "plot"))
          (PP (IN "of")
             (NP (NP (VBN "raised") (NNS "beds"))
                (CC "and") (NNS "greenhouses"))
                (PP (IN "on")
                   (NP (NP (DT "the") (NN "site"))
                      (PP (IN "of")
                         (NP (DT "a") (JJ "former")
                            (JJ "steel-galvanizing")
                            (NN "factory")))))))))

(S (NP-SBJ (NNP "Greensgrow") (TRACE 3))
   (VP (VBZ "is")
       (VP (VBG "turning")
          (NP (DT "a") (NN "profit"))))
   (TRACE 4))

(S (NP-SBJ (NNP "Greensgrow") (TRACE 3))
   (VP (VBZ "is")
       (VP (VBG "selling")
          (NP (NP (PRP-POSS "its") (JJ "own")
             (NNS "vegetables") (CC "and") (NNS "herbs"))
             (CONJP (RB "as") (RB "well") (IN "as"))
             (NP (NP (DT "a") (NN "range"))
                (PP (IN "of") (NP (NN "produce"))))
             (PP (IN "from") (NP (JJ "local") (NNS "growers")))))
   (TRACE 5))

(S (NP-SBJ (NNP "Greensgrow") (TRACE 3))
   (VP (VBZ "is")
       (VP (VBG "running")
          (NP (NP (DT "a") (NN "nursery")))))
   (TRACE 6))

(S (NP-SBJ (NNP "Greensgrow") (TRACE 3))
```

```
(VP (VBZ "is")
    (VP (VBG "selling")
        (NP (NNS "plants") (CC "and") (NNS "seedlings")))))

(DR (MEANS (TRACE 4) (TRACE 5) (TRACE 6)))

(S (NP-SBJ (DT "The") (NN "farm") (TRACE 7))
   (VP (VBD "earned")
       (NP (QP (RB "about") (CURRENCY DOLLAR-SIGN) (CD 10000)))
       (PP (IN "on")
           (NP (NP (NN "revenue"))
               (PP (IN "of")
                   (NP (CURRENCY DOLLAR-SIGN) (CD 450000)))))
       (PP (IN "in") (NP (CD 2007)))))

(S (NP-SBJ (DT "The") (NN "farm") (TRACE 7))
   (VP (VBZ "hopes") (S (VP (TO "to") (VP (VBP "make")
       (NP (NP (NP (DT "a") (NN "profit"))
           (PP (IN "of")
               (NP (NP (CD 5) (NN "percent"))
                   (PP (IN "on")
                       (NP (NP (CURRENCY DOLLAR-SIGN) (CD 650000))
                           (PP (IN "in")
                               (NP (NP (NN "revenue"))
                                   (PP (IN "in")
                                       (NP (DT "this")))))))))
       (PUNCTUATION COMMA)
       (NP-TMP (PRP-POSS "its") (JJ "10th")
               (NN "year")))))))
   (TRACE 8))

(S (NP-SBJ (PRP "it"))
   (VP (MD "can")
       (VP (VBP "open")
           (NP (DT "another") (NN "operation"))
           (PP (ADVP (RB "elsewhere"))
               (IN "in")
               (NP (NNP "Philadelphia")))))
   (TRACE 9))

(DR (EVENT-ENABLES (TRACE 8) (TRACE 9)))
```

Next, TEXTCAP adds grammatical features at the NP level to allow for eventual anaphora resolution. Given a simplified version of sentence 5 above, "Greensgrow sells vegetables.":

```
(S (NP-SBJ (NNP "Greensgrow"))
   (VP (VBZ "sells")
       (NP (NNS "vegetables"))))
```

One ad-hoc rule matches to the unmodified plural noun and marks it as being a generic class rather than an instance and stems the lexical item. Another rule notes that the subject is a proper noun that is not in its stoplist of person names. As it is not the object of a preposition, it is marked as a company name (via the WordNet sense). Additional senses are assigned if, for instance, only one sense is possible.

```
(S (NP-SBJ (NNP "Greensgrow") (TYPE COMPANY#n1)
           (GENDER NEUTRAL))
   (VP (VBZ "sells")
       (NP (NN "vegetable") (NUMBER PLURAL)
           (GENERIC YES) (GENDER NEUTRAL))))
```

Next, we map grammatical subjects and objects to logical ones, undoing passivization, etc. Then we mark verb type and semantic roles by matching selectional restrictions (currently based on ad-hoc rules) between the verb and its principal arguments. Modifiers of an NP are processed as semantic triples dependent on that NP's instance, and similarly for verbal modifiers.

```
<relation>    = (NP-SBJ (VP (VBZ "sells") NP)
                        (TRACE 5))
              --> (<agent> SELL#v? <patient>)
<agent>       = ((NNP "Greensgrow") (TYPE COMPANY#n1)
              --> COMPANY#n1(name="Greensgrow",
                            gender=neutral)
<patient>     = (NP (NNS "vegetable") ...)
              --> VEGETABLE#n?(generic=yes,
                              gender=neutral,
                              number=plural)
```

Anaphora resolution rules search NPs and their feature lists in reverse to exclude impossible coreferences; TEXTCAP currently uses the first acceptable NP as its coreferent. Next, word sense disambiguation is applied. Because we use WordNet senses as an underlying foundation, we can pass a bag of nearby senses using existing published WSD algorithms, although we are currently testing the degree of performance improvement between simple baselines and custom algorithms. After WSD, we give instance names to each type/sense and drop information on generic entities.

```
<relation>    = (<agent> SELL#v1 <patient>), trace=5
<agent>       = COMPANY#n1(name="Greensgrow",
                          inst=COMPANY549)
<patient>     = VEGETABLE#n1
```

Next, we build a list of coindexed semantic triples directly from the above representation. If no sentence-level traces or modifiers are dependent on the verbal relation, it is treated as a generic instance.

```
(COMPANY549 INSTANCE-OF COMPANY#n1)
(COMPANY549 NAME "Greensgrow")
(COMPANY549 SELL#v1 VEGETABLE#n1)
```

After repeating this process for each standard sentence-level parse, triples representing discourse relations are then included for each dependency, for instance:

```
(DR (EVENT-ENABLES (TRACE 8) (TRACE 9)))

(FARM381 MAKING287 PROFIT#n1)
(FARM381 OPENING286 OPERATION#n2)
(MAKING287 EVENT-ENABLES OPENING286)
```

6   Performance on the Shared Task

Overall, TEXTCAP performed well for its intended purpose, but many limitations were encountered on unseen texts, as expected. Principally, word sense disambiguation and pronoun resolution initially caused significant problems in terms of robustness and the capabilities of these text processing steps were significantly downgraded in order that TEXTCAP could run to completion on all seven sets of unseen texts. Thus WSD was run only for WordNet noun senses and pronoun resolution was not run across sentence boundaries within each set. Additionally, the discourse parser lacked rules to correctly convert sentences #1 and #4 in set #5, so the input sentences were manually split in that case.

However, TEXTCAP was able to do a good job at producing semantic triples for every text, and the number of triples was proportional to the length of each sentence, as expected. The use of existing lexical tools and resources allows for more time to be spent on adding and correcting semantic mappings. Some necessary lexical tools are either not available or still limited in terms of accuracy, and some resources do not exist, for instance, there is no good ontological inventory of prepositions and how they should be mapped semantically. In general, overall accuracy (as measured by human inspection) was much better on shorter sentences.

The system performed poorly in some areas such as interpreting questions and quotations involving multiple sentences. Additionally, the structure of many of the triples that TEXTCAP produced were highly reflective on the original syntactic parses — it is not clear, for instance, that they would enable a question answering system to locate correct answers reliably. However, overall, we believe that post-editing of triples with TEXTCAP would provide a significant time speedup compared to manual knowledge engineering alone, and we are looking at methods of showing this empirically.

The following data represent the performance of TEXTCAP on the 2008 STEP shared task. Sentences were processed in an average time of 4 seconds each.

```
Set #1
```

[1] "An object is thrown with a horizontal speed of 20 m/s from a cliff that is 125 m high."
Notes: (a) the parser interpreted "m/s" as a plural noun; (b) `source` is a very vague relation; (c) `cliff` was correctly recognized as a relative clause subject.

```
((OBJECT001 INSTANCE-OF OBJECT#1)
 (SPEED001 INSTANCE-OF SPEED#1)
 (M/001 INSTANCE-OF M/#0)
 (CLIFF001 INSTANCE-OF CLIFF#1)
 (NUMBER10 INSTANCE-OF NUMBER)
 (UNKNOWN-AGENT THROWING OBJECT001)
 (MANNER-WITH THROWING SPEED001)
 (SPEED001 RANGE-OF M/001)
 (M/001 SOURCE CLIFF001)
 (M/001 NUMERIC-QUANTITY 20)
 (SPEED001 CHARACTERISTICS HORIZONTAL)
 (TIME-PERIOD THROWING PRESENT)
 (NUMBER10 HAS-VALUE 125)
 (CLIFF001 BEING NUMBER10))
```

[2] "The object falls for the height of the cliff."
Notes: (a) `for` was incorrectly intepreted as purpose ("object" would be animate); (b) `of` yielded the wrong relation; (c) it's unclear what should be the 3rd element of the triple for `falling`.

```
((OBJECT001 INSTANCE-OF OBJECT#1)
 (HEIGHT001 INSTANCE-OF HEIGHT#1)
 (CLIFF001 INSTANCE-OF CLIFF#1)
 (OBJECT001 FALLING INTRANSITIVE-ARGUMENT)
 (FALLING PURPOSE-FOR HEIGHT001)
 (HEIGHT001 RANGE-OF CLIFF001))
```

[3] "If air resistance is negligible, how long does it take the object to fall to the ground?"
Notes: This sentence was not processed satisfactorily due to no rules to detect questions of the form "how [adjp]".

[4] "What is the duration of the fall?"
Notes: This sentence was processed satisfactorily.

```
Set #2
```
[1] "Cervical cancer is caused by a virus."
Notes: (a) probably better to map `cervical` to `cervix` to allow for semantic processing in, e.g., a question answering system.

```
((VIRUS001 INSTANCE-OF VIRUS#1)
 (CANCER001 INSTANCE-OF CANCER#1)
 (VIRUS001 CAUSING CANCER001)
 (CANCER001 CHARACTERISTICS CERVICAL))
```

[2 "That has been known for some time and it has led to a vaccine that seems to prevent it."
Notes: (a) the system has more trouble mapping situational referents, but it did correctly notice one was present; (b) need more mappings for `for` besides purpose; (c) need to map from grammatical tense to relational tense.

```
((SITUATION001 INSTANCE-OF UNKNOWN-REFERENT)
 (TIME001 INSTANCE-OF TIME#1)
 (VACCINE001 INSTANCE-OF VACCINE#1)
 (SITUATION001 KNOWING INTRANSITIVE-ARGUMENT)
 (KNOWING PURPOSE-FOR TIME001)
 (TIME001 QUANTIFIER-VALUE SOME)
 (TIME-PERIOD KNOWING PAST-HABITUAL-ACTION)
 (SINGLE-NEUTER-REFERENT LEADING INTRANSITIVE-ARGUMENT)
 (DESTINATION LEADING VACCINE001)
 (TIME-PERIOD LEADING PRESENT-PERFECT)
 (VACCINE001 PREVENTING001 SINGLE-NEUTER-REFERENT)
 (VACCINE001 SEEMING PREVENTING001))
```

[3] "Researchers have been looking for other cancers that may be caused by viruses."
Notes: (a) didn't map `looking` and `for` as a single verbal relation; (b) the treatment of quantifiers is too simplistic (`other`).

```
((RESEARCHER001 INSTANCE-OF RESEARCHER#1)
 (CANCER001 INSTANCE-OF CANCER#1)
 (VIRUS001 INSTANCE-OF VIRUS#1)
 (RESEARCHER001 LOOKING INTRANSITIVE-ARGUMENT)
 (RESEARCHER001 NUMBER-OF-UNITS MORE-THAN-ONE)
 (LOOKING PURPOSE-FOR CANCER001)
 (CANCER001 CHARACTERISTICS OTHER-ADJ)
 (CANCER001 NUMBER-OF-UNITS MORE-THAN-ONE)
 (TIME-PERIOD LOOKING PAST-HABITUAL-ACTION)
 (VIRUS001 CAUSING CANCER001)
 (VIRUS001 NUMBER-OF-UNITS MORE-THAN-ONE)
 (MODALITY CAUSING MODAL-MAY))
```

Set #3

We skip this set of sentences as TEXTCAP seemed to perform very well on set #3 excepting the pronouns in sentence #5.

Set #4

[1] "The first school for the training of leader dogs in the country is going to be created in Mortagua and will train 22 leader dogs per year."
Notes: (a) Mortagua wasn't treated as a city name; (b) incorrect treatment of complex passive verb phrases ("going" is not a main verb); the same semantic object school is correctly noted as being involved in both phrases.

```
((SCHOOL001 INSTANCE-OF SCHOOL#1)
 (MORTAGUA001 INSTANCE-OF PERSON#1)
 (MORTAGUA001 ACTOR-NAME "Mortagua")
 (MORTAGUA001 ACTOR-GENDER NEUTER)
 (DOG001 INSTANCE-OF DOG#1)
 (YEAR001 INSTANCE-OF YEAR#1)
 (SCHOOL001 GOING INTRANSITIVE-ARGUMENT)
 (SCHOOL001 CHARACTERISTICS FIRST)
 (GOING LOCATION-IN MORTAGUA001)
 (TIME-PERIOD GOING PRESENT-PROGRESSIVE)
 (SCHOOL001 TRAINING DOG001)
 (DOG001 PER YEAR001)
 (DOG001 NAMED-TYPE LEADER#1)
 (DOG001 NUMBER-OF-UNITS MORE-THAN-ONE)
 (TIME-PERIOD TRAINING FUTURE))
```

[2] "In Mortagua, Joao Pedro Fonseca and Marta Gomes coordinate the project that seven people develop in this school."
Notes: This sentence was processed satisfactorily.

[3] "They visited several similar places in England and in France, and two future trainers are already doing internship in one of the French Schools."
Notes: (a) not a good quantifier representation for several; (b) any proper NP is being interpreted as a person.

```
((PLACE001 INSTANCE-OF PLACE#1)
 (TRAINER001 INSTANCE-OF TRAINER#1)
 (INTERNSHIP001 INSTANCE-OF INTERNSHIP#1)
 (NUMBER11 INSTANCE-OF NUMBER)
 (FRENCH-SCHOOLS001 INSTANCE-OF PERSON#1)
 (FRENCH-SCHOOLS001 ACTOR-NAME "French Schools")
 (FRENCH-SCHOOLS001 ACTOR-GENDER NEUTER)
 (PLURAL-THIRD-PERSON-REFERENT VISITING PLACE001)
 (PLACE001 CHARACTERISTICS SEVERAL)
 (PLACE001 CHARACTERISTICS SIMILAR)
 (PLACE001 NUMBER-OF-UNITS MORE-THAN-ONE)
 (TIME-PERIOD VISITING PAST)
 (TRAINER001 DOING INTERNSHIP001)
 (TRAINER001 WRITTEN-NUMERIC-QUANTITY 2)
 (TRAINER001 CHARACTERISTICS FUTURE)
```

```
(TRAINER001 NUMBER-OF-UNITS MORE-THAN-ONE)
(DURATION DOING ALREADY)
(DOING LOCATION-IN NUMBER11)
(NUMBER11 RANGE-OF FRENCH-SCHOOLS001)
(TIME-PERIOD DOING PRESENT-PROGRESSIVE))
```

[4] "The communitarian funding ensures the operation of the school until 1999."
Notes: This sentence was relatively uninteresting.

[5] "We would like our school to work similarly to the French ones, which live from donations, from the merchandising and even from the raffles that children sell in school."
Notes: This sentence was not processed satisfactorily due to missing discourse parsing rules.

Set #5
[1] "As the 3 guns of Turret 2 were being loaded, a crewman who was operating the center gun yelled into the phone, 'I have a problem here. I am not ready yet.' "
Notes: (a) this sentence was manually split before the quotation; (b) another proper NP interpreted as a person; (c) the system in general works well with quotations, but not when they are composed of multiple sentences.

```
((GUN001 INSTANCE-OF GUN#1)
 (TURRET-2001 INSTANCE-OF PERSON#1)
 (TURRET-2001 ACTOR-NAME "Turret 2")
 (TURRET-2001 ACTOR-GENDER NEUTER)
 (CREWMAN001 INSTANCE-OF CREWMAN#1)
 (CENTER-GUN001 INSTANCE-OF CENTER-GUN#0)
 (PROBLEM001 INSTANCE-OF PROBLEM#1)
 (UNKNOWN-AGENT LOADING GUN001)
 (GUN001 RANGE-OF TURRET-2001)
 (GUN001 NUMERIC-QUANTITY 3)
 (TIME-PERIOD LOADING PAST-PROGRESSIVE)
 (CREWMAN001 OPERATING CENTER-GUN001)
 (TIME-PERIOD OPERATING PAST-PROGRESSIVE)
 (PROBLEM001 BEING READY)
 (DURATION BEING YET)
 (POLARITY BEING NEGATIVE))
```

[2] "Then the propellant exploded."
Notes: This sentence was processed satisfactorily.

[3] "When the gun crew was killed they were crouching unnaturally, which suggested that they knew that an explosion would happen."
Notes: This sentence presented more syntactic than semantic issues.

[4] "The propellant that was used was made from nitrocellulose chunks that were produced during World War II and were repackaged in 1987 in bags that were made in 1945."
Notes:

[5] "Initially it was suspected that this storage might have reduced the powder's stability."

Notes: (a) the possessive noun `powder` was incorrectly marked as a person; (b) the `time` and `modality` markers are a bit vague.

```
((STORAGE001 INSTANCE-OF STORAGE#1)
 (STABILITY001 INSTANCE-OF STABILITY#1)
 (POWDER001 INSTANCE-OF PERSON#1)
 (POWDER001 ACTOR-NAME "powder")
 (POWDER001 ACTOR-GENDER NEUTER)
 (UNKNOWN-AGENT SUSPECTING REDUCING)
 (STORAGE001 REDUCING STABILITY001)
 (TIME SUSPECTING INITIALLY)
 (TIME-PERIOD REDUCING PRESENT-PERFECT)
 (MODALITY REDUCING MODAL-MIGHT)
 (TIME-PERIOD SUSPECTING PAST))
```

`Set #6`

Data in this set was used to test TEXTCAP and so is not analyzed here.

`Set #7`

[1] "Modern development of wind-energy technology and applications was well underway by the 1930s, when an estimated 600,000 windmills supplied rural areas with electricity and water-pumping services."

Notes: (a) couldn't convert `1930s` to a date range; (b) `underway` was treated as a verb by the parser; (c) more problems mapping prepositional relations.

```
((DEVELOPMENT001 INSTANCE-OF DEVELOPMENT#1)
 (TECHNOLOGY001 INSTANCE-OF TECHNOLOGY#1)
 (APPLICATION001 INSTANCE-OF APPLICATION#1)
 (NUMBER24 INSTANCE-OF NUMBER)
 (NUMBER24 HAS-VALUE "1930")
 (WINDMILL001 INSTANCE-OF WINDMILL#1)
 (AREA001 INSTANCE-OF AREA#1)
 (ELECTRICITY001 INSTANCE-OF ELECTRICITY#1)
 (SERVICE001 INSTANCE-OF SERVICE#1)
 (UNKNOWN-AGENT UNDERWAY DEVELOPMENT001)
 (DEVELOPMENT001 RANGE-OF TECHNOLOGY001)
 (DEVELOPMENT001 RANGE-OF APPLICATION001)
 (TECHNOLOGY001 CHARACTERISTICS WIND-ENERGY)
 (APPLICATION001 NUMBER-OF-UNITS MORE-THAN-ONE)
 (DEVELOPMENT001 CHARACTERISTICS MODERN)
 (DURATION UNDERWAY WELL)
 (TIME-BY UNDERWAY NUMBER24)
 (NUMBER24 NUMBER-OF-UNITS MORE-THAN-ONE)
 (TIME-PERIOD UNDERWAY PAST)
 (WINDMILL001 SUPPLYING AREA001)
 (WINDMILL001 NUMERIC-QUANTITY 600000)
 (AREA001 HAVE-WITH ELECTRICITY001)
 (AREA001 HAVE-WITH SERVICE001)
 (SERVICE001 NAMED-TYPE WATER-PUMPING#0)
 (SERVICE001 NUMBER-OF-UNITS MORE-THAN-ONE)
 (AREA001 CHARACTERISTICS RURAL)
 (AREA001 NUMBER-OF-UNITS MORE-THAN-ONE)
 (TIME-PERIOD SUPPLYING PAST))
```

[2] "Once broad-scale electricity distribution spread to farms and country towns, use of wind energy in the United States started to subside, but it picked up again after the U.S. oil shortage in the early 1970s."

Notes: Notes: This sentence was processed satisfactorily, but only when manually split due to missing discourse parsing rules.

[3] "Over the past 30 years, research and development has fluctuated with federal government interest and tax incentives."

Notes: This sentence was processed satisfactorily.

[4] "In the mid-'80s, wind turbines had a typical maximum power rating of 150 kW."

Notes: This sentence had problems understanding the phrase "mid-'80s", perhaps as a result of the off-the-shelf parser being very generic.

[5] "In 2006, commercial, utility-scale turbines are commonly rated at over 1 MW and are available in up to 4 MW capacity."

Notes: (a) the fact that someone rates turbines isn't the same as turbines carrying a rating; `commonly` wasn't interpreted correctly; (c) the last phrase after `available` wasn't mapped to anything.

```
((TURBINE001 INSTANCE-OF TURBINE#1)
 (DATE26 INSTANCE-OF DATE)
 (DATE26 HAS-YEAR 2006)
 (UNKNOWN-AGENT RATING TURBINE001)
 (TURBINE001 CHARACTERISTICS COMMERCIAL)
 (TURBINE001 CHARACTERISTICS UTILITY-SCALE)
 (TURBINE001 NUMBER-OF-UNITS MORE-THAN-ONE)
 (FREQUENCY RATING COMMONLY)
 (TIME-IN RATING DATE26)
 (TURBINE001 BEING AVAILABLE)
 (TURBINE001 NUMBER-OF-UNITS MORE-THAN-ONE))
```

7   Conclusions

We introduced TEXTCAP, a semantic parser which uses a combination of off-the-shelf NLP technology and ad-hoc rules to produce semantic triples corresponding to the explicit semantic content in unrestricted text. We ran TEXTCAP on 7 sets of short text in the STEP 2008 Shared Task, and the system successfully generated triples for almost all inputs and provided, as we expected, a set of triples that while not fully correct, could be post-edited for accuracy and which should provide a significant speed up over completely manual production of semantic triples from text. On average, TEXTCAP processed a sentence from the corpus in about 4 seconds.

While TEXTCAP only captures explicit knowledge (but not commonsense knowledge, unmentioned knowledge, implicit relationships, etc.) it can save knowledge engineers time by providing reasonably accurate semantic representations of domain text. In future work we plan on improving methods of knowledge integration (e.g., ontology population), testing within real-world applications such as question answering systems, and empirically evaluating the time and accuracy for producing semantic triples via various methods.

References

Barker, K., B. Agashe, S. Chaw, J. Fan, N. Friedland, M. Glass, J. Hobbs, E. Hovy, D. Israel, D. S. Kim, R. Mulkar-Mehta, S. Patwardhan, B. Porter, D. Tecuci, and P. Yeh (2007, July). Learning by reading: A prototype system, performance baseline and lessons learned. In *Proceedings of the 22nd National Conference on Artificial Intelligence (AAAI)*, Vancouver, Canada.

Blythe, J., J. Kim, S. Ramachandran, and Y. Gil (2001). An integrated environment for knowledge acquisition. In *Proceedings of the 2001 International Conference on Intelligent User Interfaces*, Santa Fe, NM, USA.

Bos, J. (2008). Introduction to the Shared Task on Comparing Semantic Representations. In J. Bos and R. Delmonte (Eds.), *Semantics in Text Processing. STEP 2008 Conference Proceedings*, Volume 1 of *Research in Computational Semantics*, pp. 257–261. College Publications.

Brachman, R. J. and J. G. Schmolze (1985, April). An overview of the KL-ONE knowledge representation system. *Cognitive Science 9*(2), 171–216.

Callaway, C., E. Not, A. Novello, C. Rocchi, O. Stock, and M. Zancanaro (2005, June). Automatic cinematography and multilingual NLG for generating video documentaries. *Artificial Intelligence 165*(1), 57–89.

Carenini, G., R. T. Ng, and E. Zwart (2005). Extracting knowledge from evaluative text. In *K-CAP '05: Proceedings of the 3rd International Conference on Knowledge Capture*, Banff, Canada, pp. 11–18.

Charniak, E. (2000, April). A maximum-entropy-inspired parser. In *Proceedings of the 2000 NAACL*, Seattle, WA.

Clark, P. and B. Porter (1998). KM – the knowledge machine: Users manual. Technical report, AI Lab, University of Texas at Austin.

Clark, P., J. Thompson, K. Barker, B. Porter, V. Chaudhri, A. Rodriguez, J. Thomr, Y. Gil, and P. Hayes (2001, October). Knowledge entry as the graphical assembly of components: The SHAKEN system. In *Proceedings of the First International Conference on Knowledge Capture (KCAP)*, Victoria BC, Canada.

Collins, M. (1999). *Head-driven Statistical Models for Natural Language Parsing*. Ph. D. thesis, University of Pennsylvania.

Fellbaum, C. (1998). *WordNet: An electronic lexical database*. The MIT Press.

Gildea, D. and D. Jurafsky (2002). Automatic labeling of semantic roles. *Computational Linguistics 28*(3), 245–288.

Gliozzo, A., C. Giuliano, and C. Strapparava (2005, June). Domain kernels for word sense disambiguation. In *Proceedings of the 43th Annual Meeting of the Association for Computational Linguistics*, Ann Arbor, MI, pp. 403–410.

Lester, J. C. and B. W. Porter (1997). Developing and empirically evaluating robust explanation generators: The KNIGHT experiments. *Computational Linguistics 23*(1), 65–101.

Mann, W. C. and S. A. Thompson (1987, June). Rhetorical structure theory: A theory of text organization. Technical Report ISI/RS-87-190, USC/Information Sciences Institute, Marina del Rey, CA.

Marcus, M., B. Santorini, and M. Marcinkiewicz (1993). Building a large annotated corpus of English: The PennTreeBank. *Computational Linguistics 19*(2), 313–330.

Poesio, M. and M. A. Kabadjov (2004, May). A general-purpose, off-the-shelf system for anaphora resolution. In *Proceedings of the Language Resources and Evaluation Conference*, Lisbon, Portugal.

Reiter, E., S. Sripada, and R. Robertson (2003). Acquiring correct knowledge for natural language generation. *Journal of Artificial Intelligence Research 18*, 491–516.

Soricut, R. and D. Marcu (2003, May). Sentence level discourse parsing using syntactic and lexical information. In *Proceedings of HLT-NAACL*, Edmonton, Alberta.

Stock, O., M. Zancanaro, P. Busetta, C. Callaway, A. Krueger, M. Kruppa, T. Kuflik, E. Not, and C. Rocchi (2007). Adaptive, intelligent presentation of information for the museum visitor in peach. *User Modeling and User Adapted Interaction 17*, 257–304.

Yeh, P., B. Porter, and K. Barker (2006, July). A unified knowledge based approach for sense disambiguation and semantic role labeling. In *Proceedings of the Twenty-First National Conference on Artificial Intelligence*, Boston, MA.

Deep Semantic Analysis of Text

James F. Allen[1,2]
Mary Swift[1]
Will de Beaumont[2]

[1]**University of Rochester (USA)**
[2]**Institute for Human and Machine Cognition, Pensacola (USA)**

email: james@cs.rochester.edu

Abstract

We describe a graphical logical form as a semantic representation for text understanding. This representation was designed to bridge the gap between highly expressive "deep" representations of logical forms and more shallow semantic encodings such as word senses and semantic relations. It preserves rich semantic content while allowing for compact ambiguity encoding and viable partial representations. We describe our system for semantic text processing, which has the TRIPS parser at the core, augmented with statistical preprocessing techniques and online lexical lookup. We also present an evaluation metric for the representation and use it to evaluate the performance of the TRIPS parser on the common task paragraphs.

1 Introduction

As building rich semantic representations of text becomes more feasible, it is important to develop standard representations of logical form that can be used to share data and compare approaches. In this paper, we describe some general characteristics that such a logical form language should have, then present a graphical representation derived from the LF used in the TRIPS system (Allen et al., 2007).

The Logical Form is a representation that serves as the interface between structural analysis of text (i.e., parsing) and the subsequent use of the information to produce knowledge, whether it be for learning by reading, question answering, or dialogue-based interactive systems.

It's important to distinguish two separable problems, namely the ontology used and the structure of the logical form language (LFL). The ontology determines the set of word senses and semantic relations that can be used. The LFL determines how these elements can be structured to capture the meaning of sentences. We are addressing the latter in the paper. Consider some principles for designing useful LFs.

Preserve Rich Semantic Content in Phrasing

The LFL should allow one to express the dependencies and subtleties that are expressed in the sentence. On the simple end, this means the LFL should allow us to represent the differences between the NP *The pigeon house*, which is a type of house, and *the house pigeon*, which is a type of pigeon. On the more complicated end, the LFL should be able to capture complex quantifier structures such as those in the NPs *Nearly all peaches*, or *Every dog but one*, and phenomena such as modal operators, predicate modifiers, and explicit sets.

One might argue that capturing such complex phenomena in the LFL is premature at this time, as existing techniques are unlikely to be able to produce them reliably. On the other hand, if we don't allow such subtleties in the gold-standard LFL, we will tend to stifle long-term work on the difficult problems since it is not reflected in the score in evaluations.

Encoding ambiguity compactly when possible

This issue has a long history in the literature, with the most classic case being quantifier scoping. Underspecified representations of quantifier scoping are a prime focus in the development of modern logical form languages such as MRS (Copestake et al., 2006), and work goes all the way back to early natural language systems (e.g. Woods, 1978). Other techniques for compactly encoding ambiguity include prepositional phrase attachment, and most critically, the use of vague predicates and relations. For example, for many cases of noun-noun modification, the exact semantic relation between the nouns cannot be determined, and actually need not be determined precisely to be understood.

Enable Viable Partial Interpretations

In many cases, because of limitations in current processing, or because of the fragmentary nature of the language input itself, a system will only be able to construct partial interpretations. The LFL should be constructed in a way such that partial representations are easily compared with full representations. In particular, the interpretation of a fragment should be a subset of the full logical form of the entire sentence. It is a fortunate circumstance that representations that tend to compactly encode ambiguity tend also to have this subset property.

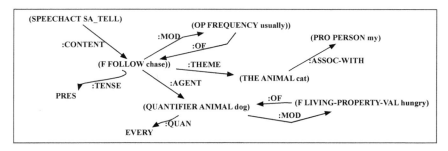

Figure 1: An LF Graph for "Every hungry dog usually chases my cat"

2 Overview of LF Graphs

An example LF-graph is shown in Figure 1. This graph introduces much of the formalism. Each node represents either a speechact, a proposition, a generalized quantifier, an operator or a kind. Nodes are labelled in three parts, the *specifier,* indicating the semantic function of node, the *type,* indicating conceptual class drawn from the ontology, and the *word* from the input. The latter allows us to relate the nodes in the LF graph back to the input. The edges are labelled with semantic roles that indicate argument structure and other critical properties such as modification relationships.

Consider each of the core node types. The first term type captures the meanings of fragments that define eventualities (i.e., events and properties). For instance, the node (F FOLLOW chase) in Figure 1 refers to an eventuality of the type FOLLOW (which would be defined in the ontology). Additional information about the eventuality is captured by the outgoing edges, which identify two arguments, the *:Agent* and the *:Theme,* and one other that provides the tense information for later contextual interpretation (PRES is the present tense).

The second node type captures generalized quantifier constructions. The node (THE ANIMAL cat) indicates a definite description referring to an object of type ANIMAL in the ontology. Generalized quantifiers that have universal import are indicated as shown in the node (QUANTIFIER ANIMAL dog), where an edge labelled :QUAN gives the specific quantifier involved. Note also the presence of a modification to the type (the :MOD) arc, which points to another eventuality, namely (F LIVING-PROPERTY-VAL hungry), which in turn has an argument (:OF) pointing back to the modified node. The :MOD link is critical for capturing dependencies that allow us to reconstruct the full logical form from the graph. For instance, it allows us to retain the distinction between head noun and the modifiers (e.g., *the pigeon house* vs *the house pigeon*).

Table 1 shows the core set of generalized quantifiers used in TRIPS (and subsequently interpreted in discourse processing, especially reference resolution. A large set of quantifiers that indicate the size (e.g., *many, some, five, at most three, a few, ...*)

are treated as an indefinite construction with a (often vague) size modifier.

Table 1: Core Generalized Quantifiers

Type	Description
THE	a definite form (we expect to be able to resolve it from context)
A	an indefinite form (we expect it to introduce new objects)
PRO	a pronoun form (we expect it to be resolved from local context)
IMPRO	an implicit anaphoric form
BARE	forms with no specifier and ambiguous between generic, kind, and indefinite
QUANTIFIER	"universally" quantified constructions (e.g., EVERY)
QUANTITY-TERM	a quantity expressed in units (e.g., three pounds)
WH-TERM	"wh" terms as in questions (e.g., which trucks)
KIND	the definition of a kind (aka lambda abstraction)

The next term type specifies modal operators, and seen in Figure 1 as the node (OP FREQUENCY usually). The operator nodes must be distinguished from the terms for predications (F) to support algorithms for quantifier and operator scoping.

The final class of node in Figure 1 is the speech act performed by an utterance: (SPEECHACT TELL). This has no third argument as it does not arise from any single word in the utterance. The semantic role :content indicates the propositional content of the speech act, and additional roles indicating the speaker and hearer are suppressed. Speech acts have modifiers in order to handle phenomena such as discourse adverbials.

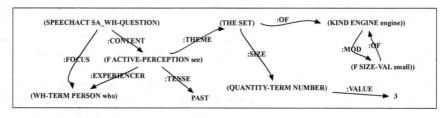

Figure 2: The LF graph for "Who saw the three small engines"

Figure 2 shows another LF graph which captures some additional key constructions. It shows another speech act, for Wh-questions, and shows the handling of plurals. LF graphs distinguish explicitly between singular and plurals by modeling sets, in which an :of argument that points to the type of objects in the set.

The KIND operator is used to define these types (aka lambda abstraction). Thus *the three small engines* is a SET of size three with elements of KIND ENGINE and which are small.

LF-graphs are interesting as they offer the possibility of comparing the semantic content of different approaches, ranging from shallow approaches that identify word senses and semantic roles, to complex representations produced by state-of-the-art deep parsers. On the shallow side, a word sense disambiguation system would produce a set of nodes with the word senses labeled from an ontology, but not indicating a specifier, and not capturing any semantic roles. A system that identifies semantic roles can capture its results using the edges of the graph.

On the other hand, we can show that the LF-graph formalism is equivalent to the TRIPS logical form language (LFL), which is a "flat" scope-underspecified representation of a reference modal logic with generalized quantifiers and lambda abstraction.

We have developed an efficient quantifier scoping algorithm on this LFL that constructs possible fully-scoped forms in the reference logic, and we can prove that we derive the same sets of possible interpretations as the representations constructed by MRS (Manshadi et al., 2008). Figure 3 shows the TRIPS logical form that produced Figure 1, and Figure 4 shows one of the interpretations produced by the scoping algorithm.

```
(SPEECHACT a1 TELL :content f1)
(F f1 (:* FOLLOW Chase)   :agent x :theme y)
(EVERY x (:* ANIMAL Dog) :mod f2)
(F f2 (:* LIVING-PROPERTY-VAL Hungry) :of x)
(A  y   (:* ANIMAL Cat))
(OP p1 (:* FREQUENCY usually) :of f1)
```

Figure 3: TRIPS Logical Form of "Every hungry dog usually chases a cat"

```
Every(x, Dog(x) ^ Hungry(f2) ^ theme(f2,x),
   Frequent(
      A(y, Cat(y),
         Chase(f1) ^ agent(f1,x) ^ theme(f1,y))))
```

Figure 4: One possible scoped interpretation shown in reference representation

Coreference

The final information encoded in the LF graphs is coreference information. Referential expressions are connected to their antecedents using a :coref arc. Note this can only encode referential relations to antecedents that actually appear previously in the text. Simple forms of bridging reference can also be encoded using the insertion of IMPRO nodes that stand in for implicit arguments, and may then co-refer with terms in the graph.

3   The LF Ontology and Word Senses

The LF ontology is the source of the semantic types and semantic roles that are used in the LF graphs. In this paper, we use the LF ontology of the TRIPS system. The TRIPS ontology also defines a rich set of semantic features that are crucial for constraining ambiguity at multiple levels of language processing. For example, the grammar uses selectional restrictions to guide word sense disambiguation and prepositional phrase attachment during parsing, and reference resolution uses the semantic features to identify valid referents and discard invalid ones.

The TRIPS LF ontology is designed to be linguistically motivated and domain independent. The semantic types and selectional restrictions are driven by linguistic considerations rather than requirements from reasoning components in the system (Dzikovska et al., 2003). Word senses are defined based on subcategorization patterns and domain independent selectional restrictions. As much as possible the semantic types in the LF ontology are compatible with types found in FrameNet (Johnson and Fillmore, 2000). FrameNet generally provides a good level of abstraction for applications since the frames are derived from corpus examples and can be reliably distinguished by human annotators. However we use a smaller, more general set of semantic roles for linking the syntactic and semantic arguments rather than FrameNet's extensive set of specialized frame elements. The LF ontology defines approximately 650 semantic types and 30 semantic roles. See Dzikovska et al. (2004) for more discussion of the relationship between FrameNet and the LF ontology. We also expanded our verb coverage by integrating VerbNet entries (Swift, 2005; Crabbe et al., 2006).

The LF ontology also differs from FrameNet in its use of a rich semantic feature set. Our semantic features are an extended version of EuroWordNet (Vossen, 1997). There are five top-level distinctions: physical object, abstract object, situation, time and proposition. Subtypes are defined to capture distinctions in lexical aspect, spatial abstractions (point, region...), origins (natural, artifact...) and so on.

We are not attempting to capture all possible word senses in our ontology. Rather, we are looking for the level of abstraction that affects linguistic processing, and leave finer distinctions for subsequent discourse processing and inference. In order not to lose information in the LF, our word senses are a tuple of form (:* <LF-type> <word-type>), where the LF-type comes from the Ontology, and the <word-type> is a canonicalized version of the word. For example, the property of a switch/device being *on* or *off* is associated with an LF type ARTIFACT-PROPERTY-VAL. Another sense of *on* is its spatial reading, of type SPATIAL-LOC, which also includes words such as *behind* and *in front of*. These two senses of *on* are:

> (:* ARTIFACT-PROPERTY-VAL ON)
> (:* SPATIAL-LOC ON).

Though we don't have the space to describe it here, TRIPS provides an ontology mapping capability that allows developers to easily map the TRIPS LF forms to a domain-specific ontology (Dzikovska et al., 2008).

4 System Overview

Much recent text processing work has focused on developing "shallow", statistically driven, techniques. We have taken a different approach. We use statistical methods as a preprocessing step to provide guidance to a deep parsing system that uses a detailed, hand-built, grammar of English with a rich set of semantic restrictions. This way, we hope to obtain deeper, more accurate interpretations. Because the parser was developed to identify likely fragments when an entire interpretation cannot be constructed, we believe it can match statistical methods in its precision and recall measures.

The TRIPS grammar is a lexicalized context-free grammar, augmented with feature structures and feature unification. The grammar is motivated from X-bar theory, and draws on principles from GPSG (e.g., head and foot features) and HPSG. The search in the parser is controlled by a set of hand-build rule preferences encoded as weights on the rules, together with a heavy use of selectional restrictions (encoded in the lexicon and ontology) to eliminate semantically anomalous sense combinations.

The TRIPS parser uses a packed-forest chart representation and builds constituents bottom-up using a best-first search strategy similar to A*, based on rule and lexical weights and the influences of the techniques addressed below. The search terminates when a pre-specified number of spanning constituents have been found or a pre-specified maximum chart size is reached. The chart is then searched using a dynamic programming algorithm to find the least cost sequence of constituents according to a cost table that can be varied by genre. For instance, when processing text as in the experiments reported here, we mostly expect UTT constituents encoding the speech act TELL, then less likely the speech acts WH-QUESTION and YN-QUESTION and we don't expect dialog-based speech acts such as CONFIRM or GREET. In addition, we also assign costs to non-sentential constituents (e.g., NPs, ADVPs, etc). The resulting least cost sequence produces a set of logical forms that are the results reported here.

Here we describe the different ways that shallow methods contribute to deep processing.

Using Preprocessors

First, statistical processing is used as a preprocessor. The TRIPS parser accepts a word lattice as input, which we have used when working with speech recognition where we want to consider multiple word hypotheses simultaneously. We have used this capability to allow for preprocessors as well. For instance, we use multiple named entity recognizers (NER) to identify names of people, companies, geographical locations, and so on. The output of the NERs are treated as additional constituent hypotheses in the input to the parser. As an example, consider the sentence *The New York Times is a newspaper.* Assuming an NER identifies *The New York Times* as a name with semantic type PUBLICATION, the input to the parser will be:

```
(word "the" 1 2)
(word "new" 2 3)
(word "york" 3 4)
(word "times" 4 5)
(constit "the new york times" 1 5
        :syn (NAME :class PUBLICATION))
(word "is" 5 6)
(word "a" 6 7)
(word "newspaper" 7 8)
```

As the parser runs, it chooses between interpreting the words individually or using the name, depending on what produces the best overall interpretation. In addition, we use a specialized recognizer that identifies possible street addresses (e.g., 15 N 25th

St NE). Note we don't need specialized NERs for dates and times as they are handled in the main grammar.

Part of Speech Tagging

We also use a part-of-speech tagger to preprocess the input and provide a likely POS tag (or set of tags) for consideration by the parser. Rather than eliminating the interpretations that do not match, the parser simply assigns more weight to interpretations consistent with the tags. This allows the parser to override bad POS assignments in some cases.

Using on-line resources

We have built a system called WordFinder that draws on WordNet (Miller, 1995) and COMLEX (Grishman et al., 1994) to construct (underspecified) lexical representations using mapping rules from high-level WordNet classes into our LF ontology. We deliberately stay at a fairly abstract level as we would rather have a few semantically abstract lexical entries rather than the many highly-specific senses found in WordNet, which we have not found useful for parsing.

Using Preferences during Parsing

Preferences (either syntactic or semantic) can be given to the parser based on statistical or other analyses. We have used the Collins parser as a preprocessor to extract hypotheses for the three constituents (NP, VP, and ADVP) which in pretests had a precision greater than 60% (Swift et al., 2004). For instance, for the sentence *The New York Times is a newspaper,* the Collins preprocessor would produce the following preferences:

(NP 1 5) (NP 6 8) (VP 5 8) (S 1 8)

With simple sentences, this information has little effect. But on longer complex sentences, we found that the preferences allow us to produce more accurate interpretations in faster time. Note again that the parser is not required to follow this advice — all this information does is add a preference for such interpretations.

Another mechanism we use is logical form preference patterns. Local form patterns of predicate types and arguments can be specified with preference scores. Consider the sentence "He put the box in the corner near the house". Although the location adverbial "near the house" could possibly describe the putting event, it is much more likely that it modifies the corner. Thus the pattern (PUT :agent :theme :destination) is preferred over the pattern (PUT :agent :theme :destination :location). We have only tested this capability so far with hand-specified patterns, though we plan to start experiments using learned patterns derived from propositions extracted from corpora (e.g. van Durme et al., 2008). The overall system, using all these techniques, is shown graphically in Figure 5.

5 An Evaluation Metric for LF Graphs

In this section we define an evaluation metric for LF-graphs that allows us to quantify our system performance against gold standard representations.

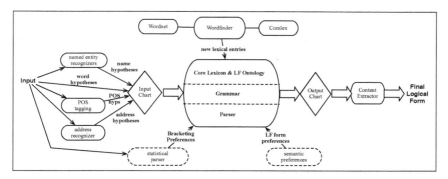

Figure 5: Using Shallow Methods to Inform Deep Parsing (the subsystems in dotted ovals were not used in the reported evaluations)

The evaluation metric between a gold LF graph G and a test LF graph T is defined as the maximum score produced by any node/edge alignment from the gold to the test LF. More formally, an alignment A is a 1-1 mapping from the nodes of the gold graph to nodes of the test graph (or to a pseudo empty node if there is no corresponding node in the test graph). Once we have defined a scoring metric between aligned nodes and edges, we define the match between a gold and test graph as the maximum score produced by an alignment. While complex scoring functions can be used, our results reported here use a simple measure:

Nscore$_A$(n) = 2 if both the indicator and word in the label of n matches the label of A(n), 1 if one of them matches, and 0 otherwise.

Escore$_A$(e) = 1 if e connect nodes n1 and n2, and there is an edge between A(n1) and A(n2) with same label, 0 otherwise.

Gscore(G,T) = max$_A$(Sum$_{n,ein}$(Nscore$_A$(n)+Escore$_A$(e)))

Once we know Gscore(G,T), we can compute semantic precision and recall measures by comparing this to the G and T graphs aligned with themselves, which gives us the maximum possible gold and test scores.

Precision(G,T) = Gscore(G,T)/Gscore(T,T)
Recall(G,T) = Gscore(G,T)/Gscore(G,G)

A more general function of node matching would be more informative. For instance, with words not in our core lexicon, we usually derive an abstract sense that is not the most specific sense in our ontology, however is an abstraction of the correct sense. A scoring function that would give such cases partial credit would have raised our scores (cf. Resnik and Yarowsky, 1997).

Evaluation Procedure and Results

To evaluate our system on the shared texts, we built gold representations for each. We did this by first generating an LF-graph by running the system, and then correcting this

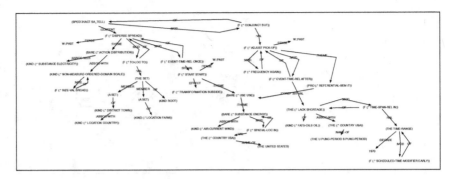

Figure 6: Hand built gold standard for "Once broad-scale electricity distribution spread to farms and country towns, use of wind energy in the United States started to subside, but it picked up again after the U.S. oil shortage in the early 1970s."

by hand using a graphical editor. Figure 6 illustrates the gold standard for a sample paragraph.

Table 2 reports the results on our baseline system, which was the first run we made on the shared texts once they became available. In addition, we report results on the latest version of the system after making some lexicon and grammar additions based on problems found in parsing the paragraphs.

Table 2: Evaluation Results

	Base System		Final System	
Text	**Prec**	**Recall**	**Prec**	**Recall**
1 "physics"	70.1%	70.1%	73.4%	80.0%
2 "cancer"	62.1%	71.9%	71.9%	79.3%
3 "dining"	86.7%	90.4%	90.8%	94.6%
4 "dogs"	63.0%	68.6%	63.8%	69.1%
5 "guns"	55.0%	64.0%	63.8%	73.4%
6 "gardens"	47.4%	53.6%	59.7%	62.0%
7 "wind"	n/a	n/a	65.8%	76.3%
Average	64.1%	69.7%	69.9%	76.4%

Specifically, we added 16 new lexical items (1 verb, 12 nouns, 2 adjectives and 1 adverb); 17 new or modified senses for existing lexical items; 3 new ontology concepts and one grammar rule, to handle the formulation of meters per second as "m/s".

6   Conclusion

We have described a graphical logical form language for expressing a significant amount of the semantic content in natural text. The representation allows for the specification of partial information extracted from sentences, yet is expressive enough to capture many of the subtleties and complications present in linguistically motivated approaches, including supporting complex processes such as quantifier scoping, reference resolution, and reasoning.

We also briefly described a hybrid system architecture centered around a domain-general, broad coverage parsing framework capable of producing deep analyses of texts. Statistical and corpora-based approaches serve to inform the parsing in order to achieve a balance between depth of analysis and broad coverage.

We find the results very encouraging, given this is our first evaluation of the system on text rather than dialog. While it is hard to quantify exactly without further detailed analysis, the remaining errors probably break down roughly evenly between gaps in grammatical coverage, word sense disambiguation errors and inadequacies in our search. Looking at grammatical coverage, the single biggest problem appears to be conjoined sentences with subject ellipsis. Regarding our search problems, because we are building semantic structures rather than syntactic, the search space is much bigger than a traditional CFG. We believe that integrating a statistical parser preprocessor and the LF-preference mechanism will start to address this problem.

Acknowledgments This work was supported by grants from the National Science Foundation (#0748942), the Defense Advanced Research Projects Agency (FA8750-07-D-0185), and the Of[fb01]ce of Naval Research (N000140510314).

References

Allen, J., M. Dzikovska, M. Manshadi, and M. Swift (2007, June). Deep linguistic processing for spoken dialogue systems. In *ACL 2007 Workshop on Deep Linguistic Processing*, pp. 49–56. Association for Computational Linguistics.

Copestake, A., D. Flickinger, C. Pollard, and I. Sag (2006). Minimal recursion semantics: An introduction. *Research on Language and Computation 3*(4), 281–332.

Crabbe, B., M. Dzikovska, W. de Beaumont, and M. Swift (2006, June). Extending the coverage of a domain independent dialog lexicon with VerbNet. In *Proceedings of the Third International Workshop on Scalable Natural Language Understanding (ScaNLU06) at HLT-NAACL 2006*, pp. 25–32.

Dzikovska, M., J. Allen, and M. Swift (2008). Linking semantic and knowledge representations in a multi-domain dialogue system. *J. Log. and Comput. 18*(3), 405–430.

Dzikovska, M., M. Swift, and J. Allen (2003, August). Integrating linguistic and domain knowledge for spoken dialogue systems in multiple domains. In *Proceedings of Workshop on Knowledge and Reasoning in Practical Dialogue Systems at the 18th International Joint Conference on Artificial Intelligence (IJCAI-2003)*, Acapulco, Mexico, pp. 383–389.

Dzikovska, M., M. Swift, and J. Allen (2004, May). Building a computational lexicon and ontology with FrameNet. In *Proceedings of Workshop on Building Lexical Resources with Semantically Annotated Corpora at The 4th International Conference on Language Resources and Evaluation (LREC'04)*, pp. 53–60.

Grishman, R., C. Macleod, and A. Meyers (1994). Comlex syntax: Building a computational lexicon. In *COLING*, pp. 268–272.

Johnson, C. and C. J. Fillmore (2000). The FrameNet tagset for frame-semantic and syntactic coding of predicate-argument structure. In *Proceedings of the first conference on North American chapter of the Association for Computational Linguistics*, San Francisco, CA, USA, pp. 56–62. Morgan Kaufmann Publishers Inc.

Manshadi, M., J. Allen, and M. Swift (2008, August). Toward a universal underspecifed semantic representation. In *13th Conference on Formal Grammar (FG 2008)*.

Miller, G. A. (1995). Wordnet: a lexical database for english. *Commun. ACM 38*(11), 39–41.

Resnik, P. and D. Yarowsky (1997, June). A perspective on word sense disambiguation methods and their evaluation. In *Proceedings of SIGLEX '97*, pp. 79–86.

Swift, M. (2005, February). Towards automatic verb acquisition from VerbNet for spoken dialog processing. In K. Erk, A. Melinger, and S. S. im Walde (Eds.), *Proceedings of Interdisciplinary Workshop on the Identification and Representation of Verb Features and Verb Classes*, pp. 115–120.

Swift, M., J. Allen, and D. Gildea (2004, Aug 23–Aug 27). Skeletons in the parser: Using a shallow parser to improve deep parsing. In *COLING '04: Proceedings of the 20th international conference on Computational Linguistics*, Morristown, NJ, USA, pp. 383–389. Association for Computational Linguistics.

van Durme, B., T. Qian, and L. K. Schubert (2008, Aug 18–Aug 22). Class-driven attribute extraction. In *COLING '08: Proceedings of the 24th international conference on Computational Linguistics*. Association for Computational Linguistics.

Vossen, P. (1997, March 5-7). EuroWordNet: a multilingual database for information retrieval. In *Proceedings of the DELOS workshop on Cross-language Information Retrieval*, Zurich.

Woods, W. A. (1978). Semantics and quantification in natural language question answering. *Advances in Computers 17*, 1–87.

PART III

SHORT PAPERS

Textual Entailment as an Evaluation Framework for Metaphor Resolution: A Proposal

Rodrigo Agerri
John Barnden
Mark Lee
Alan Wallington
University of Birmingham (UK)
email: r.agerri@cs.bham.ac.uk

Abstract

We aim to address two complementary deficiencies in Natural Language Processing (NLP) research: (i) Despite the importance and prevalence of metaphor across many discourse genres, and metaphor's many functions, applied NLP has mostly not addressed metaphor understanding. But, conversely, (ii) difficult issues in metaphor understanding have hindered large-scale application, extensive empirical evaluation, and the handling of the true breadth of metaphor types and interactions with other language phenomena. In this paper, abstracted from a recent grant proposal, a new avenue for addressing both deficiencies and for inspiring new basic research on metaphor is investigated: namely, placing metaphor research within the "Recognizing Textual Entailment" (RTE) task framework for evaluation of semantic processing systems.

1 Introduction

The RTE task and annual Challenges (Dagan et al., 2007), starting in 2005, have arisen as an evaluation framework for applied semantics in response to the fact that in NLP applications — such as *Question Answering* (QA), *Information Retrieval/Extraction* (IR, IE), etc. — the development of semantic algorithms and models have been scattered, or tailored to specific applications, making it difficult to compare and evaluate them within one framework. RTE is interesting because QA, IE, etc. can all be cast as RTE problems. In RTE, one text fragment, the *Text* T, is said to entail another one, the *Hypothesis* H, when humans considering T and H judge that H follows from T (perhaps only plausibly/defeasibly). Thus, entailment is a commonsense matter, not a precise logic-based one. An example of a T/H pair is as follows (metaphor in italics):

(1) T: Lyon is actually the *gastronomic capital* of France.

H: Lyon is the capital of France.

Metaphor can roughly be characterized as describing something (the *target*) as if it were something else (the *source*) to which it is perceived, or set forth, as being somehow analogous. Metaphor has long been identified as being ubiquitous in language (Goatly, 1997), including ordinary conversation, newspaper articles, popular novels, popular science writing, classroom dialogue, etc. In a study (Tech. Rept. CSRP-03-05 at our School, 2003) we found one metaphorical term per 17.3 words, averaging across various discourses of different genres. This is in line with other researchers' studies though counts vary widely because of theory-relativity, researchers' aims, and marked usage differences between genres. Gedigian et al. (2006) note that 90% of uses of a set of verbs of spatial motion, manipulation, and health in a *Wall Street Journal* corpus were metaphorical. Some metaphor examples arising in past RTE datasets are the Ts in T/H pairs (1–4), with human judgments No, Yes, No and No respectively.

(2) T: The technological triumph known as GPS was *incubated in the mind* of Ivan Getting.

H: Ivan Getting invented the GPS.

(3) T: Convinced that pro-American officials are in the ascendancy in Tokyo, they talk about turning Japan into *the Britain of the Far East*.

H: Britain is located in the Far East.

(4) T: Even today, *within the deepest recesses of our mind, lies* a primordial fear that will not allow us to enter the sea without thinking about the possibility of being attacked by a shark.

H: A shark attacked a human being.

Importantly, metaphor is often not just a matter of particular terms with particular metaphorical senses that are entrenched (i.e., that are commonly used, default senses; and possibly listed in dictionaries). Certainly the metaphorical senses of "capital" and "incubate" used in (1) and (2) are at least moderately entrenched. For "incubate," some dictionaries list a slow, protective sense of development (in a general, possibly non-physical sense), or for "capital" a sense like "a city [or place more generally] preeminent in some special activity" [Merriam-Websters]. But (3) shows one common type of non-entrenched metaphor, of the general form "the X of Y", where X and/or Y are often named entities. The point of such a metaphor is typically only clear with the help of context. Reference to recesses of a mind as in (4) is common, and a lexicon could reasonably include a metaphorical sense of "recess" that was directly applicable to minds (though WordNet 3.0, e.g, does not), or include "within the recesses of [X's] mind" as a stock phrase with a sense of relative inaccessibility or unmodifiability of a thought or feeling. But the phraseology can be productively varied: e.g., "deepest" can be omitted or replaced by "dim", "darkest", "foulest", "hidden", etc. — by *any* compatible qualifier that emphasizes hiddenness or obstacles to accessibility. And the fact that such access difficulties are being *emphasized* is a matter for general semantic reasoning about the qualifier.

2   Why Metaphor in NLP?

Generally, in metaphor understanding research, a specialized system has been fed a relatively small number of metaphorical inputs, and the correct outputs have been dictated by the researcher, (e.g. Fass, 1997; Falkenhainer et al., 1989; Martin, 1990; Barnden et al., 2003). However, metaphor in particular and figurative language in general suffers a chronic lack of shared resources for proper evaluation of systems (Markert and Nissim, 2007). In using the RTE evaluation framework, computational metaphor researchers may for the first time have sizable, shared datasets, and a uniform evaluation method based on systematically and transparently collected human judgments. Also, metaphor researchers will be challenged and inspired to connect metaphor more than before to other complex linguistic phenomena.

NLP applications that RTE serves have mostly not addressed metaphor, and neither have RTE systems themselves. Indeed, despite examples (1-4), RTE datasets have tended to avoid metaphor of more difficult types. Metaphor in general can introduce additional context-sensitivity and indeterminacy in entailment, whereas RTE Challenges have mainly concentrated on T/H pairs supporting relatively crisp, uncontroversial judgments (Zaenen et al. (2005); RTE organizers (personal communication); our own analysis of existing RTE datasets in Tech. Rept. CSRP-08-01, 2008). In fact, on examples such as (1), a system must interpret "capital" metaphorically, but as Bos and Markert (2006) reported, the inability of their system to process metaphor meant that it was incorrect on this example.

Further evidence is given by results on example (1) of the four RTE-1 systems available to us (out of 16 systems; the 4 include the 1st, 3rd and 4th best systems in terms of accuracy over whole dataset). Only one reported system run was correct. The systems mostly performed worse across (1) together with 10 other metaphor cases than on the whole dataset, with statistical significance at 0.05 level (Fisher's independence test); only one system run gave a better performance. In RTE-2 (23 systems), analysis of 10 system runs shows that, across 9 metaphorical examples in the dataset, the systems (including the most accurate one over the whole dataset) performed worse than they did over the rest of the dataset; in 7 of the 10 RTE-2 runs compared the deficit was statistically significant at < 0.05 level (Fisher's test, see Tech Rept. CSRP-08-01).

3 RoadMap: Datasets and Metaphor Processing

Our initiative mainly consists of (**A**): Create a public, annotated, metaphor-focussed text dataset suitable for RTE evaluation and testing of metaphor processing systems; and (**B**): Develop a prototype RTE system centred on processing (at least) the types of metaphor arising in (A). We will mainly address point (B) in this paper. As for A, metaphors vary along several dimensions of interest, such as: the target subject matter (e.g., Lyon's food, GPS development, Japanese foreign politics, shark fear in examples 1–4); the source subject matter; what particular, familiar metaphorical views (e.g., Idea as Living Being, in (2)) are used; whether the meaning in context is listed in dictionaries, WordNet, etc; whether the wording is (a variant of) a familiar idiom; the syntax used. Based on such dimensions, we will analyse the **types of metaphor** present in past RTE datasets and in the genres of text (e.g., newspapers) they drew from. One particular source will be the 242K-word metaphor-orientated corpus that we derived from the British National Corpus. To find metaphor examples elsewhere, we will use known metaphorical phrases and lexical/syntactic templates as seeds for automated search over general corpora or web. We will also investigate the use or adaptation of other researchers' automated detection/mining techniques (e.g. Birke and Sarkar, 2006; Gedigian et al., 2006).

4 Metaphor Processing

We will develop metaphor processing algorithms on an integrated spectrum going from relatively "shallow" forms of processing to relatively "deep" forms. The deeper are for when more inference is necessary and feasible; when less necessary or feasible, the shallower are appropriate (but they can still involve at least partial parsing, approximate semantic analysis, etc.). A significant research issue will be how to choose the attempted depth(s) of analysis and how to choose or combine different methods' results. The deeper and shallower ends of the spectrum will take as starting points our two previous metaphor-understanding approaches, from our ATT-Meta and E-Drama projects respectively (Barnden et al., 2003; Wallington et al., 2008).

For detecting metaphor, we can extend methods from our E-drama project (Wallington et al., 2008). This involves a mixture of light semantic analysis via tools such as WordNet and recognition of lexical and syntactic signals of metaphoricity (Goatly, 1997). We aim also to recognize specific idiomatic phrases and systematic variations of them. We will consider looking for semantic restriction violations, which sometimes accompany metaphor (cf. Fass (1997) and Mason (2004)), and using statistical techniques borrowed from such work as Gedigian et al. (2006).

Example (4) about "recesses" is similar to metaphor examples studied in the ATT-Meta project, and ATT-Meta-style reasoning could handle the Text. As for (2), note that the word "incubate" may have a directly usable lexicon-listed meaning (e.g., *help to develop* much as in WordNet 3.0). However, if the system's lexicon did *not* contain such a sense, ATT-Meta-style processing would apply. ATT-Meta processing would involve commonsense reasoning in source-domain terms (here, biological and other physical terms): e.g., to infer that the idea was a living being, Getting's mind was a physical region, the idea was kept warm in that region, and the idea consequently biologically developed there. Hence, there was a *relatively protracted, continuous process*; the idea *became more functional* as a living being; and the idea needed *protection* from physical harm (= *disenablement* of *function-inhibiting* influences). These default conclusions can then be translated into reality (target-based) terms: there was a protracted, (non-physical) continuous process of change; the idea needed protection during it; and the idea ended up being more functional. The basis for such translation is *View-Neutral Mapping Adjuncts*, a special type of mappings that cover the shape of events and processes, temporal properties and relationships, causation, functioning, mental states, emotional states, value judgments and various other matters (Agerri et al., 2007; Barnden et al., 2003).

RTE-2 organisers claimed there has been a trend towards using more deep inference and that this has been beneficial *provided* that it is based on enough knowledge. (See also Bos and Markert (2006) and Clark et al. (2007)). The depth and knowledge needs of ATT-Meta's processing are like those of deeper parts of existing RTE systems, but ATT-Meta is currently equipped only with small, hand-constructed knowledge bases. So, our main focus in deeper processing will actually be on a shallowed, broadened form of ATT-Meta-style reasoning. In this sense, we aim to look at common-sense knowledge resources such as ConceptNet 3.0 which contains relationships such as causation, function, etc. — the types of information transferred by some of ATT-Meta's VNMAs — or modified WordNets enriched by extra, web-mined knowledge (Veale and Hao, 2008), where the extra knowledge is especially relevant to metaphorical usages.

ATT-Meta's reasoning is by backwards chaining from goals derivable from context surrounding a metaphor. This relevance-based inference-focussing will be key in other processing we develop, and is highly RTE-compatible. An RTE Hypothesis can act as (part of) a reasoning goal, with the metaphor's within-Text context supplying further information or goal parts. T's own original context is of course unavailable, but this obstacle faces human judges as well.

We will also further extend our E-Drama project's methods, based there on robust parsing using the *Rasp* system and computation over WordNet. The methods are currently largely confined to metaphors of "X is Y" form where X is a person and Y is some type of animal, supernatural being, artefact or natural physical object. We will generalize to other categories for X and Y, and to cases where the categorization is only implicit. We will make the syntactic/semantic analysis of WordNet synset-glosses and the way the system traverses the network more advanced. We will extend our associated treatment of metaphorically-used size adjectives (as in "little bully").

However, the methods are also currently confined to detecting emotional/value judgments about X (unpleasantness, etc.), and mainly exploit metaphorical information that is already implicitly in WordNet, e.g., "pig" meaning a coarse, obnoxious person, in one synset. Substantial research is needed to go beyond these limitations. One avenue will be to apply VNMAs: when a synset gloss couches a metaphorical sense, we could extract not just affect but other types of information that VNMAs handle (causation, process shape, etc.); and when a gloss couches a non-metaphorical sense, we could translate some aspects of it via VNMAs.

5   Concluding Remarks

This paper aims to provide an avenue for giving metaphor-understanding the promi-
nence it merits in NLP applications and in RTE, and thereby also to engender basic
and applied research advances on metaphor by ourselves and others.

RTE researchers and NLP applications developers will benefit, as systems will gain
added accuracy and coverage by addressing metaphor. Beneficiary application areas
aside from QA, IR, etc., include Knowledge Management, Information Access, and
intelligent conversation agents.

References

Agerri, R., J. Barnden, M. Lee, and A. Wallington (2007). Metaphor, inference and
    domain independent mappings. In *Proceedings of Research Advances in Natural
    Language Processing (RANLP 2007)*, Borovets, Bulgaria, pp. 17–24.

Barnden, J., S. Glasbey, M. Lee, and A. Wallington (2003). Domain-transcending
    mappings in a system for metaphorical reasoning. In *Companion Proceedings of
    the 10th Conference on the European Chapter of the Association for Computational
    Linguistics (EACL-03)*, pp. 57–61.

Birke, J. and A. Sarkar (2006). A clustering approach for the nearly unsupervised
    recognition of nonliteral language. In *Proceedings of the 11th Conference on the
    European Chapter of the Association for Computational Linguistics (EACL 2006)*,
    Trento, Italy, pp. 329–336.

Bos, J. and K. Markert (2006). Recognizing textual entailment with robust logical
    inference. In J. Quiñonero-Candela, I. Dagan, B. Magnini, and F. d'Alché Buc
    (Eds.), *MLCW 2005*, Volume 3944 of *LNAI*, pp. 404–426. Springer-Verlag.

Clark, P., W. Murray, J. Thompson, P. Harrison, J. Hobbs, and C. Fellbaum (2007). On
    the role of lexical and world knowledge in RTE3. In *Proceedings of the Workshop
    on Textual Entailment and Paraphrasing*, Prague, pp. 54–59. ACL 2007.

Dagan, I., O. Glickman, and B. Magnini (2007). The PASCAL Recognising Tex-
    tual Entailment challenge. In J. Quiñonero-Candela, I. Dagan, B. Magnini, and
    F. d'Alché Buc (Eds.), *MLCW 2005*, Volume 3944 of *LNAI*, pp. 177–190. Springer-
    Verlag.

Falkenhainer, B., K. Forbus, and D. Gentner (1989). The structure-mapping engine:
    algorithm and examples. *Artificial Intelligence 41*(1), 1–63.

Fass, D. (1997). *Processing metaphor and metonymy*. Greenwich, Connecticut:
    Ablex.

Gedigian, M., J. Bryant, S. Narayanan, and B. Ciric (2006). Catching metaphors. In
    Proceedings of the 3rd Workshop on Scalable Natural Language Understanding,
    New York, pp. 41–48.

Goatly, A. (1997). *The Language of Metaphors*. Routledge.

Markert, K. and M. Nissim (2007, June). Semeval-2007: Metonymy resolution at semeval-2007. In *International Workshop on Semantic Evaluations (SemEval-2007)*, Prague, pp. 36–41. Association for Computational Linguistics (ACL-07).

Martin, J. (1990). *A computational model of metaphor interpretation.* New York: Academic Press.

Mason, Z. (2004). CorMet: a computational, corpus-based conventional metaphor extraction system. *Computational Linguistics 30*(1), 23–44.

Veale, T. and Y. Hao (2008). Enriching WordNet with folk knowledge and stereotypes. In *Proceedings of the 4th Global WordNet Conference*, Szeged, Hungary.

Wallington, A., R. Agerri, J. Barnden, M. Lee, and T. Rumbell (2008, May). Affect transfer by metaphor for an intelligent conversational agent. In *Proceedings of the LREC 2008 Workshop on Sentiment Analysis: Emotion, Metaphor, Ontology and Terminology (EMOT 08)*, Marrakech, Morocco, pp. 102–107.

Zaenen, A., L. Karttunen, and R. Crouch (2005). Local textual inference: Can it be defined or circumscribed? In *Proceedings of the ACL 05 Workshop on Empirical Modelling of Semantic Equivalence and Entailment*, pp. 31–36.

Representing and Visualizing Calendar Expressions in Texts

Delphine Battistelli

Univ. Paris-Sorbonne (France)

email: Delphine.Battistelli@paris-sorbonne.fr

Javier Couto

INCO, FING, UdelaR (Uruguay)

email: jcouto@fing.edu.uy

Jean-Luc Minel

MoDyCo, CNRS-Univ. ParisX (France)

email: Jean-Luc.Minel@u-paris10.fr

Sylviane R. Schwer

LIPN, CNRS-Univ. ParisXIII (France)

email: Sylviane.Schwer@lipn.univ-paris13.fr

Abstract

Temporal expressions that refer to a part of a calendar area in terms of common calendar divisions are studied. Our claim is that such a "calendar expression" (CE) can be described by a succession of operators operating on a calendar base (CB). These operators are categorized: a pointing operator that transform a CB into a CE; a focalizing/shifting operator that reduces or shifts the CE into another CE, and finally a zoning operator that provides the wanted CE from this last CE. Relying on these operators, a set of annotations is presented which are used to automatically annotate biographic texts. A software application, plugged in the platform Navitext, is described that builds a calendar view of a biographic text.

1 Introduction

Taking into account temporality expressed in texts appears as fundamental, not only in a perspective of global processing of documents, but also in the analysis of the structure of a document.[1] The analysis of temporality within texts has been studied principally by considering verbal times (e.g. Song and Cohen (1991); Hitzeman et al. (1995) and temporal adverbials (see below).

Our approach is focused on temporal adverbials — in French — that refer directly to text units concerning common calendar divisions, that we name "calendar expressions" (CEs for short). Several analyses of this kind of expressions has generated a lot of interest, ranging from their automatic recognition and annotation in texts to their analysis in terms of discursive frames (Charolles, 1997; Tannen, 1997), following work of Halliday (1994) which put the emphasis on the importance of the temporal adverbial expressions as modes of discursive organization.

Nowadays, in the field of temporality processing, automatic identification and annotation tasks of CEs are the most developed, mainly because identifying and annotating expressions which contain calendar units are considered — *a priori* — as trivial tasks. Those tasks have been particularly explored in three contexts:

1. Systems which aim to set events on a time scale depending on their duration and according to a hierarchy of unities called granularities (Schilder and Habel, 2001);

2. Systems for summarizing multi-documents (Barzilay et al., 2001); and

3. QA systems (Pustejovsky et al., 1993; Harabagiu and Bejan, 2005).

Please note that the proposition of the well-known standard temporal meta-language named TimeML (Pustejovsky et al., 2003) initially took place in the context of a QA systems worshop (Pustejovsky, 2002), and mainly integrates two schemes of annotations — namely TIDES TIMEX2 (Ferro et al., 2004) and Sheffield STAG (Setzer and Gaizauskas, 2000) — which were essentially put forward from the analysis of CEs.

In this paper, we propose a formal description of CEs in written French texts, by explicitly distinguishing several classes of linguistic markers which must be interpreted as successive operators. This work is driven in order to propose a set of fine and well-defined annotations which will be used to navigate temporally in an annotated document. Our approach differs from the preceding ones in two crucial ways:

- Our goal is not to link a CE to an event, neither to fix it on a "temporal line", using a set of values relying on ISO 8601 standard format (Mani and Wilson, 2000; Setzer and Gaizauskas, 2000; Filatova and Hovy, 2001); instead our goal is to link CEs between themselves, that is to say to establish their qualitative relative positions (the set of those relations is named "proper text calendar");

- We design CE semantics as algebraic expressions.

---

[1] This research is funded with an ANR grant (Projet Blanc Conique).

The remainder of this paper is organized as follows. In the next section, we introduce an algebra of CEs. In Section 3 we describe a software application, which exploits functional representation, built with previous way exhibited operators and plugged in the NaviTexte platform, aiming to support text reading. Finally, conclusions and future research directions are presented in Section 4.

2 An Algebra for Calendar Expressions

We postulate that a CE, say E, used to refer to a calendar area can be described by a succession of operators applied on an argument, named *calendar base* (CB), say B, that bears a granulariry and a value for anchoring allowing fixing it in the calendar system used and that gives access at the calendar area described by the CE.

Each operator gives a piece of the processing following a specific order: on B is applied a *pointing* operation, usually expressed by a determinant, whose result is an CE, E_1 part of E. On E_1 is applied a second kind of operator expressing the useful part of this base (all, the beginning, the middle, the end, a fuzzy area around) given as result a new CE E_2 which is part of E and is associated with a piece of the calendar that cuts the time line in three areas (illustrated by Figure 1):

- the former half-line (A),

- the Useful portion (U),

- posterior half-line (P)[2].

The useful part can also be obtained either by shifting, like in "trois semaines plus tard" (three weeks later), or by zooming, as in "l'automne de cette année là" (the autumn of this present year).[3] A third kind of operator gives access at the area described by the complete CE E: selecting one of the three portioned areas, like in "jusqu'en avril 2006" (until April 2006).

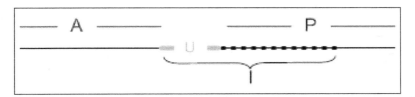

Figure 1: Partition of the time line for a unary CE

The order of operators is the following: a pointing operator *OpPointing*, followed by one or more focalising or shifting operators $OpFocalising/Shifting^{+}$ and finally at least one zoning operator $OpZoning^{\oplus}$.[4] Some operators can be omitted, usually when

---

[2]This Time line is pragmatically limited bounded. For instance, (P) can be naturally limited by the present moment, as we do in Figure 1.

[3]For such deictic CEs, the CB has the granularity *year*, and the value *current*.

[4]Usually one, but we also can find two zoning operators, for instance in "jusqu'à avant Noël (until before Christmas"). In this case, the order of the operators is more constraint than the order of Focalising/Shifting operators. Therefore we use the $\oplus$ symbol instead of $+$

they do not provide any new information. In sum, the representation of CEs has the following generic form: $OpZoning^{\oplus}(OpFocalising/Shifting^{+}(OpPoin\text{-}ting(CB)))$.

For instance, let us analyse the CE E="Avant le début de la fin de l'année 2008" (before the beginning of the end of the year 2008). B="année 2008". Firstly, the operator of pointing, triggered by the identification of "l'" (the contraction of "le") is applied, given E_1=L'année 2008".[5] Secondly, two operators of focalising/shifting are applied successively: the first one triggered by "la fin de" , provides E_2' and the second one, triggered by "le début de", provides E_2. Finally an operator of zoning is associated with "avant", provided E. Consequently, the CE "avant le début de la fin de l'année 2008" is produced as *avant (le début de (la fin de(l'(année 2008))))*. The sequence of this CE is depicted and visualized in Figure 2.

l'(année 2008)	○
la fin de (l'(années 2008))	◐
le début de (la fin de (l'(année 2008)))	◑
avant (le début de (la fin de (l'(année 2008)))	▬▬▬▬▬

Figure 2: Computation of "avant le début de la fin de l'année 2008"

Each operator is characterized by its arity (the number of its arguments) and type. With regard to arity, in this paper we focus on unary operators.

2.1 Unary operators

Three types of operators have been defined: pointing, focalising/shifting and zoning. The pointing operator is trivial (it transforms B into a CE of type $E1$) but the two others need some refinements.

Focalising/Shifting operators

Focalising/Shifting operators transform a CE of type $E1$ into a CE of type $E2$. Several kinds of focalising/shifting time may be expressed. For instance, in the expression "au début de mai 2005" (at the beginning of may 2005) the focalising/shifting is localised inside the BC (mai 2005), whereas in the expression "trois semaines avant mai 2005" (three weeks before may 2005) it is outside the BC. Consequently, six sub-operators have been identified and are shown Table 1. It should be noted that ShiftingBeginning and ShiftingAfter operators refers to a family of operators, because for these ones it is necessary to precise two parameters, the granularity and the value of the shifting.

For some reasons of implementation, except for the operator IdShifting, which refers at the identity, all others operators are treated as idempotent. In other words, we consider as equivalent these two expressions "au début du début des années 1980" (at the beginning of the early eighties) and "au début des années 1980" (in the early of eighties). The next version will improve at this point.

Zoning operators

A Zoning operator transforms a CE of type $E2$, associated to the useful portion U of Figure 1, into the CE E analysed. A Zoning operator refers to one of the six possible

---

[5]This pointing operator, as mentioned previously, is not an operator of the CE algebra, but all the other operators are part of the CE algebra.

Table 1: Focalising/Shifting operators

Operators	Examples
IdShifting	– *en* 1945
	– *au* mois d'août
ZoomBeginning	– *à l'aube de*s années 1980
	– *au début de* mai 1945
ZoomMiddle	– *au milieu de*s années 1980
ZoomEnding	– *à la fin de*s années 1980
ShiftingBefore (granularity, -n)	– *10 jours avant* le 14 juillet 2005
ShiftingAfter (granularity, +n)	– *10 jours après* le 14 juillet 2005

zones[6] built from A, P and U: that is A, A+U, U, U+P, P, A+P. These six kinds of zoning are associated with a set of prepositions, whose prototypes are shown Table 2. Fuzzy expressions like "peu avant" (short before) can double this number. Table 2 also illustrates the the ZoningAbout operator <U>. Further, note that ZoningId is not expressed, but has to be taken into account.

Table 2: Zoning operators

Operators	Expression
ZoningBefore [A]	*avant* fin avril 2008
ZoningUntil [A+U]	*jusqu'*à fin avril 2008
ZoningId [U]	[∅] fin avril 2008
ZoningAbout <U>	*vers* la fin avril 2008
ZoningSince [U+P]	*depuis* la fin avril 2008
ZoningAfter [P]	*après* fin avril 2008
ZoningApart [A+P]	*excepté* fin avril 2008

2.2 N-ary or sequence operators

As mentioned before, it is necessary to use several N-ary operators to represent some CE. For instance, a binary operator is used for representing an expression like "entre fin mai 2005 et avril 2006" (between the end of may 2005 and april 2006). This operator, *Between*, applies to two CEs, so for the preceding expression the representation is Between ((ZoomEnding(Pointing(may 2005), Pointing(april 2006)). Moreover, a sequence operator is needed to represent a CE like "le mardi 21, le mercredi 22 et le vendredi 24 mai 1980" (on Tuesday 21, Wednesday 22 and Friday 24 of May). The study of these operators, associated with even more complex CEs with quantifications, is currently under investigation.

---

[6]The empty zone, expressed by "jamais" (never) and the full zone, that is A+U+P, expressed by "toujours" (always) are CE, but not associated with unary operators associated to a BC, as defined here, hence excluded of our precedent study.

3   Application

Many applications which exploit temporal expressions in texts, in particular in the area of information extraction, have been implemented (Pazienza, 1999). Our application is plugged into the textual navigation workstation NaviTexte (Couto, 2006; Couto and Minel, 2007), in order to combine a traditional linear reading with a chronological one. With this intention, we have undertaken the construction of a computerized aided reading of biographies. Consequently, we have addressed two issues. First, identifying temporal expressions and ordering chronologically text segments in which they are included. Second, building calendar views of the text and navigating through these views.

3.1   Identifying and ordering calendar expressions

From the linguistic study presented above, we have defined a set of annotations which are used to automatically annotate biographic texts. This process is carried out by transducers which put XML[7] annotations through the processed text. These annotations describe on the one hand, the granularity of CEs, and on the other hand, the kind of identified operator. For instance, the following XML code illustrates how the temporal expression "avant le début de la fin de l'année 2008" (Before the beginning of the end of the year 2008) will be annotated:

```
<UT Type="Expression Calendaire" Nro="7">
  <Annotation Nom="Grain">Annee</Annotation>
  <Annotation Nom="Annee">2008</Annotation>
  <Annotation Nom="RelationCalendrier">Absolue</Annotation>
  <Annotation Nom="OpTempRÂÕgion1">Avant</Annotation>
  <Annotation Nom="OpTempDÂÕplacement1">FocalFin</Annotation>
  <Annotation Nom="OpTempDÂÕplacement2">FocalDebut</Annotation>
  <Chaine>
  avant le debut de la fin de l'annee 2008
  </Chaine>
</UT>
```

From these annotations, an automatic ordering relying on values of CEs can be carried out. A first implementation took only into account disjoined CEs, because they are linearly ordered. Intersecting CEs, like "En juin 2007 (...) en été 2007" (in June 2007 (...) in summer 2007) requires a more powerful formalism. A formalism relying both on S-Languages (Schwer, 2002b) and granules (Schwer, 2002a) is required to provide a full automatic ordering.

3.2   Building a text calendar view

A new kind of view, a calendar one, has been built in the NaviTexte platform. This view is built from texts which contain CEs annotated as described above. An example is shown in Figure 3. Conceptually, a calendar view is a graph coordinated with a two-dimensional grid. In the left part of the view, lexical chains of various occurrences of CEs in the text are displayed. By default, those are ordered according to their order of appearance in the text, but it is possible to display a chronological order,

---

[7]A DTD is defined in Couto (2006)

by using options offered in the panel located in bottom of the view. Nodes in the graph represent these lexical chains. The visual representation of a CE depends of the functional representation computed as described before Figure 2.

A simple CE, with only a pointing operator like in "l'année 2008" (the year 2008) is always visualised like a white ellipse. An operator of focalising/Shifting like "la fin de" (the end of) selects an area of the ellipse and blackens it. Finally, a zoning operator like "avant" (before) is visualised by a bold line displaying the area that is referred to.

The plug-in is implemented with the JGaph package and we largely use some of its functionalities, like zooming or the partial layout cache. We also use html tooltip text in Swing to contextualise a CE in the original text. For example, in Figure 3, the whole paragraph which contains the CE "en 1953" (in 1953) is displayed and the occurrence of a CE is highlighted.

3.3 Evaluation

Two kinds of evaluation could be performed on this work: (i) evaluation of automatic recognition and semantic annotation of CEs in text, (ii) evaluation of the calendar view. The former calls for a classical protocol in NLP, whereas the latter is more complex to carry out.

So far, only recognition has been carried out by Teissedre (2007) who computed recall and precision on three kinds of corpora. Due to the fact that an annotation is made up of several fields the recall has been computed like this: a score zero when a CE is not identified, a score 1 when the identification is total, and 0.5 when the identification is partial. Applying these rules, recall is 0.8 and precision is 0.9.

We would like to make two remarks on this result. First, quantified CEs like "tous les mardis" (every Tuesday) or "un mardi sur deux" (one Tuesday out of two) and n-aries ($n \geq 3$) CEs like "entre 2008 et 2009 et en juin 2010" (between 2008 and 2009 and in june 2010) are identified but are not yet taken into account in the semantic annotation process. Second, syntactic ambiguities like in "il a dormi deux jours avant Noël" (he slept two days before Christmas) are not taken into account either. However in this example, there are two possible syntactic structures. In the first case, "avant Noël" is the CE and the operator is the Regionalisation one; in the second case, "deux jours avant Noël" is the CE and the operator is the Shifting one. Presently, our analysis provides only the second one like in Aunargue et al. (2001) but we intend to upgrade it in order to provide both analyses.

Evaluation of the calendar view should be studied from a cognitive point of view and is highly dependent on the application. We plan to work with cognitive scientists to build a relevant protocol to study this aspect of evaluation which calls for the specification of a set of navigation operations based on the algebra of operators.

4 Conclusion

We proposed an algebra of CEs with three kinds of operators to analyse calendar expressions and build a functional representation of these expressions. We described an implementation of this approach in the platform NaviTexte and we have shown how the functional representation is used to visualise a calendar view of a text. In future work, we will rely on a methodology presented in Battistelli and Chagnoux (2007) in

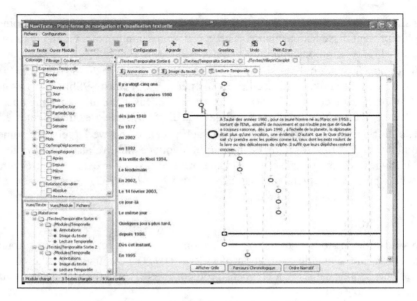

Figure 3: Example of calendar view in NaviTexte

order to take into account several temporal axis, and thus several calendar structures, which are expressed in texts by different levels of enunciations, like citations.

References

Aunargue, M., M. Bras, L. Vieu, and N. Asher (2001). The syntax and semantics of locating adverbials. *Cahiers de Grammaire 26*, 11–35.

Barzilay, R., N. Elhadad, and K. McKeown (2001). Sentence ordering in multidocument summarization. In *First International Conference on Human Language Technology Research (HLT-01)*, pp. 149–156.

Battistelli, D. and M. Chagnoux (2007). Représenter la dynamique énonciative et modale de textes. In *actes TALNÕ07 (Traitement automatique du langage naturel*, pp. 13–23.

Charolles, M. (1997). LÕencadrement du discours – univers, champs, domaines et espaces. In *Cahiers de recherche linguistique*, Volume 6 of *LANDISCO*, pp. 1–73. Université Nancy 2.

Couto, J. (2006). *Modélisation des connaissances pour une navigation textuelle assistée. La plate-forme logicielle NaviTexte*. Ph. D. thesis, Université Paris-Sorbonne.

Couto, J. and J.-L. Minel (2007). Navitexte, a text navigation tool. In , *Lecture Notes in Artificial Intelligence 4733*, pp. 251–259. Springer-Verlag.

Ferro, L., L. Gerber, I. Mani, B. Sundheim, and G. Wilson (2004). Standard for the annotation of temporal expressions. Technical report, timex2.mitre.org, MITRE Corporation.

Filatova, E. and E. Hovy (2001). Assigning time-stamps to event-clauses. In *Workshop on Temporal and Spatial Information Processing, ACLŌ2001*, pp. 88–95.

Halliday, M. A. K. (1994). *An introduction to functional grammar*. London: Edward Arnold.

Harabagiu, S. and C. A. Bejan (2005). Question answering based on temporal inference. In *AAAI-2005 Workshop on Inference for Textual Question Answering*.

Hitzeman, J., M. Moens, and C. Grover (1995). Algorithms for analyzing the temporal structure of discourse. In *EACLŌ95*, pp. 253–260.

Mani, I. and G. Wilson (2000). Robust temporal processing of news. In *Proceedings 38th ACL*, pp. 69–76.

Pazienza, M. T. (1999). *Information Extraction, toward scalable, adaptable systems*. New York: Springer-Verlag.

Pustejovsky, J. (Ed.) (2002). *TERQAS 2002: An ARDA Workshop on Advanced Question Answering Technology*.

Pustejovsky, J., J. Castano, R. Ingria, R. Sauri, R. Gaizauskas, A. Setzer, and G. Katz (2003). Timeml: Robust specification of event and temporal expressions in text. In *IWCS-5 Fifth International Workshop on Computational Semantics*.

Pustejovsky, J., R. Knippen, J. Lintman, and R. Sauri (1993). Temporal and event information in natural language text. *Lexique 11*, 123–164.

Schilder, F. and C. Habel (2001). From temporal expressions to temporal information: Semantic tagging of news messages. In *Proceedings of ACL'01 workshop on temporal and spatial information processing*, pp. 65–72.

Schwer, S. R. (2002a). Reasoning with intervals on granules. *Journal of Universal Computer Science 8 (8)*, 793–808.

Schwer, S. R. (2002b). S-arrangements avec répétitions. *Comptes Rendus de l'Académie des Sciences de Paris Série I 334*, 261–266.

Setzer, A. and R. Gaizauskas (2000). Annotating events and temporal information in newswire texts. In *Proceeedings 2rd LRC*, pp. 64–66.

Song, F. and R. Cohen (1991). Tense interpretation in the context of narrative. In *9th AAAI*, pp. 131–136.

Tannen, D. (1997). *Framing in Discourse*. Oxford: Oxford University Press.

Teissedre, C. (2007). La temporalité dans les textes : de lŌannotation sémantique à la navigation textuelle. Master's thesis, Université Paris-Sorbonne.

Addressing the Resource Bottleneck to Create Large-Scale Annotated Texts

Jon Chamberlain

University of Essex (UK)

email: jchamb@essex.ac.uk

Massimo Poesio

University of Essex (UK) & Università di Trento (Italy)

email: poesio@essex.ac.uk

Udo Kruschwitz

University of Essex (UK)

email: udo@essex.ac.uk

Abstract

Large-scale linguistically annotated resources have become available in recent years. This is partly due to sophisticated automatic and semi-automatic approaches that work well on specific tasks such as part-of-speech tagging. For more complex linguistic phenomena like anaphora resolution there are no tools that result in high-quality annotations without massive user intervention. Annotated corpora of the size needed for modern computational linguistics research cannot however be created by small groups of hand annotators. The ANAWIKI project strikes a balance between collecting high-quality annotations from experts and applying a game-like approach to collecting linguistic annotation from the general Web population. More generally, ANAWIKI is a project that explores to what extend expert annotations can be substituted by a critical mass of non-expert judgements.

1 Introduction

Syntactically annotated language resources have long been around, but the greatest obstacle to progress towards systems able to extract *semantic* information from text is the lack of semantically annotated corpora large enough to be used to train and evaluate semantic interpretation methods. Recent efforts to create resources to support large evaluation initiatives in the USA such as Automatic Context Extraction (ACE), Translingual Information Detection, Extraction and Summarization (TIDES), and GALE are beginning to change this, but just at a point when the community is beginning to realize that even the 1M word annotated corpora created in substantial efforts such as Prop-Bank (Palmer et al., 2005) and the OntoNotes initiative (Hovy et al., 2006) are likely to be too small.

Unfortunately, the creation of 100M-plus corpora via hand annotation is likely to be prohibitively expensive. Such a large hand-annotation effort would be even less sensible in the case of semantic annotation tasks such as coreference or wordsense disambiguation, given on the one side the greater difficulty of agreeing on a "neutral" theoretical framework, on the other the difficulty of achieving more than moderate agreement on semantic judgments (Poesio and Artstein, 2005).

The ANAWIKI project[1] presents an effort to create high-quality, large-scale anaphorically annotated resources (Poesio et al., 2008) by taking advantage of the collaboration of the Web community, both through co-operative annotation efforts using traditional annotation tools and through the use of game-like interfaces. This makes ANAWIKI a very ambitious project. It is not clear to what extend expert annotations can in fact be substituted by those judgements submitted by the general public as part of a game. If successful, ANAWIKI will actually be more than just an anaphora annotation tool. We see it as a framework aimed at creating large-scale annotated corpora in general.

2 Creating Resources through Web Collaboration

Large-scale annotation of low-level linguistic information (part-of-speech tags) began with the Brown Corpus, in which very low-tech and time consuming methods were used; but already for the creation of the British National Corpus (BNC), the first 100M-word linguistically annotated corpus, a faster methodology was developed consisting of preliminary annotation with automatic methods followed by partial hand-correction (Burnard, 2000). Medium and large-scale semantic annotation projects (coreference, wordsense) are a fairly recent innovation in Computational Linguistics (CL). The semi-automatic annotation methodology cannot yet be used for this type of annotation, as the quality of, for instance, coreference resolvers is not yet high enough on general text.

Collective resource creation on the Web offers a different way to the solution of this problem. Wikipedia is perhaps the best example of collective resource creation, but it is not an isolated case. The willingness of Web users to volunteer on the Web extends to projects to create resources for Artificial Intelligence. One example is the Open Mind Commonsense project, a project to mine commonsense knowledge (Singh, 2002) to which 14,500 participants contributed nearly 700,000 sentences. A more

---

[1]http://www.anawiki.org

recent, and perhaps more intriguing, development is the use of interactive game-style interfaces to collect knowledge such as von Ahn et al. (2006). Perhaps the best known example of this approach is the ESP game, a project to label images with tags through a competitive game (von Ahn, 2006); 13,500 users played the game, creating 1.3M labels in 3 months. If we managed to attract 15,000 volunteers, and each of them were to annotate 10 texts of 700 words, we would get a corpus of the size of the BNC.

ANAWIKI builds on the proposals for marking anaphoric information allowing for ambiguity developed in ARRAU (Poesio and Artstein, 2005) and previous projects. The ARRAU project found that (i) using numerous annotators (up to 20 in some experiments) leads to a much more robust identification of the major interpretation alternatives (although outliers are also frequent); and (ii) the identification of alternative interpretations is much more frequently a case of implicit ambiguity (each annotator identifies only one interpretation, but these are different) than of explicit ambiguity (annotators identifying multiple interpretations). The ARRAU project also developed methods to analyze collections of such alternative interpretations and to identify outliers via clustering that will be exploited in this project.

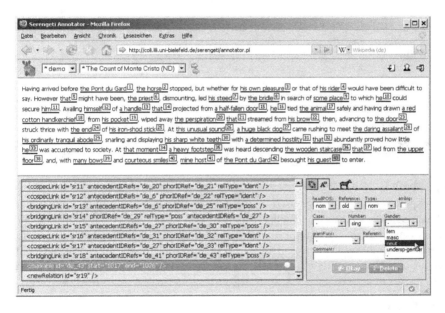

Figure 1: A screenshot of the Serengeti expert annotation tool.

3 Annotation Tools

Attempts to create hand annotated corpora face the dilemma of either going for the traditional CL approach of high-quality annotation (of limited size) by experts or to involve a large population of non-experts which could result in large-scale corpora of inferior quality. The ANAWIKI project bridges this gap by combining both approaches to annotate the data: an expert annotation tool and a game interface. Both

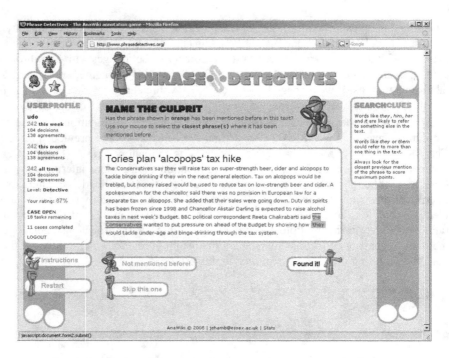

Figure 2: A screenshot of the Game Interface (Annotation Mode).

tools are essential parts of ANAWIKI. We briefly describe both, with a particular focus on the game interface.

3.1 Expert Annotation Tool

An expert annotation tool is used to obtain Gold Standard annotations from computational linguists. In the case of anaphora annotation we use the Serengeti tool developed at the University of Bielefeld (Stührenberg et al., 2007). The anaphoric annotation of markables within this environment will be very detailed and will serve as a training corpus as well as quality check for the second tool (see below). Figure 1 is a screenshot of this interface.

3.2 Game Interface

A game interface is used to collect annotations from the general Web population. The game interface integrates with the database of the expert annotation tool but aims to collect large-scale (rather than detailed) anaphoric relations. Users are simply asked to assign an anaphoric link but are not asked to specify what type (or what features) are present.

Phrase Detectives[2] is a game offering a simple user interface for non-expert users to learn how to annotate text and to make annotation decisions. The goal of the game is to identify relationships between words and phrases in a short text. Markables are

---

[2]http://www.phrasedetectives.org

identified in the text by automatic pre-processing. There are 2 ways to annotate within the game: by selecting the markable that is the antecedent of the anaphor (Annotation Mode — see Figure 2); or by validating a decision previously submitted by another user (Validation Mode). One motivation for Validation Mode is that we anticipate it to be twice as fast as Annotation Mode (Chklovski and Gil, 2005).

Users begin the game at the training level and are given a set of annotation tasks created from the Gold Standard. They are given feedback and guidance when they select an incorrect answer and points when they select the correct answer. When the user gives enough correct answers they graduate to annotating texts that will be included in the corpus. Occasionally, a graduated user will be covertly given a Gold Standard text to annotate. This is the foundation of the user rating system used to judge the quality of the user's annotations.

The game is designed to motivate users to annotate the text correctly by using comparative scoring (awarding points for agreeing with the Gold Standard), and retroactive scoring (awarding points to the previous user if they are agreed with by the current user). Using leader boards and assigning levels for points has been proven to be an effective motivator, with users often using these as targets (von Ahn, 2006). The game interface is described in more detail elsewhere (Chamberlain et al., 2008).

4   Challenges

We are aiming at a balanced corpus, similar to the BNC, that includes texts from Project Gutenberg, the Open American National Corpus, the Enron corpus and other freely available sources. The chosen texts are stripped of all presentation formatting, HTML and links to create the raw text. This is automatically parsed to extract markables consisting of noun phrases. The resulting XML format is stored in a relational database that can be used in both the expert annotation tool and the game.

There are a number of challenges remaining in the project. First of all, the fully automated processing of a substantial (i.e. multi-million) word corpus comprising more than just news articles turned out to be non-trivial both in terms of robustness of the processing tools as well as in terms of linguistic quality.

A second challenge is to recruit enough volunteers to annotate a 100 million word corpus within the timescale of the project. It is our intention to use social networking sites (including Facebook, Bebo, and MySpace) to attract volunteers to the game and motivate participation by providing widgets (code segments that display the user's score and links to the game) to add to their profile pages.

Finally, the project's aim is to generate a sufficiently large collection of annotations from which semantically annotated corpora can be constructed. The usefulness of the created resources can only be proven, for example, by training anaphora resolution algorithms on the resulting annotations. This will be future work.

5   Next Steps

We are currently in the process of building up a critical mass of source texts. Our aim is to have a corpus size of 1M words by September 2008. By this time we also intend having a multilingual user interface (initially English, Italian and German) with the capacity to annotate texts in different languages although this is not the main focus.

In the future we will be considering extending the interface to include different annotation tasks, for example marking coreference chains or Semantic Web mark-up. We would like to present the game interface to gain feedback from the linguistic community.

Acknowledgements

ANAWIKI is funded by EPSRC (EP/F00575X/1). Thanks to Daniela Goecke, Maik Stührenberg, Nils Diewald and Dieter Metzing. We also want to thank all volunteers who have already contributed to the project and the reviewers for valuable feedback.

References

Burnard, L. (2000). The British National Corpus Reference guide. Technical report, Oxford University Computing Services, Oxford.

Chamberlain, J., M. Poesio, and U. Kruschwitz (2008). Phrase Detectives: A Web-based Collaborative Annotation Game. In *Proceedings of the International Conference on Semantic Systems (I-Semantics'08)*, Graz. Forthcoming.

Chklovski, T. and Y. Gil (2005). Improving the design of intelligent acquisition interfaces for collecting world knowledge from web contributors. In *Proceedings of K-CAP '05*, pp. 35–42.

Hovy, E., M. Marcus, M. Palmer, L. Ramshaw, and R. Weischedel (2006). OntoNotes: The 90% Solution. In *Proceedings of HLT-NAACL06*.

Palmer, M., D. Gildea, and P. Kingsbury (2005). The proposition bank: An annotated corpus of semantic roles. *Computational Linguistics 31*(1), 71–106.

Poesio, M. and R. Artstein (2005). The reliability of anaphoric annotation, reconsidered: Taking ambiguity into account. In *Proceedings of the ACL Workshop on Frontiers in Corpus Annotation*, pp. 76–83.

Poesio, M., U. Kruschwitz, and J. Chamberlain (2008). ANAWIKI: Creating anaphorically annotated resources through Web cooperation. In *Proceedings of LREC'08*, Marrakech.

Singh, P. (2002). The public acquisition of commonsense knowledge. In *Proceedings of the AAAI Spring Symposium on Acquiring (and Using) Linguistic (and World) Knowledge for Information Access*, Palo Alto, CA.

Stührenberg, M., D. Goecke, N. Diewald, A. Mehler, and I. Cramer (2007). Web-based annotation of anaphoric relations and lexical chains. In *Proceedings of the ACL Linguistic Annotation Workshop*, pp. 140–147.

von Ahn, L. (2006). Games with a purpose. *Computer 39*(6), 92–94.

von Ahn, L., R. Liu, and M. Blum (2006). Peekaboom: a game for locating objects in images. In *Proceedings of CHI '06*, pp. 55–64.

A Resource-Poor Approach for Linking Ontology Classes to Wikipedia Articles

Nils Reiter
Matthias Hartung
Anette Frank
University of Heidelberg (Germany)
email: reiter@cl.uni-heidelberg.de

Abstract

The applicability of ontologies for natural language processing depends on the ability to link ontological concepts and relations to their realisations in texts. We present a general, resource-poor account to create such a linking automatically by extracting Wikipedia articles corresponding to ontology classes. We evaluate our approach in an experiment with the Music Ontology. We consider linking as a promising starting point for subsequent steps of information extraction.

1 Introduction

Ontologies are becoming increasingly popular as a means for formal, machine-readable modelling of domain knowledge, in terms of concepts and relations. Linking ontological concepts and relations to their natural language equivalents is of utmost importance for ontology-based applications in natural language processing. Providing larger quantities of text that clearly belongs to a given ontological concept is a prerequisite for further steps towards ontology population with relations and instances. We thus consider this work as a point of departure for future work on populating and lexicalizing ontologies, and their use in semantic processing.

In this paper we present a method that provides relevant textual sources for a domain ontology by linking ontological classes to the most appropriate Wikipedia articles describing the respective ontological class. The paper is structured as follows: We discuss related work in Section 2. Section 3 presents our method for linking ontology classes to Wikipedia articles. The method is implemented and tested using the music ontology (Raimond et al., 2007) and a Wikipedia dump of 2007. We present this experiment in Section 4 and its evaluation in Section 5. Section 6 concludes and gives an outlook on directions of future work.

2 Related Work

Our goal is to detect the most appropriate Wikipedia article for a given ontology class. As Wikipedia is a domain-independent resource, it usually contains many more senses for one concept name than does a domain-specific ontology. Thus, one of the challenges we meet is the need for disambiguation between multiple candidate articles with respect to one specific ontology class.[1] Therefore, we compare our approach to previous work on sense disambiguation. Since in our approach, we aim at minimizing the degree of language- and resource dependency, our focus is on the amount of external knowledge used.

One method towards sense disambiguation that has been studied is to use different kinds of text overlap: Ruiz-Casado et al. (2005) calculate vector similarity between a Wikipedia article and WordNet glosses based on term frequencies. Obviously, such glosses are not available for all languages, domains and applications. Wu and Weld (2007) and Cucerzan (2007) calculate the overlap between contexts of named entities and candidate articles from Wikipedia, using overlap ratios or similarity scores in a vector space model, respectively. Both approaches disambiguate named entities using textual context. Since our aim is to *acquire* concept-related text sources, these methods are not applicable.

A general corpus-based approach has been proposed by Reiter and Buitelaar (2008): Using a domain corpus and a domain-independent reference corpus, they select the article with the highest domain relevance score among multiple candidates. This approach works reasonably well but relies on the availability of domain-specific corpora and fails at selecting the appropriate among multiple in-domain senses. In contrast, our resource-poor approach does not rely on additional textual resources, as ontologies usually do not contain contexts for classes.

---

[1]Mihalcea (2007) shows that Wikipedia can indeed be used as a sense inventory for sense disambiguation.

3 Linking Ontology classes to Wikipedia articles

This section briefly reviews relevant information about Wikipedia and describes our method for linking ontology classes to Wikipedia articles. Our algorithm consists of two steps: (i) extracting candidate articles from Wikipedia and (ii) selecting the most appropriate one. The algorithm is independent of the choice of a specific ontology.[2]

3.1 Wikipedia

The online encyclopedia Wikipedia currently comprises more than 2,382,000 articles in about 250 languages. Wikipedia is interesting for our approach because it is semi-structured and articles usually talk about one specific topic.

The structural elements in Wikipedia that we rely on are links between articles, inter-language links, disambiguation and redirect pages. Inter-language links refer to an article about the same topic in a different language. Disambiguation pages collect the different senses of a given term. Redirect pages point to other pages, allowing for spelling variations, abbreviations and synonyms.

3.2 Extracting the candidate articles

The first step of our algorithm is to extract candidate articles for ontology classes. The method we employ is based on Reiter and Buitelaar (2008). The algorithm starts with the English label L_C of an ontology class C, and tries to retrieve the article that bears the same title.[3] Any Wikipedia page P retrieved by this approach falls into one of three categories:

1. P is an *article*: The template {{otheruses}} in the article indicates that a disambiguation page exists which lists further candidate articles for C. The disambiguation page is then retrieved and we proceed with step 2. Otherwise, P is considered to be the only article for C.

2. P is a *disambiguation* page: The algorithm extracts all links on P and considers every linked page as a candidate article.[4]

3. P is a *redirect* page: The redirect is being followed and the algorithm checks the different cases once again.

3.3 Features for the classifier

We now discuss the features we apply to disambiguate candidate articles retrieved by our candidate extraction method with regard to the respective ontology class. Some features use structural properties of both Wikipedia and the ontology, others are based on shallow linguistic processing.

---

[2]It is still dependent on the language used for coding ontological concepts (here English). In future work we aim at bridging between languages using Wikipedia's inter-language links or other multi-lingual resources.

[3]We use common heuristics to cope with CamelCase, underscore whitespace alternation etc.

[4]Note that, apart from pointing to different readings of a term, disambiguation pages sometimes include pages that are clearly not a sense of the given term. Distinguishing these from true/appropriate readings of the term is not trivial.

Domain relevance

Wikipedia articles can be classified according to their domain relevance by computing the proportion of domain terms they contain. In this paper, we explore several variants of matching a set of domain terms against the article in question:

Class labels. The labels of all concepts in the ontology are used as a set of domain terms.

- We extract the nouns from the POS-tagged candidate article. The relative frequency of domain terms is then computed for the complete article and for nouns only, both for types and for tokens.

- We compute the frequency of domain terms in the first paragraph only, assuming it contains domain relevant key terms.

- The redirects pointing to the article in question, i.e., spelling variations and synonyms, are extracted. We then compute their relative frequency in the set of class labels.

Comments. As most ontologies contain natural language comments for classes, we use them to retrieve domain terms. All class comments extracted from the ontology are POS-tagged. We use all nouns as domain terms and compute their relative frequencies in the article.

Class vs. Instance

It is intuitively clear that a class in the ontology needs to be linked to a Wikipedia article representing a class rather than an instance.[5] We extract the following features in order to detect whether an article represents a class or an instance, thus being able to reject certain articles as inappropriate link targets for a particular class.

Translation distance. Instances in Wikipedia are usually named entities (NEs). Thus, the distinction between concepts and instances can, to a great extent, be rephrased as the problem of NE detection. As our intention is to develop a linking algorithm which is, in principle, language-independent, we decided to rely on the inter-language links provided by Wikipedia. The basic idea is that NEs are very similar across different languages (at least in languages using the same script), while concepts show a greater variation in their surface forms across different languages. Thus, for the inter-language links on the article in question that use latin script, we compute the average string similarity in terms of Levenshtein Distance (Levenshtein, 1966) between the title of the page and its translations.

Templates. Wikipedia offers a number of structural elements that might be useful in order to distinguish instances from concepts. In particular, the `infobox` template is used to express structured information about instances of a certain type and some of their properties. Thus, we consider articles containing an `infobox` template to correspond to an instance.

---

[5] We are aware of the fact that the distinction between classes and instances is problematic on both sides: Ontologies described in OWL Full or RDF do not distinguish clearly between classes and instances and Wikipedia does not provide an explicit distinction either.

4 Experiment

4.1 The Music Ontology

We test our approach on the Music Ontology (MO) (Raimond et al., 2007). The MO has been developed for the annotation of musical entities on the web and provides capabilities to encode data about artists, their albums, tracks on albums and the process of creating musical items.

The ontology defines 53 classes and 129 musical properties (e.g. melody) in its namespace, 78 external classes are referenced. Most of the classes are annotated with comments in natural language. The MO is connected to several other ontologies (W3C time[6], timeline[7], event[8], FOAF[9]), making it an interesting resource for domain relevant IE tasks and generalisation of the presented techniques to further domains. The MO is defined in RDF and freely available[10].

4.2 Experimental Setup

The experiment is divided into two steps: candidate page selection and classification (see Section 3). For candidate selection we extract Wikipedia pages with titles that are near-string identical to the 53 class labels. 28 of them are disambiguation pages. From these pages, we extract the links and use them as candidates. The remaining 25 are directly linked to a single Wikipedia article.

To test our classification features, we divide the overall set of ontology classes in training and test sets of 43 and 10 classes, respectively, that need to be associated with their most appropriate candidate article. We restrict the linking to one most appropriate article. For the classification step, we extract the features discussed in Section 3.

Since the candidate set of pages shows a heavily skewed distribution in favour of negative instances, we generate an additional training set by random oversampling (Batista et al., 2004) in order to yield training data with a more uniform distribution of positive and negative instances.

5 Evaluation

For evaluation, the ambiguous concepts in the ontology have been manually linked to Wikipedia articles. The linking was carried out independently by three annotators, all of them computational linguists. Each annotator was presented the class label, its comment as provided by the ontology and the super class from which the class inherits. On the Wikipedia side, all pages found by our candidate extraction method were presented to the annotators.

The inter-annotator agreement is $\kappa = 0.68$ (Fleiss' Kappa). For eight concepts, all three annotators agreed that none of the candidate articles is appropriate and for ten all three agreed on the same article. These figures underline the difficulty of the problem, as the information contained in domain ontologies and Wikipedia varies substantially with respect to granularity and structure.

---

[6]www.w3.org/TR/owl-time/
[7]motools.sourceforge.net/timeline/timeline.html
[8]motools.sourceforge.net/event/event.html
[9]xmlns.com/foaf/spec/
[10]musicontology.com

Candidate article selection. Candidate selection yields 16 candidate articles per concept on average. These articles contain 1567 tokens on average. The minimal and maximal number of articles per concepts are 3 and 38, respectively.

Candidate article classification. We train a decision tree[11] using both the original and the oversampled training sets as explained above.

Table 1: Results after training on original and over-sampled data

	Positives		Negatives		Average	
	orig.	samp.	orig.	samp.	orig.	samp.
P	1	0.63	0.87	0.97	0.94	0.80
R	0.17	0.83	1	0.91	0.58	0.87
F	0.27	0.71	0.93	0.94	0.75	0.83

Table 1 displays precision, recall and f-score results for positive and negative instances as well as their average. As the data shows, oversampling can increase the performance considerably. We suspect this to be caused not only by the larger training set, but primarily by the more uniform distribution.

The table shows further that the negative instances can be classified reliably using the original or oversampled data set. However, as we intend to select positive appropriate Wikipedia articles rather than to deselect inappropriate ones, we are particularly interested in good performance for the positive instances. We observe that this approach identifies positive instances (i.e., appropriate Wikipedia articles) with a reasonable performance when using the oversampled training set. It is noteworthy that not a single feature performs better than with an f-measure of 0.6 *when used alone*. The figures shown in Table 1 are obtained using the combination of all features.

Table 2: Results for combination of best features only

	Positives	Negatives
P	0.60	1.00
R	1.00	0.88
F	0.75	0.94

In Table 2, we present the results for the best performing features taken together (using oversampling on the training set): `nountypes-classlabels` (F-measure: 0.6), `langlinks` (0.5), `redirects-classlabels` (0.5), `nountokens-classlabels` (0.44), `fulltextclasslabels` (0.44). Recall improves considerably, while there is a small decrease in precision.

6   Conclusions

We have presented ongoing research on linking ontology classes to appropriate Wikipedia articles. We consider this task a necessary step towards automatic ontology lexicalization and population from texts.

---

[11]We used the ADTree implementation in the Weka toolkit `www.cs.waikato.ac.nz/ml/weka/`.

The crucial challenge in this task is to deal with the high degree of ambiguity that is introduced by the fact that Wikipedia covers a large amount of fine-grained information for numerous domains. This leads to a great number of potential candidate articles for a given ontology class.

Our approach to this problem is independent of the particular ontology that is used as a starting point. Moreover, it merely depends on a set of rather shallow but effective features which can be easily extracted from the domain ontology and Wikipedia, respectively. From the results we derived in our experiments with the Music Ontology, we conclude that our approach is feasible and yields reasonable results even for small domain ontologies, provided we can overcome highly skewed distributions of the training examples due to an overwhelming majority of negative instances. In future work we will apply the methods described here to different domain ontologies and use the selected Wikipedia articles as a starting point for extracting instances, relations and attributes.

Acknowledgements. We kindly thank our annotators for their effort and Rüdiger Wolf for technical support.

References

Batista, G., R. Prati, and M. C. Monard (2004). A Study of the Behavior of Several Methods for Balancing Machine Learning Training Data. *SIGKDD Explorations 6*, 20–29.

Cucerzan, S. (2007). Large-Scale Named Entity Disambiguation Based on Wikipedia Data. In *Proc. of EMNLP*, Prague.

Levenshtein, V. I. (1966). Binary codes capable of correcting deletions, insertions, and reversals. *Soviet Physics Doklady 10*, 707–710.

Mihalcea, R. (2007). Using Wikipedia for Automatic Word Sense Disambiguation. In *Proc. of NAACL-07*, Rochester, New York, pp. 196–203.

Raimond, Y., S. Abdallah, M. Sandler, and F. Giasson (2007). The Music Ontology. In *Proc. of the 8th International Conference on Music Information Retrieval*, Vienna, Austria.

Reiter, N. and P. Buitelaar (2008). Lexical Enrichment of Biomedical Ontologies. In *Information Retrieval in Biomedicine: Natural Language Processing for Knowledge Integration*. IGI Global, *to appear*.

Ruiz-Casado, M., E. Alfonseca, and P. Castells (2005). Automatic Assignment of Wikipedia Encyclopedic Entries to WordNet Synsets. In *Proc. of the 3rd Atlantic Web Intelligence Conference*, Volume 3528, Lodz, Poland, pp. 380–385.

Wu, F. and D. S. Weld (2007). Autonomously Semantifying Wikipedia. In *Proc. of the Conference on Information and Knowledge Management*, Lisboa, Portugal.

Top-Down Cohesion Segmentation in Summarization

Doina Tatar
Andreea Diana Mihis
Gabriela Serban
University "Babeş-Bolyai" Cluj-Napoca (Romania)
email: dtatar@cs.ubbcluj.ro

Abstract

The paper proposes a new method of linear text segmentation based on lexical cohesion of a text. Namely, first a single chain of disambiguated words in a text is established, then the rips of this single chain are considered as boundaries for the segments of the cohesion text structure (Cohesion TextTiling or CTT). The summaries of arbitrarily length are obtained by extraction using three different methods applied to the obtained segments. The informativeness of the obtained summaries is compared with the informativeness of the pair summaries of the same length obtained using an earlier method of logical segmentation by text entailment (Logical TextTiling or LTT). Some experiments about CTT and LTT methods are carried out for four "classical" texts in summarization literature showing that the quality of the summarization using cohesion segmentation (CTT) is better than the quality using logical segmentation (LTT).

1   Introduction

Text summarization has become the subject of an intense research in the last years and it is still an emerging field (Orasan, 2006; Radev et al., 2002; Hovy, 2003; Mani, 2001). The research is done in the extracts (which we are treating in this paper) and abstracts areas. The most important task of summarization is to identify the most informative (salient) parts of a text comparatively with the rest. A good segmentation of a text could help in this identification (Boguraev and Neff, 2000; Barzilay and Elhadad, 1999; Reynar, 1998).

This paper proposes a new method of linear text segmentation based on lexical cohesion of a text. Namely, first a single chain of disambiguated words in a text is established, then the rips of this chain are considered. These rips are boundaries of the segments in the cohesion structure of the text. Due to some similarities with TextTiling algorithm for topic shifts detection of Hearst (1997), the method is called Cohesion TextTiling (CTT).

The paper is structured as follows: in Section 2 we present the problem of Word Sense Disambiguation by a chain algorithm and the derived CTT method. In Section 3, some notions about textual entailment and logical segmentation of a text by LTT method are discussed. Summarization by different methods after segmentation is the topic of Section 4. The parallel application of CTT and LTT methods to four "classical" texts in summarization literature, two narrative and two newspapers, and some statistics of the results are presented in Section 5. We finish the article with conclusions and possible further work directions.

2   A top-down cohesion segmentation method

2.1   Lexical chains

A lexical chain is a sequence of words such that the meaning of each word from the sequence can be obtained unambiguously from the meaning of the rest of words (Morris and Hirst, 1991; Barzilay and Elhadad, 1999; Harabagiu and Moldovan, 1997; Silber and McCoy, 2002; Stokes, 2004). The map of all lexical chains of a text provides a representation of the lexical cohesive structure of the text. Usually a lexical chain is obtained in a bottom-up fashion, by taking each candidate word of a text, and finding an appropriate relation offered by a thesaurus as Rodget (Morris and Hirst, 1991) or WordNet (Barzilay and Elhadad, 1999). If it is found, the word is inserted with the appropriate sense in the current chain, and the senses of the other words in the chain are updated. If no relation is found, then a new chain is initiated.

Our method approaches the construction of lexical chains in a reverse order: we first disambiguate the whole text and then construct the lexical chains which cover as much as possible the text.

2.2   CHAD algorithm

It is known that in the last years many researchers studied the possibility to globally disambiguate a text. In Tatar et al. (2007) is presented CHAD algorithm, a Lesk's type algorithm based on WordNet, that doesn't require syntactic analysis and syntactic parsing. As usually for a Lesk's type algorithm, it starts from the idea that a word's dictionary definition is a good indicator for the senses of this word and uses the definition in the dictionary directly. The base of the algorithm is the disambiguation of a triplet of words, using Dice's overlap or Jaccard's measures. Shortly, CHAD begins with the disambiguation of a triplet $w_1 w_2 w_3$ and then adds to the right the following words to be disambiguated. Hence it disambiguates at a time a new triplet, where first two words are already associated with the best senses and the disambiguation of the third word depends on the disambiguation of these first two words.

Due to the brevity of definitions in WordNet (WN), the first sense in WN for a word w_i (WN 1st sense) must be associated in some cases in a "forced" way. The **forced condition** represents the situation that any sense of w_i is related with the senses of the words w_{i-2} and w_{i-1}. Thus the **forced condition** signals that a lexical chain stops, and, perhaps, a new one begins.

Comparing the precision obtained with CHAD and the precision obtained by the WN 1st sense algorithm for 10 files of Brown corpus (Tatar et al., 2007) we obtained the result: for 7 files the difference was greater or equal to 0.04 (favorable to WN 1st), and for 3 files was lower. For example, in the worst case (Brown 01 file), the precisions obtained by CHAD are: 0.625 for Dice's measure, 0.627 for Overlap measure, 0.638 for Jaccard's measure while the precision obtained by WN 1st sense is 0.688. Let us remark that CHAD is used to mark the discontinuity in cohesion, while WN 1st sense algorithm is unable to do this.

2.3 CHAD and lexical chains

The CHAD algorithm shows what words in a sentence are unrelated as senses with the previously words: these are the words which receive a "forced" first WN sense. Of course, these are regarded differently from the words which receive a "justified" first WN sense. Scoring each sentence of a text by the number of "forced" to first WN sense words in this sentence, we will provide a representation of the lexical cohesive structure of the text. If F is this number, then the valleys (the local minima) in the graph representing the function $1/F$ will represent the boundaries between lexical chains (see Figure 2).

Lexical chains could serve further as a basis for an algorithm of segmentation. As our method of determination of lexical chains is linear, the corresponding segmentation is also linear. The obtained segments could be used effectively in summarization. In this respect, our method of summarization falls in the discourse-based category. In contrast with other theories about discourse segmentation, as Rhetorical Structure Theory (RST) of Mann and Thompson (1988), attentional/intentional structure of Grosz and Sidner (1986) or parsed RST tree of Marcu (1997), our CTT method (and also, as presented below, our LTT method) supposes a linear segmentation (versus hierarchical segmentation) which results in an advantage from a computational viewpoint.

3 Segmentation by Logical TextTiling

3.1 Text entailment

Text entailment is an autonomous field of Natural Language Processing and it represents the subject of some recent Pascal Challenges. As is established in an earlier paper (Tatar et al., 2007), a text T entails an hypothesis H, denoted by $T \rightarrow H$, iff H is less informative than T. A method to prove $T \rightarrow H$ which relies on this definition consists in the verification of the relation: $sim(T,H)_T \leq sim(T,H)_H$. Here $sim(T,H)_T$ and $sim(T,H)_H$ are text-to-text similarities introduced in Corley and Mihalcea (2005). The method used by our tool for Text entailment verification calculates the similarity between T and H by *cosine*, thus the above relation becomes $cos(T,H)_T \leq cos(T,H)_H$ (Tatar et al., 2007).

3.2 Logical segmentation

Tatar et al. (2008) present a method named *logical* segmentation because the score of a sentence is the number of sentences of the text which are entailed by it. Representing the scores of sentences as a graph, we obtain a structure which indicates how the most important sentences alternate with ones less important and which organizes the text according to its logical content. Simply, a valley (a local minimum) in the obtained logical structure of the text is a boundary between two logical segments (see Figure 1).

The method is called Logical TextTiling (LTT), due to some similarities with the TextTiling algorithm for topic shifts detection (Hearst, 1997). The drawback of LTT, that the number of the segments is fixed for a given text (as it results from its logical structure), is eliminated by a method to dynamically correlate the number of the logical segments obtained by LTT with the required length of the summary. Let us remark that LTT does not require a predicate-argument analysis. The only semantic structure processing required is the Text Entailment verification.

4   Summarization by segmentation

4.1   Scoring the segments

An algorithm of segmentation has usually the following function:

INPUT: a list of sentences $S_1, ..., S_n$ and a list of scores $score(S_1), ..., score(S_n)$;

OUTPUT: a list of segments $Seg_1, ..., Seg_N$.

Given a set of N segments (obtained by CTT or LTT) we need a criterion to select those sentences from a segment which will be introduced in the summary. Thus, after the score of a sentence is calculated, we calculate a score of a segment. The final score, $Score_{final}$, of a sentence is weighted by the score of the segment which contains it. The summary is generated by selecting from each segment a number of sentences proportional with the score of the segment. The method has some advantages when a desired level of granularity of summarization is imposed.

The summarization algorithm *with Arbitrarily Length of the summary (AL)* is the following:

INPUT: The segments $Seg_1, ...Seg_N$, the length of summary X (as parameter),
$Score_{final}(S_i)$ for each sentence S_i;

OUTPUT: A summary SUM of length X, where from each segment Seg_j are selected
$NSenSeg_j$ sentences. The method of selecting the sentences is given by definitions $Sum1, Sum2, Sum3$ (Section 4.2).

Remark: A number of segments Seg_j **may** have $NSenSeg_j > 1$. If $X < N$ then a number of segments Seg_j **must** have $NSenSeg_j = 0$

In Section 5 (Experiments) the variant of summarization algorithm as above is denoted as **Var1**. In the variant **Var2** a second choice of computing the score of a segment is considered. Namely, the score is not normalized, and it is equal with the sum of its sentences scores, without been divided to the segment length. The drawback of **Var1** is that in some cases a very long segment can contain some sentences with a high score and many sentences with a very low score, the final score of this segment will be a small one and those important sentences will not be included in the final summary. The drawback of **Var2** is that of increased importance of the length of the segment in some cases. Thus, the score of a short segment with high sentences scores will be less then one of a long segment with small sentences scores, and again some important sentences will be lost.

4.2 Strategies for summary calculus

The method of extracting sentences from the segments is decisive for the quality of the summary. The deletion of an arbitrary amount of source material between two sentences which are adjacent in the summary has the potential of losing essential information. We propose and compare some simple strategies for including sentences in the summary:

- Our first strategy is to include in the summary the first sentence from each segment, as this is of special importance for a segment. The corresponding summary will be denoted by Sum_1.

- The second way is that for each segment the sentence(s) with a maximal score are considered the most important for this segment, and hence they are included in the summary. The corresponding summary is denoted by Sum_2.

- The third way of reasoning is that from each segment the most informative sentence(s) (the least similar) relative to the previously selected sentences are picked up. The corresponding summary is denoted by Sum_3.

5 Experiments

In our experiments for CTT method each sentence is scored as following: $Score(S_i) = \frac{1}{nuw_i}$ where nuw_i is the number of words "forced" to get the first WN sense in the sentence S_i. If $nuw_i = 0$ then $Score(S_i) = 2$. The graph of the logical structure for the text **Hirst** is presented in Figure 1 while the graph for the cohesion structure for the same text is presented in Figure 2.

We have applied CTT and LTT methods of segmentation and summarization to four texts denoted in the following by: **Hirst** (Morris and Hirst, 1991), **Koan** (Richie, 1991), **Tucker1** (Tucker, 1999) and **Tucker2** (Tucker, 1999).[1] The denotations are as following: LS_i for LTT with Sum_i method, CS_i for CTT with Sum_i method. Also an ideal summary (IdS) has been constructed by taking the majority occurrences of the sentences in all LS_i and CS_i summaries. IdS is the last raw of the table. For the text **Tucker1** the summaries with five sentences obtained by us and the summary obtained by the author with CLASP (Tucker, 1999) are presented in Table 1.

---

[1] All these texts are shown on-line at http://www.cs.ubbcluj.ro/~dtatar/nlp/ (first entries).

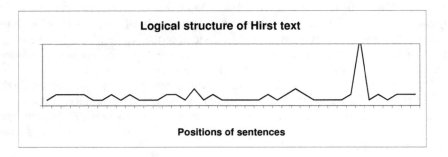

Figure 1: The logical structure of the text **Hirst**

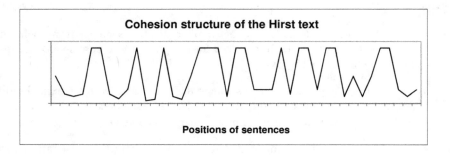

Figure 2: The cohesion structure of the text **Hirst**

Table 1: The summaries with the length 5 for the text **Tucker1** compared with the author's summary

Method	5 sent	Tucker1
LS1	$1, 16, 17, 34, 35$	$6, 8, 16, 23, 34$
LS2	$1, 16, 17, 34, 35$	
LS3	$1, 32, 34, 43, 44$	
CS1	$1, 23, 31, 34, 40$	
CS2	$8, 23, 31, 35, 43$	
CS3	$1, 9, 27, 34, 39$	
IdS	$1, 16, 17, 34, 35$	

Table 2: The average informativeness of *CTT* and *LTT* summaries for all texts

Method	Var1	Var2	Var1 + Var2
*LS*1	0.606538745	0.603946109	0.605242427
*LS*2	0.580429322	0.577647764	0.579038543
*LS*3	0.594914426	0.600104854	0.59750964
*CS*1	0.607369111	0.603053171	0.605211141
*CS*2	0.592993154	0.589675201	0.591334178
*CS*3	0.631625044	0.594702506	0.613163775
average	0.602311633	0.594854934	0.598583284
LTTaverage	0.593960831	0.593899576	0.593930203
CTTaverage	**0.6106624**	**0.5958102**	**0.6032363**

5.1 Evaluation of the summarization

There is no an unique formal method to evaluate the quality of a summary. In this paper we use as a measure of the quality of a summary, the similarity (calculated as *cosine*) between the summarized (initial) text and the summaries obtained with different methods. We call this similarity "the informativeness".

The informativeness of the different types of summaries Sum_1, Sum_2, Sum_3 (see Section 4.2) and of different lengths (5, 6 and 10) is calculated for each text. Then, the average informativeness for all four texts is calculated. A view with the these average results of informativeness, calculated with different methods, in variants **Var1** and **Var2**, is given in the Table 2.

Let us remark that for obtaining summaries with different lengths, after a first segmentation with CTT and LTT methods the algorithm *AL* from Section 4.1 is applied.

Table 2 displays the results announced in the abstract: the quality of CTT summaries is better than the quality of the LTT summaries from the point of view of informativeness.

5.2 Implementation details

The methods presented in this paper are fully implemented: we used our own systems of Text Entailment verification, Word Sense Disambiguation, top-down lexical chains determination, LTT and CTT segmentation, summarization with Sum_i and *AL* methods. The programs are realized in Java and C++. WordNet (Miller, 1995) is used by our system of Word Sense Disambiguation.

6 Conclusion and further work

This paper shows that the text segmentation by lexical chains and by text entailment relation between sentences are good bases for obtaining highly accurate summaries. Moreover, our method replaces the usually bottom-up lexical chain construction with a top-down one, where first a single chain of disambiguated words is established and then it is divided in a sequence of many shorter lexical chains. The segmentation of text follows the sequence of lexical chains. Our methods of summarization control the length of the summaries by a process of scoring the segments. Thus, more material is extracted from the strongest segments.

The evaluation indicates acceptable performance when informativeness of summaries is considered. However, our methods have the potential to be improved: in CTT method we correspond a segment to a lexical chain. We intend to improve our scoring method of a segment by considering some recent method of scoring lexical chains (Ercan and Cicekli, 2008). Also, we intend to study how anaphora resolution could improve the lexical chains and the segmentation. We further intend to apply the presented methods to the corpus of texts DUC2002 and to evaluate them with the standard ROUGE method (for our experiments we didn't have the necessary human made summaries).

Acknowledgments

This work has been supported by PN2 Grant TD 400/2007.

References

Barzilay, R. and M. Elhadad (1999). Using lexical chains for Text summarization. In J. Mani and M. Maybury (Eds.), *Advances in Automated Text Summarization*. MIT Press.

Boguraev, B. and M. Neff (2000). Lexical Cohesion, Discourse Segmentation and Document Summarization. In *Proceedings of the 33rd Hawaii International Conference on System Sciences*.

Corley, C. and R. Mihalcea (2005). Measuring the semantic similarity of texts. In *Proceedings of the ACL Workshop on Empirical Modeling of Semantic Equivalence and Entailment*, Ann Arbor.

Ercan, G. and I. Cicekli (2008). Lexical cohesion based topic modeling for summarization. In *Proceedings of the Cicling 2008*, pp. 582–592.

Harabagiu, S. and D. Moldovan (1997). TextNet – a textbased intelligent system. *Natural Language Engineering 3*(2), 171–190.

Hearst, M. (1997). Texttiling: Segmenting text into multi-paragraph subtopic passages. *Computational Linguistics 23*(1), 33–64.

Hovy, E. (2003). Text summarization. In R. Mitkov (Ed.), *The Oxford Handbook of Computational Linguistics*. Oxford University Press.

Mani, I. (2001). *Automatic summarization*. John Benjamins.

Marcu, D. (1997). From discourse structure to text summaries. In *Proceedings of the ACL/EACL '97 Workshop on Intelligent Scalable Text Summarization*, pp. 82–88.

Miller, G. (1995). WordNet: a lexical database for english. *Comm. of the ACM 38*(11), 39–41.

Morris, J. and G. Hirst (1991). Lexical cohesion computed by thesaural relations as an indicator of the structure of text. *Computational Linguistics 17*(1), 21–48.

Orasan, C. (2006). *Comparative evaluation of modular automatic summarization systems using CAST*. Ph. D. thesis, University of Wolverhampton.

Radev, D., E. Hovy, and K. McKeown (2002). Introduction to the special issues on summarization. *Computational Linguistics 28*, 399–408.

Reynar, J. (1998). *Topic Segmentation: algorithms and applications*. Ph. D. thesis, Univ. of Penn.

Richie, D. (1991). The koan. In Z. Inklings (Ed.), *Some Stories, Fables, Parables and Sermons*, pp. 25–27.

Silber, H. and K. McCoy (2002). Efficiently computed lexical chains, as an intermediate representation for automatic text summarization. *Computational Linguistics 28*(4), 487–496.

Stokes, N. (2004). *Applications of Lexical Cohesion Analysis in the Topic Detection and Tracking Domain*. Ph. D. thesis, National University of Ireland, Dublin.

Tatar, D., A. M. G. Serban, and R. Mihalcea (2007). Text entailment as directional relation. In *Proceedings of CALP07 Workshop at RANLP2007*, Borovets, Bulgaria, pp. 53–58.

Tatar, D., A. Mihis, and D. Lupsa (2008). Text entailment for logical segmentation and summarization. In *13th International Conference on Applications of Natural Language to Information Systems*, pp. 233–244.

Tatar, D., G. Serban, A. Mihis, M. Lupea, D. Lupsa, and M. Frentiu (2007). A chain dictionary method for wsd and applications. In *Proceedings of the International Conference on Knowledge Engineering,Principles and Techniques*, pp. 41–49.

Tucker, R. (1999). *Automatic summarising and the CLASP system*. Ph. D. thesis, University of Cambridge.